Burmese Super-naturalism

Transaction Books by Melford E. Spiro

Burmese Super-naturalism

Expanded Edition

Melford E. Spiro

With a new introduction by the author

Transaction Publishers

New Brunswick (U.S) and London (U.K.)

New material this edition copyright © 1996 by Transaction Publishers, New Brunswick, New Jersey 08903. Expanded edition originally published in 1978 by the Institute for the Study of Human Issues. Original edition published in 1967 by Prentice-Hall, Inc.

This book is printed on acid-free paper that meets the American National Standard for Permanence of Paper for Printed Library Materials.

Library of Congress Catalog Number: 95-50654
ISBN: 1-56000-882-2
Printed in the United States of America

Library of Congress Cataloging-in-Publication Data

Spiro, Melford E.
    Burmese supernaturalism / Melford E. Spiro ; with a new introduction by the author. — Expanded ed.
    p. cm.
    Originally published: Philadelphia : Institute for the Study of Human Issues, ©1978.
    Includes bibliographical references and index.
    ISBN 1-56000-882-2 (pbk. : alk. paper)
    1. Burma—Religious life and customs. 2. Animism—Burma. 3. Supernatural. I. Title.
BL2051.S66 1996
291.1'09591—dc20   95-50654
                                                              CIP

To My Parents

CONTENTS

I

INTRODUCTION

II

THE TYPES OF

SUPERNATURALISM

III
THE THIRTY-SEVEN
NATS

IV

ILLNESS AND
SUPERNATURALISM

V

SUPERNATURAL
PRACTITIONERS

VI
CONCLUSION

Introduction to the
Transaction Edition

The worldview of most of the world's great civilizations is informed not by one, but by two or more religious traditions—an indigenous religion, and at least one other brought in from outside. In some cases, elements from each have been combined in various ways and in various proportions to produce one syncretistic religion. Thus, although Catholicism is the dominant religion in Latin America, it is a Catholicism that represents a syncretism of Christian, indigenous, and African elements, in which the Christian, however, is hegemonic. In other cases, the different religions remain distinct, and devotees profess allegiance to both. The Japanese, for example, worship both at Buddhist temples and (pre-Buddhist) Shinto shrines.

An analogous situation obtains in Burma (now called Myanmar), as well as the other societies of mainland Southeast Asia, in which the religious landscape includes both an indigenous spirit cult and one of the great world religions, Buddhism, an import from India. The spirit cults are often referred to as a "folk religion," not however because their devotees are ordinary folk whereas the elite are devotees of Buddhism—all are devotees of both—but because the former is based on an oral, the latter on a written tradition. Since I have described Theravada Buddhism in my *Buddhism and Society: A Great Tradition and Its Burmese Vicissitudes*, this book deals instead with the Burmese spirit cult.

For reasons adduced in the following chapters, the spirit cult and Buddhism are, in my view, two separate, albeit interrelated religions, not a single syncretistic one. Since, however, this "two religions thesis" (as it has since been dubbed) has engendered much controversy among Southeast Asian scholars, much of the Preface to the Expanded Edition of this book examines this controversy. Hence, here I wish to examine two other issues, one substantive, the other theoretical, related to my treatment of the spirit cult. I shall begin with the former.

In rereading this book I was struck by the fact, which I was not when I wrote it, that fully half the text is devoted to what today would be called "traditional medicine." Thus, to describe the theology of this folk religion is, from our point of view, to describe *inter alia* a theory of illness, and to describe its rituals is to describe *inter alia* a technology of healing. That is, the malevolent supernatural beings of this religion (witches, ghosts, demons, and punitive spirits) are the supernatural agents of "illness," mostly "mental illness"; its benevolent supernatural beings are the supernatural agents of "healing"; and its ritual specialists are the human agents of "healing."

That being so it could now be suggested that rather than conceiving of this book as a study of a folk religion, I might have conceived of it instead as a study of folk medicine; and by means of a somewhat different Introduction, a different conceptual emphasis, and a different organization, the book might then have been titled not *Burmese Supernaturalism*, but *Burmese Medicine*. That I did not so conceive of it, however, is that while illness and healing, again from our point of view, constitute important elements of the spirit cult, nevertheless the Burmese themselves do not regard it as a medical system. This is not because the concept of a medical system, distinct and separate from other cultural systems, is unfamiliar to them. On the contrary, Burmese villagers, let alone city folk, know of and participate in, not only one, but two medical systems, both explicitly recognized and designated as such: indigenous (herbal) medicine and Western (or, as it is sometimes called) cosmopolitan medicine, each with its own physicians, diagnostic methods, therapeutic techniques, and pharmacopoeia.

Despite the fact that the spirit cult also deals with illness and healing, nevertheless the Burmese do not regard it as a medical system any more than Pentecostal Christianity (which is explicitly conceived as dealing with illness and healing) is regarded by its followers as a medical system. Rather, both are regarded as religious systems, not only because illness and healing is a byproduct of their central concern with religious issues, but also because they are dealt with in a "religious," not a "medical" mode. Let us examine this proposition as it applies to the spirit cult.

As I have already noted, it is mental illness (as we would call it) that is the concern of the spirit cult, whereas physical illness is the concern of the two medical systems. That being so, it might be argued that in Burma, contrary to what I have said, the spirit cult is not separate from, but is a part of, the cultural domain of medicine, within which, however, there is, as there is in the West, a division of labor: physical illness is treated by indigenous and Western medical specialists, while mental illness is treated by the cult (i.e., ritual) specialist.

Hence, from that point of view—the standard view of medical anthropology—the ritual specialist may be regarded as a psychiatrist or psychotherapist.

I do not find this argument convincing on two accounts. Thus, the person whom a Western psychotherapist would view as suffering from some form of mental illness, is viewed by the cult specialist as suffering, instead, from witchcraft or spirit possession; in short, for him such a person is not a patient, but a victim. Moreover, whereas the Western psychotherapist would regard a patient's belief that he has been bewitched or possessed as a symptom, a paranoid delusion, and would attempt to cure him of it, the cult specialist regards such a belief as veridical, and hence attempts to drive out or drive off the supernatural culprit. In sum, the cult specialist is an exorcist, not a psychotherapist. This is not to deny that exorcism, from our point of view, may have therapeutic functions; it does, indeed, and I explicitly discuss such functions in some detail. But to therefore designate the Burmese exorcist as a psychotherapist makes no more sense than to designate a Roman Catholic exorcist as one. In neither case do the exorcists themselves, their clients, or their flock conceive of the exorcistic role in this way.

Before leaving this substantive issue and, as a point of entry to the theoretical issue I wish to turn to next, it is pertinent to observe that although the first edition of this book was published almost thirty years ago, nevertheless I have not changed the text for this edition. This is not, however, because the book says all there is to be said on the spirit cult (which it surely does not), nor yet again because it contains no errors (which it doubtless does), but because any addition or change requires further research, which, for political reasons discussed below, has not been possible.

The present text was based on fieldwork conducted in Upper Burma in 1961–62 when, following a long hiatus occasioned by World War II and its aftermath, the resumption of anthropological research in Burma was just beginning. As noted, however, in the Preface to the Expanded Edition, that window of opportunity was abruptly and tightly closed when, following a military coup in March 1962, the military government abolished the nascent Burmese democracy, and also, a few months later, expelled all nonofficial foreigners from the country, thereby bringing my research to an end. Moreover, because this military regime, which has held power ever since, has (with a few exceptions) continued to bar foreign scholars from the country, it has not been possible to resume my research. (Since, according to Amnesty International, this is one of the most repressive governments in the world, its exclusion of foreign scholars, as well as journalists—both of whom might have been expected to report its dismal record—is hardly surprising).

This book, however, is not only a descriptive report of the Burmese folk religion, it is also an investigation into its social and psychological foundations; and since, in its essentials, this religion is much like folk religions elsewhere, this investigation is *pari passu* a theoretical inquiry into the foundations of folk religion more generally. Hence, while lack of access to the field site accounts for the absence of changes in the descriptive sections of the book, it does not, however, explain why its theoretical structure has not been modified, or why I do not expound upon it more fully here.

I do not expound upon the theoretical structure because I did so earlier in the Preface to the Expanded Edition. That I have not, however, modified that structure is a function both of my own thinking regarding the theoretical issues raised in the book, as well as of recent developments in anthropological theory. As for the former, my thinking regarding these theoretical issues has not changed sufficiently to require anything more than minor modifications in the book's theoretical structure. On the other hand, recent theoretical developments in anthropology have been sufficiently dramatic as to require nothing less than a wholesale overhauling of that structure. Seeing, however, as I do not subscribe to these developments—on the contrary, I view them as auguring the end of anthropology as we have known it—I see no need to overhaul it, which brings me to the theoretical issue I wish to discuss here.

Over the past fifteen years, or so, the most prominent development in anthropology (and the other human sciences) has been the rise of what has come to be called "postmodernism." Although this term refers to a congeries of concepts and assumptions, the ones most germane to the present discussion include wholesale cultural determinism, radical cultural relativism, a near-limitless view of cultural diversity, and epistemological relativism.

Based on these interrelated concepts and assumptions, postmodernists reject the foundation stones that underlie the theoretical structure of this book, namely, the concept of human nature (formerly called the "psychic unity of mankind"), the viability (based on the latter concept) of a transcultural psychological theory, a universal social science, and (hence) the possibility of causal explanations of social and cultural phenomena. Postmodernists reject the concept of human nature as "essentialist," psychological theory as "reductionist," social science as "imperialist" (a species of "symbolic domination"), and causal explanation as "positivist."

Though rejected by postmodernism, these four notions are critical to the theoretical structure of this book because its central theoretical question—how might we explain the cognitive and emotional salience of the Burmese belief in spirits, demons, witches, and the like?—is precipitated by these notions, and the proposed explanations are derived from them. But if, according to postmodernism, these notions are conceptually, morally, and methodologically flawed, then the explanations that are derived from them are similarly flawed. Indeed, according to the previously stipulated postmodernist assumptions, the only valid explanation for the salience of this Burmese belief is that it is culturally determined, or (as it is more frequently put) culturally constituted.

While this explanation—never mind that it invokes the abjured positivist notion of causation—is certainly true as far as it goes, it does not, however, go far enough. For of the many propositions (religious, economic, political, and the like) that comprise the cultural heritage of any group, only some are internalized by social actors as salient (strongly held) beliefs. Hence, to understand why some cultural propositions, and not others, are so internalized by them, it is necessary to discover the psychological grounds—cognitive, perceptual, and motivational—for their doing so, and this is what this book attempts to do in regard to the propositions comprising the Burmese folk religion.

Such an inquiry, however, is superfluous if, like the formation of beliefs, cognitive, perceptual, and motivational processes are also culturally constituted. Hence, to propose, as this book does, that these psychological processes (though not their content) may instead be universal—a proposal derived from the notion of a universal human nature—is to encounter the postmodernist riposte that the radical diversity of cultures precludes such a generalization. In short, if cultural diversity is near-limitless, hence if every culture is unique, then each culture produces its own psychological processes. The latter claim has generated two, rather different, postmodernist stances regarding the possibility of understanding the religious (or any other) beliefs of non-Western peoples.

Thus, if each culture is unique, then, according to one stance, cultures are incommensurable one with another, and if moreover virtually all human psychological characteristics are culturally constituted, then non-Western peoples are Other, that is, unknown and unknowable. That being so, their religious (and all other) beliefs are opaque to the understanding of the Western anthropologist.

The epistemological nihilism of this, the "strong" stance, may now be distinguished from the epistemological relativism of the "weak" stance. Although it does not regard non-Western peoples as Other, not at any rate radically Other, still this stance holds that a genuine understanding of non-Western beliefs can only be based on indigenous cultural theories, not on anthropological theory. That is so because anthropology—like any other "Western" science—is merely, so it claims, a Western ethnoscience, and there is no valid warrant for "privileging" its theories over those of any non-Western ethnoscience. Consequently, while it is legitimate, based on native theories, to *interpret* the beliefs of non-Western peoples—that is, to explicate their meanings—it is not legitimate, however, to *explain* them—that is, to provide causal accounts, based on anthropological theory, of why they hold them.

It is now perhaps evident why the acceptance of even this weak stance would require, as I previously observed, a wholesale overhauling of the theoretical structure of this book. For while I am at pains to describe the meanings that the Burmese themselves attribute to the doctrines and rituals comprising their spirit cult, and to explicate their reasons for believing that they are true and efficacious, respectively, nevertheless this is only one of my goals. My other goal is to provide a theoretical account, that is, a causal explanation, for these Burmese understandings.

In my view all ethnographic studies have—or, at any rate, ought to have—both descriptive and theoretical goals. The theoretical goal, which is sometimes misunderstood, has two aspects, which, to invoke Kroeber's distinction referred to in the text, can be characterized as "historical" and "scientific," respectively. In its historical aspect, the theoretical goal is particularistic: to explain some particular society or culture in all of its particularity. In its scientific aspect, this goal is comparative: to discover general principles and theories that might explain not only the society or culture in question, but societies and cultures more generally. Put differently, in the historical-theoretic mode, the field-worker employs such principles and theories to construct a plausible account of some ethnographic particulars, while in the scientific-theoretic mode, the field-worker deploys the ethnographic particulars to test these principles and theories. Analytically, these modes are separate and distinct, but since fieldwork is intellectually messy at best, pragmatically it never works that way. Rather, the historical and the scientific modes are like the two sides of the same coin, and the field-worker is continuously tacking between them.

Let me now emphasize, however, that although the scientific-theoretic goal is to test some theory or theories, nevertheless no single ethnographic study has the power to confirm nor disconfirm them. For while the ethnographic particulars may support or fail to support some theory—that is, theory and data exhibit, or fail to exhibit, a "goodness of fit"—such support, or lack of it, is not sufficient to confirm or disconfirm the theory. Rather, its confirmation or disconfirmation requires that it be further tested by comparable studies conducted in a broad range of ethnographic contexts.

This requirement, however, raises two questions. First, if some social or psychological theory has already been confirmed by studies in the West, why then should it be tested yet again by comparative studies in non-Western societies? Such tests surely are redundant. Second, if Western studies suggest that the cognitive status of the theory is unclear, hence requiring further testing, why should such tests also be conducted in non-Western societies? Surely, additional Western studies should be sufficient.

The anthropological answer (or at any rate the standard anthropological answer) to these questions is the same for both. Thus, even though some theory seems to have been confirmed by Western studies, nevertheless in the light of the wide diversity—social, cultural, and psychological—across human societies, the theory must be regarded as culture-bound until it is supported by comparable studies in non-Western societies. Without this support, then however frequently it may have been supported by Western studies, from a comparative anthropological perspective the latter constitute an N of 1, and hence its confirmation is more apparent than real.

Put differently, the scientific-theoretic purpose of non-Western research— I shall examine its historical-theoretic purpose below—is to discover whether social science theories, even if apparently confirmed in the West, are also valid *ceteris paribus* in other social-cultural-psychological contexts. In short, the latter contexts constitute the crucible in which these theories are put to the critical test. Should a theory fail that test, then seeing that a comparative anthropology denies cultural incommensurability and affirms psychic unity, such a theory is mostly likely to be false, and its apparent confirmation in the West may be an artifact of some peculiarity of Western society or culture.

I say that such a theory is most likely to be false, not certainly false, because the latter is not necessarily the case. For just as the confirmation of a theory in Western contexts may be more apparent than real, that may also be the case for its disconfirmation in non-Western contexts, and for at least two reasons. Thus, the theory may perhaps have been disconfirmed because it was inappropriately formulated for non-Western contexts; alternatively, because it was improperly calibrated—it was either too finely tuned, or too coarsely tuned—for such contexts. In sum, its apparent disconfirmation may have been an artifact of some peculiarity of non-Western society or culture.

It is important that anthropologists in particular attend to this cautionary note, for if non-anthropologists are often too quick to accept a theory that has apparently been confirmed in Western societies, then anthropologists are often too quick to reject a theory that has apparently been disconfirmed in non-Western societies. Thus, if its disconfirmation is a function of inappropriate formulation or improper calibration, then the theory might yet be confirmed when modified accordingly.

It may now be suggested that the implementation of the scientific-theoretic goal of ethnographic fieldwork may have four, not merely two, scientific consequences. It may increase our confidence that the theory is true; it may increase our confidence that the theory is false; it may alert us to the necessity to reformulate the theory; it may alert us to the necessity to modify the theory.

As I suggested previously, the implementation of the scientific-theoretic goal of ethnographic fieldwork is also important for the achievement of its historical-theoretic goal. For if the latter goal is to explain or interpret the cultural systems and social institutions of some particular society, then presumably it is important to offer not just any old explanation or interpretations, but valid ones. Unless, however, they are ad hoc (in which case they are uncontrolled speculations), our explanations and interpretations are derived from one or another social science theory, and if these theories are false, then these explanations and interpretations are invalid. Hence, even those anthropologists for whom the theoretical goal of ethnography is exclusively historical—and who may view its scientific goal as a species of positivism and cultural imperialism—even they ignore the scientific goal at a heavy price. For until or unless the latter goal is achieved, it cannot be known to what degree, if any, their interpretations are not only plausible, but true. (To be sure, if they view truth as an "essentialist" concept, they will not be troubled by this possibility.)

We may now return to the study of the Burmese spirit cult described below. In addition to its descriptive goal, this study exemplifies, for better or for worse, the two theoretical goals of ethnographic fieldwork, the historical and the scientific. On the one hand, it employs various social and psychological theories to explain the major beliefs and rituals comprising this folk religion; on the other hand, it deploys these beliefs and rituals as data for testing these theories. Although these data, it will be seen, support the theories—that is, the two exhibit a goodness of fit—they do not, for the reasons presented above, confirm them. In short, until these theories are tested by comparable investigations in still other non-Western contexts, the explanations that I offer for the various components of the spirit cult should be regarded as hypotheses whose cognitive status remains unclear.

Preface
to the Expanded Edition

Since this book was first published more than a decade ago, it is hardly surprising that I no longer subscribe to all its formulations. Nevertheless, except for the correction of typographical errors (which were kindly brought to my attention by Professor Richard Gombrich), the text of this edition is identical with the original. There are two reasons for this decision. First, the military dictatorship that illegally seized power in Burma in 1962 has refused to allow foreign scholars to conduct research in the country since that time, so that neither I nor anyone else has been able to collect new data. Second, despite my new thoughts about certain details of the theoretical formulations that organize the materials and (hopefully) render them intelligible, my general views regarding the topics discussed in the book have remained more or less unchanged.

Unhappily, modern Burmese ethnography was in its infancy when the military coup cut off further field work. Often, therefore, this book, like others on the subject, is forced by lack of data to become speculative. Much more systematic work is required to solve the problem of the *mizain-hpazain* nat, for example, or to fully understand the role of the *gaing* in Burmese society, or the significance of the *hsaya* for Burmese personality. A more thorough investigation of these topics (and, for that matter, of almost every other topic treated in this book) would not only enrich the value of this volume as an ethnographic study of Burmese religion, but would also permit a more thorough exploration of the theoretical structure underlying the ethnographic presentation. At the present time neither aim can be fulfilled. What I will do in this new Preface, then, is to discuss some of the underlying theoretical issues that were of necessity skimmed over in the original edition, as well as a major debate that has been evolving since its publication.

Religion as a Cultural Belief System

This is a book about culture or, more specifically, about that domain of culture that relates to religious beliefs and behavior. By "belief" I mean any cognition concerning human beings, society, or the world that is held to be true. By "religious belief" I mean any belief that directly or indirectly relates to beings who are held to possess greater power than humans and animals, with whom human beings sustain relationships (interactions and transactions), and who can affect human lives for good or for evil. In short, "religious" beliefs are beliefs related to supernatural beings. Although the term "supernatural" poses many conceptual difficulties—I prefer "superhuman"—I have retained it in this volume because of its long usage in religious scholarship. By "religious behavior" I mean any behavior (including, but not exclusively consisting of, ritual) that is related directly or indirectly to beliefs concerning these supernatural beings.

Not all religious beliefs, of course, are part of culture, nor is all religious behavior culturally constituted. "Culture," as that term is used here, refers to *tradition*. Hence, insofar as religious beliefs are culturally constituted, they are *traditional* beliefs, i.e., they are beliefs that arise and develop in the history of a social group, and that are transmitted from one generation of the group to the next through those social processes that are variously denoted by such terms as "education" and "enculturation." In this book we are concerned with religious beliefs and behavior insofar as they are culturally constituted.

Cultural beliefs never stand alone. Rather, they are related in complex ways to the other beliefs comprising an institutional domain, such that the total set of beliefs associated with the domain may be said to constitute a "system." This holds, of course, for noncultural no less than for cultural beliefs. Typically, however, cultural belief systems are more complex than noncultural belief systems because, as the products of history, the beliefs comprising a cultural system are more numerous, the number of actors who have contributed to the pool of beliefs is larger, and (since the beliefs are acquired by instruction rather than through experience) there is often considerable "slippage" between the beliefs-as-transmitted and the beliefs-as-acquired. Much of the paradoxical quality that scholars and theologians purport to see in religious belief systems derives not from some special characteristic of religious thought, but from this Rashomon-effect that is attendant upon the transmission of any cultural belief system.

Since religious beliefs comprise a cognitive system, the intellectual task confronting the student of religion is manifold. First, the boundaries of the system must be delineated. Second, the variables comprising the system—its component beliefs—must be described. Third, the structure or organization of the system must be explicated. Fourth, the grounds for holding the beliefs must be uncovered. Fifth, the functions served by the beliefs—the consequences, either for the social actors or for their society, of holding the beliefs—must be discovered. Although the first three tasks are *emic* in nature, i.e., they require that the system be described from the point of view of the actors, the last two are partially *emic* and partially *etic,* i.e., they require that the system also be described by reference to processes and meanings of which the actors may be unconscious.

In this connection, the term "unconscious" is ambiguous. On the one hand it may refer to cognitive processes that are out of awareness because they are habitual and automatic. When linguists say that native speakers are unconscious of the rules of their grammar, or when structuralists say that the basic structure of myths, for example, is unconscious, it is this meaning of "unconscious" that is intended. But "unconscious" may also refer to processes and meanings that are out of awareness because, being threatening to the conscious self, they are repressed. The latter usage refers to the "dynamic unconscious," as that expression is used in psychoanalysis. In this book "unconscious" is used in both senses, and the text usually makes clear which of the two is intended.

But I have run ahead of myself. When we speak of the "meanings" of cultural beliefs (whether conscious or unconscious), we are, of course, speaking elliptically. Cultural beliefs, taken as cognitive statements about the world, do not "contain" their meanings; the latter are "located" not in the beliefs themselves, but in the minds of the actors who hold them. Thus, for example, when we ask, "What does this Christian belief mean?", we are really asking, "What does this belief mean to Christians?", for the belief has entirely different meanings—if indeed it has any meaning at all—to non-Christians.

If, then, religious beliefs, as culturally constituted beliefs, are acquired through instruction (rather than experience), and if their meanings are located in the minds of the believers, these meanings depend on the psychological "level" at which they have been learned. Briefly, and in ascending order of cognitive salience, we may delineate a hierarchy of five levels at which cultural beliefs may be learned. a) The actors *learn about* the beliefs, that is, they acquire an acquaintance with them. b) They not only learn about them, but they *understand* their traditional meanings, as these are understood, for example, in authoritative texts or by recognized specialists. c) They not only understand the traditional meanings of the beliefs, but—to change from the noun to the verb—they *believe* that they are true, correct, or right. When beliefs are learned at this level we may say that they are genuine beliefs, rather than cultural clichés. d) That actors hold a belief to be true does not in itself indicate that it occupies a prominent position in their cognitive structure. One may believe that Kabul is the capital of Afghanistan without its making any difference to one's life. Hence, at the fourth level, in addition to being held to be true, the belief is cognitively salient; that is, it informs the actors' *behavioral environment,* serving to structure their perceptual world and to guide their action. e) Sometimes cultural beliefs go beyond guiding action to instigate or serve to initiate action. At this psychological level cultural beliefs possess motivational and affective, as well as cognitive, properties. Thus, a Christian who has acquired the belief in hell at this level has not only incorporated this belief as part of his cosmography, but has *internalized* it as part of his motivational system. It arouses strong affect which, in turn, motivates him to action (whose purpose is the avoidance of hell).

This delineation of the psychological levels at which the learning of cultural beliefs may take place is more than a scholastic exercise, for it is crucial to the explanatory task of a religious (or any other) ethnography. Any explanation of the grounds for holding religious beliefs, and any assessment of the functions of these beliefs, must deal in the first instance with whether they possess cognitive or motivational salience for the actors, or whether they are merely clichés to which the actors pay lip service. The theoretical neglect to mark these distinctions and the empirical failure to ascertain these levels can lead—and has led—to misguided interpretations of the role of religion in human affairs. This is especially true in the case of the great historical religions whose doctrines are encapsulated in canonical texts. Popular writers and journalists, as well as some scholars (who ought to know better), frequently explain the behavior of the devotees of these religions by reference to doctrines which, in fact, many of the followers do not understand, and whose meanings are not incorporated as part of their cognitive structures. Not surprisingly, therefore, one can read in numerous books on Buddhist Asia that poverty, or authoritarian governments, or lack of planning, or high suicide rates (to mention only a few items) are the result of such Buddhist doctrines as *anatta* (the doctrine that there is no permanent self), when, in fact, most Buddhists do not understand the meaning of this complex metaphysical concept, even if they have heard of it.

This same problem is only slightly less troublesome in the study of folk or nonliterate religions. Since the latter do not have authoritative texts, investigators often turn to religious specialists as their informants, and it is their beliefs that are described as the religious belief system of the society under investigation. Now the beliefs of religious specialists may or may not constitute the normative belief system of their society, but in

assessing the relationships between social behavior and religious beliefs—
even assuming that such relationships exist—it is hazardous to rely on the
beliefs of religious specialists alone. First, there is no a priori reason to
assume that the meanings attributed to these beliefs by religious virtuosi
are shared by the other members of the group. Second, even if their
meanings are shared, unless we know at which psychological level the
beliefs have been learned, we cannot determine the grounds on which the
actors hold the beliefs, on the one hand, or the consequences (functions)
of their holding them, on the other.

Failure to specify the level at which cultural beliefs are learned, or
even to recognize that this is a relevant issue, stems from either of two
types of error. The Type 1, or culturological, error consists in assuming
that because some belief is part of the cultural heritage of a group, it is
necessarily held at the fifth (the "deepest") of the five psychological levels
adumbrated above. Culturological theorists simply assume, without examin-
ing the belief systems of individual actors, that their behavior is determined
by the beliefs of their culture. The Type 2 error consists in making the
contrary assumption. For certain theorists (stemming from both Marxist
and Freudian traditions), there is little point in ascertaining the psychological level at which cultural beliefs have been acquired since, it is assumed,
belief systems merely comprise the rhetorical forms that justify and ra-
tionalize—rather than determine—behavior. The "real" determinants of
behavior, so it is thought, are to be sought elsewhere. Since the research
reported in this book was designed to avoid both types of error, the cultural beliefs of individual actors were examined extensively and intensively,
and an attempt was made to assess the psychological level at which they
were acquired.

Anthropology as "History" and "Science"

What, then, can we say about the cultural beliefs that are the objects
of this study? All these beliefs relate to classes of "supernatural" beings
who, with one exception, are viewed as malevolent, and whose primary
activity, so far as their relationship to human beings is concerned, consists
in inflicting suffering. The exceptional class comprises the gods, or *devas,*
who can be called upon for protection against, or for the alleviation of,
the suffering perpetrated by the other classes (ghosts, witches, and evil
spirits, or *nats*). For anthropologists, at least, the beliefs and practices
related to these supernatural beings are especially fascinating. Nevertheless, in writing this book, I was constantly confronted with the problem
of the degree to which they should be described in their details. Anthropology is often charged with having fascinating data, but little theory; like
psychiatric case studies, ethnographic studies, it is claimed, make for good
cocktail-party conversation or entertaining lectures, but often lack theoret-

ical importance. Though this claim is sometimes well taken—I certainly have no wish to defend unequivocally the ethnographic enterprise—it is surely false as a general statement. To be sure, anthropologists, like clinicians, are often wary about abstract formulations, especially when (as they so often do) the latter denude social life of its richness and complexity. Hence, instead of (or in addition to) publishing disembodied theoretical tracts, we anthropologists often embody our theories in ethnographic description and analysis. In doing so, however, we must always face the problem of what constitutes the optimum ratio of theory to facts.

Except for area specialists or seekers after esoterica, very few scholars are interested, *per se,* in the ethnographic minutiae of a village in Upper Burma, any more than I (as a nonspecialist in African studies) am interested in the ethnographic details, *per se,* of a village in eastern Nigeria. Hence, when we read an ethnography, we hope to be informed not only about the microscopic domain which is its ostensible concern, but also about the macroscopic domain—the human career—which is (or ought to be) at the center of its author's purpose. An ethnography that does not give us a picture, however indirect and muted, of the universal as it is reflected and refracted in the particular may possess great importance for the area interests of the specialist, but is of limited significance for the more general humanistic concerns of those who work in the social sciences and humanities. With respect to these concerns, any particular culture is important to the nonspecialist insofar as it is (or can be) seen as a variation on a universal human theme.

Given these considerations—which I mention briefly on pages 5–6 of the original text—I was conscious in writing this volume of the requirement that it attempt to treat its materials at two levels simultaneously. On the one hand, it must recognize that it is dealing with certain universal themes, and yet its analysis must be sufficiently *contextual* that it does not lose sight of the trees for the forest. On the other hand, while recognizing that cultures differ in their approaches to these themes, its analysis must yet be sufficiently *conceptual* that it does not lose sight of the forest for the trees. An overly conceptual monograph satisfies the needs of the theorist while neglecting those of the area specialist; an overly contextual monograph enriches the specialist's knowledge at the expense of saying little of significance to the student of human culture who has no special interest in Southeast Asia.

In delineating these two approaches to the writing of ethnography—the contextual versus the conceptual—I am following Kroeber's distinction between two conceptions of anthropology which he termed, respectively, "history" and "science." The practitioner of anthropology as "history," immersing himself in the local setting, is concerned with the latter in all its uniqueness. The practitioner of anthropology as "science," placing the local setting in a theoretical context, is concerned with the local as a variant of—and therefore a means for understanding—the universal. Although this book steers a course between these two approaches, it is clear that its concerns are closer to the latter than to the former.

For anthropology conceived as history, the question of why the Burmese today believe in ghosts, witches, evil spirits, and the like evokes an unambiguous answer: as part of the cultural heritage of their society, these beliefs have been acquired by the present generation of Burmese from previous generations. Having said that, the practitioners of the historical approach would be interested in discovering how these beliefs are related to other aspects of Burmese culture and society such that, together, they comprise an integrated "system." To the extent that they are interested in additional explanation these anthropologists would then turn in one of two directions. An older generation, concerned with diachronic questions, would have attempted to discover when and under what conditions in the history of Burma the beliefs were invented or borrowed. A younger generation, concerned with problems of "meaning," would pose its questions in semiotic terms: what are the cultural symbols by which the Burmese express and represent their beliefs, and what do these symbols "signify"?

Anthropology conceived as "science" is no less interested in these questions, but it is not content to say that the Burmese believe in their various types of supernatural beings because such beliefs are culturally determined. This statement contains a number of implicit assumptions that pose further problems for research. We know, for example, that the beliefs comprising the cultural heritage of any group sometimes die out or are so transformed over time that they become unrecognizable. We know, too, that even when they persist many cultural beliefs are held with little cognitive conviction or emotional involvement. Hence, if we are interested in distinguishing genuine beliefs from cultural clichés, it is not enough to say that traditional beliefs are held by the members of a social group because they are "culturally determined." Such an explanation is the beginning rather than the end of inquiry, for if genuine beliefs are those which are cognitively and affectively salient, there is no escaping the task (which some anthropologists relegate to "psychology") of attempting to ascertain the cognitive orientations and motivational dispositions of the social actors who hold them.

But even if it were to be granted that this is a worthwhile task, how, it might be asked, does it lead us from history to science? Although such an inquiry might provide a richer texture against which particular cultures might be better understood, how does it enable us to proceed from the local and parochial dimensions of particular cultures to their general and universal dimensions?

To answer these questions one might begin by observing that despite the plasticity that characterizes human beings, their cognitive orientations and motivational dispositions are hardly limitless: indeed, the limits are much narrower than anthropologists are usually prepared to recognize. Thus, when cultural beliefs from a diversity of human societies are examined under a psychological microscope, it is usually possible to demonstrate that underlying their broad range of surface-structure variability there is a narrow range of deep-structure variability. If so, although cultural beliefs can be explained, on the one hand, by reference to the particular historical characteristics of the groups in which they are found, they can also be explained by reference to certain generic characteristics of the human mind. This, indeed, is what was attempted in this book. The Burmese religious beliefs described here are traced not only to historical processes specific to Burma, but also to psychological processes that are presumed to operate everywhere.

This presumption is based on the traditional anthropological premise of (what is called) the "psychic unity of mankind," a premise that no longer evokes universal assent within the anthropological community. Some anthropologists, espousing an extreme form of cultural relativism (one that borders on what might be termed cultural solipsism), contend that each culture is a unique configuration that can be understood only in its own conceptual terms. Although admitting that it is usually possible to gloss the concepts of another culture, they believe that it is never possible to render their meanings by the concepts of a trans-cultural anthropological science.[1] Hence, it is contended, even if the members of different societies are assumed to share the same kind of mind, their incommensurable culturally acquired conceptual systems forever render its characteristics unknown and unknowable. For radical cultural relativism, as for radical behaviorism, the mind is a black box.

This book, in contrast, assumes that despite the variability in culture, the minds of culture bearers are characterized by pan-human properties ("psychic unity of mankind"); that these properties are the products of a shared biological and cultural phylogeny, on the one hand, and a shared social ontogeny, on the other; that the diversity in culture represents various attempts of the human mind to solve the existential and adaptive problems of social life, which vary with historical experience and ecological conditions; that although cultural diversity is found at the level of "surface" structure, it is associated with trans-cultural regularities at the level of "deep" structure; that the trans-cultural regularities of deep structure are transformed into the diversity of surface structure by means of historically conditioned, and therefore culturally parochial, symbols and symbol systems; that the interpretation of cultures consists in part in the translation of surface-structure cultural symbols into deep-structure meanings; that

---

[1]This view, of course, not only precludes the possibility of a comparative anthropology—is there any other kind?—but logically entails that ethnographies can only be written by and for native speakers in their native language. Thankfully, most of the spokesmen of this view have not followed the logic of their own position.

since deep-structure meanings are grounded in the psychic unity of mankind, their symbolic representation (in the parochial symbols of surface structure) can be described by the concepts of a trans-cultural anthropology. This last, among other things, is what this book has attempted to do.

The Psychological Basis for Belief in Mythico-Religious Systems

Having described the general framework within which this book was written, I now wish to examine two problems of interpretation which have been addressed by certain of its critics. The first problem relates to the theoretical question of the psychic unity of mankind, and, more specifically, the assumption that culturally parochial symbols may have pan-cultural meanings, both conscious and unconscious. The second problem relates to the ethnographic question of whether the religious beliefs and practices described here comprise a separate religious system, analytically and phenomenologically distinguishable from Buddhism (as is argued in this book), or whether they, together with Buddhist beliefs and practices, comprise one religious system (as some critics argue). Let us begin, then, with the first problem.

That human beings attempt to maximize pleasure, that pleasure consists in the gratification of wishes and desires, that many of the latter (since all human beings belong to the same biological species and are members of culturally constituted human groups) are pan-human—these putative characteristics of the human mind would, I take it, evoke fairly wide assent. That wishes and desires must be fulfilled by transactions with the environment, and that these transactions are based on perceptual and cognitive processes, many of whose characteristics are universal, are also widely accepted assumptions. Thus, if perception were not (for the most part) veridical, it would be difficult to explain the survival of the species, and if there were some society in which this was not the case, it would be difficult to account for its persistence. In short, if there ever was a society whose members could not typically distinguish fantasy from reality, or hallucinatory from veridical perception, that society, surely, is now part of the fossil record of human history. Cloistered scholars may speculate about the "social construction of reality," but in their transactions with nature even they must either adapt or perish.

The same considerations hold with respect to cognitive processes. Societies whose members were unable to assess causal relationships, to see logical connections, to arrive at valid inductive generalizations, or to make valid deductive inferences—these are societies in which even simple economic activities, such as hunting and gathering, would have had no possibility of success. In a word, such societies would not have survived. The cognitive processes alluded to here comprise a form of thinking which is governed by normally accepted rules of logic, and in which ideas and thoughts are represented by verbal symbols which are combined and manipulated by conventional rules of grammar and syntax. At the cultural level this mode of thinking is institutionalized in cultural systems that govern those adaptive activities that we denote as economic, technological, and so on.

In his study of dreams, fantasy, and related phenomena, however, Freud discovered yet another form of thinking, one in which ideas and thoughts are represented in visual symbols and other forms of imagery, and whose logic is analogous to that exhibited in metaphor, metonymy, and other tropes and figures of speech. Following Freud, we may term this mode of thinking the "primary process" mode, in contrast to the first, which he termed "secondary process." If, at the cultural level, economic and technological systems are based on secondary process thinking, mythico-religious and ritual systems are based on primary process thinking. Hence, the decoding of these latter systems presents some of the same problems encountered in decoding a dream. Just as in dreams we must attend to both manifest and latent content, so in religious systems we must attend to both surface and deep structure. Before turning to this decoding problem, however, we must first address a prior problem.

To claim that religion and myth, like dreams, are based on primary process thinking is to claim not only that they possess a certain kind of symbolic structure (which we shall describe below), but also that the mythico-religious world is a symbolic construction which the actors take to be real rather than symbolic. It is to claim, in short, that mythico-religious beliefs are based on a form of thinking in which, as in dreaming, fantasy is taken for reality, symbols are taken for things, images in the inner world are taken for objects in the outer world. Despite this comparison of religion and myth with dreams, we cannot ignore the fact that the latter differ from the former in one crucial respect. When dreamers awaken from their sleep, they recognize (at least in some societies) that the dream which they had taken as an occurrence in the external world was in fact a nocturnal fantasy, a creation of the mind. If, then, religion and myth, like dreams, are based on primary process thinking, why is it that religious believers do not awaken, as it were, from their religious slumber and recognize that the mythico-religious world is in fact a fantasy world? In short, why are the objects and events portrayed in the dream-as-recalled recognized as fantasy, while those portrayed by religious beliefs are believed to be real? The answer, I think, is twofold. It consists, first, in an obvious difference between mythico-religious symbols and dream symbols, and, second, in certain characteristics of the human mind, both of which predispose the actors to accept the reality of the mythico-religious world. These, at least, are the answers implicitly suggested in this book, and which now I wish to make explicit. I shall begin with the first answer.

The world of the dream is *invented* by the actor himself; it is a mental representation, in the form of *private* visual symbols (images), of ideas and thoughts of his own creation. The dream-as-recalled is a mental representation in memory—hence, a reproduction—of the dream-as-dreamt. That it is a memory of actual events (which is how they are construed in the dream-as-dreamt), rather than of fantasied (symbolically constructed) events, is supported by no independent evidence. By contrast, beliefs concerning the world of myth and religion, rather than being invented by the actor himself, are *transmitted* to him by his social group by means of cultural or *public* symbols: they are conveyed by language (external verbal symbols) and represented in ritual and sacred drama (external visual symbols) which proclaim their truth. From the messages conveyed in these socially transmitted cultural symbols, the actor constructs a mental representation, in the form of visual symbols (images), of the mythico-religious world; and in accordance with his culturally acquired beliefs, he locates this world in external reality.

In short, for the waking actor one difference between the nonreality of the dream world and the reality of the mythico-religious world is that the former is constructed from private symbols, the latter from culturally constituted symbols. This means that: 1) The reality of the mythico-religious world is not only proclaimed by the full authority of tradition, but is also confirmed by the ever-present (and socially compelling) public symbols from which the actor's representation of this world was constructed in the first place. 2) The fantasy (primary process) quality of symbolic representation by means of images is blunted in the case of the mythico-religious world by its simultaneous representation in verbal (secondary process) symbols. Whereas, upon awakening, the chaotic, fragmentary, and often bizarre quality of the dream challenges one's belief in the reality of the dream world, the systematic and coherent character of myth and religion present no challenge to the reality of the mythico-religious world. 3) Since culturally constituted symbols are public (and therefore shared), the belief in the reality of the mythico-religious world is supported by the fact that any actor's mental representation of that world is confirmed by the consensual validation of his fellows.

Although enhancing the belief in the reality of the mythico-religious world, these characteristics of cultural symbols are hardly a sufficient explanation for the belief. They do not explain why it persists in the face of competing, and often compelling, counter-claims of fact or reason: if the latter render the belief irrational or absurd, actors resolve their cognitive dissonance not by abandoning the belief, but by resting it in faith. This suggests, as William James observed long ago, that religious belief ultimately rests in the "will to believe," which perhaps finds its most extreme expression in Tertullian's *credo quia absurdum est*—I believe because it is absurd. From the strength of the will to believe in the reality of the mythico-religious world, it may be assumed that this belief satisfies some powerful needs, an assumption that brings us back to the relationship between the interpretation of cultures and the psychic unity of mankind.

Mythico-religious systems, as Max Weber has observed, have two universal functions, both being related to the vexatious problems raised by human suffering. First, these systems provide answers to the *existence* of suffering—illness, death, drouth, loss, madness, and so on—and to its seemingly unfair and inequitable distribution. Second, they provide various means for *overcoming,* if not avoiding, suffering. If, then, despite the remarkable cross-cultural diversity in their structure and content, religion and myth have (at least) these two universal functions, it follows that human actors universally have two corresponding needs which preadapt them to believe in the reality of their mythico-religious worlds. These include a need to explain and find "meaning" in phenomena that are seemingly inexplicable and meaningless, and a need to conquer the intolerable anxiety attendant upon painful and frightening situations that are beyond the ability of human actors to affect or control. If the proposition that these needs are universal characteristics of the human mind seems banal, it is because all of us, including radical cultural relativists, are so accustomed to perceive human beings in this fashion that we take this proposition to be self-evident. Self-evident or not, the universality of these needs shows that the relativity of cultural symbols does not imply a corresponding relativity of the human mind—not, at least, in all its dimensions.

But the will to believe, however powerful the needs from which it is derived, could not in itself explain the belief in the reality of the mythico-religious world unless there were also some cognitive basis for the belief, and this book argues that such is indeed the case. Just as human actors are affectively preadapted, they are also cognitively preadapted to believe in that world's reality. Although the preadaptive cognitive orientations are not innate (as the preadaptive needs seem to be), their universality derives from three universal characteristics of human infancy: prolonged helplessness, extended dependency, and relatively late acquisition of language.

Because of these characteristics, cultural systems (political, religious, economic, etc.) are neither the only sources from which social actors construct their representational world, nor the first. Beginning from birth—prior to their acquisition of the *culturally constituted* conceptions of the world made possible by language—children develop *socially constituted* conceptions of the world on the basis of their social experiences (ongoing encounters and transactions) with parents and the other "significant others" comprising their behavioral environment. Hence, inasmuch as infants are entirely helpless and absolutely dependent on these parenting figures, they construct mental images of incredibly powerful beings long before they learn about the existence of the supernatural beings postulated by their culture. These images, of course, are highly distorted, exaggerated, and even bizarre representations of the actual parenting figures, and after children acquire language and mature egos, they are usually relinquished (often, however, with considerable struggle) in favor of more realistic conceptions. In the case of infants, the mental representations of these powerful beings are constrained neither by the rational (secondary process) thinking made possible by language, nor by the reality-testing made possible by mature ego-functioning. (For an authoritative discussion of such mental representations, see Schafer 1968.)

That infants possess neither language nor mature ego-functioning has yet another important consequence for their distorted conceptions of the parenting figures in their behavioral environment. Typically, real parenting figures are in varying degrees, but simultaneously, both good and bad, helpful and harmful, dependable and undependable, controllable and uncontrollable, and so on. This, however, is not how they are represented by infants: first, because they have not achieved object-constancy; second, because they have not acquired language. Prior to the cognitive stage of object-constancy—which is not achieved until about 18 months, according to Piaget—different types of experience with one and the same person are not yet organized to form a single, integrated conception of him; rather, each type of experience produces a separate image of the same person. Hence, instead of constructing conceptions of beings who are simultaneously good *and* bad, helpful *and* harmful, and so on, infants form images of beings who are good *or* bad, helpful *or* harmful. But even with the achievement of object-constancy, integrated conceptions of parenting figures are precluded by the absence of language. When these figures are symbolically represented in images rather than in words, the representation in a single symbol of different—let alone opposed—conceptions of the same person is impossible. Hence, the infant (no less than the artist or the dreamer) must represent the different attributes of the same person in separate images. For both reasons, then, parenting figures are symbolically represented not in a single, integrated image, but (by a process known as "splitting") in separate images of powerful beings, some of whom are good, some bad, some helpful, some harmful.

It should now be apparent that the mental representations which young children form of the parenting figures comprising their family world are highly similar to those which they form much later of the supernatural beings comprising the mythico-religious world. Moreover, since their mental representations of their parenting figures are constructed from actual experiences with real beings, and therefore denote real beings, they are cognitively preadapted to believe that their mental representations of supernatural beings (which are constructed from conceptions of them conveyed by religion and myth, rather than from direct experience) also denote real beings. Since the former are real, there is no reason, surely, to doubt the reality of the latter.

To summarize, then, myth and religion are examples of symbolic representation in the primary process mode because they represent fantasy in the guise of reality. They succeed in achieving this end because, universally, human actors are preadapted to believe in the reality of the mythico-religious world. First, they possess innate needs which are satisfied by, and hence motivate the belief in, the reality of this symbolic world. Second, as a result of their prolonged helplessness and consequent protracted dependency on parenting figures, they develop cognitive structures (images, fantasies) related to the real world which seem to validate their belief in the reality of this symbolic world.

Deep Structure and Surface Structure in Religious Symbols

Thus far I have been treating the symbols comprising myth and religion at the level of their (culturally specific) surface structure only. But these cultural systems also exhibit a (universal) deep structure—or so, at least, it is argued in this book—which means that their symbols have unconscious, as well as conscious, meanings. To explicate the unconscious meanings of cultural symbols, we must examine yet another characteristic of symbolic representation in the primary process mode. To do this, we must return to the representational world of infancy and childhood.

The cognitive *stage* of the infant, as I have already observed, is similar in many respects to the cognitive *state* of the dreamer. The latter, whose reality-testing (while sleeping) is impaired, cannot distinguish inner from outer experience, or, to put it differently, cannot distinguish the symbol from that which it symbolizes. Hence, although the dream-as-dreamt occurs as images in the internal world of the mind, these images are both *reified* (i.e., they are believed to *be* rather than to *represent* the objects and events they denote) and *externalized* (i.e., they are believed to occur in the external world of space). The dream, in short, is a nocturnal hallucination. These same cognitive distortions that characterize the sleeping thoughts of the dreamer characterize the waking thoughts of the infant, not because his reality-testing is impaired, but because it is still undeveloped. Thus, the infant's mental images of his parenting figures are often reified and experienced either as autonomous agents existing in the inner world (whence they are labeled, in the terminology of psychoanalysis, as "introjects") or, since the infant's inner and outer boundaries are blurred, as externalized agents (projections) in the outer world. As the ego develops, these reifications are gradually given up, although (as children's imaginary playmates indicate) this mode of primary process thinking is not relinquished easily. Those few individuals who do not give them up exhibit severe psychopathology—borderline and schizophrenic states in the case of persistent introjects, paranoia in the case of persistent projections (cf. Schafer 1968).

The externalized reifications of parental images may, however, undergo yet another fate, which is our concern here. When there is a fair degree of integration between social and cultural systems, the character of parent-child interaction (which is governed by the socialization system) produces in the child conceptions of parenting figures which are structurally isomorphic (on such dimensions as power, control, benevolence, etc.) with the attributes of the supernatural beings comprising the mythico-religious system. This being so, when images of these supernatural beings are constructed by the child, they may be merged (identified) with the images of his parenting figures to form a single representational world. Under these circumstances, the externalized (projected) reifications of early parental images may not be relinquished (and yet result in no pathological consequences), for they may be construed as those very supernatural beings whose external reality is taught by religion and myth. If so, the belief in the external reality of these supernatural beings is assured by their being identified with the reified and externalized images of the parenting figures.[2] This, at least, is the hypothesis adopted here. In rapidly changing societies, however, in which—because of differential rates of social and cultural change—there may be much less integration between social and cultural systems, the self-evident status of religious beliefs is maximally jeopardized, with the result that the beliefs may either be relinquished or (as we have already observed) proclaimed as an article of faith.

If this analysis of the relationship between the mental representations of parenting figures and those of supernatural beings is correct, it may be inferred that when, for example, God is referred to by Christians as "our Father who art in heaven," the expression may be said to have two simultaneous meanings. Consciously, "Father" is taken figuratively, for God surely is not thought to *be* one's father (whether genitor or pater); rather, with respect to certain attributes—justice, mercy, love, etc.— He is thought to be *like* a father (pater). Unconsciously, however, "Father" is to be taken literally, for "God" represents one of the reified and externalized mental representations of the pater of childhood.

If, to express it more generally, the child's mental representations of supernatural beings are merged with his reified and externalized mental representations of his parenting figures, the various cultural symbols for these supernatural beings—whether they take the form of words, icons, sculptures, paintings, or any other—have both surface-structure and deep-structure meanings simultaneously. At the level of surface structure, these symbols represent the *culturally constituted* conceptions of the supernatural

---

[2]If, as sometimes happens, parental introjects are not relinquished, or if, having been projected, they are again introjected, the merging of parental and supernatural images in the inner world may be experienced as supernatural possession; that is, a god, spirit, or the like is experienced as having entered into and having seized control of the person.

beings portrayed by religion and myth—Jahweh, Allah, the Madonna, Siva, Durga, and so on. This is their conscious meaning. At the level of deep structure, they represent the *socially constituted* conceptions of the parenting figures of childhood. This is their unconscious meaning. (This analysis might be contrasted with that of Durkheim who, it will be recalled, viewed God as a symbol—at the level of deep structure—for society.) In sum, underlying the cross-cultural diversity in the surface meanings of the symbols of mythico-religious beings, there are important cross-cultural uniformities in their deep-structure meanings: the culturally parochial external symbols constitute symbolic transformations of culturally universal internal symbols.

If, then, the culturally parochial meanings of these mythico-religious symbols are associated (as we have seen) with culturally invariant (manifest) functions related to universal characteristics of the human mind, this should also be the case, a fortiori, for the (latent) functions associated with their culturally universal meanings. To aid us to understand the latter functions and characteristics, we shall turn once again to the symbolic form of the dream, as well as of poetry, for assistance.

Should a poet wish to represent some attribute of a friend—his strength, for example—he may convey this attribute either in simple prose ("Charles is strong"), in a figure of speech ("Charles is [strong] like a lion"), or in a trope ("Charles is a lion", or, more succinctly, "the lion"). In the trope, "lion" is intentionally used as a metaphorical, not a literal symbol: it is intended to express the poet's conception of Charles (he is strong), rather than to represent a carnivorous feline. Should the poet then proceed to portray some behavior of the "lion," he is still using this symbol metaphorically to denote Charles.

A dreamer, however, whether poet or policeman, has fewer degrees of freedom to express his conception of a friend. The attribute of strength—like any attribute that is conveyed in verbal symbols by means of adjectives and adverbs—is difficult to express directly in the visual symbols that constitute dreams. One of the ways that the dreamer (like the painter or sculptor) can solve this problem is to express his thought by means of a visual trope; he may, for example, represent his conception of his friend by an image of a lion. If so, the dreamer, like the poet, represents his conception by a symbol which, inasmuch as it literally represents something else, is an apparently inappropriate symbol. In the poem, a conventionally inappropriate verbal symbol is substituted for a conventionally appropriate one because the poet believes that he can express his thought more effectively, forcefully, or artistically by a figurative than by a literal symbol. In the dream, a visually inappropriate symbol is employed not as a substitute for one more appropriate, but because the symbolic medium does not provide the dreamer with an appropriate symbol.

In addition to the representational constraints imposed by the symbolic medium, there are other reasons that dream thoughts might be represented by inappropriate visual symbols. (Indeed they are the same reasons that a poet, in addition to stylistic and craft considerations, might represent his thoughts by conventionally inappropriate symbols. Since, however, we are on surer ground with the dream, I shall choose it as my example.)

If it be granted that motivation may have extra-cultural as well as cultural roots, it might then be expected that some of our thoughts relate to wishes and desires that conflict with our culturally acquired values. Although our commitment to these values usually leads us to suppress such thoughts, their suppression (as anyone who attends to his waking fantasies, if not to his dreams, can testify) does not mean their extinction. One way of coping with the moral anxiety aroused by this conflict is to *re*press the forbidden thoughts, i.e., to ban them from conscious awareness. Let us suppose, now, that someone has repressed a forbidden thought concerning a friend—the thought, for example, that he would like him to die. Let us suppose, too, that while he is sleeping this thought continues to press for expression, and that by substituting an image of a lion for that of his friend, he dreams of a dead lion or, perhaps, of himself killing a lion. In short, by disguising the identity of the victim, this symbolic substitution permits the dreamer to express a hostile wish, albeit in a distorted form.

Notice the difference between the use of an inappropriate symbol in this dream, on the one hand, and in the poem and the first dream, on the other. In all three cases, a symbol for a lion—"lion" in the poem, an image of a lion in the dreams—is used to represent a human being. In the first dream and the poem, the figurative meaning of the symbol is its *consciously* intended and exclusive meaning. In the other dream, it is its literal meaning that is consciously intended, but this is not its exclusive meaning, for its figurative meaning is also, although *unconsciously,* intended. In other words, in the poem and the first dream, the lion symbol is used as a *trope,* while in the second dream it is used as a *defense mechanism.* In a trope, the figurative meaning of a symbol is consciously intended because the actor's purpose in choosing a manifestly inappropriate symbol is to more effectively *express* his thought. In a defense mechanism, the figurative meaning is unconsciously intended because the actor's purpose in choosing a manifestly inappropriate symbol is to *disguise* his thought.

Since our concern here is with defense mechanisms rather than with tropes, we may now summarize the characteristics of the defensive use of symbols in the technical psychoanalytic terms which are employed, but not defined, in the chapters that follow. When a symbol is used defensively, a) the motivation of the actor is *overdetermined,* i.e., he has more than one purpose in choosing the symbol. On the one hand, he wishes to express a forbidden thought; on the other hand, he wishes to disguise the thought so that, having been rendered morally acceptable, it does not arouse guilt. b) This disguise is achieved by means of an unconscious process known as *displacement,* in which an inappropriate is substituted for an appropriate symbol as the vehicle for representing the thought. By this process (which follows the same logic exemplified in such verbal tropes as metaphor, metonymy, and synecdoche) the affects, as well as the thoughts, related to the original (appropriate) symbol are transferred to the substitute (inappropriate) symbol. c) Hence, the substitute symbol is characterized by *condensation* (polysemy), i.e., it has two or more intended meanings, at least one of which is unconscious. d) The literal, or *manifest,* meaning of the symbol is conscious, while its figurative, or *latent,* meaning is unconscious.

We may now apply this analysis of the defensive meaning of private symbols to the culturally constituted symbols of religion and myth. That these latter symbols have figurative, as well as literal, meanings is, of course, a commonplace observation for those scholars who are exclusively concerned with their surface structure. If, however, we also attend to their deep structure, and if at this level these symbols may denote (among other things) the reified and externalized images of the parents of childhood, we can then understand how they may also be *used* defensively. The word *used* is italicized because, in order to understand the defensive meaning of religious symbols, it is important to distinguish religion-in-belief from religion-in-use, a distinction which is analogous to Saussure's distinction between *langue* and *parole.*

Religion-in-belief refers to the actor's organization of religious symbols into a system of meanings (ideas, beliefs, conceptions, and the like). The actor, however, not only organizes these symbols, he uses them; and, as has already been observed, the uses to which he puts them relate to the explanation, reduction, and overcoming of suffering. To achieve these ends, he engages in ritual transactions with the supernatural beings represented by his religious symbols, and he also (necessarily) thinks about his relationship with them. Some of these beings are conceived to be (because they are taught as being) kindly and benevolent; others are conceived as aggressive and malevolent. The former are turned to for assistance and aid, while the latter are pacified, warded off, and (when necessary) driven away and exorcised. The former evoke longings for dependency and nurturance, the latter attitudes of fear and hatred.

All of these thoughts, affects, and activities are not just consistent with the surface-structure meanings of the symbols by which the supernatural beings are represented; they are also appropriate to the religious contexts in which they are displayed. It is obvious, however, that many of these affects and actions are almost universally inappropriate when displayed by adults in contexts other than religion. Although dependency is a legitimate posture of childhood, adults are expected to be self-reliant and independent actors. Similarly, within the culturally defined boundaries of the in-group, aggression is usually prohibited, and most children in all societies eventually learn to inhibit their aggressive needs, so that they are seldom exhibited in adult behavior. This does not mean that feelings of dependency and aggression, and the motivation to behave in a dependent or aggressive fashion, are extinguished in adults. Indeed, it is commonplace that such feelings and motives, however strongly suppressed, are capable of arousal in certain contexts and under certain provocations. That they are usually suppressed is a measure of both the strength of the cultural norms that prohibit their expression and the effectiveness of the actors' enculturation. That they are nevertheless arousable is a measure of their intensity.

There is one context, in particular, in which aggression and dependency are especially problematic and uniquely disruptive. This context, of course, is the family. As the child's most significant others, his parenting figures are at once his most salient frustrators (and, consequently, the most important targets of his aggressive feelings) and his most important nurturers (and, consequently, the most important objects of his dependency feelings). At the same time, these figures are the objects concerning whom the prohibitions against dependency and aggression are most severe. Human and social survival demand that the child relinquish his dependency on his family of origin and, having achieved autonomous status, become a parent himself and an object for the dependency of his own children. Similarly, intra-family aggression—even more than incest, though for some of the same reasons—is entirely disruptive of the family and of its important social functions. In most societies, moreover, the conscious awareness of feelings of dependency or aggression in relationship to parents can be expected to arouse moral anxiety in the actors, not, to be sure, because of the objective requirements alluded to above, but because in the course of their socialization and enculturation they have internalized the prohibitions against expressing such feelings. The moral anxiety aroused by aggressive feelings against parents is probably the more intense because parents are usually viewed as objects of affection and love.

Given, then, the strength of the cultural prohibitions on the expression of aggression and dependency in relationship to parenting figures (and other family members), and given the strength of the moral anxiety aroused by these affects when they enter conscious awareness, it is hardly surprising that they are not only strongly suppressed, but usually repressed, i.e., they are excluded from conscious experience. This being so, they can achieve gratification only in a disguised form: they must be displaced or gratified by some kind of defensive maneuver. The condensation which is characteristic of religious symbols—their denoting of supernatural beings at the level of surface structure, and (among other things) the parenting figures of childhood at the level of deep structure—enables religion to be used in exactly this manner. That is, given this polysemic character of religious symbols, religion can be used as a culturally constituted defense mechanism for the unconscious gratification of the needs for dependency on and aggression against parents. In coping with suffering, the Burmese, for example, invoke the assistance of *devas* (gods), and they exorcise nats (evil spirits). In doing so, they consciously gratify dependency and aggressive needs, respectively, but only in relationship to beings who are their culturally appropriate objects and targets. To the extent that these supernatural beings are also the externalized reifications of benevolent and malevolent parental images, it may also be suggested that the Burmese are simultaneously, but unconsciously, gratifying prohibited dependency and aggressive needs with respect to their parents.

This example is not intended to suggest that these are the only latent functions served by religion. Rather, this example was chosen to illustrate one postulated universal function of religion as it relates to the interaction between one universal meaning of the deep structure of religious symbols and two especially important characteristics of the human mind—the needs for aggression and dependency. As this book abundantly shows, religious symbols may have other deep-structure meanings, some of which vary from culture to culture. The following chapters describe some of the deep-structure meanings of Burmese religious symbols, and the ways in which the latter are used to gratify still other needs, both conscious and unconscious. (For a more extended treatment of the functions of witchcraft, see Spiro 1969.)

Nat Religion and Buddhism

Having dealt with the first problem raised by this book—that of the pan-cultural meaning of culturally parochial symbols—we may now briefly turn to the second, or ethnographic, problem, one that has come to be referred to in the anthropological literature on Southeast Asia as the "two religions" problem. I argue in this book (especially in Chapter 14) that the beliefs concerning the supernatural beings discussed therein, particularly those known as nats, the rituals and festivals related to them, and the religious specialists that are the central figures in their cultus comprise a distinctive religious system which, in many respects, is not only different from but is also incompatible with the other religious system of the Burmese—Theravada Buddhism. (For a description of Burmese Buddhism, see Spiro 1970.) Each of these religions has separate doctrines, rituals, and specialists, and although both are concerned with the essential problem of any religion—the problem of suffering—each addresses a different dimension of this problem. For Buddhism, suffering is ultimately an existential problem, being viewed as inherent in the very nature of life. Hence, the solution to the problem is achievable only at the end of the long cycle of rebirth, with the attainment of nirvana. For the religious system described here—let us call it the nat religion—suffering is a pragmatic problem; it concerns illness, loss of cattle, destruction of crops, and the like, the solution to which is achievable by practicing various types of ritual.[3]

If their conceptions of and modes of dealing with suffering were their only differences, we would not want to view Buddhism and the nat religion as distinctive, let alone inconsistent, religious systems; rather, we would view Buddhist beliefs and rites as the soteriological dimension, and nat beliefs and rites as the nonsoteriological dimension, of a single Burmese religious system. I view them as separate religious systems on two different grounds. First, viewed from the outside, the very premises of nat beliefs and the practice of many nat rites are incompatible with—indeed they are often opposed to—essential elements of the metaphysics, ethics, and ethos of Buddhism (as Chapter 14, among others, indicates). Like all of the great salvation religions, Buddhism is an ethical religion, requiring commitment to and practice of a moral code as the first step to the achievement of salvation, both the proximate salvation of rebirth in one of Buddhism's heavens and the ultimate salvation of the attainment of nirvana. As a symbol of the ethical principles of Buddhism and of the renunciation of the world that eventually attends their implementation stands the world-renouncing Buddhist monk. The nat religion, on the other hand, is an amoral, magical religion, whose world-embracing cult specialist (*nat kadaw*) is the Dionysian inversion of the Buddhist monk. Second, many Burmese themselves are keenly aware of this incompatibility, and they themselves maintain that Buddhism and the nat cult comprise separate and distinctive systems. Many of them go so far as to say that only their Buddhist beliefs and rites should be designated a "religion." (Despite this emic view, I have designated nat beliefs and rites as a "religion" because they satisfy all the criteria for the etic definition enunciated at the beginning of this Preface.)

However much they may disagree with *my* view of the relationship between Buddhism and the nat cultus, it is rather strange, in the light of the abundant evidence supplied in the following chapters, that the critics of the "two religions" thesis have chosen to ignore the *Burmese* view. Tambiah, who *is* concerned with the Burmese view, and whose own views, as we shall see, are similar to my own, nevertheless claims that the inconsistencies to which I point between Buddhism and the nat cult are derived entirely from my "own understanding of what true Buddhism really

---

[3]In one of its aspects, Buddhism too is concerned with suffering as a pragmatic problem. It contains not only a theology, but also an elaborate ritual system for dealing with it. Even in this aspect, however, Buddhism differs from the nat religion in that these beliefs and rituals have been ethicized, the supernatural protectors are Buddhist, and the rites are performed by Buddhist monks. (See Spiro 1970:chs. 6, 11.)

is," and do not represent the perception of the Burmese (Tambiah 1970:42). It is certainly true, of course, that the incompatibility that I delineate between these two systems is based, in the first instance, on a comparison of nat beliefs and rites with Buddhist doctrines enunciated in the canonical texts. Tambiah is in error, however, when he claims that although sophisticated Burmese may be aware of some of these inconsistencies, villagers are not aware of them. In support of this claim, Tambiah offers the following quotation from page 46 of this book: "None of the villagers, however, showed any awareness of the basic inconsistency." To be sure, even this one quotation would have been sufficient to support his claim were it germane to the topic under discussion. As even a brief glance at page 46 reveals, however, this quotation does not refer to nat beliefs and rites at all. It refers instead to certain aspects of the beliefs concerning Buddhist gods (*devas*).

Since the section from which this quotation is taken is entitled *Devas,* and since the entire section is devoted to this one topic exclusively, Tambiah's misreading is rather surprising. It is all the more surprising that Tambiah did not present the data which describe the Burmese awareness of the incompatibility between Buddhism and the nat religion, not to mention the conflict which it engenders in them. I shall turn to Tambiah's own views concerning this issue below.

Most critics of the "two religions" thesis hold that Buddhism and the spirit cults of Southeast Asia (nat in Burma, *phii* in Thailand, and so on) comprise instead one syncretistic religion. For Kirsch such a "syncretic" relationship means that "elements derived from several historically discrete traditions have combined to form a single distinctive tradition. In such a situation, individuals may simultaneously hold beliefs or practice rituals derived from different traditions, without any apparent sense of incongruity" (Kirsch 1977:241). Not too many pages later, however, Kirsch proceeds to show that the spirit cult and Buddhism are not one, but distinctive and separate systems; that on some dimensions they are not only different, but opposed; and that this is recognized by the actors themselves. Consider the following statement, among others.

> In contrast to the respect accorded to Buddhist and Folk Brahman features . . . considerable ambivalence is expressed about the entire animist domain . . . most animist practitioners have little respect among their fellows. There are clearly deep-seated cleavages between animistic elements and Buddhism and Folk Brahmanism. In many respects, animism stands in symbolic opposition to that which Buddhism values most highly: asceticism, self-control, and predictability. The superior potency of Buddhism over animistic threats is taken as axiomatic by Thai . . . [p. 259].

To characterize a situation in which separate religious traditions retain their distinctive beliefs, rites, and specialists; in which there are "cleavages" between them; in which one stands in "symbolic opposition" to the other—to characterize such a situation as "syncretic" is, surely, to use that term in a strange way. It is no less strange to claim, on the one hand, that the devotees exhibit "considerable ambivalence" about one of these traditions, and, on the other, that they hold to both systems "without any apparent sense of incongruity."

If, nevertheless, we still wish to characterize the relationship between Buddhism and the spirit cults as one of syncretism, we must then invent a new term for the "syncretism" that is usually alleged to have obtained when, for example, the fusion of Hebrew and Greek thought produced Christianity, or the fusion of Muslim and Hindu notions produced Sikhism, or—more aptly—the fusion of Christian and pagan beliefs almost everywhere produced folk Christianity. Consider, for example, the famous Virgin of Guadalupe. In pre-contact Mexico, Tepayec (the modern Guadalupe) was the site of the cult of the mother-goddess Tonantzin. Following the Christian conquest, Tonantzin was fused with the Virgin Mary, producing the Virgin of Guadalupe. In the process, Tonantzin (whose attributes have been assimilated to that of the Virgin) has disappeared as a distinctive deity, as have the rites associated with her worship. Today, there is only one mother goddess, the Christian, whose conception is integrated with the other conceptions comprising Christian theology, who is worshipped in a Christian church, whose mode of worship is Christian, whose worship is led by a Christian specialist, and so on. If, then, this is a paradigmatic situation of "syncretism"—as most religious scholars take it to be—it is surely confusing to similarly characterize the relationship between Buddhism and the spirit cults as it is described by Kirsch (with whose description I agree).

Although he does not use the term "syncretism," Keyes, another critic of the "two religions" thesis, holds that Buddhism and the spirit cults of Southeast Asia comprise "a single religious system" in which, however—he cautiously concedes—"a tension between Buddhist and animist beliefs may sometimes exist" (Keyes 1977:115). As an example of such tension, Keyes cites the difference between Buddhism and the spirit cults with respect to their explanations for suffering, the former attributing it to karma, the latter to spirit causation. He does not, however, think these explanations conflicting; rather, they merely denote a difference between "proximate" and "ultimate" causes. The logic of this attempt to deny conflict is rather elusive. According to the doctrine of karma the actor himself is responsible for his suffering, which is moral retribution for sinful action, and the agent of retribution is impersonal. The spirit doctrine, on the other hand, assumes that the actor has no responsibility for his suffering, that it is caused by a malevolent or capricious agent, and that this agent (a spirit or a sorcerer) is personal.

In support of his view that these are not contradictory but merely different explanations, Keyes offers the example of an infertile woman who could either attribute her difficulty to karma or else seek the assistance of the *devas*. She opted for the latter choice because she "obviously finds it psychologically more satisfying to continue to perform ritual offerings . . . in the hope of becoming fertile than to resign herself to her condition" (p. 115). This is a curious example, for two reasons. First, this case cannot possibly involve a tension between Buddhism and the spirit cults since the *devas* are part of Buddhism: their propitiation may represent a "tension" within Buddhism, but not between Buddhism and the spirit cults. To the extent, however, that the case is intended to illustrate Keyes' contention that karmic and non-karmic theories of causation are different, but not contradictory, the logic is clearly misguided for, of course, it shows just the reverse. The woman had to decide whether to attempt to change her unhappy state, or merely to resign herself to it. As Keyes sees it (and I entirely agree) she chose the more satisfying of these mutually exclusive options. But to say that mutually exclusive explanations are merely different, rather than contradictory, is to invoke a curious logic.

Keyes (like some other critics of the "two religions" thesis) twists not only logic but also facts in order to sustain his view. Thus, in criticizing my contention that nat and Buddhist beliefs are in conflict concerning (among other things) the persistence of some kind of spiritual essence after death, Keyes contends that though this may be the case in Burma (which he doubts), it is not the case in Thailand. Although he concedes that in northeast Thailand it is believed that "consciousness" survives through successive rebirths, this, he claims, is an entirely "orthodox Buddhist" belief. To support this seemingly heterodox contention, he cites the authoritative opinion of Buddhaghosa. There is, however, one problem with the citation: Buddhaghosa says the very opposite of what Keyes purports him to have said. Indeed, in the very opening section of the *Visuddhi-Magga,* quoted by Keyes, Buddhaghosa unequivocally denies Keyes' claim: "There is no entity, no living principle; no elements of being transmigrated from the last existence into the present one." After this opening passage, which Keyes seems to have overlooked, Buddhaghosa proceeds to describe the process of death, in which, as one by one the vital organs begin to fail, "consciousness residing in that last refuge, the heart, continues to exist by virtue of karma . . ." (in Warren 1953:238). It is this passage which Keyes interprets to mean that "consciousness" persists into the next birth.

Keyes' interpretation of this passage is not only contradicted by the immediately preceding passage, but is just as clearly contradicted by the succeeding passages. Consciousness, Buddhaghosa goes on to explain, does not persist into one's next rebirth—though it is the locus of "desire" which is the cause of rebirth—for as soon as a person dies his *former* consciousness passes out of existence, and a *new* consciousness comes into existence. So that there might be no misunderstanding concerning this conclusion, Buddhaghosa repeats it yet once more. "But it is to be understood that this latter consciousness did not come to the present existence from the previous one . . ." (in Warren, p. 239). In short, if Buddhaghosa is to be taken as our authority, the belief that "consciousness" persists from one birth to the next is *not* an "orthodox Buddhist" belief. With respect to this one doctrine at least—the doctrine of *anatta,* or the impermanence of the soul—there is a clear contradiction between Buddhism and the spirit religion.

Let us now turn to Tambiah who, unlike these other writers, fully recognizes the opposition between Buddhism and the spirit cults. The Thai villagers he studied view the spirit cults "as belonging in a separate and even opposed domain of religious action" from that of Buddhism (Tambiah 1970:264). Hence, Buddhist monks do not participate in the spirit cults (p. 264), the motivations for making offerings to Buddhism and the spirit cults are entirely different (p. 264), their rites may not be performed on the same days (p. 268), their specialists and their modes of recruitment are differentiated by sex, morality, and temperament (pp. 283, 286), their "theology" and ethics are opposed (p. 309), and so on. Realizing that such a situation (which is precisely like that in Burma) can hardly be characterized as "syncretism," and yet objecting to the notion of two religions, Tambiah sees Buddhism and the spirit cults as comprising a "single field" characterized by "hierarchy, opposition, complementarity, and linkage" (p. 377).

One cannot help wondering, then, why Tambiah objects to the "two religions" hypothesis, for despite the differences in terminology, it would seem that he and I are saying very nearly the same thing. We both recognize that there are two distinctive systems, Buddhism and the spirit cults; that on many dimensions these two systems are based on logically incompatible premises ("opposition"); that each serves certain functions not served by the other ("complementarity"); that though the actors in both systems are the same (linkages"), Buddhism enjoys a position of primacy ("hierarchy"). To be sure, there is a difference of sorts between a "single field," comprising opposed but complementary systems (Tambiah), and "one culture," comprising opposed but complementary religions (Spiro), but why should a difference of such small magnitude have provoked a polemical reaction?

Perhaps Tambiah's reaction may be explained by the fact that in this book I examine religion not only culturally, but also psychologically, and for Tambiah this is not acceptable. "The systematic arrangement and structuring of the religious field as such," he argues, *"has* to be sought not at the level of the individual actor but elsewhere—at the level of collective representations composed of religious ideas and formalized rituals" (p. 340, italics supplied). On this point Tambiah and I are in complete disagreement. This book assumes that the religious field—and, for that matter, any other—is best understood when it is studied at both "levels." This being so, data are presented here which, I believe, refute Tambiah's claim that it is both "mischievous" and a "misunderstanding" to view Buddhism and the nat religion as sustaining a relationship of (as Tambiah puts it) "uneasy co-existence" (p. 41). For these data show that the "opposition" which Tambiah perceives only at the level of "collective representations" is also perceptible at the level of the "individual actor." More importantly, they show why it is that the peoples of Southeast Asia have retained the spirit cults despite their strong devotion to Buddhism and despite the fact that these two religions are often in conflict. In short, these data explain why syncretism has *not* occurred.

References

KEYES, CHARLES F.
1977   *The Golden Peninsula.* New York, Macmillan.

KIRSCH, A. THOMAS
1977   "Complexity in the Thai Religious System." *Journal of Asian Studies,* 36:241–266.

SCHAFER, ROY
1968   *Aspects of Internalization.* New York, International Universities Press.

SPIRO, MELFORD E.
1969   "The Psychological Function of Witchcraft Belief: The Burmese Case." In *Mental Health Research in Asia and the Pacific,* William Caudill and Tsung-yi Lin, eds. Honolulu, East-West Center Press.

1970   *Buddhism and Society.* New York, Harper and Row.

TAMBIAH, S. J.
1970   *Buddhism and the Spirit Cults in North-East Thailand.* Cambridge, Eng., Cambridge University Press.

WARREN, HENRY CLARKE
1953   *Buddhism in Translations.* Cambridge, Mass., Harvard University Press.

I

INTRODUCTION

CHAPTER ONE

The Study of
Supernaturalism

THE PROBLEM

Although religion, like all cultural systems, has numerous functions, and although different religions may have different functions, they all help their devotees to cope with the problem of suffering. They serve this function in two ways: first, by offering an explanation for (if not the origin of) suffering, and second, by providing techniques—consistent with their respective explanations—by which suffering may be avoided or its burden diminished.

Since no cultural system is entirely self-consistent, religion may provide alternative, logically incompatible explanations for the phenomena it purports to explain. The believer, often unaware of the incompatibility of these explanations, may hold both explanations simultaneously. This occurs most frequently when he is the heir to more than one religious tradition, a situation which obtains not only in cases of religious syncretism, but also in those cases in which dual religious allegiance is permitted. A Chinese, for example, may say his devotions at both Taoist and Buddhist temples; a Japanese might worship the gods of both Buddhism and Shinto; a Singhalese might make religious offerings to a Hindu *deva* as well as to the Buddha Gautama.

That Buddhism, in both its Theravadist and Mahayanist forms, is never the exclusive religion of its lay devotees can now be accepted as a truism.

Wherever it is found, Buddhism is accompanied by some other religious (using "religious" very broadly) system. In Burma and in the other countries of Southeast Asia, the latter system comprises a folk religion which postulates the existence of "supernatural" beings and which includes a set of rituals relating to them.[1] Whether Buddhism and this companion religion (which is usually termed "animism") are distinct and mutually exclusive systems, as some authors believe, or whether they are hopelessly interfused, as others believe; whether animism is the "basic" religion, while Buddhism is a mere veneer, or whether animism has been superseded by Buddhism, the former persisting as a "survival"—these, and still other, controversies can be profitably discussed and analyzed. I shall discuss some of them in subsequent chapters. What is rather to be emphasized here is that no one who is at all acquainted with the ethnography of, or who has himself undertaken research in, a Buddhist society can have avoided encountering those animistic beliefs and practices which, viewed as a system, can be referred to as "supernaturalism." Since Buddhism and supernaturalism are very different religions, it is not surprising that each offers its own explanation for suffering and its own techniques for its resolution. It is hardly surprising, too, that their explanations and their techniques are often incompatible. Such is the case in Burma, whose system of supernaturalism is the subject of the present study.

As a study of Burmese supernaturalism, this study attempts to describe and explain a variety of "supernatural" beliefs—ghosts, demons, witches, and those spirits whom the Burmese call *nats*. Of these four types of beings, it is the nats who loom most important in Burmese thought and behavior, their cultus comprising an organized and an elaborated system of beliefs, rituals, and practitioners. Although these four types of beings are substantively distinct, they are functionally similar. They are all "supernatural" in that their power is greater than man's; they are all either harmful or potentially harmful; and they all, therefore, are believed to use their power to cause human suffering. According to Burmese animism,

---

[1]Typical is De Young's description of a Buddhist village in Northern Thailand (1955:143): ". . . in almost every incident of a peasant's daily life, from his birth to his cremation, the spirits, or *pi*, are still propitiated. Spirits exist in many forms —ghosts of the dead; wandering astral spirits of the living; spirits of trees, the ground, the house, and a host of natural objects. The variety is great, but the one common element is that the spirits are evil or will become so if not properly propitiated."

In this respect Hindu society is no different from its Buddhist counterpart. "To the newcomer," writes Carstairs (1957:89) of an Indian village, "it is the latter elements [i.e., "primitive animism, magical fantasy and superstition"] which are immediately apparent: the multitude of wayside shrines, the stories of ghost-afflictions, of witchcraft and of sorcery. The very houses are congested with spirits. . . . The open countryside is scarcely less haunted. . . . Ghosts and demons are protean . . . a wise man was always on his guard against being thus deceived." For a general discussion of the relationship between animism and the high religions of South Asia, see Mandelbaum (1966).

then, supernatural intervention is the primary, if not the exclusive explanation for suffering—an explanation which is remarkably different from that proposed by Theravada Buddhism, as it is taught and practiced in Burma.

In analyzing the Buddhist treatment of suffering, it is important to distinguish its explanation for the *origin* of suffering from its explanation for its *cause*. For Buddhism, the origin of suffering is to be found in desire, or, as the Buddhist term *taṇhā* is more accurately rendered, in craving and clinging. Since, however, desire is an attribute of all sentient beings, it follows that suffering can be eliminated only by the transcendence of sentient existence, i.e., by the attainment of nirvana. In most cases, however, this goal may not be attained even after thousands upon thousands of rebirths, so that the most that the average person can hope for in any one rebirth is the gradual reduction of suffering by the gradual reduction of desire, a process which is achieved by grasping the Four Noble Truths of Buddhism and by following its Noble Eightfold Path.

But the *origin* of suffering, in this generic sense, does not explain the *cause* of personal existential suffering. Illness, the loss of one's cattle, the death of one's child, pressing poverty, and so on, are attributed by Buddhism to the inexorable working out of one's karma, which consists of the consequences of the good and evil deeds committed in all one's previous existences. Suffering, therefore, is the karmic consequence of one's past sins, or, as Buddhism calls them, demerits. This being so, one cannot escape, or even alleviate, present suffering; one can only hope to preclude future suffering by eliminating those desires which produce the sins, which produce the karma, which produces the suffering.

However satisfying it may be intellectually, the Buddhist explanation for the cause of suffering is less than fully satisfying emotionally. It not only places the responsibility for his suffering exclusively on the sufferer, but it precludes any possibility of coping with it: there is no escape from one's karma. Supernaturalism provides not merely an alternative explanation for the cause of suffering, but one which is more satisfying emotionally. Since, according to the supernaturalist explanation, suffering is caused by evil witches, harmful nats, and so on, the sufferer in some cases is entirely blameless—he happens to be the victim of an evil witch who, from malice, has chosen him as a victim. In other cases he is only inadvertently responsible—he has unwittingly offended or neglected a nat who, annoyed by his behavior, punishes him. In both cases, moreover, he can alleviate his suffering by appropriate ritual techniques. He can make restitution to the nat; he can call upon any number of supernatural practitioners to combat the witch; or, paradoxically enough, he can utilize Buddhist power, channeled through a variety of rituals, to combat his supernaturally caused harm. It is little wonder, then, that supernaturalism, given its explanation- and resolution-potential for suffering, has been a perduring feature of Burmese culture, despite the latter's pronounced Buddhist cast.

This function of Burmese supernaturalism is at once its most obvious and its most important function. Because it is so obvious it is taken for granted, rather than tediously reiterated, in the explanatory sections of the chapters which follow. But if the importance of this explanatory hypothesis is taken for granted, we are then confronted with two problems to which this explanation does not address itself, and it is to these problems that the explanatory sections of this book are addressed: namely, a) What are the conditions—cultural, social, and psychological—that produce and maintain supernaturalism, rather than some other system which might serve the same function of explaining and resolving suffering? b) Given that supernaturalism, rather than some other system, does serve this function, what are its consequences for the other systems— cultural, social, psychological—with which it interacts? In attempting to answer these questions, I have derived my explanations primarily from two theoretical traditions: functional anthropology and culture-and-personality.

It should be emphasized, then, that in its theoretical concerns this study is not so much an exercise in the testing of theory as it is in its application. To be sure, the logical line that separates these twin aspects of the theoretical enterprise is a thin one, for every application of a theory is at the same time a validation procedure. Thus a good "fit" between theory and data *ipso facto* provides additional support for the theory; and, by strengthening one's confidence in the validity of the theory, it enhances its "subjective probability." Conversely, if the fit is not good, one's confidence in the validity of the theory, or in the explanation derived from it, is weakened, with the consequence that one or both may be revised if not discarded. Still, despite their logical similarities, there is an important substantive difference between the testing of a theory and its application. In the latter case the investigator has a substantive interest in a set of social or cultural data, and his intellectual task is to explain these data by reference to a body of theory which, for the purposes of this task, he accepts as valid. In the former case, however, the theoretical structure is taken as problematic, and the data are of interest to him only insofar as they are relevant to his intellectual task of testing the validity of the theory; they are of interest, that is, evidentially rather than substantively.

Although my interest in Burmese supernaturalism is substantive, it is markedly dissimilar from the substantive interest (and, therefore, from the approach) of what has come to be known as the "new ethnography." I am not interested, that is, in Burmese supernaturalism *per se*, nor am I interested, as an end in itself, in "how the natives think" about their supernatural beliefs or in the criteria by which they classify and order them. For me these are intellectually trivial questions, "trivial" with respect to what I consider the main tasks of inquiry in the social sciences—*viz.*, the discovery of regularities in social and cultural phenomena and of the causal laws by which they may be explained. This being so, *Burmese* supernaturalism is of scientific interest only as an empirical instance of the type *supernaturalism*. (Similarly, "supernaturalism" is of interest as a subtype of "religion," which, in turn, is of interest as a subtype of "cultural belief system.") From this it is evident that my interest, unlike that of the new ethnography, is not in "reproducing" Burmese supernaturalism by means of Burmese categories (which in any event I believe to be impossible); rather, I am interested in explaining it by means of theoretically relevant categories. For if the task of the anthropologist, *qua* anthropologist, is to explain Burmese culture and not (however much he may wish to do so, *qua* citizen) to emulate it, then the categories that are relevant for anthropological inquiry are not the categories through which the "natives" order the world, but those through which it is ordered by anthropological theory.

As between the "emic" and "etic" approaches, then, my approach is unabashedly etic. The former approach leads to a descriptive and relativistic inquiry whose interest begins and ends with the parochial. The latter approach leads to a theoretical and comparative inquiry in which the parochial is of interest as an instance of the universal. If the former issues in ethnography, the latter (although based on ethnography) issues in science. Since I am interested in science, the explanations offered in this study use concepts which are analytic rather than substantive; their reference is usually to a theoretical construct rather than to an ethnographic category; and their domain is usually the class "supernaturalism," and not merely Burmese supernaturalism.

Like science in general, the scientific approach to social and cultural inquiry rests on the assumption that nature (including society and culture) is lawful, and that underlying its manifest diversity there is a discoverable regularity. It is my personal assumption, which I wish to make explicit from the very start, that the regularity which underlies the manifest (cross-cultural) diversity in cultural *forms* rests on a common psychobiological "human nature," and that within any cultural domain (and frequently across domains) the *wide* range of diverse forms constitutes a set of structural variations for the satisfaction of a *narrow* range of common psychobiological needs. To put it somewhat more technically, these diverse forms represent functionally equivalent structural alternatives. Since, *ex hypothesi*, human nature is a constant, the diversity in cultural forms must be explained by reference to the diverse ecological contexts to which societies must adapt and to the diverse historical contexts in which cultures arise, persist, and are transmitted. With respect to supernaturalism, then, any of its parochial forms—Burmese supernaturalism, for example—must be explained by reference both to its (unique) contexts and to its (universal) processes and functions.

Despite the current revolt against functionalism, therefore, I remain an unregenerate functionalist. (It should be noted, however, that although derived from functional theory, my explanations are cast, for reasons described in Chapter 5, in a causal mode). Hence, although entirely sympathetic with Lévi-Strauss' strategic emphasis on the analysis of cultural symbols (and, especially, with his attempt to discover "structural" universals), I believe his exclusive concern with the formal properties of symbolic systems to be misconceived. This is not to deny that such systems as myth and ritual have an underlying logical structure: Such an assumption would be given the lie by Lévi-Strauss' brilliant demonstrations to the contrary. It is to deny, however, that these systems stem primarily from some need, as it were, to "play" with symbols, or that the discovery of their logical properties is our most important task. For me, at least, to know that mythical themes exhibit a binary oppositional structure is not to know enough, and to argue that totems exist because they are good for thinking is not good enough. Although humans may like to think, and although sometimes they may even think logically, human thought, like the rest of human behavior, is generally goal-directed. And if culturally constituted symbol systems represent the historical distillation of human thought, it is surely part of our job to discover at least the ends, both conscious and unconscious, to which they are directed. For if it is their meaning for social actors with which we are concerned (the analysis of these symbol systems may be concerned, of course, with other kinds of "meaning"), it is in these ends (their manifest and latent functions), rather than in their formal properties, that this meaning will be discovered.

For me, then, the approach of Lévi-Strauss cannot substitute for the more traditional approaches of functional anthropology and culture-and-personality, although, unlike the new ethnography, it importantly augments them. In both of these traditional approaches, culture is of interest not merely for its formal (logical or lexical), but for its functional, attributes. This is so probably because these latter two approaches not only take culture seriously, but they also take man and society seriously. Indeed, for both of them, culture (taken as a cognitive system) is the handmaiden, as it were, of man and society. It is the indispensable instrument by which men, both individually and collectively, adapt to the physical environment, their fellow men, and themselves. Since, for both of them, man is not only a rational animal, but also a biological and social animal, culture is the means *par excellence* for controlling the nonrational and irrational forces inherent in biology and society. And since, for both of them, conflict (both social and psychological) as well as order is present either potentially or actually in all men and in all groups of men, culture is necessary to reduce conflict and to promote integration. Finally, since for both of them man seeks for "meaning" even more than he seeks for order, cultural systems classify the universe, not merely to render it intelligible, but also (as Weber puts it) to make it "meaningful." Thus, to return to the theme broached at the beginning of this section, since suffering (and especially its unequal distribution) both poses an intellectual problem and is experienced as an existential condition, the Burmese classification of their supernatural world not only orders their supernatural beings according to discoverable criteria, but, in doing so, also gives "meaning" to their problem of suffering. It provides an answer, in part, to their intellectual problem and it enables them to cope with the existential condition.

That both these approaches—the one concerned with the social and psychological consequences of symbolic action, the other with its instigations—present both technical and methodological difficulties cannot be denied. In the absence of experimental controls, it is difficult to arrive at more than an educated guess concerning the functions of symbolic systems; and, since a variety of motives might serve to instigate the same act, generalizations about the motives which assure their persistence are always hazardous. Despite their difficulties, however, these approaches are not haphazard. Theoretical advances in social systems analysis permit us to check our functional interpretations against theoretical expectations; and, since the motives with which we are concerned are those which are relevant to the maintenance of these systems, we need not attend to a society's entire "motivational pool." Still, the problems remain, and they cannot be swept under the rug. I would say only that in the debate between those who would sacrifice theoretical importance for technical precision and those who, in order to pursue significant problems, are willing to tolerate some degree of cognitive ambiguity, I am happy to join the latter.

SETTING

Most of the materials described in this study were collected in 1961–62, during the course of anthropological field work centered in Yeigyi, the pseudonym for a village in Upper Burma, about ten miles from the city of Mandalay. Although this study is concerned with Burmese supernaturalism, it should be emphasized at the outset that the various phenomena which I have subsumed under this rubric were not my primary concern. My main reason for undertaking field work in Burma was to explore the relationships among an otherworldly religious system (exemplified in Buddhism), the personality patterns by which it is maintained, and the social (and, specifically, the political) system by which group life is organized. These interests were aroused by Weber's sociology of religion, and especially by his essay on the social psychology of the world religions (Weber 1946). Although "otherworldliness" was my focal concern, the fact that much of the basic spadework in Burmese ethnography, despite Scott's classic monograph (Shway Yoe 1896), was still to be performed necessitated a general ethnographic study of Yeigyi prior to undertaking the more intensive study of "otherworldliness." This decision stemmed from a sense of responsibility to ethnological science, as well as from the anthropological truism that most theoretical problems in the social sciences must be explored within a total social and cultural context. The study of supernaturalism, then, was undertaken as part of a more general ethnographic investigation of Burmese society and culture, the findings of which will be published separately.

Since fourteen months hardly constitute sufficient time to accomplish the somewhat ambitious goals of this type of study, and since field work, however carefully designed, is at best a spotty and haphazard enterprise, I am painfully aware that my materials, and therefore this study, are filled with many, often wide gaps. When planning my Burma research, I originally intended to return to Burma for a series of trips in which, hopefully, these anticipated gaps would have been progressively narrowed. Had I been able to execute this original plan, publication would have been deferred until further field work could have been undertaken. Unfortunately, the visa policies of the present military Government have made it impossible to conduct research in Burma. The reader should be warned, therefore, that since the data are incomplete, some of their interpretations, by that token, may well be in error.

Although most of my research efforts were centered in the village of Yeigyi, they were not confined to this village. Since I was interested in understanding Burmese society and culture, rather than in describing the Burmese village system, my work took me to a number of other villages in Upper Burma, as well as to the cities of Mandalay and Rangoon. I chose a village as the base of my operations because it seemed to be the most manageable functional unit in which the patterns of Burmese culture and the structure of Burmese society might be studied. Hence I was not interested in Yeigyi *qua* village, but as a locale in which those patterns and that structure might be exemplified.

In order, however, to test the assumption that I was studying Burmese society and culture (refracted, to be sure, through a village prism), rather than a—or even *the*—Burmese village system, it was necessary to compare the data collected in Yeigyi with data obtained in other settings. Hence my excursions to other villages for periods ranging from a week to a month, as well as to Mandalay and Rangoon. I spent much more time in Mandalay than in Rangoon because, although I lived in Yeigyi, my family lived in Mandalay, and I returned there twice a week for almost a year to be with them. While visiting them, I was able to meet and talk with our many Mandalay friends and to interview a variety of other Mandalay informants. My stay in Rangoon was confined to a period of one month following our arrival in Burma and another month prior to my departure. Nevertheless, since I lived in Yeigyi for nine of the fourteen months which I spent in Burma, and since most of the materials presented here are based, therefore, on my research in this one village in Upper Burma, a brief description of Yeigyi will be of some value.

With a population of approximately five hundred people, Yeigyi is situated on a central irrigation canal. Since this is the dry zone of Upper Burma, irrigation is indispensable for wet rice cultivation, the dominant economic activity of the village. The village comprises 119 houses, each of which, typically, is inhabited by a nuclear family. Although most villagers were born and raised in Yeigyi or in one of the neighboring villages, a few families, mostly basket makers and loggers, who have emigrated from a district about forty miles northwest of Mandalay, are relatively recent arrivals to Yeigyi. These immigrants occupy a low position in the social structure, and their houses—which, like most village houses, are constructed of bamboo poles and coconut thatch—tend to be concentrated within one section of the village.

Surrounded on three sides by paddy fields—blue with water during the transplanting season, and golden in the growing season—and by the foothills of the purplish Shan hills on the fourth, and protected from the cruel tropical sun by clumps of shade trees, the village offers a most attractive approach. Like most villages in Upper Burma, however, Yeigyi is reached only after traveling for four or five miles on a dirt road which, in this case, connects with the highway leading to Mandalay.

Although the oxcart is the main means of transportation—the few wealthy villagers use bicycles—the proximity of Mandalay means that this, the former capital of Burma and its second largest city, is relatively accessible to Yeigyi. The city's main bazaar is used by the villagers for important shopping, its famous pagodas beckon on Buddhist holy days and pagoda festivals, and its money lenders and rice merchants are important mainstays of their agricultural economy. This, then, is not an isolated village, remote from outside contacts or influence. On the other hand, although the British conquered Upper Burma in 1885 and administered it (except for the brief interlude of the Japanese occupation) until Burmese independence in 1948, Yeigyi and its environs show much less British cultural influence than villages in Lower Burma. From the early nineteenth century the Mandalay region was, and continues to be, the heartland of traditional Burmese culture.

From very early times Yeigyi and its neighboring villages were part of the economic and cultural orbits of the various royal courts of Upper Burma, and especially of the court at Mandalay. Prior to the British conquest of Upper Burma, Yeigyi performed services of various kinds for the government in Mandalay, and after the conquest it was caught up in the insurgency and unrest that attended the exile of King Thibaw. Although having little contact with the British Raj during the fifty-year period prior to the Japanese occupation of Burma, the British political presence was felt by the villagers and, in retrospect at least, respected and appreciated. World War II ushered in a long period of tension and unrest, which continues to the present. The Japanese occupation, harsh and brutal, was experienced directly by the village. Similarly, the achievement of independence was followed by a series of insurrections against the central government which, in some parts of Burma, still continue, and which were experienced by Yeigyi as late as 1959. The area around Yeigyi witnessed numerous battles between government and insurgent troops, and Yeigyi itself was occupied and reoccupied by at least two of the insurgent groups. Indeed, a small number of men, and a few women as well, joined one or another of these groups for short periods. The most recent upheaval impinging on the village, one to which I have already alluded, was the *coup* of 1962 which replaced the civilian with a military government. Although the villagers had frequently expressed many criticisms of the civilian government, the military takeover left them bewildered and anxious.

Despite these changes and upheavals, there were few differences between the basic social and cultural patterns which I encountered in Yeigyi in 1961–62 and those described in early—indeed, in the earliest—published reports on Burmese life by western writers. Paddy cultivation continues to be the basic economic and subsistence activity. The nuclear family household, related through bilateral kin ties to other households both within and outside the village, remains the basic social unit. The village continues to be governed by a village headman—who, however, is now an elected, rather than a hereditary official—and a council of village elders; and it is to them, rather than to government courts or magistrates, that most intra-village disputes are brought. Buddhism continues to be the single most important cultural force in the village, and certainly its most important basis for social integration. There are three monasteries in Yeigyi, with a combined population of four resident Buddhist monks and a somewhat larger number of temporary and transient novices. As in the past, every male child is ordained as a temporary member of the monastic order; and, as in the past, Buddhist devotions are recited, holy days are observed, and pilgrimages are undertaken by almost every villager. Technologically, too, the village has undergone few changes. Yeigyi has no radios, no tractors, no electricity; all tasks are performed by either man power or ox power. Farming and sex, gossip and intrigue, worship and celebration, pilgrimage and festival—these continue to be the major axes along which the sociocultural matrix of life in Yeigyi (and in Burma in general) can be ordered.

It is a matrix, I hasten to add, within which the Burmese are reasonably content. Unlike the inhabitants of most other parts of Asia, few Burmans ever lack for food or other physical needs. There are plenty of frustrations, of course, but when life gets too difficult, the Burman can find some surcease in saying his beads, in worshiping at the pagoda, in watching a play, in participating in a festival. If necessary, he can retreat, temporarily or permanently, to a monastery. But always he can perform numerous acts of merit by means of which he can hope for a better existence in his next birth, perhaps as a wealthy man, perhaps even as a blissful inhabitant of one of many Buddhist heavens. (For detailed descriptions of contemporary Burmese village life, *cf.* Pfanner 1962, and Nash 1965).

RESEARCH METHODS

My initial material on supernaturalism was obtained in the course of a house-to-house census of Yeigyi in which questions about nats were routinely included as a part of a general schedule designed to elicit information on household composition, kinship, economics, values, and religion. In addition to these respondent interviews, I conducted a series of informant interviews with villagers known to be knowledgeable about supernaturalism. These interviews were designed to elicit cultural beliefs about the nat cultus, ghosts, witches, and so on, rather than information concerning the personal beliefs and practices of the informants.

My knowledge of Burmese being limited to simple conversations, I conducted all formal interviews through an interpreter. Since, however, I had four different interpreters during my stay in Burma, I was able to check the reliability of these interview data by comparing the information obtained through each of these four different human media. Although interpreter reliability was very high, it would be rash to deny that interpreters are a source of error; and although I believe that the margin of error from this source was small, I cannot be sure that this was the case.

From these informant interviews information was obtained concerning known cases of nat possession and other types of confrontation with nats, and, whenever it was possible those villagers who had had these experiences were interviewed. Gradually, as the villagers learned that I was interested in these phenomena, they began to inform me of any cases that occurred either in Yeigyi or in neighboring villages. Thus, it was possible to interview current cases as well as to observe the performance of the rituals by which they were treated. In the same fashion I came to know a number of the practitioners—doctors, shamans, and exorcists—who, in quite different ways, were involved in the nat cultus. From them I obtained not only professional information, but biographical and psychological data as well. They were important sources, too, for information on witches and witchcraft, so that, in addition to the few cases of witchcraft that I was able to observe during my period of study, I had access to former victims of witchcraft or to their friends and relatives. Witchcraft data, like nat data, were obtained both through respondent and informant interviews, as well as through participant observation in exorcistic rituals.

But Yeigyi, as I have already indicated, was not the only source of data. Key informants were interviewed in a variety of other villages in the area, as well as in Mandalay and Rangoon. Questions concerning supernaturalism were routinely included in the interviews conducted with monks, both in villages and in the cities. English language newspapers were scanned for relevant information from other parts of the country, and my interpreters translated relevant articles which appeared in Burmese language newspapers.

Observations of and participation in supernatural rituals proved to be the most valuable source of data. In addition to participating in exorcistic and divinatory ceremonies, I was fortunate in being able to attend three important nat festivals, including the supremely important Taungbyon Festival. Living in Taungbyon for seven days, observing both the formal and informal behavior, and interviewing both laymen and shamans provided highly important insights into the meaning of the nats and the nat cultus for Burmese society and personality.

The same techniques which were employed for the collection of data about supernaturalism were employed for the collection of data about Buddhism, a topic which is especially important in the last chapter. In the case of Buddhism, needless to say, Buddhist monks, like shamans in the case of supernaturalism, served as key informants for eliciting normative doctrine.

Having briefly described the techniques of data collection, something must be said about the nature of the sample and, more generally, of the sampling problem in cultural studies. (A cultural study, in brief, is a study of a historically transmitted and socially shared system of ideas and of the symbolic actions attendant upon that system.) When working with simple societies, anthropology short-circuited the sampling problem by arguing that in these small and putatively homogeneous societies, a key informant was an adequate source of both cultural and social data— "adequate," at any rate, for discovering their basic social and cultural patterns. When, however, it began to investigate complex societies, in which social relations were not confined to small face-to-face groups, it became apparent that, at least for sociological-type studies, key informants were not adequate, and that valid generalizations required some kind of sampling procedure. From informants alone it was not possible to make reliable statements about, for example, the frequency of litigation, the distribution of power, the incidence of matrilocality, the prevalence of polygyny, and so on.

Recently, as anthropology has broken away from the dogma, promulgated for the past twenty-five years by a doctrinaire subbranch of social anthropology, that the study of culture is all but irrelevant for the understanding of behavior and that, in any event, it is less susceptible of scientific analysis than the study of society, cultural studies have become prominent once again. With this renewed interest in culture, the notion has developed, at least in some quarters, that the key informant (or a small set of informants) is a sufficient source even in complex societies for the collection of cultural data. For, it is argued, since the study of culture is the study of rules, norms, beliefs, and so on, the frequency of matrilocality, for example, or the incidence of polygyny are irrelevant for the study of residence rules or marriage norms. Hence, unlike the study of society, the study of culture can ignore the sampling problem because, in cultural studies, behavioral measures are superfluous. Often, but not always, structural linguistics is held up as the model which justifies this stance. Just as the linguist can construct a grammar (the rules of a language) on the basis of one informant, so too the anthropologist, it is argued, should be able to construct a culture (the rules of a society) by the same procedure.

Seductive as it is, this argument cannot be sustained. In the first place—and ignoring for the moment the linguistic model—how can we know that the beliefs, norms, and so on, elicited from one informant are cultural rather than idiosyncratic? Surely some sampling procedure is required in order to discover into which category the beliefs and norms elicited from him fall. Moreover, excluding children, deficients, and abnormals, by what criterion—and surely it must be a quantitative criterion—is any belief or norm assigned to the category of the "cultural"? Must it be held by the total population? 80 per cent? 51 per cent? Since, clearly, there is no ready answer to this question, any investigator must know, at least in some rough way, the distribution of a belief or norm which he claims to be cultural. In the case of nat beliefs, for example, he would want to know to what extent they are found among women as well as men, the rich as well as the poor, urbanites as well as peasants, and so on; and this he cannot discover by means of a key informant. He would want to know, too, the range of variation concerning various of the dimensions of some norm or belief. Given, for example, that the belief in nats is widely distributed, the investigator would want to know the range (and distribution) of beliefs concerning such of their attributes as benevolence, power, temperament, sex, punitiveness, knowledge, and so on. And this too he cannot discover without sampling his population.

Only after satisfying himself about the distribution and range of a belief, derived from the investigation of a variety of informants, can the anthropologist proceed to the analytic task of constructing the "organization" or the "structure" of a cultural belief system. Without such an investigation, and limiting himself to a key informant, he can only construct the "organization" of his informant's belief system which, for all he knows, may be idiosyncratic rather than cultural. Those anthropologists who defend the key informant technique argue that the sampling procedure is a means merely for discovering the range of opinions which informants hold about a belief system, rather than a means for constructing the "structure" of the system. But this argument, surely, can be sustained only if they are then prepared to argue that cultural systems "exist" in an ontological realm independent of the belief systems of living social actors.

Contrary, then, to some current opinions, I would claim that cultural, no less than sociological, studies must confront the problem of sampling. But I would claim even more. Although concerned primarily with idea systems, cultural studies cannot avoid the task of studying behavior as well as ideas. For if culture consists, for example, of norms, and if cultural norms (by definition) govern social behavior—much as grammatical norms govern linguistic behavior—then an informant's statements cannot be taken as normative until they are tested against behavior—his own and that of others. If an anthropologist were then to discover that some putative norm is not reflected in behavior—if, that is, behavior does not comply with its requirements, or if noncompliance entails no punitive sanctions, or if, though noncompliant, the actor experiences no guilt—would he persist in labeling the informant's statement, although it exhibits no normative properties, as a cultural "norm"? The conclusion would seem to be obvious: cultural research cannot neglect to study behavior if, that is, the notion of "norm" is not to be shorn of all meaning, and if culture (as a system of norms) is taken to be an important component of action.

The notion that cultural studies can ignore behavior because "culture" has an ideational rather than a behavioral referent is all the more surprising when proposed by those who point to structural linguistics as their model. The linguist's grammar, after all, is not derived from an informant's statements about grammatical rules. Rather, it is constructed by the linguist on the basis of inferences which he draws from the informant's language behavior. Deprived of behavioral data—and, please note, the linguist samples his informant's behavior—the linguist could not even begin to do his job. To be sure, a grammar is different from a culture in that (among other differences) the members of a speech community can seldom articulate the rules which govern their language behavior, while the members of a cultural community can articulate most of the rules which govern their social behavior. By the same token, however, it is the existence of other differences between language and culture which enables the linguist to use only one informant while requiring the anthropologist to use a sample.

But suppose some anthropologist, despite these *caveats*, was prepared to argue, and to face the *reductio*, that informants' statements, even when they have no behavioral consequences, are nevertheless cultural norms.

Suppose, then, that he were prepared to concede that the statement, "All men are created equal," even when elicited from informants in Mississippi, is a statement of a cultural norm. How, then, would he proceed to evaluate its cultural importance? And even he, I assume, is interested at some time in distinguishing "important" from "unimportant" norms. Surely, to return to the subject of this study, it would not be enough for him to conclude that Burmese Buddhism is more important than supernaturalism because an informant, or even a random sample of informants, told him that this is so. At some point he would have to test their statements against some independent criterion, and what other criterion could he use except their behavior? Scholars may disagree over the appropriate behavioral indices of "importance"—that is an easily resolved technical disagreement —but they would not disagree, surely, that the independent criterion must be a behavioral criterion.

Few field studies, of course, can do more than approximate the research model implicit in the above discussion. Although in the study reported here behavioral as well as ideational data were collected, the sampling techniques were more opportunistic than systematic. Although data were collected from the range of important sociological categories—age, sex, occupation, wealth, education, locality, population size, and so on—I do not know to what extent the samples chosen from these categories were either random or representative. I can be reasonably sure of only one thing, *viz.*, that the data reflect almost the entire range of possible beliefs and practices pertaining to supernaturalism. With respect to belief variables, the range extends from complete orthodoxy (as defined by verbal statements of "orthodoxy") through skepticism and disbelief. When evaluated by the same criterion, the range of ritual practices extends from strict observance of normative practice through nominal practice and (in a very few cases) nonobservance. Only in the case of Yeigyi, however, can I be confident about the distribution of beliefs and practices, as well as of their range. Since the non-Yeigyi data reveal the same range as those found in Yeigyi, it is not implausible to assume that their distribution, too, is similar, and that the general patterns found in Yeigyi are typical of those to be found in other parts of Buddhist Burma. Still, since there are some differences between my findings and the findings of scholars who have worked in Lower Burma, and even in Upper Burma, these differences, to the extent that I am aware of them, are noted in the text, and most of my own generalizations are accompanied by a description of the sample(s) from which they are derived, and of the range and distribution of the data on which they are based.

Before concluding this section, it should perhaps be added that although field work is the anthropologist's most important research tool, his data must be placed in a wider context for their meanings to be more fully probed. The two most immediately relevant contexts include the historical and the regional. Hence, in addition to combing the historical materials on Burma for information concerning supernaturalism, I attempted, upon returning from the field, to familiarize myself with the literature on cognate phenomena in other societies within the Burmese cultural orbit. These historical and regional comparisons provided important clues for, as well as checks on, the many interpretations which are offered for the phenomena which I observed at first hand.

A Note on Spelling and Terminology

The thesis that the meaning of exotic concepts can never be satisfactorily rendered in translation has become a fetish in recent ethnographic theory. But even granting the truth of this notion, I would nevertheless suggest that the use of English words, properly defined, constitutes much less of a communication barrier than the use of a spate of native terms whose meanings are almost impossible to remember. On this assumption I have decided to follow the first of these two alternatives throughout this book. Thus, after a Burmese or Pali term is introduced for the first time, and its meaning is rendered in English, it is usually replaced in subsequent contexts by its most appropriate English equivalent. Only in those few instances in which English equivalents, except through the use of complex locutions, are unavailable, are the exotic terms retained. In such instances, however, the term with which the Western reader is presumably most familiar is the one which is used. Thus, for example, rather than using the Burmese *kan*, or the Pali *kamma*, the Sanskrit *karma* is consistently used on the assumption that it is the most familiar to the Western eye.

It should be emphasized that the meanings which I have assigned to Burmese terms and religious concepts are those obtained from informants in Yeigyi and elsewhere. Frequently these meanings, both of Burmese and of Pali terms, are different from their dictionary definitions, and I often indicate the discrepancy between these colloquial meanings and the technical or scholarly meanings of these terms. Nevertheless, as an anthropologist I am concerned with Burmese religious beliefs as they are conceived by the Burmese themselves, and it is with their colloquial meanings, therefore, that I work. This, of course, is one of the reasons for interviewing a variety of informants; for it is the consensus of their meanings, rather than those of historical or linguistic scholars, which are important for the field worker and which form the bases for his interpretations. Similarly, when I quote the opinion of an "expert" nat informant—i.e., a villager acknowledged by his fellows to be an expert—it is not with the intention of deciding an issue in historical scholarship. Indeed, he may be, and he often is, quite wrong in his historical or linguistic derivation of the meaning of a belief or concept—and therefore highly inexpert from the point of view of a historical or linguistic scholar—but he remains an "expert" for me because, to the extent that his opinions help to influence and shape those of his fellows, he tells me what I as a field worker want to and must know, *viz.*, the meanings and conceptions which the Burmese themselves attach to their beliefs.

The absence of a standard system for the transliteration of Burmese continues to present a problem for those who write on Burma. After experimenting with various alternatives, I decided (despite its drawbacks) to employ, with some few changes, the more or less conventional English spellings of Burmese words. The following, then, is a rough guide to the pronunciation of Burmese terms found in the text. (The spelling of Pali terms is taken from the Pali-English Dictionary of the Pali Text Society).

i	as *ee* in *seen*
e	as *e* in *yet*
au	as *o* in *for*
ai	as *i* in *kite*
ei	as *ei* in *veil*
ou	as *ou* in *soul*
au	as *ou* in *out*
a	as *a* in *father*
u	as *oo* in *roof*
th	as *th* in *think*
đ	as *th* in *that*
ky	as *ch* in *chat*
sh	as *sh* in *shine*
gy	as *g* in *germ*
g	as *g* in *game*

Aspirated consonants are preceded by an *h* (thus, *hsaya, hti*). Consistent with conventional usage, glottal stops are indicated, variously, by *t* or *k*. Tones are not rendered.

Acknowledgments

I can hardly hope to acknowledge all the assistance, both direct and indirect, which I received in the course of writing this book and during the research which preceded it. Most of what I know about Burmese supernaturalism I learned from the people of Yeigyi, my gracious hosts and patient informants. Numerous other Burmese were willing to share their beliefs and to expose their behavior to the anthropological eye. I am especially indebted to the sensitive and intelligent cooperation of my two main assistants, U Ba Thaw, a proud heir of traditional Burma, and U Aung Thein, a tutor at the University of Rangoon and a representative of modern Burma. U Ko Ko, professor at the University of Mandalay and my Burmese *hsaya*, was always prepared to place his vast knowledge of Burmese and Pali at my disposal.

For their comments and criticisms of an earlier draft of this book I am particularly indebted to five people. David Schneider's critical comments not only helped to sharpen some of my arguments, but even when rejected, they compelled me to reexamine and to spell out theoretical positions and methodological stances which I had normally taken for granted. Sarah Bekker, E. Michael Mendelson, F. K. Lehman, and Theodore Stern, whose expertise in certain topics dealt with in this study far exceeds mine, called my attention to numerous ethnographic points and saved me from many ethnographic blunders. Mendelson's assistance is especially apparent in the last two chapters, as the many references to his comments (and his publications) indicate. Lehman not only criticized the text but also performed the prodigious task of providing both a running commentary on the meaning of all Burmese terms and advice concerning their spelling. Mrs. Bekker's assistance was particularly helpful in connection with Shamanism, as was Stern's in relationship to problems of an historical nature. It should be said, lest these scholars be criticized for my errors, that I did not always follow their advice. Finally, I wish to express my gratitude to the National Science Foundation for its generous support of the field work on which this book is based.

II

THE TYPES OF
SUPERNATURALISM

CHAPTER TWO

Witches

THE BELIEF SYSTEM

Although it is assumed by some Burmese that witches are evil spirits in the form of humans, it is not their questionable status as spirits that is the basis for including them in this study, but rather that they, like evil spirits, are believed to possess supernatural power to cause suffering.[1] The epistemological status of this belief is no different from that of the belief in ghosts, demons, and other spirits. Witches and spirits alike are "known," in the first instance, through the learning of a culturally transmitted cognitive (belief) system, rather than through encounters with such beings. On the basis of this transmitted "knowledge," witches, like ghosts and other spirits, may indeed be "encountered," and they may be "perceived" to possess those attributes postulated by the cultural tradition. But the belief in their existence, like the belief in the existence of ghosts or nats, is acquired by learning about them, rather than by experiences with them. In this sense, the actual existence of witches is not at issue here, for even if their ontological status were different from that of spirits

---

[1]Belief in witches and in witchcraft is endemic, of course, in South and Southeast Asia, this belief being found within Hindu, Buddhist, and animist cultures alike. It would be instructive to compare Burmese witchcraft with that of such tribal groups in Burma as the Pa-O (Hackett 1953: 558ff.), Indian Hindus (cf. Carstairs 1957: 89ff.), or non-Burmese Buddhists such as the Singhalese (cf. Gooneratne 1866).

—a dubious assumption, at best, since no one has ever seen (or is reported to have seen) the actual practice of witchcraft—their epistemological status is identical: in both cases knowledge of their existence and of their attributes is derived from a cultural (belief) system.

Following Evans-Pritchard (1937) it has been customary in anthropology to distinguish two types of evil magical power exercised by human agents—sorcery and witchcraft. According to this distinction the witch is a person who possesses innate power to work harm against others, while the sorcerer achieves his ends by magical techniques which he has learned. In the former case the power resides in the practitioner, in the latter it resides in the magic. Although this is still viewed as a useful classification for much of the African materials (Middleton and Winter 1963), it has only limited utility for the classification of cognate Burmese phenomena; indeed, whatever utility it possesses is vitiated by the confusion which its adoption would entail. To be sure, the Burmese, too, distinguish between innate and learned techniques of magical harm, but this distinction is of almost no significance for them, and they are both referred to by the same term. The Burmese classification cuts across the dichotomy suggested by Evans-Pritchard, and since, functionally, the former classification is much more useful for my purposes, it is the one employed here.

There are various types of practitioners of evil in Burma, and different informants give somewhat differing lists, as well as different terms for the types comprising their lists. There is, however, near-consensus about the two major types with which this chapter deals.[2] These two major types are termed, in Burmese, *souns* and *aulan hsayas*. The distinction between them is based partly on the criterion of sex—with almost no exceptions, *souns* are female, and without exception all *aulan hsayas* are male; partly on motive—typically, the *soun* practices from personal spite, the *aulan hsaya* for a client; partly on power—the *aulan hsaya* is much more powerful than the *soun*; and partly on technique—typically, the *soun* achieves her evil ends either through her innate power or by the use of spells, rites, and material substances, but the *aulan hsaya* utilizes ghosts, nats, and other evil spirits. Using the Burmese distinction, I shall arbitrarily refer to the *aulan hsaya* as "master witch," and to the *soun* as "witch."

Master Witches

Although Burmans are reluctant to discuss witches, they will do so under certain circumstances and for certain incentives. It is much more difficult, however, to elicit information concerning master witches, and, with but one exception, all my informants in Yeigyi said that there were

---

[2]Certain differences remain between the data offered here and those found in the literature (cf. Shwe Zan Aung 1912). In all such cases the types and the terms by which they are designated are those derived from my own data.

none in that village. They admitted, however, that master witches existed in other villages, naming both the villages and the practitioners. Although it is certainly possible that the villagers do not believe that there are master witches in Yeigyi, I am more inclined to think that their responses reflect fear rather than truth. It should also be added, of course, that it is almost impossible, short of observing the actual practice of witchcraft, to identify a master witch. Skilled in the arts of deception, a master witch talks and acts like a pious Buddhist, saying his beads, worshiping at pagodas, and so on.

The Burmese term which I am rendering here as "master witch" is a compound, consisting of the noun, *hsaya*, and the adjectival expression, *aulan*. The Burmese call any expert or master by the appellation, *hsaya*. Thus a native doctor is a *hsei* (= medicine) *hsaya*, a teacher is a *kyaung* (= school) *hsaya*, a pedicab driver is a *seika* (= side-car) *hsaya*, etc. Similarly, expert practitioners, or masters, of the occult arts are also known as *hsayas*. But here, a distinction is made between good and evil practitioners. The former are known as *ahtelan* (= upper path) *hsayas*, the latter as *aulan* (= lower path) *hsayas*.[3] Sometimes the same person may practice both good and evil arts—this was alleged to be the case concerning the one inhabitant of Yeigyi identified by one informant as an *aulan hsaya*—but typically these roles are performed by different persons.

While the *ahtelan hsaya* cures illness caused by witches and evil spirits by invoking the assistance of beneficent spirits, the *aulan hsaya*, or master witch, causes illness and death by his ability to control the evil spirits, including nats. This ability, which is based on acquired knowledge rather than on innate power, is coercive; obtaining power over a spirit, the master witch compels him to do his bidding.[4] To control ghosts, the master witch feeds them raw meat and, when they become dependent on him for their food supply, they carry out his bidding. Power over nats is acquired in a somewhat more complicated fashion. They must be made an offering consisting of opposite, sacred and profane (*mato-mate*), elements. Typically, the profane elements might consist of the beak of a crow, the penis of a dog, a woman's skirt, and earth from a cemetery, a latrine, and a nat shrine. The sacred elements might consist of a streamer adorning a Buddha image and earth taken from a Buddhist ordination chamber. The master witch then sets fire to this mixed offering under the shrine of the Mahagiri nat, a nat who is repelled by fire, and thereby gains control over the nat whom he has chosen as his agent. Should this technique prove ineffectual, he smears the face of a nat image with this mixture, a technique which invariably succeeds in gaining control over the nat.

It must be emphasized that, although the master witch practices his arts

---

[3]Lehman (personal communication) informs me that technically these are better rendered as "aboveboard way" and "hidden way," respectively.

[4]For a similar technique in Ceylon, see Gooneratne 1866: 95; Pertold 1929: 319.

at the bidding and in the employ of a client, his motivation is not merely monetary. He is conceived of as an essentially evil person, harboring feelings of malice and ill will toward others. Since few people are either willing, because of fear, or sufficiently informed to talk about them, my information concerning master witches is scanty.

Information on actual cases of master witchcraft is even scantier. The only cases I was able to uncover are from Mandalay rather than from Yeigyi. In one case the technique, somewhat different from the one described above for village master witches, seems unduly complicated relative to the simple ends achieved. This case involved a philandering husband and his wife's attempt to break up his latest affair. For a fee of K 30 (about $6.00), the master witch coerced some nats to cause the husband and his mistress to quarrel during coitus. The violence of their quarrel led to their arrest and jailing. The master witch achieved this end in the following way. From the wife he obtained the husband's horoscope, which he placed on the ashes of an *in* (a cabbalistic square). He then chanted certain spells (*gahtas*),[5] repeating them eighteen times, while holding in his hand one end of a string, the other end of which was attached to his big toe. Using this "charmed" string as its wick, he manufactured a candle on which he etched some more cabbalistic figures. He then carried the candle, together with a tray holding flowers, beef, fish, and charcoal, to a cemetery. There he lit the candle and, while chanting more spells, placed his heel over the candle, thus inducing certain nats, in the form of flies, to come and eat the food on the tray. Having eaten his food and thus come under his power, the nats carried out his orders. (F. K. Lehman, in a personal communication, points out that this practice is deeply involved with the etiquette of giving not only among the ethnic Burmese, but among Burma's tribal peoples as well. "To force someone to enjoy what you give is to gain power over him.")

Witches

Unlike the case of master witches, the Burmese are either more knowledgeable or more willing to talk about witches (*souns*). In either event, we know much more about them. Witches, in the first place, are much more prevalent than master witches. Some villagers believe—and this belief was also recorded by a previous generation of scholars (Shwe Zan Aung 1912:45)—that "out of seven houses, there must be one witch." This belief most probably accounts for an expert estimate of their incidence in Yeigyi. When I asked a village expert on witches how many there were in Yeigyi, he said he would have to consult his *weikzas*[6] for this

---

[5]A *gahta*, technically, is any Buddhist Scriptural stanza. Villagers use it to refer to any spell, whether derived from Scripture or from some other source.

[6]*Weikzas* are men who, through alchemic and cabbalistic techniques, enjoy vastly prolonged lives and various types of supernatural power.

information. The latter "informed" him that there were approximately twenty witches in the village. (Since there are 146 households in Yeigyi and its sister village, the ratio is approximately one in seven.) Although this ratio of one witch to seven houses may be somewhat inflated, every villager—every villager, that is, who believes in witchcraft—believes that there is at least one witch in every village. "Without witches we cannot build our villages," is a Burmese proverb which was quoted to me in every village in which I inquired about witchcraft. Since one can never be sure about the identity of witches, it can always be assumed, so it is believed, that there are more witches than can be identified. The Yeigyi expert, who estimated the number of witches in Yeigyi to be twenty, did not identify them for me. Other villagers, willing to identify the Yeigyi witches, produced a core list of no more than six.

Although it is not believed possible to identify all witches, certain signs are obvious indicators: a witch's eyeballs are only dimly colored; the pupils of the eyes do not reflect external stimuli except when the witch looks directly at people, and then the image is reversed—it is upside down. For this reason—and this is another indicator—a witch will never look directly at another person if doing so can possibly be avoided. She will instead bend her head or turn her face away.

The use of the feminine pronoun in the preceding sentence is not accidental. Although it is possible for a male to be a witch, this rarely happens. Indeed, one of the prevalent synonyms for *soun* is *ywasu*, literally, "female villager." (This term, of course, not only suggests what the Burmese assume the sex of their witches to be, but also how prevalent they assume them to be.) All the alleged witches in Yeigyi are female.[7]

Except for sex it is difficult to make many generalizations about the attributes of witches from the six alleged witches in Yeigyi. Five of the six are old, being in their fifties and sixties; all of them are dominant persons, dominating especially their husbands and their children; all are, or have been, married. Except for these attributes, however, these (putative) Yeigyi witches exhibit no other common features—none, at least, that are obvious. Some are widowed, others are not; some are poor, others well-to-do; some are natives of Yeigyi, others have come from outside the village; some are healthy, others are afflicted with illness. All, of course, are believed to be capable of causing illness and death, and two of them are believed to have, in fact, caused the death of fellow villagers.[8]

[7]Although, literally, "female villager," women are not called *ywasu* because, as Lehman reminds me, *ywa* is also a polite term for witchcraft. Hence only witches, when referred to politely, are called by this term.

[8]Unlike the case in certain Indian villages (Carstairs 1957:89), in which witchcraft is attributed to members of (religious) communities other than one's own—Hindus attribute it to Muslims, etc.—Burmese villagers, like those in Ceylon, believe that witchcraft is practiced within the in-group. It is interesting to note, however, that in Burma this does not produce the intra-village bloodshed and crime that it produces —or, at least, that it produced in the past—in Ceylon (Gooneratne 1866:108).

As is the case for almost all other Burmese beliefs, there are wide differences, even among experts, in the description of witches, their powers, and their techniques. The following account represents a synthesis of discussions held with different, and differing, informants. In the first place, the Burmese, as I have noted, distinguish between those witches whose powers are innate (*wundwin soun*) and those whose powers are learned (*you-you soun*; alternatively, *eindelein soun*). The former, though more powerful than the latter, are believed to be less vicious, for they have become witches because of bad karma—and hence they have no choice but to perform their evil acts—while the latter have deliberately learned their art in order to perpetrate evil on others.

Innate witches can not only cause illness and death, but they possess other forms of magical power as well. They can fly in the air, transform themselves into animals, transform inanimate into animate objects. When flying in the air during the day, they usually assume the form of bats or vultures; at night they fly without heads, their entire bodies covered by their skirts. Their flights are most frequently observed during the waxing or waning of the moon. Some informants report having shot at them in the air, only to have them disappear.[9] Illness caused by other witches can usually be cured by an exorcist (*ahtelan hsaya*); illness caused by innate witches, however, is usually fatal, the witch being invulnerable to the exorcistic arts. Thus should the exorcist, believing the witch to be in the lower part of the patient, beat his buttocks with a cane, she will move to his head; if he beats the patient's head, she will move to his buttocks.

Both types of witches are believed to be fond of eating human excrement. This is usually achieved by the witch severing her head from her body; the head rolls along the ground toward the excrement and eats it. One informant recounted the following case as an illustration. Some years ago a villager went into the fields to defecate and, seeing what he believed to be a large fruit, he picked it up. Putting it to his nose, he recognized by its smell that it was a human head. Fearing that it was the head of a witch, he seized it by the hair (but not before the head had bitten him in the face) and struck it against the trunk of a tree. With the shouts of the witch ringing in his ears, he fled to the village.

Whether their powers are innate or acquired, witches are believed to harm others either from malice or—and this happens very infrequently—for a client. A few examples of the former motive will probably suffice.

In one case of a man complaining of stomach pains, the witch informed the exorcist[10] that she had attacked this victim because he was a busybody. In another case, a witch killed a mother and her two daughters because, so

---

[9] It is of interest to note that in Burma, as in Africa (Middleton and Winter 1963:3), it is only the innate witches who possess such powers.

[10] The exorcist, in an exorcistic seance, induces the witch to possess her victim, who, while in trance, serves as her medium. (see Chapter 11.)

she informed the exorcist, the woman had insulted her. In yet another case, in which a teen-age girl was bewitched, it was because the girl had rejected the witch's home, where she had been living, in favor of a friend's house.

Many if not most of the personal malice cases are, interestingly enough, based on sexual jealousy. In one case, for example, a man was bewitched by his former wife because of his intention to marry another woman. In yet another case a young woman was bewitched for having refused to marry the witch's son. Sexual jealousy was the basis of what is probably the most dramatic case of witchcraft to be called to my attention, a case in which four persons were simultaneously attacked by one witch. It seems that two of the four victims—a young man and woman—had fallen in love, while the other two had acted (in traditional Burmese fashion) as their intermediaries. The witch, who was herself in love with the young lover, vented her spleen on all four.

Whatever their motives, witches attempt to harm their victims by causing illness and/or death. Typically, the illness consists of eye trouble, intestinal complaints, or "madness." Since cases of witch-caused illness, especially of mental illness, are described elsewhere (see Chapter 10, pp. 163–71), it will suffice here to mention a case—an especially dramatic one—of witch-caused death. The case begins with a woman who, without any previous symptoms, died while bathing at the village well. A few days later her elder daughter died of a scorpion bite and her younger daughter was smitten with a strange swelling of the body from which, shortly after, she too died. That the nearly simultaneous deaths of a mother and two daughters could not have been coincidental is, for the Burmese, a proposition so self-evident that it remained only to determine whether the deaths were caused by a witch or a nat. (For a variety of reasons it was decided that they were caused by a witch.)

To achieve their maleficent ends, witches are believed to employ a variety of techniques. Some informants believe, for example, that the witch accomplishes her purpose by calling on the help of nats and other evil spirits (ghosts, demons, etc.); others believe that these spirits assist the witch only when invoked by the power of her spells; others deny that she is assisted by these spirits, claiming, rather, that she achieves her ends by the power of her mind and the thought-processes which it emits. Innate witches, of course, are born with this power. Other witches, however, can acquire this power, not from other witches, but from the various evil spirits alluded to above. The would-be witch goes to a cemetery with a master witch (aulan hsaya), and there, digging a pit, she buries herself up to her neck. The master witch then calls upon various evil spirits to enter the woman (through her mouth), and they instruct her in the use of magical power.

Typically, however—this, at least, is the most prevalent belief—the witch achieves her ends by the malevolent use of food. Here there are four techniques available to her. One technique is to offer a normal meal—curry, boiled rice, pickled tea, betel leaves—to a prospective victim, and then to utter a curse in the form of "Let X (the name of the victim) suffer from disease Y (the intended illness)." A second technique, which does not involve a curse, is to introduce some foreign body—usually human hair, but sometimes leather, raw beef, or a bit of animal sinew—into the victim by mixing it with his food. This foreign body is known as *apin*,[11] and its consequent disease is especially dreaded, it being believed that the *apin* multiplies and fills the entire stomach. In a third technique, the witch causes illness by transforming excrement into beef curry and feeding it to her victim. The witch can use still a fourth technique: after transforming a palm frond into a fish, she straddles it and then feeds it to her victim. (The lower part of the body is associated in Burma with negative, evil qualities). In all these cases the Burmese refer to the food as having been "poisoned" by the witch.

In addition to those already described, at least two other techniques should be mentioned. Sometimes witches collect a person's spittle, hair, excreta, etc., and, by reciting a curse over these exuviae, achieve their nefarious ends. Sometimes, too, they work their evil by capturing a victim's soul (*leikpya*, which leaves the body during dreams), and illness and death ensue if it is not returned. Although I did not encounter this latter belief in my own field work, it is reported for the Burmese by Temple (1911:22) and by Shway Yoe (1896:388–89), by Hackett for the Pa-O (1953:558), and by Lehman for the Kayah (forthcoming).

THE RITUAL SYSTEM

Fearing their attacks, the Burmese employ three types of protection against master witches and witches: preventive, therapeutic, and offensive. The existence of these types does not, of course, say anything about their efficacy, and there are many villagers who believe that none of them is efficacious against an especially powerful or malevolent witch. We may examine each type in turn.

If witches are hungry, they may annoy young children, causing them to cry persistently. Taking this as a warning, parents can prevent more serious trouble by placing food on a tray outside the house. Arriving at night in the guise of a black dog, the witch will eat the food and, if satisfied, will desist from further harm. If not satisfied, she will leave a clod of earth in the tray, and if she is not appeased by additional food, she will cause serious harm to the child.[12]

---

[11]This technique is also mentioned by Fytche (1878:80–81) and others.

[12]A similar practice is reported by Taw Sein Ko (Scott and Hardiman 1900:74), and by Lehman (personal communication) for the Haka Chin, a Burmese tribal group.

More general protection is afforded by the wearing of amulets (*lehpwe*) and by the practice of Buddhism. These are discussed in the following chapter on ghosts. The protective power of Buddhism is especially stressed by pious informants, who claim that "good" Buddhists are invulnerable to witchcraft.

If a witch has already caused a person to become ill, the only remedy is exorcism. Since, however, possession and exorcism are similar for both witches and nats, and since these phenomena are instructive for a variety of other problems, exorcism is discussed below in a separate section (see Part IV).

If a witch kills someone, an attempt is made, by enlisting the aid of someone even more powerful, to harm the witch in return. Thus, one of the putative witches in Yeigyi is a blind woman who was allegedly blinded by a master witch hired for this purpose by the relative of a man whom she had killed. Sometimes the witch is killed, rather than merely harmed, the fate met by the Yeigyi witch (described above) who had killed a mother and her two daughters. The son of one of her victims—himself an exorcist (*ahtelan hsaya*)—attempted to discover, by a special method of concentration, the identity of the witch. After worshiping the Buddha, he put his mind to the task and her identity was revealed to him. He then showed his power, destroying the witch by a technique used by master witches (see above, pg. 23). Taking some hair from a young child (hair which is ordinarily used to tie together the toes and thumbs of a corpse), a turban worn by a nat image, some pieces of cloth cut from the robe of a Buddhist monk, and cloth cut from the skirts of laborers, he twisted them all together in a triangular shape. Using this as a wick, he placed it, together with an *in*, in a saucer filled with fuel oil. He then lit the wick, and after the fire consumed both the wick and the *in*, the witch died.[18]

Under the Burmese kings witchcraft was recognized as a crime punishable by law. If a woman accused of witchcraft murder confessed her crime, she was banished from her village and sent to ". . . someplace where the air is unwholesome." If she denied the charge she was ". . . placed upon a little bier, supported at each end by a boat, and a vessel of ordure

---

[18]That an exorcist (*ahtelan hsaya*) should publicly admit to practicing the art of the master witch (*aulan hsaya*) confirms the average Burman's suspicion of, and ambivalence concerning, the exorcist: he can control both good and evil spirits, and he can do both good and evil. This exorcist was not unaware of the implications of his behavior and, having recounted the story, he felt constrained to provide his action with a Buddhist justification, not only because of the moral ambiguity of his action, but because even witches, however evil they may be, are protected by the Buddhist ban against harming living creatures. By killing the witch he had acted, so he claimed, like the Buddha himself who, when challenged by an "evil nat," proclaimed himself to be the Buddha, thereby drowning his enemy in the ensuant flood. (This tale, obviously, is a somewhat garbled version of the famous Withoudaya myth, see pg. 46.)

is emptied upon her. The boats are then slowly drawn from each other till the woman falls into the water. If she sinks, she is dragged out by a rope of green herbs tied around her middle, and is declared innocent; but if she swims, she is convicted as a witch . . ." (Sangermano 1893: 150).[14]

THE QUALITY OF BELIEF

Although a tiny minority of villagers profess not to believe either in their existence or in their power—in a village census, three persons, all males, expressed these sentiments—most Burmans, including sophisticated city dwellers, believe in the existence of witches; they are concerned lest they become the victims of witchcraft; and they are frightened when they encounter a putative witch.

In one sense it might be said that witches evoke more concern than do either ghosts or nats. As spirits, the latter are only rarely encountered, and when they are, they are unambiguously identifiable as one or the other. Witches, on the other hand, are human beings; superficially, they are like any other human being. One can never be sure, therefore, that some ordinary-looking person—and one is living with at least a few hundred ordinary-looking persons—is not really a witch. Everyone, therefore, is carefully observed to detect any sign that might identify him as a witch. (The psychological basis for this attitude is examined in Chapter 5.) Thus, for example, the headman of Yeigyi told me that some people had had doubts about me: they were convinced that I had magical power, but they were not sure whether I used this power for good or for ill. My interpreter, upon questioning some of his close village friends, was able to discover at least some of the grounds for suspicion. First, I slept on my stomach, rather than (as the Burmese do) on my back. This queer habit must mean something. Second, I was never observed to spit on the ground. From this it was inferred that I was afraid that my spittle might be used by a witch to harm me, and such excessive caution concerning witchcraft might indicate that I myself was a witch.

The villagers' anxiety about witchcraft is again most tellingly revealed in connection with my own experience, specifically in their attribution of witchcraft anxiety to me—an attribution which, of course, can only be explained projectively. Thus, I made a practice while in the village of eating any freshly cooked food which was offered me, but of avoiding uncooked or left-over food (which had already attracted flies). Since much of the food offered me was of the latter category, my polite demurrers were taken to mean that I was afraid the food had been "poisoned."

---

[14]Witches would float because, according to Taw Sein Ko, who reports that the practice continued until the British conquest, they were believed to have charmed gourds or bladders in their stomachs. (Scott and Hardiman 1900:74).

Invariably, in the two villages in which I worked intensively, and whose residents felt comfortable enough to discuss such matters, I was told that I need not be anxious about the food; they were my friends and I could be sure that the food had not been "poisoned."

If witchcraft beliefs arouse anxiety in the Burmese, encounters with specific witches or with cases of witchcraft evoke their fear. Although a few villagers were willing, in absolute privacy, to reveal the identity of witches, most people (as we have seen) were unwilling to do so, either because—some said—the witches would then harm them, or because—others said—they might be sued for defamation. Since my request was almost invariably met by the Burmese with great perturbation and upset, the latter explanation struck me as a rationalization for their fear of punitive consequences. It is not surprising, then, that no one is ever openly accused of witchcraft, for the fear of retaliation is too great.

Witch fear is most clearly observed, of course, in concrete instances of alleged bewitchment. I have seen terror in the faces of villagers when confronted with such cases. A young man, for example, began to behave violently, so that neighbors and kinsmen had to attempt to restrain him. When it was agreed that he had been bewitched, and especially after an initial attempt to cure him had failed, the villagers' ordinary attitude of precaution turned to intense fear. The fear was sufficiently great to overcome their reluctance to approach me at night while I was in conversation with a group of monks concerning sacred matters. Their apologies were profuse and their demeanor deferential, but they were frightened and they needed help—they wanted me to drive them to a famous exorcist. They were effusively apologetic (*anade*) for disturbing me because, of course, they could have gone by bicycle. But since the witch had announced that she would attack anyone who went for the exorcist, they decided reluctantly to ask me. (I don't know whether they viewed me as especially powerful, or whether they believed my car to be invulnerable, or what their reason may have been.) As the leader of the delegation, in an obviously distressed state, put it, "This is no longer human to human; it is witch to human."

Even more interesting, however, was the behavior of the exorcist, whom we reached after a half-hour drive. When the patient's symptoms were described to him, he became visibly upset. Trembling, he uttered some spells (*gahtas*), touched his beads, consulted a horoscope, and finally announced that he could not accompany us because the planets were not propitious either for him or for the patient. As we drove off, my village friends interpreted his refusal to accompany us exactly as I had—he was frightened. To them, although his refusal was shocking (see Chapter 13, pg. 233), he had reason to be frightened; this was an especially powerful witch, and the fact that a man is an exorcist does not render him immune from attack. He lost face in their eyes not because he was frightened by the danger—it was only natural to be frightened—but because he refused to meet it.

The belief in and fear of witches are not restricted to uneducated villagers. They are found on all levels of Burmese society and among all educational strata. Although my nonvillage sample is by no means systematic, it is sufficiently variegated to carry conviction. A few examples will suffice.

The Township Officer (T.O.) of Amarapura, a graduate of Mandalay University and a major in physics and chemistry, is an unabashed believer in witchcraft. Queried about possible inconsistencies between witchcraft and science, he replied, "It is a very complicated problem, very difficult to explain. I can only say that their [witches'] existence is beyond question."

A senior medical student at Mandalay University, a Muslim, explained that he, unlike his "superstitious" family, held beliefs on "scientific" grounds alone. His belief in witchcraft, he insisted, satisfied the empirical criteria of science. He had once witnessed the stomach operation of a man who claimed to have been the victim of witchcraft, and he himself saw the hair—"a sure sign of witchcraft"—with which it was filled.

The Township Officer for Yeigyi, a Baptist leader and a science graduate of the University of Rangoon, has seen flying witches with his own eyes. Like my medical friend, he insisted that his belief, therefore, was empirically based. He hastened to add, however, that his belief is also sanctioned by the Bible.

A wealthy woman of Rangoon, a graduate of its University, widely traveled in Europe and America, and, because of her sophistication, a close friend of the Western colony, accused a man whom I had believed to be one of her best friends of practicing witchcraft against her father and grandfather. This man, she said, envious of her husband's good fortune—her husband within a relatively short time had acquired great wealth—had "killed" her father and grandfather by placing a curse on them. Nothing could dissuade her from this belief.

Witch beliefs know no ideological boundaries. Thus communists, though frequently anti-Buddhist, may continue to believe in witchcraft. An officer in the communist underground was convinced that a certain woman, after quarreling with his wife, had killed his daughter by means of witchcraft; he ordered her executed for this alleged crime (*The Nation*, October 22, 1963).

CHAPTER THREE

Ghosts and Demons

THE BELIEF SYSTEM

Technically, "ghost" may be used in comparative religion to refer to any disembodied spirit of the dead. In this all-embracing sense, the Burmese may be said to believe in three kinds of ghosts. First, there are the souls (*leikpya*) of the dead who, improperly escorted from their human habitat, remain to haunt people. Since any soul is potentially dangerous at the time of death, certain mortuary rites are performed to prevent it from remaining within the house or village. If such rites are not performed, the soul, still attached to the scene of its previous existence, remains within the settlement and, in effect, becomes a ghost, haunting the inhabitants. The souls of deceased government officials are believed to be especially attached to their positions; to prevent them from remaining in their offices, a special document is prepared, signed, and sometimes recited by the superior officer of the deceased, discharging the soul from all connections with his erstwhile position. This ceremony (known as *ameindaw pyan*) is still performed in many government offices, at least on the district level. I do not know if it still performed in Rangoon.[1] According to Sarah Bekker

[1]Grant Brown (1916) cites the case of the spirit of a deceased civil surgeon who, because the above ceremony was not performed, persisted in disturbing his former patients until, at the request of his widow, Brown, the District Commissioner, signed an order discharging him from government service.

this ceremony is performed, in Rangoon at least, not only for government servants, but for persons in other occupations as well, and the discharge statements are buried in the grave with the deceased. In her experience (personal communication) "this practice is still scrupulously observed."

Although technically "ghosts," these souls of the dead are not included among those ghosts with which this chapter is concerned—those whom the Burmese call *tasei* or *thaye*, and who are known to Buddhism as *pretas*. Unlike these latter ghosts, the former are mildly harmful spirits who represent the persistence, rather than the rebirth, of the spirit of the deceased. They are easily banished by the performance of simple mortuary rites. The *tasei-thaye*, on the other hand, are beings who, as a consequence of evil committed in their past lives, have been reborn into their present disembodied state. Inhabiting their own realm of existence (*loka*), the realm of *pretas*, they remain "ghosts" until, having worked out their karmic fate, they are reborn into another realm.

These ghosts, to whom we shall shortly return, are to be distinguished from the nats who, in the all-embracing and technical sense, could also be classified as "ghosts." The nats, however, are quite different from the *tasei-thaye* on a number of dimensions, and the Burmese quite properly classify them separately. In this chapter, then, "ghost" will be restricted to those beings whom the Burmese call *tasei* or *thaye*.

Despite my reference to ghosts as "spirits," it is difficult to decide from discussions with informants whether Burmese ghosts are physical or spiritual beings.[2] For the most part they are invisible, but under certain circumstances they can become visible. When visible they are reported to possess flimsy and resilient materiality—much like a pillow, according to one informant who was once engaged by a ghost in personal combat. Those who have seen ghosts, or who have heard about them from others, describe them as monstrous in size—at least seven feet tall, which is very tall for a Burman—very dark, if not black, with huge ears, long tongues, tusklike teeth, and repulsive in every way.

Ghosts generally live on the outskirts of villages, especially near cemeteries, where they feed on corpses. They also enjoy the flesh of living people, however, and at times—when feeling especially hungry or malevolent, or when under the control of a witch—they enter a village in order to attack and eat one of its inhabitants. (In this sense their relationship to man is in contrast to that of the nats: whereas the latter are fed *by* people, ghosts feed *on* people.) It should not be supposed, however, that they enter the village only for such dramatic ends. Most frequently they enter to cause illness, although in my experience the illness which they cause is minor. A baby cries persistently, he is feverish for two or three days,

---

[2]Although my informants were undecided, Maung Tin (1913a) states categorically that ghosts are physical. For a collection of ghost stories see Maung Tin (1913a, 1913b).

and so on, and it is assumed that he has been attacked by a ghost. Their favorite times for entering a village are at high noon and after sunset; those who are especially concerned about ghosts are particularly cautious at these times.

In addition to ghosts, the Burmese believe in a number of other evil creatures which, for lack of a better term, I shall call "demons." The most important of these demons are ogre-like beings known as *bilus*. Ogres, like ghosts, feed on people. Images of ogres are frequently encountered on pagoda platforms and in ornamental wood carvings in monasteries and elsewhere. Although no villager encountered an ogre during my stay in Yeigyi, cases of such encounters in other villages were reported in the press. Especially interesting are the accounts of babies who, born deformed, are believed to be ogres. The following report (*The Nation*, February 17, 1962) is typical. A child born to parents in Lower Burma had a "big body, hairy arms and legs, bushy eyebrows, enormous eyes, and protruding teeth that look like fangs." Villagers who viewed the baby decided that he was an ogre. His mother, horrified by the baby and subject to nightmares from the time he was born, refused to breast-feed him. At the time of the press report the villagers were still debating the ultimate disposition of the child. In the meantime, monks had been requested to "drive away the evil spirit which they believe is incarnate in the luckless child." In at least two other such cases reported in the press, the baby was less fortunate: the mothers, believing their deformed offspring to be ogres, killed them. If my Yeigyi experience is typical, these ogres, and other types of demons, despite their sculptural prominence, play a relatively insignificant role in Burmese thought and behavior, although they are sometimes used to frighten children. This is in marked contrast with other societies which share with Burma a common Hindu-Buddhist mythology. In Ceylon, for example, the various Hindu-Buddhist demons— *bhutas, raksas, yaksas*, etc.—play the same prominent role as they play in Hindu India, from where they were derived. (Cf. Gooneratne 1866, Ryan 1958, Sarathchandra 1953, Wirz 1954.) One has the impression that the Singhalese demons are similar to the Burmese nats, to which they play an analogous role. If so, the prominence of the nats in Burma would in part explain the relative unimportance of the demons.

THE RITUAL SYSTEM

Although there is no specific charm or talisman which is used to ward off ghosts and demons, there are a variety of more general amulets, known generically as *lehpwe*, which are believed to offer protection against all forms of harm, including those caused by demons and ghosts.[3] The amulet

[3]For a summary of the major types of amulets, see Hildburgh 1909; Scott and Hardiman 1900: 79–82.

most frequently used in Yeigyi is a metallic foil, attached to a piece of string or a strip of bamboo, worn around the neck or about the wrist, and over which a spell or incantation has been recited by a magical practitioner.[4] A small number of men also use magical squares containing cabbalistic symbols (*in*) as amulets; others use a tiny alchemic ball (*datloun*), generally made of mercury or iron; still others use tatooing for this purpose. There are various kinds of *ins*—or, as Htin Aung (1962:54) calls them, runes—most of them consisting of a piece of paper divided into squares on which various kinds of cabbalistic symbols—usually, but not always, alphabetic—are inscribed. Sometimes the symbols are inscribed on a piece of metal which is then inserted underneath the flesh. I have not encountered the latter technique, but it is reported by earlier authors (Sangermano 1893:148; Trant 1827:88). Sometimes, too, these symbols are used for the representation of some object. The bull, depicted below, is composed of letters of the Burmese alphabet. If painted on a handkerchief and placed on the house altar, it will protect the inhabitants from harm. (see Chapter 11, pg. 176 for a similar depiction of the Buddha.)

FIGURE 1.   *Magical symbol of a bull, constructed from letters of the Burmese alphabet.*

The *datloun* is the end-product of the Burmese alchemic process, a process whose goal is the prolongation of life—at least until the coming of the Future Buddha. This goal can be achieved by means of a special *datloun*. Although most *datlouns* do not have the power to prolong life, many of them have other kinds of magical power, including the power to protect against snakes, demons, ghosts, and so on.

Highly favored in the past as a means of protection against malevolent power, tatooing is falling into disuse today. Until the very recent past

----

[4]Amulets made by powerful practitioners are especially desirable. When I gave such a talisman—it was made by one of the most famous practitioners in Upper Burma—to a village friend, he was literally rapturous for several minutes; eyes closed, lips trembling, he began to utter some *mantras*. Two days later the village headman, hearing of my gift, came to ask for one for himself.

every male was tatooed from the navel to the knee,[5] but today it is rare to see extensive tatooing on any male under forty. Tatooing, like amulets, *ins, datlouns,* and so on, provides protection against natural, as well as supernatural harm.[6]

Like the *lehpwe,* all these techniques afford generalized protection against harm, rather than specific protection against demons and ghosts. In addition to these general prophylactics, there are other techniques which afford specific protection from ghosts. Thus, when entering the village gate, a person can prevent a ghost from accompanying him to his home by uttering "phyi! phyi!" and spitting. I observed this practice most particularly in the case of women who, returning from the fields, were concerned about their children. Children are believed to be especially vulnerable to ghostly attack.

When an epidemic, especially of plague or cholera, breaks out or is believed to be imminent, a ceremony is performed to frighten the ghost (or nat) that is believed to be its agent. Since plague-bearing ghosts are believed to be especially virulent during seasonal changes, this ceremony is performed at infrequent but regular intervals. Although I did not observe the ceremony in Yeigyi, my encounter with it in Mandalay was similar (although not identical) to the reports in the older literature. (Cf. Conder 1826:81; Shway Yoe 1896: Chapter 41; Taw Sein Ko 1893:185; Vossion 1891:3.) Thus, one night in January fires were suddenly lit in a number of quarters of Mandalay and, without warning, there banged out a dinning cacophony of sounds, caused by the simultaneous beating of gongs, tin roofs, wooden doors, and, indeed, of anything that happened to be handy, and by the shouting of human voices. All this was intended to frighten away the ghosts that are believed to be responsible for the plague. The next day, to make sure that the ghosts would stay away, a group of monks, reciting *pareittas* (sections from the Buddhist *Suttas*) and walking in procession, circled those quarters in which the din had been created the previous night. This latter, Buddhist, part of the ceremony might be viewed as a kind of spiritual inoculation.[7]

[5]"The principal tatooing is confined to that portion of the body from the navel to below the knee. . . . The figures imprinted consist of animals, such as lions, tigers, monkeys, and hogs, with crows, some fabulous birds, Nats, and Balus or demons. Occasionally are added cabbalistic letters and figures intended as charms against wounds. . . . The process is not only painful but expensive. . . ." (Crawfurd 1834: 95–96. See also Sangermano 1893:148; Cuming 1893:97–99.)

[6]The use of tatooed charms of this kind was believed to render soldiers invulnerable in battle. Thus, we find such "invulnerables" in the first Anglo-Burman war (Winter 1858:219)—and presumably in the others as well—and we find them again, over one hundred years later, in the famous Saya San Rebellion (Harvey 1946:73).

[7]Consistent with their attack on all forms of "superstition," some of the Mandalay newspapers denied that the noisemaking comprised a ceremonial type of preventive medicine. It was occasioned, they claimed, by the people's desire to cast shame upon a blatantly adulterous government official. Our servants, who had participated in the ceremony, scoffed at this evasive interpretation.

In addition to specific prophylactic rituals of this kind, Buddhism—as we shall see—provides general immunity against danger. If a person is truly pious, adhering to the Buddhist precepts, worshiping the Buddha, and reciting his beads, he can expect to be immune from attacks by demons and ghosts, as well as from other forms of danger.

THE QUALITY OF BELIEF

Although some few villagers express skepticism about the existence of demons and ghosts, the vast majority entertain no doubts. Their conviction about the existence of these beings is based on a number of factors. First, their existence is taught by Buddhism, and, as devout Buddhists, few villagers would challenge the veracity of Buddhist cosmology. Second, villagers point to instances of illness allegedly caused by ghosts as evidence for their existence. Cases of successful therapy, moreover, not only testify to the skill of the practitioner, but also contribute to the evidential basis for the truth of the belief. Third, there have been first-hand encounters with ghosts which, again, provide empirical underpinning for the belief. Since these cognitive bases for belief will be examined elsewhere (see Chapter 5), what is of importance for us in this chapter is not so much the cognitive as the affective dimensions of ghost belief.

Although the data for ghosts, unlike those for witches and nats, are meager, there is little question but that ghosts are greatly feared. Given their character and behavior, it is little wonder that this is so. Especially feared are those ghosts who are the spirits of women who died in childbirth. These are known as *Thabe*. Fear takes a number of forms. A pious Buddhist says he does not engage in Buddhist meditation because he would then be especially vulnerable to attack by ghosts. A village elder does not go to a village meeting because his wife is afraid to be left alone at night lest a ghost attack her. A young man, fearing an attack by ghosts, will not venture out at night to return a stray ox unless a friend agrees to accompany him. Ghosts are sufficiently salient in Burmese consciousness to have comprised the almost unanimous response category, both for adults and children, to a TAT picture of a hideous-looking human being.

Despite the Burmese fear of ghosts, it would be false to convey the impression that their fear is obsessive, as it sometimes is among other peoples. Surrounded though they are by these and other malevolent beings, the Burmese attitude toward their ghosts is similar to that described by Ryan for the Singhalese.[8] They know that they exist and that precautions

---

[8]"No one should suppose, as well one might from this evidence of a fearful demon world, that Pelpolans live in terror of the supernatural. Just as one may fear serious disease yet lead a normal life of exposure without much thought of falling sick, so do Pelpolans live in the midst of a potentially threatening supernatural world." (Ryan 1958:112)

are required, but normally their concern is no greater than that of a city dweller who, knowing the dangers entailed, drives his car in heavy traffic. This is especially evidenced by the fact that although ghosts cause illness and even death, almost every case of ghost-induced illness which I was able to uncover was so diagnosed not by the patient or his relatives, but by the medical practitioner to whom the patient was taken. To be sure, the diagnosis was accepted without demur by the patient—or, in the case of children, by their parents—but the fact that this explanation did not immediately spring to mind refutes, I believe, any notion that the fear of ghosts constitutes an obsessive fear among the Burmese.

CHAPTER FOUR

Nats

THE BELIEF SYSTEMS: A TYPOLOGY

Introduction

Although nats, witches, ghosts, and demons are substantively different, they are all included in this volume because, as I have already pointed out, they share one functional attribute: they cause pain and suffering. Nats differ from witches in that the latter are humans while the former are spirits; they differ from ghosts (who are also, according to some informants, spirits) in that the latter are terrestrial while the former reside in a nonhuman abode. More importantly, however, the nats—unlike these other beings—are the objects of an elaborate cultus which, from the point of view of comparative religion, can only be viewed as part of an organized *religious system*. Resting on a complex mythological charter, the nat cultus consists of an elaborated ritual system under the supervision of socially recognized cult leaders and practitioners. Although, from the Burmese point of view, the nat cultus does not constitute a religion, the fact remains that it rivals Buddhism in its elaborate cognitive, ceremonial, and organizational systematization. The nats with which we shall primarily be concerned are the so-called Thirty-Seven Nats. Since, however, the term "nat" is used to designate other types of supernatural beings as well, these types must be distinguished before we can turn to the Thirty-Seven, the nats *par excellence*.

Generically, "nat" refers to a class of supernatural beings who are more powerful than man and who, therefore, can affect him either for good or for evil. That power is a salient component of the meaning of "nat" is suggested by a variety of contexts in which the term, presumably by extension, is used metaphorically. Thus, the senior male in the household (i.e., the husband-father) is referred to as the *ein ya in u nat*, the nat who lives in the front of the house. In the formal structure of the Burmese family, the husband-father has power over his wife and children. Similarly, the king is called the *loka thamudi nat*, the nat in the language of convention; the Buddha himself is designated as the *withoudi nat*, the pure nat. The Burmese king, of course, had absolute power over his subjects, and the Buddha possessed the greatest power of all—the power to attain nirvana and Buddhahood.

Since "nat" is used to refer to different types of supernatural beings, it is necessary, before describing these types, to make two observations concerning the derivation of the typology. In the first place, although the average Burman can distinguish three types of nats, it would be false to imply that his conception of each of these types—or, for that matter, his notion of the meaning of "nat" in general—is clearly delineated. On the contrary, the Burmese conceptions of the nats (like many of their other conceptions) are marked by inconsistency, contradiction, and by what might be called cognitive looseness. It is not at all unusual, for example, for a man to deny—and to adduce evidence for his denial—that the nats exist, or, at the least, to deny that they have power, and then to recount some incident which presupposes both their existence and their power. This cognitive looseness is reflected in many ways, but perhaps one more instance will suffice. The following reasons are usually given as alternative explanations for the characterization of the Thirty-Seven nats as *meihsa*, or evil.[1] They are "evil" because they are malevolent; because they died violent deaths; because they died suddenly, without an opportunity to think about the Buddha prior to their deaths. (Unexpected deaths, for which preparation cannot be made, are known in Burma as "green deaths.") In a discussion of the nats with *the* village nat expert, the latter proffered the first explanation: the Thirty-Seven nats are "evil" because they are malevolent. But then why, I asked him, should the village nat, who protects the village from harm, be thought of as malevolent? To this he replied that although the village nat is characterized as malevolent, he does not perform malevolent acts. Indeed, "He is really a good nat; he is only *called* an evil

---

[1]Meihsa is a Pali loan word, meaning heterodox or heretical. My Burmese informants, however, render it as "evil," and I shall follow their usage. F. K. Lehman reminds me that all nats not converted by the Buddha and, therefore, not bound by the Law are *meihsa*.

nat." The impresario of the famous Taungbyon nat festival answered the question in a slightly different fashion: although the Taungbyon nats are called *meihsa* "by the people," this is not to be taken seriously since "the people are ignorant."

The second point to be emphasized in connection with the nat typology is that the Burmese, like the members of any other society, differ considerably both in interest and in knowledge concerning their own culture. Thus, for example, in an intensive study of the nat beliefs of fifteen villagers, three could recount the myth of their own "hereditary" nat in detail, seven did not know it at all, and the others knew only the barest outline. It follows, then, that the typology to be presented here is derived from informants who are both more knowledgeable and more analytic than their fellows. This is not to say that the others would not recognize it. On the contrary, although the typology is not one which every Burman would volunteer, its constituent types represent emic rather than etic categories. The typology, in short, is one which the average Burman would most certainly recognize, and to which he would undoubtedly subscribe: its terms and concepts are part of his lexicon, and he himself employs them on the appropriate occasions in ordinary discourse. Nevertheless, for the average Burman the types are not as sharply differentiated as the typology would suggest, and the resultant classification of the various beings called "nats" is in fact somewhat more ambiguous than the typological criteria delineated below would imply.

With these provisos, then, we may say that the average Burman recognizes three types of nats. First, there is a type which comprises nature spirits of various kinds—spirits with differing degrees of power, of jurisdiction, of character, and of prominence, all of whom, however, are associated with such natural phenomena as trees, waterfalls, hills, paddy fields, and so forth. A second type, referred to collectively as *devas*, resides in various of the Buddhist heavens and is characterized as the guardian or protector of the Buddhist religion (the *sāsana*). A third type, each of whose members possesses a historically (or mythologically) identifiable biography, is known as "the Thirty-Seven" nats. They, like the nature nats, are called *meihsa* nats. In addition to these three fairly well delineated types of nats, there is a mixed type which is treated separately at the end of this chapter.[2]

Although the average Burman is unable to identify all the members of these three types, and although in some cases he would be hard put to decide to which type a given nat "belongs," or, having decided, would have difficulty justifying his decision, the types themselves are for him phenomenologically real. The nats of each type are characterized by a number of distinctive (substantive, functional, jurisdictional, character-

[2]Theravada Ceylon distinguishes, too, between *devas* and a class of spirits known as *yakas*, who, functionally speaking, are almost identical with the other types of Burmese nats. (cf., Ames 1964; Yalman 1964).

ological, and even historico-genetic) attributes which are, for him, cognitively salient. If the boundaries between these types are fluid, the permeability is between the first and third, both of which comprise the *meihsa*, or "evil" nats. They are to be contrasted with the second type whose members (the *devas*) are uniformly conceived to be "good." Indeed, the *devas* are really not nats at all; although they share a common label with the other "nats"—they are designated as *upapati nats*—the *devas* are clearly distinguished by the Burmese from the other beings designated by that label. For the Burmese, the *devas* are conceptually a part of Buddhism, and Buddhism, in turn, is sharply distinguished by them from nat propitiation. More importantly, the *devas* are omnibenevolent, while the other nats are, at best, neutral; the *devas* alleviate suffering, the other nats cause suffering, the *devas* are moral, the other nats, at best, are amoral. Hence, although referred to as "nats," the *devas* comprise a type, *sui generis*—a type which is excluded from the nat cultus to be described below. Nevertheless, some brief attention must be paid to the *devas* because they throw the other types, the genuine nats, into sharp relief, and because Western observers have all too frequently failed to distinguish them from these other types when describing Burmese "animism."[3]

Devas

The word *deva* is the Sanskrit term for deity. In the Burmese context, *devas* are "good" nats; they protect the people from harm and accede to their requests for assistance. In Buddhist cosmology there are twenty-six *deva* abodes ("heavens"), ranging along a continuum from materiality to immateriality. In my research I encountered very few monks and no laymen who could even name these abodes, let alone describe their distinguishing features. The average Burman, monk and layman alike, distinguishes two types of devas: *thamma devas* and *byahma devas*. Although the latter are believed to occupy a more exalted position in the hierarchy of devas,[4] they play almost no role in Burmese religious thought or practice. The *devas* which most Burmese aspire to become, and who serve as

[3]Although qualifying his statement with the proviso that ". . . sometimes [*deva*] suggests the more blessed of heavenly spirits," Winston King, in a contemporary work, perpetuates this older view when he writes: "In Burmese Buddhism they [the *devas*] have been generally merged with the nats, nature spirits and spirits of dead persons . . ." (King 1964:66).

[4]In Buddhist cosmology there are thirty-one planes of existence, divided into three spheres or worlds (*lokas*). The first sphere, known as *kama-loka*, includes the hells, and the animal, ghost, demon, and human worlds, as well as the six lower *deva* abodes. The remaining twenty planes of existence, inhabited by the *brahma* (Burmese *byahma*) *devas*, are divided into two spheres: sixteen planes of *rupa-loka*, in which the *brahmas* retain a tenuous corporeality, and four planes of *arupa-loka*, in which there is no corporeality at all. The Burmese refer to the inhabitants of the six lower *deva* abodes as the *thamma devas*. For a more extended summary of Buddhist teachings concerning the *devas*, see La Vallée Poussin (1911a, 1911b, 1917) and Thomas (1920).

objects of religious ritual, are the *thamma devas*. It is they who are the subject of this section.[5]

The *thamma devas* do not comprise a uniform type of supernatural beings. Some of them are "gods," in the Western sense of superhuman beings, who possess power over at least certain segments of both the physical and the animal worlds, including man, and who have existed as gods for interminable periods. These *devas*, of course, are the Hindu-derived deities who, demoted in power, function, and prestige, comprise the named deities of the Buddhist pantheon. These are to be distinguished from a large, undifferentiated group of unnamed *devas* who inhabit the same abodes and enjoy the same blissful existence, but who are without the powers and functions associated with the first type. To be sure, according to Buddhist belief both types had once been humans who, because of their highly favorable karma, were reborn in one of the Buddhist heavens (*deva* abodes); and both will be reborn again and again until they eventually pass out of the wheel of *saṁsāra*, or cycle of rebirths. Pragmatically, however, a distinction is made between *devas* who function as gods—the named deities of a (Hindu-derived) pantheon, brought into Burma with Buddhism—and *devas* who are merely the denizens of Paradise.[6]

In a random sample of thirty households of Yeigyi, 85 per cent were fairly consistent in their conceptions of the *devas*. They are conceived to be spirits of pious people who live in one of the Buddhist heavens, who

[5]This discussion, including the distinction between these two types of *devas*, is based on village interviews; it represents what villagers (and most other Burmese Buddhists) believe. That their beliefs are frequently distortions of canonical doctrine is not surprising. The Burmese *thamma deva* is a corruption of the Pali *samma deva*, or "free of error deity," which refers to all benevolent *devas*. In (Pali) Buddhist cosmology, then, the *brahma devas* are a subclass of the generic *samma devas*, who occupy the twenty highest planes of existence (the *rupa* and *arupa* spheres). In Burmese thought, however, the *brahma* and *samma devas* are distinct classes. The latter are active *devas*, intervening in human affairs, while the former have no concern with the mundane world.

[6]The cognoscenti include the four World Guardians among the *samma devas*. These Guardians, inhabitants of Mt. Meru, watch over the cardinal points of the compass, and control various types of evil beings with which Buddhism, appropriating them from Hinduism, populates the world. The Guardians themselves are, of course, four of the eight Hindu Protectors-of-the-World or *Lokapālas*. (Cf. Daniélou 1964: 129–32.) According to some informants, the chief of these Guardians, Daterata, who guards the eastern side of Mt. Meru, controls the evil nats; Wirulaka, on the southern side, controls the monsters (*gounban*); Wirupeka, on the western side, controls the mythical garuda birds (*galoun*) and the mythical serpents (*naga*); Kuweira, on the north, controls the ogres (*bilu*). These four *devas* are almost invariably invoked during exorcistic ceremonies.

Although technically *ariyas*, mention should also be made here of the four Burmese Buddhist saints whose favors, like those of the *devas*, can be solicited by means of spells (*gahtas*). These are Shin Upagok, Shin Thiwali, Shin Angulimala, and Shin Peindola. Duroiselle (1922–23) reports the existence of shrines in their honor and of images, in the form of monks, which represent them. I have seen neither. According to Sarah Bekker (personal communication) Shin Thiwali is often associated with Ananda (one of the early disciples of the Buddha Gautama), whose tiny image is carried by travelers for protection.

guard the Buddhist doctrine (*sāsana*), and who are always benevolent. The *devas* need not be feared. Unlike the other nats, they need not be propitiated because of some apprehension that, inadvertently, they may have been offended, or that, having neglected to make an offering to them, they will cause illness, loss of livelihood, or other forms of suffering. If prayers are recited or offerings are rendered to the *devas*, it is to express one's gratitude for their protection, or to solicit their continuing protection, or to seek their assistance in time of trouble or distress.[7] One frequently hears stories of shipwrecks, plane crashes, insurgency attacks, and other calamities, in which all concerned were killed, maimed, or harmed, except for those who had sought and received the protection of the *devas*.

In addition to the use of prayer, the assistance of the *devas* is invoked by ritual offering of food, usually as part of some ceremony. The offering (*kadaw pwe*) may consist of a coconut and three bunches of bananas, or it may consist of objects of lesser value, such as rice, vegetables, fruit, sweets, or mineral water.[8] Because, as Hindu-derived gods, they are vegetarian, *devas* are never offered meat; and since, unlike the situation in Buddhist Ceylon, there are in Burma no temples or shrines for the *devas*,[9] these offerings may be made in any ritually clean place.

Deva images are frequently to be seen on pagoda platforms or in monastic compounds, and many casual (and sometimes not so casual) observers of Burma, seeing the proliferation of these "nat" images on, for example, the famous Shwedagon pagoda platform in Rangoon, have concluded that the pre-Buddhist nat cultus persists in, and is part of, Buddhist worship. In fact, however, nats and small nat shrines are only rarely and inconspicuously found in pagoda compounds. With one important exception,[10] the only conspicuous "nats" to be found in any Buddhist holy place

---

[7]Various prayers and charms are widely used. Thus, for example, for continuous protection the recitation of the *Mangala Sutta* and of the "Virtues" (*guṇam*, Pali; *goundaw*, Burmese) of the Buddha are believed to be efficacious, but for critical situations a famous prayer, known as *Thamboutei*, is believed to be especially efficacious.

[8]The combined offering of coconut and bananas constitutes the essential core of Burmese religious offerings. In Buddhist ceremonies it consists of one coconut and three bunches of bananas, and in nat ceremonies it consists of one coconut and two bunches of bananas. Although any offering is literally a *kadaw pwe* (*kadaw* = to do homage; *pwe* = oblation) this term is most usually used to refer to the core offering—the coconut and bananas—exclusively.

[9]Buddhist worship in Theravada countries, such as Ceylon or Thailand, generally occurs in a temple. (Except for those in Pagan, Burma has no temples, and worship takes place at pagodas.) In Ceylon almost every Buddhist temple (*Vihara*) is associated with a temple for the *devas* (*Devale*), the faithful invariably proceeding from one to the other.

[10]The exception is in the famous Shwezigon pagoda in the ancient capital of Pagan. When he began construction of this pagoda in 1059, King Anawrahta, who introduced Theravada Buddhism to the Burmese, had the images of the original Thirty-Seven nats moved to the new pagoda. "Men will not come for the sake of the new faith," he is alleged to have said. "Let them come for their old gods and gradually they will be won over" (Harvey 1925:33).

or holy structure in Burma are the *devas*, the orthodox Buddhist nats. Probably the most popular of these *deva* images is that of the female *deva*, Wathoundaye (alternatively, Withoudaya; in Pali, Vasundhara), the heroine of a famous Buddhist myth. When the embryo Buddha was about to be ousted from his place under the Bo tree by Mara, the Buddhist Satan, Withoudaya, the earth goddess, put the Evil One and his hosts to flight in the flood of water which she wrung from her hair, wet with libations commemorating the meritorious deeds performed by the future Buddha.[11] In contemporary Burma some people interpret the Buddhist water libation ceremony (*yeizetkya*) as calling the attention of Withoudaya to the worshiper's sharing of his merit with all creatures—including, incidentally, the *devas* and other nats.

That the belief in the intercession of *devas* is inconsistent with the Buddhist notion of karma (all events are a consequence of merit and demerit) is explicitly recognized by the more sophisticated villagers. Attempts to resolve the inconsistency usually employ one or both of the following arguments. Although the *devas* are the protectors of Buddhism and Buddhists, they will not automatically protect any Buddhist, even if he should seek their assistance. They will only protect those who are pious and who live in accordance with the five Buddhist precepts. In a variant of this attempted resolution, others argue that if one's karma is bad, neither ritual nor prayer can be of any assistance—the *devas* will not help. If, on the other hand, one's karma is good, the *devas* will assist without the need for ritual or prayer. None of the villagers, however, showed any awareness of the basic inconsistency: if one's life fate is determined by an impersonal karma, then the *devas* can have no effect on one's existence—whether his karma is good or bad, whether he is pious or impious.

Nature Nats

This type includes a variety of spirits, who can be classified in many ways and who are uncertainly and ambiguously conceived by the Burmans themselves. After interviewing in forty-five households—almost 40 per cent of the households in Yeigyi—it became clear that beliefs concerning these nats are not only vague and amorphous, but that they exhibit wide differences. An unnamed spirit for one informant is named for another; a proper name of a nat for one informant is a generic name for another; a category of nats for one informant is only one nat for another. Thus, depending upon the informant, it might be the case that each tree has its own tree spirit (unnamed), that each forest has its own tree spirit, that all trees in all forests have the same tree spirit. Different informants use

---

[11]This myth, according to Duroiselle (1921–22) is not found in any written form in Burma, although it is recorded in Thailand and Cambodia. Curiously, too, although little known in Indian Buddhism, this deva is widespread in Indo-China.

Youkhazou[12] either as the proper noun or as a generic term for one or for all of these different categories. Others do not know this name, and speak rather of a "tree nat" or a "forest nat."

However vague their knowledge or conception of these nats, informants are unambiguous concerning their character and behavior. The natural world, as seen through Burmese eyes, is a potentially dangerous world. A stream may flood and drown the people along its bank; a tree may fall and kill the person walking in its path. The forest is trackless, and it is easy to lose one's way and die of privation; wild beasts are unpredictable and may attack a harmless victim. None of these events occurs by chance. Sometimes, of course, they are the result of one's karma; at other times, however, they are instigated by one of many nats (of the forest, the field, the hill, the stream, etc.), offended by trespass on his domain or by neglect in making him an offering. The nature nat, then, is a jealous suzerain of his domain, harming those who do not properly acknowledge his suzerainty. At the same time, however, he protects those—sometimes the protection is only from his own easily aroused anger—who recognize his suzerainty by proper propitiation. Hence, although petty and irascible, capable of great pain and harm—and therefore termed "evil" (*meihsa*) —these nats are also viewed as protectors or guardians. Thus the various nature nats are termed, for example, *taw-saun nat*, the guardian nat of the forest (*saun* = to protect, to guard; *taw* = forest); *le-saun nat*, the guardian nat of the wet fields (= *le*); *taung-saun nat*, the guardian nat of the hill (= *taung*); and so forth. There is little question, however, that it is their potentially dangerous quality, and the attendant fear of the harm which they may perpetrate, which provide the motivational basis for their propitiation.

In Yeigyi the important nature nats are those of the trees, the hills, and the fields. The forest nat (Youkhazou), for example, is propitiated whenever a villager ventures into the woods, and especially when a tree is about to be felled. During our stay in Yeigyi an entire family in a near-by village was "killed" by Youkhazou for cutting a tamarind tree without first propitiating this nat. Typically,. after offering him a small quantity of betel, pickled tea leaves, or cooked rice, the nat is then requested to protect the petitioner (as well as his cattle, if they are grazing in the forest) from "harm," from "thorns" ("thorns" is to be taken both literally and figuratively), from wild beasts, and from going astray. This propitiation, as implied above, is double-edged. It is intended to protect the person from the nat who, if not propitiated, might send wild beasts, cause one to become lost, and so on; and it is intended to solicit the assistance of the nat if, due to other causes, these events should transpire.

---

[12]Professor U Ko Ko of Mandalay University informs me that Youkhazou is a Burmese-Pali name, *sou* (Burmese) meaning "to rule" and *rukkha* (Pali) meaning "tree."

In addition to offerings and to petitions, other precautionary measures may be taken when in the forest. Some villagers will not urinate on a tree while others refrain from the use of obscenity lest, in either instance, the nat be offended and cause harm. But there are numerous other ways by which the forest nat (and other nats) may be offended, and offense, as Spear has observed, need not be intentional. "Vengeance is just as sure to come upon the guilty person if, unknowingly, he harms or offends the nat" (Spear 1928:41). Hence, offerings to the nats are intended to placate them for any unknowing or unwitting offense that might be committed.

In addition to individual propitiation of the tree nat(s) in the forest, in the village there is an annual public propitiation (*nat pwe*) for You-khazou (now taken to be the proper name of a single nat, the Nat of all the trees, who lives in huge trees—especially bo trees). Following the calendrical ceremony for the village nat (described in Chapter 7), the assembled group proceeds to a bo tree about fifty yards from the shrine of the village nat, where two women, charged with this responsibility, place a banana and coconut offering (*kadaw-pwe*) on a mat before the tree and offer it to the nat. Lighted candles are also placed before the tree, accompanied by popular music played by the village orchestra. No prayers are recited. The participants, a large percentage of the village population, are entirely casual in their demeanor, showing neither respect nor fear. The musicians are lively and gay, looking for all the world as if they were performing at a dance, rather than propitiating a potentially harmful spirit.[13]

Hills as well as forests are inhabited by nats. Indeed, unlike the forests which, at least in the minds of some, are under the jurisdiction of one forest nat, each hill has its own nat. The most important hill adjacent to Yeigyi is a Buddhist pilgrimage center, to which the devout come from a large area to worship at the pagodas and Buddha images found in its many caves. This hill, however, also has its nat, a female spirit known as *Yeidigoun taung Thakinma*, the Lady of Yeidigoun hill. This hill is the haunt of tigers, snakes, and other wild beasts, and unless this nat is properly propitiated—the procedure is the same as for the forest nat—she will order these animals to harm those who venture onto it.[14] In addition to

[13]As is true for other non-Buddhist beliefs, the more pious Buddhists, when they don't reject the cultus of the nature nats entirely, attempt to invest it with Buddhist sanction. Thus, U Cit Ti, a villager who later became a monk, hastened to inform me at the conclusion of the ceremony that Youkhazou is really a *samma deva*, that he is "pious," and that both his existence and his arboreal habitation were "taught by the Buddha." When asked why, then, it was necessary to propitiate him—since the *devas*, as we have seen, are benevolent—he lapsed into the typical explanation for nature nats: if offended, Youkhazou might cause harm.

[14]The juxtaposition (but physical separation) of Buddhism and nat worship is seen nowhere more clearly than on hills. There is almost no hill in Burma which does not have its pagoda and which, at the same time, is not the abode of some nat. One might speculate that pagodas were erected on hills not only because of the nearly universal association of religion and high places, but also as an explicit attempt to

individual propitiation of this nat, there is in Yeigyi at least one annual public ceremony (*nat pwe*) in her honor. The ceremony I observed, which was held in an afternoon in January, was a paltry affair. In addition to the members of the orchestra, the participants consisted merely of four old women, nine young girls, and a handful of young boys. After two women placed lighted candles in a tree on the side of the canal, the usual coconut and bananas were offered to the nat. I do not know what prayers, if any, were recited.

Nats have jurisdiction over cultivated fields, as well as over forests and hills. The paddy field nat in Yeigyi is a female spirit called *Tabindain Thakinma* ("Our Solitary Lady") or, alternatively, *Aungpinle Thakinma* ("Our Lady of Aungpinle," a dry lake near Yeigyi). Because she sends snakes (among other types of punishment) when angered, she is propitiated in the paddy field during the transplanting season when snakes are most prevalent. In addition to food offerings (pickled tea, cooked rice, jaggery, and plantains), she is offered face powder, a mirror, a ribbon, and a comb. After the offering she is asked to protect the laborers from snakes, skin rash, and all forms of illness acquired by working in the fields, and to expedite their labor.[15]

Protection is also required from the nat of the non-irrigated land, on which primarily sesamum and peas are grown. It is difficult to say whether this nat, also female, is also the nat of the irrigated paddy land. Unfortunately, I learned about her existence only near the end of my study, and had no opportunity to make inquiries beyond the information given by one informant. He called her the *nedoshin* (= "Lord of the field") *nat*

---

replace the nat cultus with Buddhist devotion and, as Lehman suggests, to conquer the nat.

[15]There are light moments connected with nat propitiation. After food offerings are made to the nats, they are typically consumed by or distributed among the participants. In this case there are usually many fewer objects comprising the offering than there are laborers in the field, and the offering is therefore distributed by casting lots. Pieces of paper are placed in a container, some of them having the name of one of the offered objects, others containing some witty saying. Each worker draws a slip from the container; the ones who draw slips with the name of an offering acquire it. The sayings written on the losing slips usually express mock frustration at being unlucky in the lottery. The following sayings, found on the losing slips for one day, are typical: It is a shame for one who wants something, but who cannot get anything.—One cries because one cannot get a mirror by drawing lots.—I couldn't get anything in the past, and I cannot get anything now. I feel ashamed of it.—I don't want to draw lots. I feel ashamed of doing so.—I like to apply powder on my face, but I can't get it by drawing lots.—I am not happy in receiving it because nobody's going to use it or look at it.—I will buy something for you although you cannot get anything by drawing lots.—It is useless to feel sorry for you.—My man: Your karma is not good.—Hello there! Don't think highly of yourself.—Feeling sorry for you; you cannot get what you want.—It is nothing although you have received something after drawing lots.—You all take great delight by drawing lots. Ha! Ha! Ha!—Dear friend! Don't feel angry.—Your karma is bad. You don't need to feel ashamed.—Oh! What a miserable world.—It is not good because I cannot get it.—It is nothing to be "wide." It is only you who think so.

—alternatively, *pedoshin* (*ne = pe*) *nat*—and insisted that she was to be distinguished from the paddy field, or *le-saun*, nat. Like the latter, she is asked to provide protection from snakes, and she receives the same food offerings. She is especially offended by human excrement and by abusive language, and when offerings are made to her she is asked to forgive anyone who may have inadvertently committed either offense in her fields.

Neither of these field nats is to be confused with still another female nat, called Bounmagyi, who is also associated with agriculture. Bounmagyi is propitiated at the harvest (usually in the month of Tabaung), either on the threshing floor or in the granary. At that time she is offered sticky rice, fried peas, and pickled tea leaves, with the expectation that she will continue in the future to grant a good harvest. If she is not pacified, the harvest will be poor. Although she is a spirit like all nats, images of Bounmagyi in clay are often found in the fields during the harvest. These images are elongated, rounded lumps of clay, built as nests by a certain wasplike insect. With sufficient imaginative projection, they can be perceived, as the Burmese do in fact perceive them, as humanlike figurines. Surrounded by paddy plants, the figurine is brought to the house where it is carefully protected until the paddy is stored in the granary, at which time it is placed on top of the paddy. It is believed that the quantity of paddy will be thereby increased. When the image is placed on the paddy, the following curious prayer is recited. "Please eat here; please reside here; please urinate and defecate here." When asked why she is requested to excrete in the granary, informants respond with the usual refrain for questions to which they have no answer: "This is the custom in Burma."[16]

One old man from Yeigyi told me that in the past, before the construction of the Mandalay canal, Bounmagyi would signal the beginning of the plowing season by possessing a villager and informing him of the date of the impending rains. With the construction of the canal, and the

[16]Bounmagyi very likely is the Burmese variant of the Southeast Asian rice mother. Hatt (1951) describes the Indonesian practice of using a sacred sheaf of rice (the rice mother) to "attract and preserve the soul-stuff of the rice field." It, too, is placed in the granary. In Thailand peasants perform rituals invoking the Rice Goddess to "dwell in the fields and to be very fertile, to return to the threshing floor after harvest without taking offense at the brutal dismemberment of stalk, . . . and to remain in the storage bin until the next year's planting" (Pfanner and Ingersoll 1962:354).

For Lower Burma, Temple (1906b:25), quoting an unnamed source, describes an almost identical practice among the Mons and the Burmans of the Delta, in which the figure of a woman, fashioned out of straw, is placed in the granary. Pfanner (1962:378) and Htin Aung (1962:122) also report the same named nat and her propitiation in Lower Burma. According to the latter author she is depicted as "a goddess with big breasts and a huge belly." Only Furnivall (J.S.F. 1911a), however, reports Upper Burma beliefs and practices associated with a spirit called Bounmagyi and similar to those reported here from Yeigyi. E. M. Mendelson (personal communication) discovered in Central Burma figures made of dough and representing carts, bulls, agricultural tools, and so on, which were placed in the barn for Bounmagyi.

consequent assured water supply, her intervention was no longer necessary.[17]

Although obviously non-Buddhist, the belief in Bounmagyi, like the belief in Youkhazou, is related to Buddhism by those who need to provide a Buddhist "charter," however tenuous, for all beliefs and rites. The following tale, provided by one old informant, is tenuous indeed. At the time of the Buddha there was a wealthy man who took two sisters for his wives. The elder sister was sterile, while the younger conceived but died during her pregnancy. Her death, it was assumed by all, was (magically) caused by her sister because of jealousy. While on her deathbed, the younger sister vowed that in her next birth she would have her revenge. In their next births, the elder sister, who was born as a deer, was killed and eaten by the younger sister, who was born as a tigress. After a series of rebirths, the elder sister was reborn as a human and became the mother of two children. Her sister, who was reborn as an ogress, killed and ate the elder of the children. When, shortly after, she attempted to seize the second child as well, the woman fled with her child to the Buddha asking for his help. The Buddha prevailed upon both of them to live together amicably. They returned to the home of the woman, where the ogress, transforming herself into a wasp, lived for a long time. Eventually she became a spirit and moved from the house, first to the edge of the village, and then to the paddy fields, where, as Bounmagyi, she continues to dwell among the paddy stalks.[18]

In addition to these nature nats which most villagers either propitiate or, when queried, know of, there are others which only a few villagers know of, and which are not propitiated. Boummazou, thought to be the nat of the earth, and Akaḋazou, believed to be the nat of the sky, are among those mentioned.

The Thirty-Seven Nats

By the Thirty-Seven nats (*thounze khunna min nat*, literally, "the thirty-seven chiefs nats"), I mean those spirits who, unlike the *devas*, are potentially punitive, and who, unlike the nature nats, are conceived to be the spirits of deceased human beings who, because of their violent deaths, became nats.[19] Each of the Thirty-Seven nats is named, although the names

[17]I did not observe any harvest ritual similar to that described by Vossion (1891:4). "Before harvesting the Burmese cultivators have regularly a Nat-feast, marked by a procession around the fields, and large offerings to the Nat of the district, in order to get a good harvest."

[18]Dr. Htin Aung informs me that this is a distorted version of a tale originally found in the Dhammapada Commentary.

[19]The belief that those who meet violent deaths become evil spirits is found in India as well as in Burma. Thus Monier-Williams (1891:239) writes: "If any man is killed by a tiger or the bite of a snake, or has died a sudden violent death of any kind, away from his relations and out of reach of proper funeral ceremonies, he forthwith becomes an unquiet spirit, roaming about with malevolent proclivities."

of only a small number are known by the average villager; each has his myth, although very few villagers know the myth of more than one or two. Descriptions of the individual nats comprising this class, and accounts of their associated myths, can be found in a number of sources (cf. Temple 1906b; Htin Aung 1962, Chaps. 6–7; Ridgeway 1915:228–61; Scott 1918). Our concern here is with the structural and functional properties of the class, not with its individual members.

It should be emphasized from the very outset that "thirty-seven" is not to be taken in its literal, numerical sense. Indeed, only thirty-three nats comprised the original royal list of nats, whose images King Anawrahta placed in the Shwezigon pagoda of Pagan in 1059. These included a group of thirty-two nats, plus the Hindu-derived Buddhist *deva*, Sakka. Authorities differ over the expansion of the original thirty-three to thirty-seven nats. Taw Sein Ko (1893) derived this number from the thirty-seven odes—some of these nats had more than one ode—which became associated with them. Shorto (1963) believes that the four Hindu-derived World Guardians (*lokapālas*), reinterpreted as nats, were added to the original list to make thirty-seven. Whatever may be the true explanation, many nats of the original list seem to have disappeared—they are never mentioned, they have no shamans, they have no cultus—while others, not in the original list, have been added to the list and have acquired wide prominence. As some nats became defunct and others became prominent the Burmese Court issued new lists of the Thirty-Seven. The last list, compiled at the court of Bodawpaya (1782–1819), includes a nat which was added as late as the seventeenth century (Htin Aung 1962, Chap. 7).

Although few Burmans can enumerate even the classical thirty-seven nats, there are probably three or four times that number that comprise the class of the Thirty-Seven nats. The Burmese are not at all troubled by this fact because they take "thirty-seven" to be a category, rather than an enumeration, of nats. Given that "thirty-seven" refers to a category, a further distinction must be made between the "inside" (*atwin*) and the "outside" (*apyin*) Thirty-Seven nats. Although almost all villagers use these concepts, and although some can even classify specific nats within one or the other category, few can explain the difference between them. These few have a ready explanation. The Inside Thirty-Seven consist of those nats who are included in one of the royal lists of nats, and whose cultus, therefore, was ordained by the kings. The Outside Thirty-Seven—all informants admit that "thirty-seven" was adopted purely for symmetry—consist of nats not included on any royal list. Some informants add another difference. Although both Inside and Outside nats died violently, the latter did not die by murder; some drowned, some fell from trees, others met death by other types of accidents.[20]

[20]F. K. Lehman (personal communication) suggests that not only were the Outside Thirty-Seven not included on any of the royal lists but also that, unlike the

Whatever their number, all nats comprising the category of the Thirty-Seven are characterized as *meihsa,* "evil." Essentially irascible, and quick to take offense when slighted, it is best to ignore them and have nothing to do with them. Since, however, they cannot be ignored—they live in the house, the village, etc.—and since they are very powerful, discretion dictates that they be placated. When properly propitiated, especially with food, they will use their power to protect those who propitiate them—the house nat will guard the house, the village nat will protect the village, etc. If, however, they are not properly propitiated—i.e., if they are not fed—or if in any way they are offended, they will turn their power against the members of the house or the village, causing various types of harm, ranging from accidents to death. Thus one man lost thirty cows which he had taken to pasture because he had offended the village nat by urinating in front of his shrine. When, upon the advice of a shaman, he pacified the nat with a food offering, the cows were found on the very next day.[21]

Spear's characterization of the prevailing attitude to these nats (1928: 41) is as true today as it was when he wrote almost forty years ago:

It might be said that the Burmese people pay little attention to the few benevolent nats [*Devas*]. They are concerned chiefly with those which are likely to harm them. These nats are capricious, vicious, unruly, undependable, strong, and jealous. I should say that power and quickness to resent injury or slight are their most prominent characteristics. . . . In his nat worship . . . [the Burman] wants to be free from all physical disease and harm; he wants his family and village to be free from all epidemics, storms, violence at the hands of others, and all the disaster an offended nat may send. . . . The less he has to do with them, the better he is pleased. In almost all instances he wants to be let severely alone by all of them.[22]

This attitude reflects the Burmese conception of these nats as *meihsa,* or "evil." When asked why they are *meihsa,* the Burmese, as we have seen above, offer a variety of explanations: because they do not know how to worship the Buddha; because they died violent deaths; because they were

---

Inside Thirty-Seven, they were not killed by royal authority. He suggests, too, that unlike the latter nats who had challenged the throne, the former had challenged some local authority.

[21]The similarities between these Burmese and similar Mon nat beliefs are too numerous to be accidental. Cf. O'Riley 1850.

[22]Sarah Bekker (personal communication) believes that I have unduly emphasized the negative features of the nats in this account. In her experience, "There are many relationships with the nats which are positive and protective, and which contribute to the spirit of optimism which often seems to us completely uncalled for. A Burman who would freely remark on the unreliability of nats in general may have his own personally chosen nat whom he feels as a constant companion. I do not believe your account takes these positive elements into consideration." Since Mrs. Bekker worked in Rangoon, this difference between her findings and mine may be accounted for in a number of ways. They may reflect differences between Lower and Upper Burma, or between urban and rural, or modern and traditional settings.

sinners; because they perpetrate evil; because they died without the opportunity to think about Buddhism prior to their death. The latter explanation requires brief comment. It is a common practice for a monk to recite scriptural verses to a dying man because it is believed that, by focusing his mind on Buddhism, he will achieve inner peace and consolation which, in turn, will assure him rebirth in a good abode. Should a person die suddenly before he has a chance to acquire inner peace, and should he die, moreover, from violence, his mind is agitated and filled with evil thoughts, so that it is impossible for him to have a good rebirth. As the spirits of men who died with evil thoughts, the nats continue to harbor such thoughts.

The Thirty-Seven nats are classified by the Burmese into at least three subtypes. Although these will be examined in detail (see Chapter 6), it may be useful to at least mention them here. Each house in Burma is "guarded" by the household nat. Throughout the whole of Burma the house nat is Min Mahagiri, Lord of the Great Mountain. Although his special abode is in his national shrine on Mt. Popa, he is also believed to reside in the coconut which hangs in his honor in every house in Burma.[23]

Just as each house is protected by the household nat, so each village (and town) is protected by a nat. Although there is only one house nat for all of Burma, there are a number of village nats. A group of villages within a defined district, however, share the same village nat. Each village has a shrine (*nat sin*), usually near the village gate, for its village nat. Here his cultus is performed and here he resides.

The third type of Thirty-Seven nats is the hereditary nat—"mother's side-father's side" nat. Any of the Thirty-Seven nats, with the exception of Sakka, or Thagya Min (who is really a *deva*), may serve as a nat of this type. Such a nat, as we shall see below, exercises dominion over an extensive region taken, as it were, to be his fief. All those who are descended from the original inhabitants of his fief, wherever they may reside, acquire a hereditary obligation to pay annual tribute to him.

Although not all the Thirty-Seven nats can be classified according to these three types, it is these types which are named, and whose cultus is recognized throughout Burma. Other nats excluded from these named subtypes, are also included, however, among the Thirty-Seven. Many of these can be grouped together and classified as a fourth subtype, unrecognized and unnamed by the Burmese, which, for reasons to be explained below, I shall call "public works" nats.

Personal Nats

In addition to *devas*, nature nats, and Thirty-Seven nats, there is an additional, "mixed" type, representing an admixture of two of these three.

[23]This apparent inconsistency is not dissimilar from that found in the twin Catholic beliefs that patron saints dwell in heaven as well as in their numerous, widely scattered shrines.

Unlike the three main types, about which almost every villager has some information, there is little knowledge concerning, and no cultus devoted to, the latter type, known as the personal guardian, or *kousaun* (*kou* = body, *saun* = protect) nat. In twenty households, subjected to an intensive study of nats, two respondents had never heard of, four had only the vaguest conception of, and four denied the existence of this type.

The personal guardian nat, according to more knowledgeable informants, is in reality not one but a collectivity of twelve nats, consisting of six good nats (*devas*) and six evil nats. (No one is quite sure whether the latter are nature nats or Thirty-Seven nats.)[24] There is one *kousaun* nat (i.e., a unique collection of twelve nats) for each person. His six evil nats, according to some informants, entice him to do evil; according to other informants, rather than enticing him to do evil, they punish him for doing it. All informants agree that the six good nats (*devas*) encourage him to "do good," i.e., to live according to Buddhist precepts. They also protect him, especially when he is sleeping, by standing watch near his head and waking him if any danger should threaten. Since they remain with him until he washes his face in the morning, they are annoyed if he sleeps late and causes them to be tardy for the daily meeting which is held in the *samma deva* heavens. They may even curse him for sleeping late.

Miscellaneous Nats

In addition to the types of supernatural beings discussed in this and in previous chapters, there are a number of other harmful spirits—quasi-demons, quasi-ghosts, quasi-nats—which are not readily classified, but which are designated by the Burmese as "nats." Among these many quasi-nats, the most important—at least in the area in which I conducted field work—are those known as *ouktazauns*. These are spirits who, because of greed for treasure as human beings, are assigned to guard the treasures of the Buddha. Further description of these spirits and the evil they can do is deferred until Chapter 10.

THE QUALITY OF BELIEF

Since it is the "evil" nats, rather than the *devas*, with whom this study is concerned, the comments in this section will be devoted to them exclusively, and to the Thirty-Seven nats primarily. This section is much more detailed than the corresponding section on ghosts and witches, not merely because the Burmese are more concerned with nats than with the latter beings, but because my data on nats are much richer. It is not unlikely,

[24]According to Shway Yoe (1896:233), six of the *devas* are male and six female. Brown claims (1921:85) that the fact that the Burmese never strip to the nude, even in private, stems from fear of offending the six good nats.

though I have no proof for this conjecture, that the following comments on the nats apply with little modification to ghosts and witches as well.

In the sample which was subjected to intensive interviewing, I was somewhat startled to discover that almost half the males—but none of the females!—stated that they did not believe in the Thirty-Seven nats. That some degree of religious skepticism is to be found in any community can, I think, be taken for granted, but that the skepticism in this case should have been so extensive, and that it should have had so little influence on behavior—only one of these skeptics does not participate in the nat cultus —was more than a little surprising. My surprise was reduced, however, when after further probing and additional research, it became clear that the statement, "I do not believe in nats," has a number of meanings, of which the denial of their existence is the least prominent. Indeed, for only two persons in the sample did "disbelief" in the nats mean that nats do not exist.

When the interview materials are combined with other data, it is apparent that skepticism takes at least four forms: 1) disbelief in the existence or the power of the nats; 2) disbelief in their power to do good, but belief in their power to do evil; 3) disbelief in their power to do evil to those who have good karma or who are good Buddhists; 4) verbal denial of, but actual belief in, their existence and their power. Let us examine each of these seriatim.

1. Although a number of men expressed some skepticism concerning the existence and/or the power of specific nats, only two men categorically denied the existence of all nats; for them the nats, as a class of beings, are nonexistent. Kou Thwin, a man in his late thirties, denies their existence on empirical grounds. As a child he had been told about the nats, and their myths had been recounted to him, but he ceased to believe when he grew up. He will not believe in anything he cannot see with his own eyes. Nor is he willing to infer their existence from putative effects of their behavior, such as illness. For him, illness is not caused by nats; it is caused either by natural events or by contagion. To test the limits of his skepticism, I asked Kou Thwin why it was that U Nu, the incumbent prime minister whom he so greatly admired, had only recently given orders for the construction of a new national shrine for Min Mahagiri. He could not speak, he replied, for U Nu, but if he were the prime minister, he would have built a Buddhist chapel (*damayoun*), rather than a nat shrine.

Kou Maung Kou, a young man in his twenties, insisted that he is a thorough naturalist. Sickness is caused not by nats, but by karma, weather, food, and imagination. Other vicissitudes of life, both good and bad, are the results of karma, which could not be effected by the nats even if the latter could be said to exist. Basically, his skepticism is based on Buddhist doctrine. According to Buddhism no one is permanent, everyone must die; "even the Buddha had to die." Hence, he argued, though the nats may have existed in the past, they must have long ago been reborn in some other abode or some other form.

An older villager, U Shun, although obviously ambivalent about the existence of nats, offered a surprisingly modern psychological interpretation for the prevalent belief in their existence. The nats, he explained, "exist only in the mind." The believer is like a person who does not feel good and attributes his illness to a lizard that has entered his stomach. He consults a native doctor and informs him of his difficulties and of the presumed etiology. If the doctor is wise he does not try to disabuse the patient of his (erroneous) beliefs. Instead, he gives him a purgative, and at the time that it takes effect, he releases a lizard which he has in readiness for this purpose. The patient, believing that the lizard has emerged with his feces, feels cured. "So it is with the nats. Believing in their existence, people feel safer for having propitiated them."

2. If disbelief in the existence of nats has the smallest number of adherents, disbelief in their *power* to do good claims the largest number. In some cases, skepticism rests on empirical grounds: the protective power of the nats is not in evidence. Thus U Chit Ti, a practitioner of Burmese medicine and an exorcist, denies that Min Mahagiri, for example, has any protective power because, if he had such power, "why is it that there are so many dacoities [robberies] inside the house?"

Still others base their disbelief on Buddhist grounds. It is karma, rather than nats, that is responsible for good fortune. U Shun recounted the following (Jātaka) story as "proof" for this position. Maung Pein was a very poor man, so poor that he wore leaves for clothing. One day, on his way to seek advice from the Buddha, he came to a stream where he encountered a deaf and dumb girl, two fighting cocks, an alligator unable to enter the stream, and five hundred carts all stuck in the mud. When he arrived at his destination he asked the Buddha to explain these strange phenomena. As for the mute, the Buddha said that she would speak if Maung Pein asked her to do so. When Maung Pein asked her to speak, she spoke to him; and so she became his wife. When he asked the Buddha why the cocks were fighting, the Buddha said it was because there was a diamond in the head of one and an emerald in the head of the other. Maung Pein removed the jewels, which he was permitted to keep, and the cocks stopped their fighting. He then asked the Buddha why the alligator could not enter the water, and the Buddha said it was because he had a diamond in his head. Maung Pein removed the diamond, which he was also permitted to keep, and the alligator entered the water. As for the cartmen, U Shun did not remember how they were extricated from the mud, but extricated they were, and the drivers helped Maung Pein to transport his new valuables to his home. Overnight, then, Maung Pein became a wealthy man, not through the intervention of nats, but because of his karma. So it is in general—it is karma, not nats, that determines one's fate. And so it is in his, U Shun's case. He has wanted all his life to live in a pukka house, but he has never succeeded in owning one because of his bad karma, which no nat has the power to change.

3. It might have been thought, if karma is the primary determinant of good fortune, that it would also be taken to be the primary determinant of bad fortune. This, however, is not the case. Although a large percentage of the skeptics disbelieve in the power of the nats to do good, only a small number disbelieve in their power to do evil. Indeed, with the exception of the two skeptics who explicitly denied the existence of the nats, none of the other disbelievers denied the punitive power of the nats; they merely denied that the nats had the power to harm pious Buddhists or those whose karma is good. Thus U Shun denied that the nats could harm him because, being pious—he recites his rosary and worships the Buddha—he is immune from their harm. Surely, he argued, the nats "are not more powerful than the Buddha!" Similarly, U Chit Ti denies that the nats can harm him, because he is a pious Buddhist and an exorcist. "Instead of worshiping them, all the nats must worship me." He recites the ritual formula recounting the Buddha's "Virtues" (*guṇas*), and "anyone who recites the *guṇas* is like a pagoda" (i.e., nothing can harm it). Moreover, he observes the Buddhist precepts, and for this even the *devas* must watch over him.

Just as they cannot harm pious Buddhists, so the nats cannot harm those whose karma is good. Thus Ma San, a girl of seventeen, was taken ill while working in the fields and fell into a coma. Her illness was caused by the nat, Aungpinle Thakinma, because no offering had been made to her when the laborers had entered her fields. The nat had attacked Ma San, rather than the field's owner, who was responsible for the negligence, because Ma San's karma was bad while that of the owner was good.

4. Despite the varying degrees of disbelief summarized thus far, all but one of the skeptics have a coconut for the house nat in their homes and they participate, either personally or by means of a financial contribution, in the cultus of the other important nats. This seeming inconsistency is explained on a number of grounds. Some say that since it is customary to propitiate the nats, to refuse to participate would result in public criticism. Others say they participate in order to please their "superstitious" wives. Still others say that if someone in the household were to fall ill, they would be held responsible for having failed to propitiate the nats. These explanations are, I think, genuine for many of the professed skeptics. There are others, however—certainly as many as half—for whom these explanations are patent rationalizations. While claiming to be skeptics, they are obviously believers. A few examples will suffice.

In discussing the nats, U Chit Ti insisted that they were powerless and scoffed at those who believed in them. That same afternoon, in another context, he told me that sometime in the past his wife had become ill because of his negligence in propitiating the house nat. After offering a coconut to the nat, his wife's health was restored.

Similarly, U Sa Mya, a former monk, consistently denied the power of the nats when responding to the items on the interview schedule. A few days later, as he was returning from a funeral for a friend, I asked him the cause of the friend's death. He explained that with this death, an entire family had been extinguished within one year, for they had cut down a banyan tree without making an offering to the tree nats.

It is notable that although half the males in Yeigyi expressed some degree of skepticism—if only verbal—concerning nats, none of the females expressed any kind of skepticism. This is not accidental. Regardless of their degree of Buddhist piety, it is the women—and men and women alike agree on this point—who are the more deeply involved in nat propitiation. It is they who most fear the nats and who are most concerned with their cultus. Village nat shrines are almost always in the charge of women caretakers (nandein), and village nat ceremonies are attended almost exclusively by women.

Formal cultic behavior also shows sex differences. Although nats are not objects of "worship," some women may bow to them, hands pressed (in the traditional sign of respect) to their foreheads, when propitiating the nats; except for male shamans, few men do so. To any query about this formal sex difference, one receives a stock response: human males are nobler than human females. Since males already occupy a higher position than the nats within the thirty-one abodes of existence, it would be improper for them to show this mark of respect for beings who are lower than they. But females, being less noble than males, commit no impropriety in doing so.

Fearing the nats, the women not only expressed no skepticism concerning them, but also strongly dissented from the male expressions of skepticism which they heard. In most cases, they importuned the men to discontinue their skeptical comments lest the nats be offended and cause them harm. The comments of Kou Thwin's wife were typical. Kou Thwin, she said, is educated and, moreover, he is a male. It is alright for him to reject the nats. As for herself, she is not educated and she is a female. More importantly, she lives with, and is responsible for, their children. If the nats become angry, they will cause her children to fall ill. All she asks is that they not harm her children; so let him (her husband) keep his peace.

Despite the claims of many scholars, both Western and Burmese, that nat belief is confined to the untutored villager, there is abundant evidence that it is found with undiminished intensity in the more sophisticated and educated population as well. Indeed, with respect to rural-urban differences—not including the handful of Burmese intellectuals—there is reason to believe that in many instances the nat cultus is more important in urban centers, such as Rangoon or Mandalay, than in the villages. To be sure, many sophisticated Burmans disclaim any belief in nats, but for most of them these disclaimers represent the same stance I encountered among male villagers, *viz.*, verbal expressions of disbelief combined with overt indications of belief.

That supernaturalism, including spirit propitiation, does not decrease with urbanization should occasion no surprise unless urbanization is associated with an increase both in scientific knowledge and in control—including prediction—over one's environment. In Burma, and in most societies with prescientific cultures, urbanization is accompanied, on the one hand, by little increase in scientific knowledge and, on the other, by a decrease in environmental control. Except in special circumstances—drought, flood, etc.—the peasant's life is fairly predictable. Governed by the rhythm of the seasons and by traditional agricultural lore and technology, his life has an almost inevitable flow. At any given period in his life, he knows where he will be living at some future period, what he will be doing, and the general status he will occupy. The urban proletarian, his future dependent on an impersonal market, lives in a much less structured, much less predictable world. And on this dimension, the wealthier classes are not much better off. "All the rich people," exclaimed a friend in Mandalay, "believe in nats. They must, since they never know when they will meet trouble." Since, he went on to explain, the wealthy do not know when and under what circumstances they might lose their wealth, it is only through nat propitiation and consultation of shamans that they can achieve any assurance of control and predictability. In short, it is here, where chance, luck, and uncertainty reign, that we find what we would expect to find—the most attention to nats and their cultus.

Let us then briefly examine the urban concern with nats. At the highest level, for example, U Nu's devotion to the nats is well known. Indeed, one of his last official acts before the military *coup* of 1962 was to order the construction of two national nat shrines, one for Upper and one for Lower Burma, at a cost of K100,000, or more than $20,000 (*The Nation,* August 15, 1961). A week later, it was announced (*The Nation,* August 22, 1961) that the government had decided, instead, to build only one shrine, on Mt. Popa, because the funds allocated for the project were "too small to erect a grand shrine" in two places.

His decision to construct these nat shrines at government expense was not U Nu's first attempt to involve the government in the nat cultus. A defector from his first cabinet charged at a press conference that U Nu's decision to plant vast coconut plantations was not based, as he had claimed, on a desire to save foreign exchange by the domestic production of oil. It was based, rather, as U Nu had allegedly explained at a mass rally of his party, on the belief that the Mahagiri nats are fond of coconuts, and by thus incurring the favor of the nats, the party would be successful in future elections. During his incumbency in office, moreover, the government, in a ceremony attended by the president, the prime minister, and the cabinet, made an annual offering to the nats near the famous Kaba-Aye pagoda in a suburb of Rangoon.

U Nu was concerned with the nats as a private citizen, as well as a government official. During the one year which I spent in Burma, he not only contributed two new statues of Min Mahagiri and his sister to their shrine on Mt. Popa, but he regularly retired to this mountain, the ancient center of the nat cultus, for long periods of retreat and meditation.

Although the most famous, U Nu is not an atypical case of nat belief in a sophisticated, urban Buddhist. Nor are Christians any more immune to traditional nat beliefs—indeed, why should they be?—than Buddhists. A native of Moulmein and a graduate of the University of Rangoon, the township officer for the Yeigyi area is a Christian and a collector of Bibles. While touring the township he was informed by the residents of Sedaw village that they had been threatened by tigers for the past month. Both he and the villagers believed that the tigers—whose roars he heard the night he slept in the village—were sent by the nat, Sedaw Thakinma. The next day he ordered posted on the village gate an ultimatum, written in his own hand and addressed to the nat. He informed her that she resided in his township at his sufferance, that he, as the representative of the government, was more powerful than she, and that if she continued to harass the villagers, he would expel her from his township. When I queried him about this order, he said that nothing is more powerful than the government, and that the nat would have to obey his order.[25] When I met him again, about a month later, he told me triumphantly that following his ultimatum the tigers had disappeared from the Sedaw area.

Perhaps one more example, as revealing as this one, will suffice. When a young man in Yeigyi was possessed by a nat, I was asked to bring a certain exorcist to the village. Arriving at the home of this exorcist, I was told that he could be found at the home of his friend, the township officer. The latter, informed of the case, volunteered to drive the exorcist in his car. His mother, a devout Christian and the sister of a professor in a Christian seminary, begged her son not to go. This nat, she said, was especially vicious and would try to prevent the car from reaching the village. When, nevertheless, he insisted on going, she dropped to her knees, invoking the protection of Christ for her son. At the same time, in another

[25]The belief that government officials have the power to expel nats has its roots in traditional Burmese political theory (cf. Htin Aung 1933a; for a similar belief in Laos, see Halpern 1964:124). That the government is more powerful than the nats is not, however, a universally held belief. This same township officer, indignant at the troubles which a nat had caused a friend, told a group of villagers that he was "fed up" with all the nats and that he would expel them all from his township. The village elders, when queried privately, were amused by his warning. The nats, they insisted, are more powerful than any government.

corner of the room, the exorcist was invoking the assistance of the *samma devas*.

Like some peasants, many urbanites, especially the better educated, profess to be skeptical of the nats, but, like many "skeptical" peasants, their verbally expressed attitudes are belied by their behavior. Educated in a Christian high school in Mandalay, my interpreter, for example, persistently denied that the nats could affect anyone's life, although he did not deny that they existed. When, however, he shared a house with my wife and me at the Taungbyon Festival, he asked us not to sleep together near the coconut which hangs for the house nat, lest we suffer some harm. Somewhat later, when visiting his house and noticing a suspended coconut, I asked him why he, a professed skeptic, observed this ritual. Embarrassed, he explained that because he recited his beads daily, he had no fear of the nats, but because his daughter did not recite her beads, it was necessary to hang the coconut, lest she be harmed by Min Mahagiri, the house nat.

Again, U Maung Maung, a wealthy Mandalay merchant and a graduate of a Christian high school, emphasized that he, unlike the villagers, was not "superstitious." He, for example, had no belief in nats. Shortly after, however, he told me that "strange things" occur in Burma. Thus, accompanied by eight other people, a few years ago he had traveled to Maymyo by car and twice—both going and coming—he had a flat tire. Although not "superstitious," was it not strangely coincidental that the accidents happened while violating the taboo imposed by the nat Koumyoumin, which prohibits nine people from riding together when in his domain? Since then, being ever careful to comply with the taboo, he has never had a flat tire on that road.

The persistence of nat belief in the face of education, urbanization, Buddhism, and Christianity does not mean that there is no opposition to the nat cultus among sophisticated Burmans. On the contrary, skepticism and disbelief are to be found in urban areas, especially among the intellectual and military elite, just as they are found (as we have seen) in the villages. Indeed, the army, concerned with modernization and economic development, is actively opposed to the nat cultus, both for the "magical" habits of thinking that it encourages and for its draining of capital into nonproductive channels. One of the very first acts of the present military regime, for example, was to cancel U Nu's plans for the construction of a nat shrine on Mt. Popa. A year and a half later, this same government announced that the funds which had been allocated for the nat shrine were to be used, instead, "for the welfare of the peasants and workers" (*The Nation*, December 21, 1963). But this government has gone even further. Only a few months after seizing power, it issued a decree prohibiting the production of any films depicting nats, ghosts, witches, etc. This decree ". . . is part of the Revolutionary Government's efforts to remove the obscurantist influence of superstitious beliefs on the people" (*The Nation*,

August 3, 1962). In the same vein, addressing the University Training Corps, an army colonel attacked the nat cultus, complaining of the "backwardness" of Burma, ". . . where people are still worshiping nats while the rockets have been orbiting the earth more than four or five circles" (*The Union Express*, April 25, 1962).

It is not only the army that attacks the nat cultus; opposition is found among some—but by no means all—intellectuals, as well. Their attack is based, on the one hand, on their generic opposition to magic and superstition, and, on the other hand, on their perceived conflict between nat beliefs and Buddhism, a topic which we shall discuss in detail (Chapter 14). The former objection to the nat cultus is exemplified in an editorial in *The Guardian* (May 23, 1961). Commenting on the government's decision to construct two new nat shrines, the editorial states that the "majority of our readers" are opposed to this decision, not only because nat propitiation cannot be reconciled with Buddhism, but because:

they hold that Nat worship is primitive, stemming from the unreasoning belief of the primitive people who were ignorant of the laws of nature and phenomena of life, and therefore invoked the help of the spiritual beings to dispel the dangers which beset human beings in earth.

The accompanying cartoon from the same newspaper illustrates its attitude toward nat propitiation. (The figure at the left is making an offering to the nats.)

FIGURE 2. *Cartoon from The Guardian, September 1, 1961*

CHAPTER FIVE

Supernaturalism:
Some Explanations

A NOTE ON EXPLANATION

Having outlined the major types of harmful supernatural beings found in Burma, our immediate task—on the assumption that supernatural beings have no objective existence—is to examine the bases for their putative existence. The explanatory task is twofold. First, granted that beliefs in harmful supernatural beings comprise an integral part of Burmese culture —specifically, its cognitive or belief system—why is it that they are differentiated into the various types—witches, ghosts, demons, nats—which we have delineated above? If this first question is basically a cultural question, the second is essentially a psychological question. Granted that beliefs concerning these supernatural types comprise part of the Burmese culture, why is it that the Burmese accept these beliefs? In this chapter the answer to the psychological question will attend exclusively to those dimensions which are shared by all these supernatural beings; later chapters will deal with dimensions specific to particular types.

Explanation in the social sciences is usually cast in three quite different but complementary modes. For lack of better terms, these modes might be designated as causal, functional, and configurational. Explanations of religious phenomena fall within this same explanatory matrix (cf. Spiro 1966). Ideally, a complete explanation would include all three modes.

Causal explanations, briefly, comprise three subtypes. One type, the historico-genetic, accounts for a religious variable (a belief or a ritual) by reference to its historical origin within the social group in which it is found. A second type, the ontogenetic, takes origin for granted and accounts for the variable by reference to its acquisition and development in each generation of actors that comprise the group. A third type, the dynamic, is concerned with the persistence of the variable and seeks an explanation in those personality attributes of actors—cognitive, perceptual, and motivational—which instigate religious behavior (the holding of a belief or the performance of a ritual).

Unlike causal explanations, which are concerned with antecedent-consequent relationships, configurational explanations are concerned with structural relationships. For this explanatory type, a religious variable is explained by reference to other institutional variables with which it is associated and with which it forms a pattern or cluster. Embedded within a sociocultural matrix, religion is accounted for by showing its patterned relationships to other elements of this matrix.

Like causal explanations, functional explanations are also concerned with antecedent-consequent relationships. Functionalism, however, takes religion as an antecedent condition and explains it by reference to its consequences—by reference, that is, to its contributions to the maintenance of the society or the culture of which it is a part, or by its contribution to the personality integration of those who adhere to it.

At a minimum, then, an explanation for the Burmese beliefs in ghosts, witches, and nats would attempt to indicate their origin, to stipulate their functions, to delineate their relationships to other features of the Burmese social and cultural systems, and to specify the psychological bases (cognitive, perceptual, and motivational) for these beliefs and for the practices associated with them. Although I shall attempt to accomplish part of this explanatory scheme—the causal part—the data are not sufficient to accomplish it in its entirety. Moreover, I shall not even attempt to accomplish the other parts of the scheme because functional and configurational explanations, in my opinion, either are ultimately causal or else they are not explanatory. Having already indicated the insufficiency of the data, only a brief comment is necessary to explain my rejection, in the present context, of functional and configurational explanations.

Since functional explanations attempt to account for the persistence of social and cultural phenomena by reference to their consequences, it is obvious that the latter cannot explain the former unless it can be shown that these consequences are intended (either consciously or unconsciously) by the actors. But if they are intended, they are causal variables, for by their reinforcement of the actors' behavior they create an expectation that the repetition of the behavior will achieve a repetition of these consequences. This expectation, then, constitutes a motivational variable, and motivational variables, being causal variables, provide us with one kind of causal explanation.

If, on the other hand, the function of the phenomenon to be explained is an unintended consequence, it is a logical fallacy to explain the phenomenon by reference to its function. Indeed, the contrary is the case: the function is explained by reference to the phenomenon by which it is achieved. The religious phenomenon, to return to the substance of the discussion, is then seen as an antecedent condition for a given social function, its consequent condition. Notice, then, that this functional explanation of religion does not explain religion; rather, it explains a dimension of society—social solidarity, for example—by reference to religion. If religion has such unintended functions, it is important, of course, that the anthropologist identify them—and in a later chapter I hope to be able to identify some of the functions of Burmese supernaturalism—but he must then recognize what he is doing: he is not explaining religion, he is explaining society. To assert that he is explaining religion—as is frequently the case in functional analysis—is to perpetrate a fallacy. Even if the putative function of religion satisfies a functional requirement of society, it is inadmissible, surely, to argue that this unintended consequence of religion is the cause of religion.

Configurational explanations can be subjected to the same kind of analysis. When one argues that a religious belief, a kinship practice, and a political form are "related," one either means that one or more of these related variables is cause while the other is effect, or that all three are the effects of a fourth, as yet unidentified variable. In either case we are left with a causal explanation in which religion is either the dependent or the independent variable. If the latter, the religious variable is explained; if the former, the religious variable is used to explain the other variables.

With these brief comments on the logic of explanation, I can return to the original two questions: why is it that the Burmese believe in the existence of supernatural beings? and, more concretely, why is it that they believe specifically in those kinds of supernatural beings described in the previous chapters? These are related, but distinct, questions. The answer to the first must either be deduced from, or implicitly contain, a theory which will explain why not only the Burmese, but why any other people, believe in the existence of supernatural beings. The strategy to be used to answer the second is just the reverse, for what is sought is not an explanation for some generic human belief, but for its uniquely Burmese variant. Nevertheless, although ultimately requiring different answers, both questions, in a first approximation to an explanation, may be provided with a common answer.

The Burmese, in the first instance, believe in supernatural beings because, like other peoples, they have been taught that such beings exist. For the same reason their beliefs relate to certain types of supernatural beings—ghosts, witches, and nats—with specified attributes, rather than to other types with other attributes. To say this, however, is merely to push the explanatory task one step back. Granted that these beliefs are acquired in the process of acquiring the Burmese cultural tradition, we must still explain how it is that these, rather than some other types, comprise this tradition. Despite the bias against history that has characterized recent explanation in social anthropology, this question can only be answered by a historical explanation. For whatever may be the psychobiological source of the generic belief in supernatural beings, and whatever may be the functions of their uniquely Burmese variants, the fact remains that, in the first instance, the supernatural beliefs which are part of the culture of contemporary Burma derive from Burma's religious history. Unhappily that history is still to be written. Instead of attempting to write it, I shall attempt in the next section to show how Burmese supernatural beliefs parallel those found among Burmese tribal peoples, and to suggest that cognate Burmese beliefs developed from a similar aboriginal background.

THE SUPERNATURAL TYPES: A BACKGROUND EXPLANATION

The Aboriginal Influence

The belief in spirits of various kinds is found among all tribal groups within the Union of Burma—indeed throughout all of Southeast Asia—and it is at least plausible to assume that the tribal ancestors of the Burmese Buddhists had beliefs similar to, if not identical with, these other tribal groups. The spirits of these tribal groups in Burma have been classified (Taw Sein Ko 1893:177; Temple 1906b:16) into five types: 1) personal spirits, 2) family or house spirits, 3) communal spirits, 4) genii or dryads, 5) disembodied spirits of the deceased. Since all five types are found among contemporary Burmese Buddhists, it is not unreasonable to assume that, with the exception of the *devas*, contemporary Burmese spirit types represent the persistence, sometimes reinterpreted, of the types of aboriginal spirits found among their pre-Buddhist ancestors.

The spirits of Type 1 find their parallels in the "butterfly spirit" (to be examined later) and in the "personal guardian" (*kousaun*) nat of the contemporary Burmans, while those of Type 5 are similar to Burmese ghosts (*tasei-thaye*) which, incidentally, are sanctioned by Buddhism as well. The spirits of Type 4, those "who inhabit trees and rocks, hills and mountains, rivers and streams, lakes and seas" (Taw Sein Ko 1893:177), are, without change, the contemporary Burmese nature nats. Some of the earlier Burmese nature nats may, to be sure, have dropped out; others, especially influenced by Hindu and Buddhist legends and folktales, may have been added. In general, however, contemporary Burmese nature nats would seem to represent a persistence into the present of earlier Burmese nature spirits. Many of the latter have been legitimized, of course, by lexical assimilation to the Hindu-Buddhist pantheon. Thus, the nat of the trees is now named Youkhazou, after the Indian tree spirit.

This leaves the second and third type of spirits which, I would suggest, find their parallels in the Thirty-Seven nats. Because the new nats could have been easily assimilated into these latter two types, the establishment of their cultus would have encountered few cognitive obstacles. Thus, Type 3, the "communal" nats, consists in some, but by no means in all, cases of "souls of departed heroes" who are "the tutelary gods of clans or tribes" (Taw Sein Ko 1893), and their "territorial" jurisdiction is clearly defined. It is at least plausible, then, that the Thirty-Seven nats, who correspond in each of these crucial dimensions to these "communal" nats, were assimilated to this aboriginal system. Thus, for example, different districts in Burma have as their village nat one among the various nats in the pantheon of the Thirty-Seven. Regardless, however, of the specific, named nat who serves as the village nat within any given district, all these nats—all, at least, whom I have been able to track down—share a common nickname: Boubougyi, "the great—in the sense of important—grandfather." It might be assumed that this may have been an early Burmese appellation for an unnamed village nat who, when the pantheon of the Thirty-Seven was instituted, was incorporated into the latter system by the process of lexical assimilation.

Some of the "communal" nats, moreover, rather than being replaced by and/or reinterpreted in terms of some new nat, were most probably incorporated without modification into the Thirty-Seven. The latter category is not only highly fluid, but it includes a large number of nats, the Outside Thirty-Seven, who, though not part of the prescribed Thirty-Seven, have been cognitively assimilated to this category. Some of the latter nats, then, might consist of earlier Burmese "communal" nats, who were incorporated into the category of the Thirty-Seven.

Type 2, a household or family spirit, is also represented (although very much transformed) in contemporary Burma in the most famous of the Thirty-Seven nats, Min Mahagiri, the house spirit. Although in the aboriginal nat system and probably in the early Burmese system, every household has its own house spirit, it would not have been difficult, when the Throne established the cultus of Min Mahagiri, to accept the notion that he was *the* house spirit for all households.[1]

[1] For a contemporary account of the spirit types found among one Burmese hill tribe, see the description of the Chin by Lehman (1963:174–77). Although there are both substantive and functional differences between the Burmese and Chin types, the latter also include personal spirits, house spirits, communal spirits, and so on.

Not only may aboriginal spirit types explain the existence of similar types in contemporary Burma, but one of the earlier types, the personal spirit, may well provide the ontological basis for the entire animistic system. According to the *anatta* doctrine of orthodox Buddhism, the belief in an ego or a self, separate from the body and persisting after the dissolution of the body, is a false belief. In contrast to Hinduism, Buddhism teaches that there is no *ātman*, or perduring soul. Although every form of life represents the rebirth of a previous form of life, the former is not the reincarnation of some spiritual essence, liberated at the death of the latter; it is, rather, a new form of life, inhabiting one of the thirty-one abodes, or realms of existence, postulated by Buddhism.

Although many Burmans have some understanding of Buddhist ontology and its rejection of the existence of a perduring soul, Burmese animism rests on the essentially non-Buddhist belief in a personal spirit or soul, called the *leikpya*, or butterfly spirit (cf. Shway Yoe 1896, Chap. 40).[2] The *leikpya* is the essence of life; its permanent departure from the body is the ultimate cause of death, and its re-embodiment in a new form is the basis for rebirth. The belief in the persistence of the *leikpya* in an unembodied form—as a nat, ghost, demon, etc.—provides the ontological basis for Burmese animism.[3] To be sure, from a Buddhist point of view the

[2]Although *leikpya* is the traditional Burmese term for the spirit or soul, some Burmans do not know the word. In a sample of twenty villagers, five claimed not to know its meaning, and four professed not to believe in its existence. The latter, however, used other terms to refer to the concept of spirit or soul, notably *winyin* (Burmese) or *nama* (Pali).

[3]The Burmese belief in spirits of the dead raises some question about the existence of "ancestor worship" among the Burmese. Since ghosts, in the narrow sense in which that term is used here, are not propitiated, and since nats, who are propitiated, are not genealogical ancestors, the answer to the question would seem to be negative. Burmese belief and practice, in this regard, seem to be consistent with those of primitive Buddhism which, in turn, as Tachibana points out, are "strikingly contrasted" with Hinduism and Confucianism. "In spite of the fact that the Buddha attaches great stress to filial duty, that he teaches the existence of the future world, and the great merit of almsgiving, he never instructs his disciples to offer sacrifice or oblation for the welfare of departed parents or relatives" (Tachibana 1926:220).

There is no reason to believe, of course, that the absence of ancestor worship in Burma is a consequence of Burmese commitment to Buddhist orthodoxy. Chinese Buddhists practice ancestor worship, and there are indications of its practice even in an orthodox Theravada country like Ceylon, where Wijesekera, for example, sees "traces" of it. "The spirits are supposed to look after the family, help them in distress and generally act in a beneficent manner in return for acquiring merit on account of their good deeds. Hence the reason for soliciting consciously or unconsciously help from the dead parents" (Wijesekera 1949:154).

Although such beliefs are not to be found among the Burmese, there are other signs of concern with ancestors which, although not constituting ancestor worship, cannot be ignored. First, primitive Buddhism notwithstanding, the Burmese perform rituals at funerals and other occasions, for the welfare of departed ancestors, which are designed to transfer the merit of the living to his dead ancestor, thereby improving the latter's chances for rebirth in a good abode. Second, there has been a practice —which I did not observe during my field work, but which Taw Sein Ko records as late as 1893—in which "the charred bones of parents and grandparents are carefully

rebirth of an embodied soul is both heretical and unnecessary: heretical because it violates the doctrine of *anatta*; unnecessary because there are orthodox explanations for rebirth in the absence of such a belief (though monks and laymen alike are troubled by the set of paradoxes, which I cannot enter into here, which its absence entails). Nevertheless, though the belief in a reborn soul is not necessary for Burmese animism, it is in fact the belief by which village informants—and many city informants too—explain the existence of nats and other spirits. A nat or a ghost, they explain, is the reborn *leikpya* of the deceased.

It should be added, lest I be misunderstood, that the *leikpya* belief is not only the basis for Burmese animism, but it is used by the Burmese to explain the general phenomenon of rebirth. Thus when a corpse is taken to the cemetery, a relative of the deceased breaks a branch from a tree and brings it to the former home of the deceased. Here, it is widely believed, the *leikpya* rests for seven days. On the seventh day, monks arrive to chant scriptural passages (*pareittas*); their chanting, according to this same belief, serves (among their other functions) to send the *leikpya* to a peaceful abode. The *leikpyas* of those with good karma are then reborn in one of the good abodes; the others become, among other things, ghosts, nats, and demons.

Burmese spirits are not the only harmful supernatural beings that have an aboriginal background; there are striking parallels, as well, between Burmese witchcraft beliefs and those found among Burmese tribal peoples (cf. Spearman 1880:397–98; Temple 1911).

The Buddhist Influence

Burmese supernatural beings can be traced not only to the animistic ancestors of contemporary Burmans, they also have their roots in Buddhism. This is true not only of the *devas*, but of the harmful supernaturals as well. This is best understood by reference to Buddhist cosmology.

Of the thirty-one levels of sentient existence postulated by Buddhism, twenty-seven comprise the "good" or "fortunate" (*sugati*) realms. These include the twenty-six Buddhist heavens—the realms of the gods or *devas*, whose Buddhist character has already been described—as well as the human realm, which, according to some contemporary classifications, also includes the nats. The four remaining realms are known as the "states of woe." These, proceeding from the lowest to the highest, are the infernal

---

preserved in cases of glass, and daily offerings of rice and other eatables are placed before them, in the same manner as before the images of the Buddha" (Taw Sein Ko 1893:178). Finally, ancestor worship seems to have been practiced by the royal family. During the Alaungpaya dynasty, at least, it was the practice to make images of the deceased king and queen, which three times a year, on the eve of the three Buddhist holy days, were worshiped by the reigning king and queen (Harvey 1925: 327–28).

realms or hell (*niraya loka*), the realm of "ghosts" (*peta loka*), the realm of demons (*asurakāya loka*), and the realm of animals (*taricchāna loka*). The realm which any being occupies in his round of rebirths (*samsāra*) is determined by his karma, the net balance of merits and demerits acquired in all his past existences.[4] It can be seen from this very brief summary that the various beings who inhabit the Buddhist *peta* and *asurakāya* realms are not dissimilar to—in some cases they are identical with—contemporary ghosts, demons, and nats.

Buddhism assumes the existence not only of harmful spirits, but of witches as well. Despite its opposition to witchcraft and to other forms of black—as well as white—magic, there seems little question that canonical Buddhism recognizes the existence of witchcraft and concedes the power of witches (cf. La Vallée Poussin 1916). This being so, there is little reason to doubt that Buddhist beliefs concerning witchcraft were imported into Burma with Buddhism. (Buddhism, in turn, derived its witchcraft beliefs from earlier Indian notions.) Like their beliefs in harmful spirits, then, Burmese beliefs in witches can be traced to both indigenous and Buddhist sources.

As far as the nats are concerned, it is clear from this attempt to uncover the aboriginal and Buddhist roots of Burmese supernaturalism that the Burmese tripartite classification of nature nats, Thirty-Seven nats, and *devas* reflects a plausible reconstruction of the history of the nats, a history of which even the Burmese peasant, at least in some degree, is aware. The peasant in Yeigyi is aware that the non-Buddhist, non-Burmese ethnic groups in Burma propitiate many of the nature nats that he propitiates. He is aware that the Thirty-Seven nats, in their previous existence, were identifiable, historical persons, living within the kingdom of Burma. He is aware that the *devas*, on the other hand, are Buddhist "nats," and that at least some of them are Hindu in origin.

SUPERNATURAL BELIEF: A PERCEPTUAL EXPLANATION

It is obvious that no amount of historical information can explain why it is that cultural beliefs, once instituted, persist over long periods of historical time. Cultural beliefs persist, i.e., they are transmitted from one generation to the next, because social actors believe in them. Thus, although a cultural belief is an ethnographic fact, explicable by reference to the historical processes of culture, to assent to this belief, i.e., *to believe*, is a psychological fact, to be explained by reference to the psychological processes of social actors. As we have seen, the belief in nats, witches, ghosts, and demons is found on all levels of Burmese society, resisting

[4]For a more detailed description of the Buddhist cosmology, cf. Bigandet 1912: II, 217–27; Sangermano 1893, Chaps. 2–4; La Vallée Poussin 1911a; Waddell 1911.

the normally corrosive influences of science, education, Westernization, and so on. This being so, it is fair to assume that these beliefs persist because, among other things, they are rooted in, and satisfy certain aspects of, Burmese character. Hence, having examined the historical bases for the Burmese supernatural world, we must now inquire into certain perceptual and cognitive processes which infuse traditional beliefs with credibility, and into certain motivational processes which render them satisfying. It should be emphasized again, however, that this chapter is concerned only with those processes which serve to explain the common features of Burmese supernaturals, notably their punitive nature.

The credibility of any traditional belief rests, so I assume, on two classes of experience—one had prior to the acquisition of these beliefs, the other had subsequent to their acquisition—which provide it with an "evidential" basis. Thus, to begin with the first class, as a result of the child's earliest experiences with significant others—usually, but not always, with his parents—he develops a set of hypotheses or expectations concerning the structure of *his* social world, the kinds of acts which are instrumental for the gratification of his needs, the methods by which satisfying interpersonal relationships are acquired and maintained, the character of those who nurture and discipline him, the anticipated consequences of, and responses to, different types of acts, and so on. In sum, from his very earliest experiences the child develops images of powerful figures who relate to him in predictable or unpredictable ways, and of acts which can or cannot influence these figures in predictable or unpredictable ways. It is this constellation, or perceptual set, which constitutes the basis for the individual's projective system, as Kardiner (1945) uses this concept. This perceptual set is relatively perduring because it is acquired when the organism is more or less an affective and cognitive *tabula rasa* and, therefore, maximally impressionable; when the ego is undeveloped, so that the stimulus value of affect is most intense; when verbal symbolism is absent or meager, so that the intellectual comprehension of experience is minimal (or distorted); and when the boundary between fantasy and reality is still fluid, so that the former is easily confused with the latter.

When this perduring perceptual set of any actor is consistent with the cognitive set of his religious tradition—i.e., when his privately structured fantasy system, which he acquires through experience, is isomorphic with his society's culturally structured fantasy system (religion), which he acquires through instruction—then the former system, projected into the latter, provides the experiential basis for his conviction that his taught religious beliefs are true. In short, these taught beliefs provide substantive content for, and are cognitively assimilated by, these perceptual sets. For the actor, then, religious beliefs are true, not only because they are transmitted with the authority of tradition, but because he has personally experienced their truth (cf. Spiro 1953 and 1964; Spiro and D'Andrade 1958).

With this conceptual framework, we may now turn to the perceptual basis for the Burmese belief in nats, witches, demons, and ghosts. The credibility—and therefore the persistence from generation to generation—of traditional beliefs concerning harmful and potentially harmful supernatural beings must be based, we may assume, on a personal orientation to the world which includes the notion that it is populated with, among other things, hostile, dangerous, harmful beings. Given this personal orientation or perceptual set, cultural beliefs about hostile supernaturals carry conviction because they are consistent with—indeed, they are confirmed by—one's personal convictions. That the Burmese are characterized by such an orientation seems to be agreed upon by most scientific commentators on Burmese character (Gorer 1943; Hagen 1962, Chaps. 8, 18; Hitson 1959; Pye 1962; Sein Tu 1955; Steele, unpublished manuscript), and it is a conclusion strongly supported by my own observation of Burmese character. Indeed, one of the striking characteristics of the Burmese is the frequency with which they allege that they are disliked, even hated, by their fellows. In conversations with friends and informants alike, one is invariably told that "everybody hates me"—because he, the speaker, "dares" to tell "them" the truth, or because he is "afraid" of no one, or because he has the "courage" to say what is on his mind, or for numerous other ostensible reasons.

It is this perceptual stance—"everyone hates me"—that gives special salience to the belief in harmful supernaturals, for it is this stance that, consistent with belief in witches, renders everyone suspect and that, consistent with beliefs in witches and nats interprets all harm as the result of punitive or malevolent intention. Thus the suspicion that, because of my spitting habits, I might have been a witch (see pg. 30) tells us much more about the characterological basis for witchcraft than it does about witches. To have observed and noted that I did not spit on the ground—an observation whose truth had escaped me until it was pointed out—implies a cautious, watchful, attitude, constantly alert to cues which might identify an apparently harmless person as being other than what he appears or claims to be. If it be argued that there is insufficient evidence for this conclusion—I was, after all, a strange and mysterious foreigner, from whom anything might have been expected—I hasten to add that the Burmese approach each other with the same wary attitude. Suspiciousness of others, fear of their putative hostile designs, and accusations of deceit and duplicity are recurrent features of Burmese interpersonal relationships. The Burmese say that *no one* can be trusted because, in the expression that came to me as a constant refrain, "How can anyone know what is in the mind of another human being?" Since clearly one cannot know what is in the other's mind, one can only watch for cues. In the case of foreign anthropologists, one can watch for, or at least be struck by, blatant cues. In the case of fellow villagers, the signs are more subtle. "We must watch their mood and manner, their facial expressions, and then maybe we can know what kind of people they are." This is why witches are believed to turn their faces away from the speaker—a somewhat stupid tactic for any witch to adopt because, of course, that is a sure sign that he is a witch.

The true measure of the Burmese perception of others as hostile, may be gauged by the fact that although malevolence can be identified in another, benevolence can never be established with certainty. No one's *bona fides* can be taken at its face value. The most vicious witch may appear to be the most pious Buddhist; the bitterest enemy may appear to be the warmest friend. Hence, the more affectionate his smile, the more pious his devotions, the more cautious one must be.

It is my assumption, then, that it is this perceptual set—"everybody hates me"—that is reflected in the belief in harmful supernaturals; it both reinforces this belief and is reinforced by it. Thus if harm befalls someone, it is an obvious conclusion, given Burmese psychological reality, that another has intended that he be harmed; and if the harm cannot be traced to some natural agency, it is an equally obvious conclusion, given their culturally constituted reality, that it was caused by some supernatural agency. Hence, when I asked Ma Hlain, an attractive woman in her thirties, to describe the congestion in her chest of which she was complaining, she told me instead that her pain had been caused either by a witch or a ghost. When I asked how she knew this to be so, she replied, "I always feel that a witch or a ghost is about to do me some harm."

But to identify a perceptual set which, in the most general way, is congruent with a cultural belief is not enough. It is the perceptual underpinning of the concrete belief in nats and witches, supernatural beings with specified attributes, and not merely some general feeling about a hostile world, that requires explanation. Granted that perceptions arise in experience, our task is to identify those experiences which might possibly produce the personal perceptions which render these taught beliefs credible. And since these beliefs are learned in early childhood, these perceptions, too, must be acquired in the early experience of the child, even prior to the acquisition of these beliefs. In short, we must attempt to identify those childhood experiences which might possibly produce personal perceptions homologous to, or isomorphic with, the belief in nats and witches.

There are two findings that seem to bear directly on our problem. First, following a period of warm nurturance and free indulgence, Burmese children are often subjected by their parents to a series of painful experiences which add up to what might be termed parental rejection. Second, Burmese children, according to interviews with them, often perceive their parents as rejecting and even as brutal. It is not difficult to conclude that these two findings are systematically related; that the parental treatment is the cause of the child's perception. And it is this perception, I suggest, that constitutes at least part of the perceptual basis for Burmese nat beliefs. If in Burma, as in any society, parents are imbued with "supernatural" power by their children, then the Burmese belief in nats is rendered credible by the fact that on many important dimensions nats are isomorphic with parents.

Nats, like parents, are superior to the self in power, authority, and status. Both are to be offered obeisance; both are to be respected, both are to be obeyed. Nats, like parents, may protect and assist; but, like parents, they also control. More importantly for our present purposes, nats, like parents, are swift to anger and when angered they are swift to punish. Indeed, it is their punitive quality—as was repeatedly emphasized, and which will continue to be emphasized in the detailed description of the Thirty-Seven Nats—that for the Burmese is their salient quality. To be sure, nats, unlike witches, are not evil or sadistic. Nats are not so much harmful, as *potentially* harmful; it is not malevolence, but slight, which motivates their punitive behavior. Nevertheless, just as the child does not know what he might have done to have evoked the hostility ($=$ rejection) of his parents, so the adult is never sure when, and under what conditions, he might offend, and therefore evoke the wrath of the nats. Thus it is that he fears their wrath more than he desires, much less expects, their assistance.

It is my argument, then, that the Burmese child's perception of his parents, a perception derived from painful rejection experiences, provides the perceptual basis for the credibility of the taught belief in nats. An analysis of witches, however, demands still another perceptual, and therefore still another experiential, basis. Witches, it will be recalled, are malevolent beings who, though human, are endowed with magical (supernatural) powers of evil and destruction. I submit that a belief in which sheer malevolence is conjoined with magical power for the execution of one's desires can be based only in the earliest fantasies of childhood. If hostility is induced by frustration, the sheer rage, which is the emotional basis for malevolent and sadistic impulses, is the frustration-induced response of a child's immature ego—either because its frustration tolerance is low, or because its anxiety-binding processes are weak. Similarly, it is the immature ego, its reality-orientation still undeveloped, for whom the omnipotence of thought—the psychological analogue to the cultural belief in magical power—is the basis for the execution of its desires. In short, it is in childhood that private fantasies corresponding to witchcraft beliefs develop. By means of his omnipotent thought, the child, in a fitful rage, hopes to destroy the frustrating, threatening object.

This process, we have reason to believe, is universal. All children experience frustration-induced rage, and all children are characterized by the omnipotence of thought. But although the process is universal, its dimensions are culturally variable. For one thing, the intensity and frequency of rage is a function of culturally instigated threat. For another, the persistence of the cognitive stage of infantile omnipotence is a function of

culturally constituted reality. In a society like Burma in which lavish nurturance is followed by abrupt rejection, the child's frustration and, hence,
his frustration-induced rage are likely to be intense. And in a prescientific
culture, like Burmese culture, in which magical beliefs play a dominant
role, the child's private belief in the omnipotence of thought is reinforced
by his culturally transmitted magical world view.

It is my thesis, then, that the child's fantasies of his own sadistic and
destructive powers constitute the perceptual basis for his belief in witches,
just as the perception of his rejecting parents constitutes the perceptual
basis for his belief in nats. On the assumption that nats and witches have
no objective reality, the belief in their existence must be based on psychological or phenomenological reality. This psychological reality, I have
attempted to argue, is provided by the projected fantasies and perceptions
of the believers. By projecting their own phenomenological reality (fantasies and perceptions of parental and self attributes) onto the cultural
beliefs concerning nats and witches, the Burmese transform these beings
from items of belief on a cultural inventory into what they take to be
existential reality.

If this perceptual explanation for the Burmese belief in nats and witches
is correct, then we not only have one explanation for the credibility of
these supernatural beliefs, but we also have a key to their motivational
explanation.

SUPERNATURAL BELIEF: A
MOTIVATIONAL EXPLANATION

A rounded explanation for the persistence of a traditional belief must
not only account for its credibility, but it must also account for its importance—if it is important—to those who hold it. And although beliefs may
persist because of their credibility alone, their truth value (real or assumed)
cannot in itself account for their importance—if they are important—
to an actor or a group of actors. Many beliefs which are held to be true
are of little importance to those who believe in them. That Brighton is a
city in England, for example, is an unimportant belief for those (few)
Burmans who believe it to be true. This is patently not the case with
respect to their supernatural beliefs which, for the same Burmese actors,
evoke intense affect and instigate much of their behavior. Taking these
latter behavioral measures to be reliable indicators of "importance," it
can then be said that the importance which his beliefs have for an actor
must be explained by reference to their pragmatic value—i.e., by reference
to the functions which they perform for him. These functions, in turn, depend upon the set of needs which the beliefs are (consciously and unconsciously) intended to satisfy, or which they are believed to frustrate.

Put in other terms, the importance with which an actor imbues his beliefs depends on his motivational system.

Burmese nat and witch beliefs are rendered credible, so I argued in the previous section, by the believer's rejecting-parent perceptions and by his witchlike self-perceptions. These beliefs, moreover, are not only rendered credible, but they are invested with reality by the projection of these perceived attributes of parents and self onto these putative beings. That these attributes are projected onto them, rather than merely imputed to them, can be reasonably inferred from the twin observations that Burmese adults do not perceive their parents as hostile or rejecting, nor do they perceive themselves as witches. Since these attributes are not perceived to characterize the original agents, it can only be concluded that they have been divested of their attributes by their projection onto the culturally postulated nats and witches.

Now projection is a defense mechanism, and like all defense mechanisms, it represents an attempt to cope with threat. If our explanation of the perceptual basis for the belief in nats and witches is correct, then the Burmese child must cope with the perception of his parents as hostile to himself and with the perception of himself as harboring sadistic and malevolent fantasies toward others (and especially toward his parents). That these are highly threatening perceptions—arousing, in the one case, affection anxiety, and in the other case, ego anxiety—can hardly be doubted. But anxiety, like any other emotion, has both response and stimulus properties; it is not only a threat-instigated response, but also it is a response-instigating stimulus. Hence, if the belief in the existence of nats and witches can serve as a means for coping with anxiety, the latter, in turn, might serve as the motivational basis for belief (belief is one type of response). And this is indeed my thesis with respect to these supernatural beliefs. By utilizing the beliefs in nats and witches as the basis for culturally constituted projections, the Burmese can reduce the intensity and even preclude the arousal of both types of anxiety alluded to above. Let me attempt to explicate this thesis, beginning with the affection anxiety aroused by the Burmese perception of their parents as hostile.

Burmese nats, as we have seen, are isomorphic on a number of dimensions with the rejecting parents. On the assumption, then, that isomorphic stimuli may become functionally interchangeable, we may now see how Burmese children can project their perception of hostile or rejecting parents onto the nats and thereby protect themselves from the threatening perception of their parents as hostile. By means of this culturally constituted defense mechanism the original threatening perception, "my parents are hostile," is converted into the nonthreatening perception, "it is the nats (not my parents) who are hostile." The latter perception, of course, is also threatening: the Burmese rightly fear the nats. But the threat-value of the nats is small compared to the threat-value of rejecting and hostile parents. For a child, surely, the perception of hostile parents is the greatest possible threat, and the affection anxiety attendant upon this perception is the most painful of all emotions. If this is so, one would expect this anxiety to become highly motivational—that is, to instigate activity by which this threatening perception may be altered, if not extinguished.

This, then, is my first motivational hypothesis. The Burmese are motivated to believe in nats from (among other reasons) a desire to reduce the affective anxiety aroused by the perception of their parents as hostile. By utilizing this traditional belief as a means for the projection of this threatening perception, parents, shorn of their hostile qualities, are perceived as nonhostile, if not loving and affectionate. This, it must be emphasized, is especially important in an Asian society in which reverence for parents, which is expected without qualification, is an important ingredient of the social cement. It would be difficult to expect, let alone enforce, such reverence were parents regarded as hostile, hateful persons.

If affection anxiety, aroused by the Burmese perception of their parents as hostile, is an important motivational basis for believing in nats, then ego anxiety, aroused by the child's own witchlike fantasies, is an important motivational basis for the Burmese belief in witches. If witches do not exist, the psychological reality to which witch beliefs correspond must consist, as I observed in the previous section, of rage-produced childhood drives of sadistic and malevolent destruction. Drives of powerful intensity, whatever their nature, assume traumatic proportions for the immature ego; they create internal pressures which threaten to overwhelm, even to destroy, it. One means of coping with these traumatic pressures is to externalize these drives and project them onto some other being(s). By this process, they are no longer part of the ego; they have become ego-alien. Projected onto others, they no longer arouse traumatic anxiety in the self. This then leads to the second motivational hypothesis. The Burmese are motivated to believe in witches from a desire to reduce the anxiety aroused by their own rage-induced, witchlike fantasies. By using this traditional belief as a means for projecting their sadistic and malevolent impulses, they are protected from the traumatic consequences of attempting to handle powerful forces with which they cannot cope.

In passing, it should be noted that this explanation helps to explain two otherwise inexplicable ethnographic features of Burmese witch beliefs. Since almost every Burman, experiencing the trauma of rejection, develops the sadistic fantasies which, *ex hypothesi*, provide the motivational basis for believing in witches, this explanation may partially explain the Burmese belief in the prevalence (one out of every seven Burmans) of witches. Moreover, since from the child's point of view the chief rejecting parent is the mother—so that, presumably, the child's rage is directed against her primarily—it may also account for the belief that almost all witches are females. On both accounts, this explanation provides a psychological underpinning for the Burmese use of *ywasu* (literally "female villager") as a synonym for witch (*soun*).

Thus far I have been concerned with the motivational basis for the acquisition of cultural beliefs concerning nats and witches. Since these beliefs are acquired in childhood, their bases are appropriately sought in childhood needs and drives. But though acquired in childhood, these beliefs persist throughout life. Their persistence, no less than their acquisition, requires motivation. But having projected their threatening drives and painful perceptions of self and of parents onto nats and witches, the motivation for the acquisition of these beliefs cannot explain the motivation for their persistence. This does not mean that the Burmese are not troubled by aggressive drives arising in post-childhood experience—they most certainly are—and it is not unreasonable to assume that their beliefs in these harmful and potentially harmful supernaturals enable them to cope with these latter hostilities.

If affection and ego anxiety are the typical anxieties of Burmese childhood, moral anxiety is one of the typical anxieties of adulthood. In the context of a Buddhist culture, in which compassion and love for all sentient beings is a paramount value, the harboring of harmful intentions toward others is an important source of moral anxiety. One of the means, I would suggest, by which the Burmese cope with this anxiety is by the projection and displacement of this hostility onto nats and witches. Since witches are conceived to be malevolent beings, intent on harming others, while nats, though harmful, are not evil, it is witches, I suggest, that are used for the projection of the desire to harm others. Given their belief in witches, the Burmese can invest them with their own aggressive impulses. Projection, then, leads to the cognitive distortion: "It is the witches (not I) who harbor evil intentions." This, then, is the third motivational hypothesis. The Burmese are motivated to believe in witches because this belief permits them to reduce their hostility-produced moral anxiety.

If the projection of hostility is a means for its externalization, its displacement—i.e., its expression in a socially sanctioned manner—is a means for its abreaction. Believing in the reality of nats, witches, ghosts, etc., the Burmese fear them; fearing them, they hàte them. Since these supernaturals are harmful, they can be hated—despite the Buddhist admonition to love all creatures—with moral impunity: no Burman whom I encountered has any guilt feelings about expressing hostility toward witches, ghosts, or punitive nats. On the psychological assumption that all conscious hostility is accompanied by displaced (unconscious) hostility, it might minimally be argued that in their conscious hatred of these harmful supernaturals, the Burmese are also to some extent displacing their (unconscious) hostility against their fellows. By this process of cognitive distortion —"It is not my fellows, but witches and nats whom I hate"—displacement of hostility permits the discharge of this drive. This, then, is the fourth motivational hypothesis. The Burmese are motivated to believe in nats and witches because these beliefs permit them to express, and thereby reduce, their hostility against their fellows.[5]

SUPERNATURAL BELIEF: A COGNITIVE EXPLANATION

Having examined some possible motivational bases for the Burmese belief in their culturally transmitted supernatural beings, we may now return to the earlier problem concerning the nature of belief—the problem of conviction. Except in delusional systems, motivation is not a sufficient basis for belief; for however strong the motivation to believe, conviction about the truth of traditional beliefs rests on their credibility. I have already noted that there are two classes of experience which may provide the basis for the credibility of traditional beliefs. One class, consisting of experiences prior to the acquisition of belief, produces the perceptual set which provides the perceptual readiness to believe. The other class, consisting of experiences subsequent to acquisition, provides evidential confirmation for the truth of the belief. Having acquired the belief in supernatural beings, it often happens that the believer has experiences of a certain character which, in the absence of alternative explanations, are perceived as encounters with these beings. In short, just as prior experience creates a perceptual set congenial to the acquisition of traditional beliefs, so these beliefs, once acquired, constitute a cognitive set which structures subsequent experience. For our present purposes it may be said that while, on the one hand, encounters with supernatural beings depend on having beliefs concerning such beings, these encounters, on the other hand, provide empirical confirmation for these beliefs. Conviction concerning the truth of supernatural beliefs thus rests not only on the authority of tradition or on a perceptual set consistent with tradition, but also on empirical evidence which supports tradition. It is this evidence which provides the cognitive basis for belief (Spiro 1964).[6]

[5]Lest I be misunderstood, I wish to emphasize that all societies are confronted with the problems of hostility and the anxieties attendant upon it, and that all societies with prescientific cultures resolve these problems in a manner similar to that of Burma. In societies in which belief in supernaturals has been eroded by a scientific world view (and its attendant skepticism concerning supernaturals), other cultural systems are used as culturally constituted defenses against hostility-induced anxiety. Politics, for example, is often a favorite means for the projection and displacement of hostility. It is no accident, therefore, that political ideology evokes little emotional commitment from the Burmese, and that political issues for the most part leave them almost totally indifferent. For a more extensive treatment of the cognitive and motivational bases of Burmese witch beliefs and, especially, for an analysis of their social and psychological functions, cf. Spiro (in press).

[6]Empirical confirmation for their belief in nats and witches is especially important for the more sophisticated urban Burmans, caught between, on the one hand, their

Before presenting this evidence, I should like to say three things about these encounters with supernaturals. It should be noted, in the first place, that unlike the previous two sections, which were concerned only with the harmful qualities of the supernaturals, this section, when dealing with the nats (who are both helpful and harmful), will be concerned with their helpful qualities as well. It should be noted, in the second place, that the expression "encounter with a supernatural being" does not necessarily mean direct interaction with one. This does, of course, happen, and we shall examine such cases. The most dramatic examples of such encounters are afforded, of course, by possession and exorcism; since, however, these are described in detail in Section IV of this volume, they are omitted here. There are other experiences, however, which are also taken as evidential for the existence of supernatural beings, even when they are not directly encountered. Some examples of these cases, too, will be examined. It should be noted finally that, although most Burmese have had no encounters with supernaturals, they hear by word of mouth of local encounters, and they hear or read of more distant encounters by means of the frequently and prominently reported accounts in the Burmese language press. With these observations, we may now describe some of these encounters.

Ghosts

Before my arrival in Yeigyi, one of the villagers was alleged to have possessed a certain herb which, when rubbed in the eye, rendered ghosts visible. A few villagers had been able to "perceive" ghosts by this tech-

---

belief in spirits, and, on the other hand, their realization that such a belief is inconsistent with their self-image as modern men. Given this "evidence," the conflict can be resolved by arguing that their beliefs, rather than being irrational "superstitions," rest on solid empirical grounds.

In addition to the sophisticated Burmans who, despite their education, believe in supernatural beings, there exists a small number of intellectuals who genuinely reject spirit beliefs. Their response to "evidence" of the type to be presented is somewhat more interesting. Unlike the former, who use such data as empirical support for their antecedently held beliefs, the latter, when confronted with these data, have two intellectual alternatives. Unaware of possible psychological explanations for these phenomena, they can either conclude that they are in fact evidential—and thereby become believers—or they must insist that the person who claims to have had such experiences is not to be trusted. Thus, when I asked a young scientist from the University of Mandalay how he would explain a ceremony which we had both observed, and which had apparently succeeded in exorcising a nat, his answer was ready: the patient had contrived the story of possession in order to disclaim all responsibility for an episode of debauchery—i.e., drinking, gambling, and "womanizing." For this young scientist, the exorcism we had witnessed was either genuine, and therefore the nats exist, or it was simulated by the patient (who had also simulated the experience of possession), and therefore the nats do not exist. Since he did not believe in nats, and was not prepared to change his belief, he concluded that both the possession and the exorcism were fraudulent and that the patient, a mutual friend, had lied.

nique. Unfortunately, the owner of these herbs had died some years before, and the herbs had disappeared. Other villagers, however, have encountered ghosts because they have been attacked by them. I recorded two such encounters in Yeigyi; others have been reported in the older literature (Tin 1913b).

About a year prior to my arrival in Yeigyi, Kou Lwin, a villager in his late thirties, attended a wake at the far end of the village. After an evening of eating, drinking, and gambling, he, together with his son, started home at approximately 2 A.M. On the way, he felt a sudden rush of warm wind from behind him. Startled, he looked back to see a figure, about seven feet tall, most of whose face was covered by long, bristly hair. (His son did not feel the gust, nor did he see the figure). The figure seized Kou Lwin by the nape of the neck and dragged him along the ground. Attempting to resist, Kou Lwin beat the figure with his fists, but his blows were of no avail, for the figure was soft and resilient. Nevertheless, with each blow, the figure retreated slowly until, about twenty minutes later, they had come to the house of a village exorcist, one U Kyan. Instructing his son to shout for help, Kou Lwin threw himself on the ground and rolled into U Kyan's compound. U Kyan, hearing the boy's shouts, ran from his house and found Kou Lwin on the ground. Helping him to his feet, U Kyan supported Kou Lwin as he walked home.

Kou Lwin claims to have been conscious the entire time. Even after entering U Kyan's compound he continued to see the ghost, who remained standing near the gate. The ghost followed Kou Lwin and U Kyan as they walked back to Kou Lwin's house, and when they entered the house he lingered outside. After putting Kou Lwin to bed, U Kyan recited some Buddhist texts (*gahtas*) to protect him from further harm, and he gave him some medicine to drink. Kou Lwin's pains were so great that he had to remain in bed for seven days. A devout Buddhist, Kou Lwin said that his karma must have been "low" for him to have had this encounter.

While discussing ghosts with a group of village men, the headman recounted the following story. About ten years ago a Buddhist monk from a nearby village was traveling by oxcart to a neighboring village, where he was to obtain his daily alms. Midway between the two villages he came to a junction which is thought to be inhabited by a certain type of ghost. Believing that this was his intended destination, he accepted the offerings of food which the group of assembled people had prepared for him. After eating the prepared meal, he had a disturbing feeling that his hosts were ghosts rather than humans. Instructing his driver to drive him back to his monastery, he climbed into his bed upon his return and immediately died.[6a]

[6a]This anecdote is inconsistent with the strongly held belief that the Yellow Robe renders its wearer invulnerable to supernatural attack. Theodore Stern (personal communication) has found "the same categorical statement and a similar occasional hedging among the Mon and Pwo Karen."

This last story was followed by another, told by a relative of the head-man. A few years ago U Tein, a landowner from Yeigyi, went with a companion to work in his mango orchards. After driving for some distance, he realized that he had lost his way and, seeing a woman picking mangos, he asked her for directions. After leaving the woman, U Tein and his companion agreed that she seemed to be a ghost rather than a human being. Fearing to return through this area at night (ghosts do not attack during the day), they left their work in the afternoon. When they arrived at the spot where they had earlier encountered the woman, she was no-where to be seen, and more importantly, there was no evidence of the houses they had seen earlier in the day. When they returned to Yeigyi they were informed that there had never been any habitations in that area. The woman, it was concluded, had definitely been a ghost.

Other cases, as we have noted, are much more circumstantial. An infant, for example, cries persistently for two or three nights. It is sug-gested to his worried parents that he is the victim of an attack by some ghost. The parents bring the baby to a native doctor who, agreeing with the diagnosis, prescribes some medicine. In such cases the presence of the ghost is deduced, rather than directly observed, but this deduction is possible, and makes sense, only in a society in which a belief in ghosts exists. At the same time, each time such behavior occurs and a ghostly attack is deduced, conviction about the truth of the belief is strengthened.

Witches

Evidential support for belief in witches is provided most clearly by alleged cases of witchcraft and their cures. Since we have already de-scribed some cases of witchcraft (see Chapter 2, pp. 26–27), and shall have occasion to describe still others in a later chapter (see Chapter 10, pp. 163–64), this section will be confined to more general observations. In the absence of alternative explanations, cases of heretofore normal per-sons exhibiting bizarre forms of behavior—such as attacking kinsmen, roaming about without clothes, shouting obscenities at exorcists, insulting the Buddha, and so forth—constitute indubitable proof of bewitchment (and, therefore, of witches). A young man in Yeigyi who, when interviewed, had insisted categorically that witches do not exist, was the first to ask for my assistance in obtaining an exorcist when his cousin exhibited such bizarre behavior. There was now no question in his mind but that his cousin had been bewitched. When the exorcist was unable to cure the patient, this erstwhile skeptic offered the same explanation as the non-skeptics: therapeutic failure was a measure of the power of the witch, rather than the basis for skepticism concerning witchcraft. In cases of successful therapy, on the other hand, success was taken as a measure of the power of the exorcist, and as proof that the illness was indeed caused by witchcraft.

A sophisticated Mandalay official adduced the same kind of evidence to support his belief in witchcraft. After recounting the case of a bewitched village girl, he went on to describe her behavior after the exorcist, in order that he might speak with the witch, had ordered the witch to possess her. Following possession, the girl, so this official explained, behaved in a way in which no villager would have acted in the presence of a government official: she became insolent toward him, and even threw a cigarette at him. From her behavior it was obvious that it was the witch, rather than the girl, who was engaging in this behavior. Moreover, it could only have been the witch, certainly not the girl, who drank an entire bottle of rum after the exorcist had ordered her to possess the girl. Even more compelling was the fact that, having consumed the entire bottle, there were no traces of alcohol on the girl's breath.

Given the motivation to believe, evidence of course is twisted to conform to the belief. When I accompanied this official and the exorcist to the girl's village, so that the experiment might be repeated in my presence, the smell of liquor was clearly on the girl's breath after the "witch" had consumed the rum. "Oh," the official exclaimed, "the witch desired that the smell remain." But it was still obvious, he argued, that it was the witch, not the girl, who had consumed the rum, because, in the first place, the girl had agreed to drink it, and, after drinking it, she showed no signs of intoxication.[7]

Nats

Empirical confirmation for nat beliefs is afforded by many types of experience. Many villagers, quite independently, told me of the assistance of Myinbyushin, the village guardian nat, during the recent insurgency. When insurgents occupied Yeigyi, they became angry with Boubougyi (as most villagers refer to Myinbyushin) because he did not protect them from

---

[7]Comparative data from South and Southeast Asia point in the same direction. Gooneratne (1866:98), describing Singhalese demonological beliefs, writes that after listening politely to counterarguments, the Singhalese retorts with, " 'Sir, all this may be true, indeed *very* true, *but* for what I have seen with these eyes of mine.' If you ask him what those things may be which he has seen with 'his own eyes,' he will mention to you several instances of men, women, and children cured of sundry dangerous diseases by means of Charms and Demon Ceremonies, or of others who were suddenly struck down with disease by demon influence, and whom no medicine could cure until the Cattadiya performed a certain ceremony. If you try to argue with him on the possibility of any of these things happening in the ordinary course of nature without the agency of any demon or charm he will give you his reasons against such a belief. He will say, 'Oh, I have seen it with these two eyes of mine, and I know very well that it is so. It can't be otherwise. If my eyes and ears do not deceive me in other things of my daily life, why should they do so in this. Chances cannot do these things, nor the ordinary course of nature. If demons and demon-sickness and demon ceremonies be mere fictions I should be more glad of it than you, because it would save my poor earnings for other purposes; but that they are not fictions, I have often found to my cost.' "

mosquitoes, and, in retaliation, they destroyed his shrine. He, in turn, re-
taliated against them by aiding the government forces in the battle in
which the insurgents were finally defeated. When the government army,
after a pitched battle with the insurgents, entered Yeigyi at dawn, the
figure of an old man on a white horse was seen circling the village.[8]
Others point out that during the entire campaign, and although the village
was twice struck by bombs, no one was killed because of the protection
of Boubougyi. The army was sufficiently impressed by the power of this
nat that, according to one old woman, soldiers from the nearby military
camp still come to Yeigyi to make offerings to him.

There are still other kinds of evidence which testify to the power of
the village nat. A few years ago some thieves stole his representation (a
statue of a white horse) from the village shrine. Shortly after this crime,
the thieves died—killed, of course, by the nat. Again, about five years ago,
one of the village women, Daw Nwe by name, offered a turban to
Boubougyi, placing it inside the shrine. A few days later it was stolen.
While discussing the disappearance of the turban with another woman,
Daw Nwe was possessed by the nat, who, as a crowd gathered, informed
her that U Pain was the thief. At that very moment U Pain walked by,
wearing the turban. Hence, Daw Nwe claims, "All the people believed in
me [i.e., in her power to communicate with nats] and in Boubougyi."

Evidence for both the beneficent and punitive behavior of hereditary
nats is abundant. Villagers cite many cases in which negligence in ful-
filling hereditary obligations to these nats resulted in illness to the head
of a family or others of its members. Cases are cited in which a sick person is informed by a shaman that his illness is caused by an angered
hereditary nat, and after making the proper offering, the patient recovers.

Other types of "evidence," such as the story recounted by the headman
of a village adjacent to Yeigyi, are somewhat more dramatic. In his
village there was a man, U Khe, who bought a bottle of liquor to offer to
the Taungbyon Brothers (his hereditary nats) at their annual festival. A
fellow villager, U Aung Gyi, intent upon drinking the liquor, took the
bottle from U Khe. Although warned that the liquor had been designated
for the Taungbyon Brothers, U Aung Gyi took no heed and, together
with U San Gyi, consumed the entire bottle. Since U San Gyi had been
incited to the deed, he did not suffer any ill effects—indeed he is still
alive today. U Aung Gyi, however, suffered the nats' punishment. Almost
immediately after emptying the bottle, he began to vomit blood, and he
died on the same night.

[8]The village guardian nat is believed to be an old man, and he is always represented
in his shrine by a statue not of himself, but of a white horse. The association of
Myinbyushin with the Burmese army is an old one. Myinbyushin was reputed to
have fought with the Burmese against the British in the first Anglo-Burmese war of
1824 (Htin Aung 1962:98) and, seventy-five years before that, he fought with
Alaungpaya's army against the Talaing (Harvey 1925:220).

A similar tale was told to me at Taungbyon village. It seems that three men from Mandalay, who had vowed to make an offering to the Taungbyon Brothers if they won a prize in the state lottery, came to the village after their victory to fulfill their vow. Arriving in Taungbyon drunk, they made insulting remarks to the Brothers. Shortly after their return to Mandalay, one was beaten up by an unknown assailant and was maimed for life, the second became a cripple, and the third was found dead in the jungle with the marks of tiger claws on his body. (The Brothers are always depicted as riding on tigers.)

The most famous example of the punitive power of the nats is provided by the following story about King Mindon, a story for whose historicity I cannot vouch, but one which firm nat believers are especially fond of recalling. In the middle of his reign, Mindon, a pious Buddhist and a disbeliever in nats, ordered that the Taungbyon Festival be canceled. Shortly thereafter his testicles and his Queen's belly became painfully swollen. Still not convinced of the existence of the nats, nor of the argument that they were responsible for his trouble, he charged that, if the nats were real, the swords which their images at Taungbyon hold in their hands should fall to the ground. When this in fact happened, he became convinced of their existence and withdrew his order canceling the festival. Shortly after, he and his Queen recovered.

Cases are also cited of assistance by the Taungbyon Brothers. When visiting Taungbyon village I met a woman who had just offered K300, or about $60, to these nats. Having won K5000 in the state lottery after making a vow that if they assisted her she would offer them part of her winnings, she had come to fulfill her vow.

Sometimes nats assist good Buddhists who require funds to hold Buddhist ceremonies. While still a young woman, for example, Daw Thi Hla—then as now, a pious Buddhist—wished to amass sufficient funds to hold a Buddhist ordination (*shimbyu*) for her eldest son. Preparing an offering (*kadaw pwe*), she hired a male shaman to make the offering to the Taungbyon Brothers. At her instruction, the shaman asked these nats to grant Daw Thi Hla a good harvest so that she might be able to defray the considerable expense of the ordination ceremony, and he promised them that if they granted her wish, she would offer them a new Bangkok silk sarong (*pahsou*). (Bangkok *pahsous* are especially valuable.) Thanks to the nats, her harvest was exceptionally good, and Daw Thi Hla was able to hold an elaborate ordination ceremony. On the day of the ceremony she fulfilled her vow by offering the sarong to the nats. (This sarong is still used by the shaman when participating in the annual Taungbyon Festival.)

Belief in nats, including hereditary nats, is supported not only by instances of rewards and punishments, but by personal encounters. The following story, recounted by U Kyaun, a villager who calls himself a nat skeptic, is not untypical of the scores of tales which one can hear in

Burma. Shortly before the war, U Kyaun, accompanied by some friends, went to the Taungbyon Festival to make his annual offering. On the way they met a man of dark complexion, his hair parted in the middle and wearing a short-sleeved shirt and trousers. Taking him to be a madman, U Kyaun and his friends ordered the stranger away. Instead of complying with their order, the stranger approached even closer. Angered by his insolence, U Kyaun seized his dagger and attempted to chop off the head of the stranger, but the dagger slid off his neck. The stranger then seized the dagger from U Kyaun and informed him that he was the younger of the Taungbyon Brothers. Instead of returning the dagger immediately, he would deposit it, he said, at the north side of U Kyaun's house. He then vanished in the air. Returning from the Festival two days later, U Kyaun discovered his dagger where the stranger had said he would find it. This, said U Kyaun, is "proof for the existence of the Taungbyon Brothers."

In addition to nats and ghosts, there are not infrequent encounters with those beings known as *ouktazauns*, who, as we shall see (see Chapter 11), occupy a somewhat intermediate position between nats and ghosts. Two years prior to my arrival in Yeigyi, an *ouktazaun* in the form of a beautiful maiden appeared to a young boy who was herding his family's cattle. Giving him two kyats, she promised him many more if he would consent to live with her. When, after recounting the story to his parents, he opened his bag to show them the money, they found two mango leaves instead. Two days later the boy died, taken, so everyone assumed, by the *ouktazaun*.

Encounters with *ouktazauns* are not restricted to young boys; even Buddhist monks may meet them. A few years ago a monk from Yeigyi saw an *ouktazaun* while meditating on a nearby hill. She appeared unannounced in the form of a beautiful woman who, when he continued to stare at her, disappeared as suddenly as she had appeared, leaving in her place a small heap of golden tamarind fruit. When he stooped to pick them up, there occurred a rain storm, accompanied by minor earth tremors. Carrying the fruit back to his monastery, the monk placed them in his bellows—for he is an alchemist—and they instantly burst into flame and vanished.

One of the most dramatic encounters with an *ouktazaun* involved a case to which I was a witness. Because this *ouktazaun*, having possessed a young man, proved to be resistant to the therapeutic skills of a local exorcist, I was asked to bring a famous exorcist to the village in my car. When my companions and I arrived in the town in which he lived, we found him at the home of the township officer, who volunteered to bring him in his car. The latter's mother, it will be recalled from my description in the previous chapter, begged her son not to go, saying that the *ouktazaun* would surely try to prevent the exorcist from reaching the village. Her son scoffed at her apprehensions, saying that the nat would not dare to harm him, a government official. As we set out for the village

—the exorcist, the township officer, and two of his clerks in one car, and my interpreter, the village headman, and two of his assistants in my car— the township officer requested that I precede him because his headlights were dim. After traveling a few miles, the headman said that he could not see the headlights of the township officer's car, and he suggested that we wait on the side of the road till the latter caught up with us. When, after some delay, the car did not appear, my companions became visibly worried and frightened. Perhaps the car had broken down; perhaps they had met some accident; perhaps, the *ouktazaun* had interfered with their progress. In any event, it was agreed that we had to do something. Retracing our route, we discovered the car on the side of the road. Unaccountably, the car had gone out of control and had careened off the road and into a ditch. Although the clerks were uninjured, the township officer and the exorcist had both sustained injuries and were bleeding. No one at the scene questioned the fact that, far from being an accident, this was obviously the work of the *ouktazaun*. When we arrived at the village, the assembled group was unanimous in interpreting the event in this same fashion. This not only proved that the patient was indeed possessed by the *ouktazaun*—some few had previously had doubts about this—but it indicated what a powerful and evil adversary she was.

Encounters with supernaturals are not confined to rural Burma. The following account is from the autobiography of a former president and supreme court justice of the Union of Burma, a sophisticated and Anglicized Burman who had been knighted by the British Crown (Ba U 1959: 80–81).

> Just before my wife breathed her last, an extraordinary event happened. We Buddhists believe that when a person dies, he goes to either the *Natpye* (the abode of the Celestial Beings) or the *Nga-ye-pye* (the Nether World), or else is reborn as a human being or in the animal kingdom. There is also a strong belief among the Burmese and the Singhalese Buddhists that a dying person sometimes experiences premonitory visions of his destination. For instance, if on his death a person is to go to the heavenly world, he will see heavenly cars coming to convey him thereto. If, on the other hand, he is to go to the Nether World he will see inhuman beings coming to drag him away with them. In order to enable a person to go the Natpye, we generally say prayers, chant Pirith, and recite stanzas from Mingala Sutta and Metta Sutta (Buddhist scriptures) by his side. By so doing, we help the dying person, if conscious, to concentrate his thoughts and mind on Lord Buddha, His Dhamma and His Sangha. If the person dies concentrating on these Three Gems, we Buddhists believe that he goes to the abode of Celestial Beings; otherwise he goes to the Nether World. During the last moments of my wife's life, both my mother-in-law and I, overwhelmed with grief, forgot to say prayers. We just remained silent by her side. Suddenly, my wife started shouting, "Mother, Mother, there are big black men coming into the room to take me away with them. Please save me, please save me!"

I said, "There are no black men inside the room. There are only two of us, your mother and I."

My wife said, "No, no, there they are. Please help me, please help me!"

Then I realized that the black men were the denizens of the Nether World and that they had come to take away the soul of my wife; we could not see them because of their supernatural powers. I said to my mother-in-law, "Please say prayers and recite *mantras*."

She did, and I also recited prayers and stanzas from *Metta Sutta* and *Mingala Sutta*. As we did so, my wife said, "The black men have run away. Oh! Now I see Nat-thamee (fairy spirits) coming into the room to take me away with them. I now *shikoe* you, Mother, and I *shikoe* you, Ko Ba U. Please forgive any sins I may have committed." So saying, she passed away.[9]

[9]Europeans whose Christian beliefs are similar to those of their Asian hosts have been known to encounter the latter's spirits. Knox, writing in the sixteenth century, does not question the Singhalese belief in demons because he, too, given his Christian belief in demons, had encountered them during his sojourn in the island. "This for certain I can affirm, That sometimes the Devil doth cry with an audible Voice in the Night; 'tis very shrill almost like the barking of a dog" (Knox 1911:124).

III

THE THIRTY-SEVEN NATS

CHAPTER SIX

The Thirty-Seven Nats
A Typology

INTRODUCTION

The most important of the nats, and the most important of all the Burmese supernaturals, are the Thirty-Seven nats. These spirits not only occupy a preeminent place in the Burmese supernatural belief system, but they are the objects of a widespread cultus which, in its complexity and organization, rivals even Buddhism. It is necessary, therefore, to describe them in greater detail than has been done in previous chapters.

Because the category of the Thirty-Seven nats includes many nats (collectively known as the Outside Thirty-Seven nats) who are not on any of the royal lists, some authors (cf. Spear 1928:40) have erroneously concluded that the nats comprising this category are not important. This erroneous conclusion stems from a confused classification of these nats. Spear, for example, after relegating the Thirty-Seven to an unimportant position, proposes the following fourfold classification of the remaining nats (excluding the *devas*): "1) personal spirits or kohsaung (body-keeping) nats; 2) the guardian nats of the house; 3) the village nats; 4) innumerable nats which are not individualized and whose characteristics are not clearly apprehended" (Spear 1928:40). This is a wholly confused classification. We may ignore the last class (which probably refers to the nature nats) and the first class (which presents a special problem to be discussed below), but the second and third classes, rather than being distinct from the class of Thirty-Seven nats, are the most important members of it.[1]

More recent classifications have also been confusing. Unlike Spear, M. Nash and J. Nash recognize that the household and village nats are members of the category of the Thirty-Seven, but each commits other errors. M. Nash (1965:167) distinguishes between "territorial," "village," "inherited," and "activity" nats. Since this classification confuses different dimensions, however, it implies that these classes are mutually exclusive when, in fact, they are not exclusive at all. Most of the Thirty-Seven nats are "inherited," perform some "activity," and are "territorial" or "village" nats simultaneously. Nash's attempt to relate each class of nats to different categories of social groups is also confusing. Thus, for example, his association of village nats with the community is correct if "community" refers to the unit of propitiation; it is incorrect if "community" refers, as it probably does, to the nat's domain.

J. Nash (1966) erroneously characterizes both the Mahagiri nat, who is, and the *mizain-hpazain* nats, who are not, as "household" nats. Similarly, she does not distinguish the Thirty-Seven from the nature nats, and, like M. Nash's, her criteria for classifying the former nats according to "structural levels" are somewhat confusing. That the class of Thirty-Seven nats can be subclassified according to a limited number of types, and that these types can in turn be ordered in accordance with "structural levels," is undeniable. Indeed, the Burmese themselves (as we have already seen) classify the Thirty-Seven nats according to three universally found subtypes, and their typology is based, in part, on such structural criteria as the type of social unit with which the nat is associated. What is at issue here, therefore, is not the notion of "structural level," but the criteria for the construction of the types with which these "levels" are associated.

Hoping to bring greater order into these materials, I shall first examine these subtypes in detail and then analyze the criteria by which they are constructed.

HOUSE NAT

Almost every house in Burma contains a coconut, hanging from the southeast pillar of the house, which is simultaneously a representation of, an offering to, and the residence of the most famous of the Thirty-Seven nats—Min Mahagiri, the house nat. The conventional explanation for the coconut is that its cool juice soothes the pains of this nat who died of burning. Min Mahagiri is believed to guard the house and is known, there-

---

[1]Spear's error is probably due to lack of information. When he writes that "the Burmans are glad to talk about Buddhism, but they do not speak of nats so freely" (p. 41), he indicates that his information is less than satisfactory. I should add that in my experience Burmese villagers, at any rate, are not at all reluctant to talk about nats.

fore, as the *eindwin* nat (the "nat within the house")[2] or, alternatively, as the *einsaun* nat (the "nat who guards the house"). In Yeigyi there was only one house at the time of our study which did not have an *oundaw* (*oun* = coconut; *daw* = honorific), as the coconut for Min Mahagiri is called. Typically it is replaced whenever the stem falls off, or about every four months. At this time offerings are made to Min Mahagiri of various combinations: bananas, jaggery, sticky rice, sandalwood, pickled tea leaves, and cooked plain rice.

Knowledge and belief in Yeigyi exhibit a narrower range of variability concerning Min Mahagiri than for any other major nat. In the sample of twenty households in which nat beliefs were subjected to intensive study, all but three knew this nat by his proper name and classified him as the *einsaun* nat. Only half, however, were able to recount his myth. Since the latter is accessible in a number of sources (Temple 1906b, Chap. 10; Htin Aung 1962, Chap. 6; Scott and Hardiman 1920:19–23; and especially Tin and Luce 1960:45–46), I shall present only its general outline here.

In his human existence Min Mahagiri was a blacksmith named U Tin De, who lived in the village of Tagaung. U Tin De was famous as the most powerful man in the kingdom. The king of Tagaung, fearing that he would raise a rebellion, took U Tin De's elder sister as his queen—some versions say in order to appease U Tin De, others say as a ruse. Still fearing the blacksmith, the king asked his queen to summon her brother to the palace so that he might offer him an appointment in his (the king's) service. When he arrived at the palace, U Tin De was seized and, at the order of the king, thrown into a fire burning under a jasmine tree. His sister, granted permission to take farewell of her brother, threw herself into the flames. Seeing this, the king ordered the flames extinguished, but it was too late to save his queen. She perished together with her brother, only their heads remaining unburned.

Brother and sister now became nats, inhabiting the tree under which they died. Because it was their habit to kill and eat all those who came into the shade of their tree, the king ordered that the tree be uprooted and cast into the Irrawaddy. Floating down the river, it came ashore on a bank near Pagan, where the nats continued to kill and eat anyone who approached the tree. Appearing one night before the king of Pagan, the nats told him their story. The king thereupon ordered that their heads be removed from the trunk of the tree and placed in a shrine on Mt. Popa, where the two nats might be propitiated as the guardians of the mountain. (Hence the name Min Mahagiri, Lord of the Great Mountain.) He further ordered that an annual festival (*nat pwe*) be held in their honor in the month of Nayon, when offerings (including animal sacrifices) were to be made to them. Centuries later, during the reign of the great Kyansittha, it was ordered that, because of their assistance to this king, every household

---

[2]According to Lehman, *dwin* literally means "pertaining to" rather than "within" (personal communication).

in Burma should honor these nats by hanging a coconut inside the house. Gradually, although the sister (Shwei Myet Hna) is still one of the Thirty-Seven nats, it was the brother (U Tin De) with whom the coconut became identified.[3]

Although there exists in Yeigyi a variety of beliefs concerning Min Mahagiri, there are some important consensual elements. It is typically believed that, if properly propitiated, Min Mahagiri protects the house from thieves, dacoits, and other enemies. If insulted in any way, or if not propitiated, he may cause illness, poverty, domestic squabbling, as well as (in a general and vague way) "misery" or "harm." Min Mahagiri, like all the nats, is easily offended. Since he lives inside the house, there are specific activities related to the house which are offensive to him. Thus, the coconut must be removed during childbirth because the house is polluted at this time. Similarly it must be removed when someone dies, and it cannot be replaced for seven days, because the house is inauspicious (a-mingala) during that period. Not to do so would result in "harm." It is especially offensive to have sexual intercourse on the southeastern side of the house—the side where the coconut hangs—because the brother and sister nats are offended by the sight of sexual activity. It is for this reason that spouses never sleep on this side of the house.

Although in general the fear of offending him is stronger than any expectation of his beneficence, there are occasions—when the coconut is changed, for example, or when one is experiencing some difficulty—when the assistance of Min Mahagiri might be sought. The following is a typical prayer (hsutaung) recited when the coconut is changed: "Oh, Mahagiri, please receive and taste this offering of a coconut, bananas, etc. Bounzahi, Bounzahi, Bounzahi (untranslated). Please take and enjoy these offerings. Allow us, thereby, to avoid all thorny pricks and all kinds of snares. Be our protector, and grant us prosperity and all favors."

Some villagers continue the ancient practice of making an offering to Mahagiri at the time of a child's cradle ceremony—usually, but not always, on the seventh day after birth—with the expectation that he will protect the infant from harmful spirits. A new coconut is hung in place of the old one and a white cotton string is tied about the infant's wrists to indicate to these spirits that he is protected by the house nat. Sometimes this protection is expressly solicited by the mother, who, when the coconut is changed, addresses the nat as follows: "One more slave has been born to serve you; take care of him."[4]

Despite these solicitations of favor, it is fear of his anger which is the more prominent Burmese attitude toward this nat. The person in Yeigyi, an elderly woman, who placed the greatest emphasis on the potentially

---

[3]Although Min Mahagiri is the household nat, there are seven Mahagiri nats: U Tin De himself, as well as his elder sister (Shwei Myet Hna), his younger sister (Ma Htwei Byu), his wife (the dragon, Shwei Na Bai), his sons (Shin Byu and Shin Nyou), and the daughter of his younger sister (Ma Ne).

[4]I did not record this formula in my own work, but it is reported by Smart (1931).

beneficent quality of Min Mahagiri, nevertheless concluded her remarks by saying, "but these nats, Min Mahagiri and all the rest, always do evil; one must always fear them."

Although historically Mahagiri is probably the oldest of the Thirty-Seven nats, the persistence of the belief in his power can be gauged by the modern rituals that are associated with him. Thus, whenever a loudspeaker —which is always used to amplify the gramophone records which are played at festivals, feasts, and other joyous occasions—is hired, an offering (*kadaw pwe*) to Mahagiri is placed next to the speaker. Since Mahagiri was a blacksmith in his human existence, it is unwise to ignore him when using anything made of metal. If this offering is omitted, the loudspeaker will not function properly and other difficulties will be encountered in connection with the music.

VILLAGE NATS

Near the entrance to villages within a large district in Upper Burma is a small hutlike structure attached either to a tree or to a long pole and usually containing a cup of water, bits of food in a dish, flowers, and/or a bundle of leaves. This nat shrine (*nat sin*) sometimes contains as well a wooden, doll-like white horse. The former objects are offerings to, and the wooden horse is a symbol of, one of the Thirty-Seven nats, Myinbyushin ("Lord of the white horse"). In these villages, Myinbyushin is the village nat, a type referred to alternatively as the *ywa-saun* nat ("village guardian nat") or *ywa-dawshin* ("Lord of the village as a royal domain"). Villages in other districts have as their village nat another one of the Thirty-Seven nats. These districts, however, may be extensive, for E. M. Mendelson (personal communication) has discovered that Myinbyushin is the village nat for "a very large area of Central Burma."

In Yeigyi and in the surrounding villages it is extremely difficult to obtain any information about the identity of Myinbyushin. In the entire village only one person could recount his myth, and the myth he recounted corresponds with none of the published myths identified with this nat.[5]

[5]Myinbyushin, according to this village informant, had been a gambler as a human being. One night, while returning home on his white pony after gambling late into the night, he rode unknowingly into a creek and was drowned.

Harvey (1925:52–53) identifies Myinbyushin with Nga Pyi, the equerry in the following story. King Naratheinhka, having designs on his brother's wife, ordered his brother to march on a fictitious enemy in the north, following which he made his sister-in-law his queen. Nga Pyi, the brother's equerry, who had left at the court because his master suspected some ruse, rode out to inform his master of the king's action. Because he tarried on the way, his master became angry and slew Nga Pyi, who became the nat Myinbyushin. (See also Tin and Luce 1960:136–38.)

Htin Aung, who recounts the story of Nga Pyi (1962:96–97), does not, however, include him in his list of the Thirty-Seven nats, although Myinbyushin—without a story—is included by him in a supplementary list of nats. Temple (1906b), on the other hand, does not include either Myinbyushin or Boubougyi (his synonym) in his list. Langham-Carter (1934), who identifies Myinbyushin as the village guardian nat

Strangely, too, very few villagers can explain why he is represented by his horse alone, rather than by his own image. Only U Cit Ti, the village nat expert, even attempted an explanation beyond the usual, "it is the custom." His hardly convincing explanation was that if an image of the nat himself were placed in the shrine, someone might steal it. Lehman suggests that the identification of this nat is clouded by the fact that *any* lord rides a white horse, the latter being a sumptuary symbol (personal communication).

As if to compound the confusion, many villagers either do not know or do not use the proper name Myinbyushin, referring instead to Boubougyi, "Great Grandfather." ("Grandfather," of course, is used here as an honorific.) This, however, is a generic term by which other villages, with different village nats, refer to their nats. The same practice, according to Pfanner (1962:370), obtains in Lower Burma. Finally, to confuse things even more, there are two village nat shrines in Yeigyi, at the eastern and at the northern gates, and some villagers—obviously distinguishing between Boubougyi and Myinbyushin—claim that the latter resides in the eastern, the former in the northern shrine.[6]

The conception of the village nat is almost identical with that of the house nat. If properly propitiated, and if not offended, he will guard the

---

for almost all of Upper Burma, finds him associated with three different tales. For the Kyaukse area, the tale recounted by Harvey is standard. In the Meiktila area, Myinbyushin is the spirit of a villager, killed when kicked by a pony. In the latter area, however, there is still another tale associated with this nat, according to which the nat is the spirit of a servant of King Anawrahta, who charged him with discovering if the Meiktila lake extended as far as Mt. Popa. Riding hard to carry out his mission, he returned to the king in an exhausted condition, and barely managed to gasp out the answer before he and his horse died and became nats.

But this is not all. From a nat expert in Mandalay, I obtained the following tale, which differs from both of the others recounted. During the reign of Sawhnit, the Shans rebelled against the king, who sent his son to suppress the rebels. While encamped in a site near Thazi, the prince neglected his duties in favor of cock-fighting, and the king as a consequence had him executed. Both the prince and his mother, who died of sorrow, became nats, the prince being known as Myinbyushin. Htin Aung (1962:97) records this story, but identifies its hero with yet another nat, not with Myinbyushin.

[6]All of this illustrates again the cognitive looseness concerning nats which reflects, to be sure, a complicated history of syncretism and reinterpretation. Boubougyi (translated as the "Old Man of the Banyan Tree") is one of the Thirty-Seven nats in Htin Aung's collection (1962:93). Htin Aung believes that he represents an older tree nat, and I am inclined to agree with him. In Yeigyi, immediately following the public ceremony for Myinbyushin-Boubougyi at the nat shrine, there is a ceremony at a nearby banyan tree for the nat whom the villagers call Youkhazou and who, as we have seen, is the old Hindu-derived god of the trees. It is not improbable that in this village parts of three different nats have been both separated and fused.

Lehman, who incidentally is skeptical of this interpretation (personal communication), adds that in much of Upper Burma Boubougyi is the divination nat, represented by an upturned rice-basket. Among the Kayah, where he is called "Grandpa Rice-Basket," he is also a divination nat, and after the annual divination ceremony he is "sent" to the edge of the village where he is enshrined in a shelter mainly in the form of a model horse—though not, presumably, a white one.

village against illness, witches, insurgents, and dacoits; otherwise, he will send illness and wild animals into the village, and he will leave it unprotected against dacoits and other marauders. Although he can protect the village from witches, he cannot, according to some informants, protect it from master witches. Indeed, there are some who believe (as I have already noted) that under certain circumstances, all nats, including the village nat, will even assist the master witches to carry out their evil intentions. In general, the village nat can protect the village only from external enemies, but not from enemies from within: he cannot protect one villager against a fellow villager. Moreover, he has no power to protect the village from natural calamities such as storms, lightning, and so on.

Just as the house nat is propitiated at childbirth, so the village nat is propitiated during two other *rites de passage*. During the *shimbyu* ceremony, prior to his becoming a novice in the Buddhist monastery, every boy is taken to the shrine of the village nat, who receives an offering. At the marriage ceremony, too, an offering is made to the village nat, as well as to the hereditary nats of the bride and groom. The village nat is propitiated not only as part of rite of passage ceremonies, but also in special ceremonies held in his honor (see Chapter 7).

I have already observed that although each village has a village nat, and although all the villages in a wide geographic area may share the same nat, different areas have different village nats. Typically a Burman is either unaware of, or unconcerned with, the village nats of other areas. If, however, he should enter the domain of some other village nat, he is careful to comply with the regulations pertaining to him. Thus, for example, the people of Yeigyi and its surrounding area frequently travel within the domain of a famous Shan nat, Koumyoumin (the "Lord of the Nine Towns"), whose district encompasses a large part of the irrigated area around Kyaukse. This nat dislikes, and will cause harm to, anything consisting of nine units. When people travel within his domain, they are careful that their vehicle contain either more or fewer than nine people. If there are nine travelers, they will place in their cart or truck a stone to represent the tenth passenger. Should this precaution be neglected, they will meet with an accident.

"MOTHER'S SIDE-FATHER'S SIDE" NATS

Although one's "Mother's Side-Father's Side" nat is in some respects the most important of the Thirty-Seven nats, this subtype is not mentioned in any of the classical descriptions of the nats, and contemporary descriptions are not entirely satisfactory.[7] Given this state of affairs, as well as

[7]Nats of this type are not "family" nats in the sense that M. Nash (1965:168) uses the term, nor are they "household" nats, as J. Nash (1966:120) claims.

the technical problems which are raised by this type, a more extended discussion is required.

When I first began to investigate those nats whom the Burmese call *mizain-hpazain*, and whom I am designating as "mother's side-father's side" nats,[8] I expected to find a very small number of such nats in any one village. I was somewhat surprised to discover, after taking a census of Yeigyi, that there are fourteen such nats represented in this village. (Since the nats Talain and Talain-Meingyi may represent the same nat— or, as Sarah Bekker informs me, the same group of nats—and since Boubougyi may represent any number of nats, the actual number may be twelve rather than fourteen.) These nats and the number of their adherents are shown in Table 6.1 (see pg. 100). I was even more surprised and puzzled by the uneven distribution of these nats within the village, ranging from Taungbyon, the nat of fifty-five people, to Popa Medaw, the nat of only one person. Finally, I could not understand why a few persons had two *mizain-hpazain* nats, when most had only one. It was while inquiring into these questions, both in Yeigyi and at the famous Taungbyon nat festival, that the structural features of this nat type began to emerge.

When respondents were asked how it was that they had Talain, for example, or Popa Medaw as their *mizan-hpazain* nats, rather than Taungbyon or Koumyoumin, the response—from those who knew enough to answer the question—invariably indicated migration to Yeigyi from another part of the country, from Lower Burma or from the Lower Chindwin. It soon became apparent that each of the nats included in Table 6.1 was the *mizain-hpazain* nat for people who had emigrated from a particular region—indeed it is possible to trace family origins from a knowledge of a person's *mizain-hpazain* nat—and that, in general, each of these nats is associated with a different region of the country. In short, just as each "district" has one of the Thirty-Seven nats as its village nat, so each "region" has one of these nats as its *mizain-hpazain* nat. Since, however, an immigrant, and all his descendants after him, continue to propitiate the nat associated with his region of origin—rather than the nat of the region to which he has migrated—it follows that the basis for the propitiation of *mizain-hpazain* nats is descent rather than residence. To put it in slightly other terms, the principle of recruitment to their cultus is not territorial, like that of the house or village nats, but hereditary.[9] Given this hereditary basis for their propitiation, and given the fact that offerings to them at their annual festivals (*nat pwe*) are made, not by individuals, but by groups of kinsmen (or by a member of the group acting as its

---

[8]*Mi* and *hpa* are, respectively, "mother" and "father" in Burmese. *Hsain* means "to be connected to," "related to," "to have jurisdiction over," "to have responsibility for."

[9]A similar spirit type is found among the tribal peoples of Burma, as well. Thus, among the Plains Chin, although a woman becomes a member of her husband's patrilineage, she continues to "honor her own ancestral spirits." (Stern 1962:5).

representative), it would not be inappropriate to render the locution "mother's side-father's side" nat as "family nat," if the latter expression were unambiguous, which, as we shall see, it is not.

Prior to the British conquest of Lower Burma it would have been difficult to determine whether the basis for the propitiation of a "mother's side-father's side" nat was hereditary or territorial. Since emigration from the fairly large region which constituted the domain of any nat of this type was all but nonexistent, almost everyone who propitiated a particular family nat lived within the region over which the nat exercised dominion. The fact that the "family" was the unit for his cultus would not have necessarily suggested that his propitiation was hereditary; it could have been concluded, instead, that the members of the family, living more-or-less contiguously, formed a convenient cult unit. To be sure, "family" refers, as we shall see, to a (loosely defined) group of agnatically related kinsmen, but even that would not have been an unambiguous indicator of the hereditary basis for propitiation, since kinsmen of either the father's or the mother's side would have had the same family nat.

With the British conquest, however, and the consequent large scale migration from Upper to Lower Burma, and, moreover, with the general increase in internal migration within the last century, the territorial base of the adherents of each of these nats has undergone a marked change. It is this change which enables us to determine the hereditary basis for the dominion of these nats. As a result of these population movements, descendants of the original inhabitants of any nat's region may now be scattered throughout the entire country (although in most instances a plurality, if not a majority, continue to live within the original domain); but since these descendants, no matter where they may now be scattered, continue to recognize his dominion and persist in performing his cultus, it is obvious that the basis for dominion is hereditary rather than territorial.[10] Unlike the premodern period, therefore, in which the adherents of their cult inhabited geographically differentiated and mutually exclusive regions, today their contemporary residence patterns exhibit a crazy-quilt pattern of overlapping geographic regions. The same *mizain-hpazain* nat may be shared by persons living in widely scattered parts of the country, and, conversely, different *mizain-hpazain* nats may coexist even within one village.

Given, then, that the propitiation of these nats is based on descent, we should like to know what the descent principle might be. This is not an

[10]After writing this section I discovered that fifty years ago, Furnivall (1913) had proposed a similar interpretation. Although he did not discover a specific category of nats termed *mizain-hpazain*, he was struck by the fact that some nats were hereditary (he calls them "tribal") rather than territorial, and he concluded that all nats had originated as "tribal" nats, some having later become territorial. He also suggested that, if this is the case, migration patterns might be reconstructed from a distribution study of the nats, and expressed the hope that someone might undertake such a study. Unhappily his hope, as I have already indicated, is still to be fulfilled.

easy question to answer, and we are best advised, therefore, to examine some additional data from Yeigyi before attempting to suggest one. It can be noted, in the first place, as Table 6.1 reveals, that the Taungbyon Brothers (either alone or combined with another nat) are the *mizain-hpazain* nat of more than 60 per cent of the villagers, the remaining thirteen nats being distributed among the other 40 per cent. Since the village of Yeigyi is included within the territory originally granted to the

TABLE 6.1 *Distribution of the Mizain-hpazain Nats in Yeigyi Village (N=97)*

NAME OF NAT	SEX OF RESPONDENT		TOTAL
	M	F	
Taungbyon	29	26	55
Badoun	7	5	12
Koumyoumin	2	10	12
Taungbyon-Badoun	4	2	6
Zidaw	5	0	5
Myinbyushin	1	2	3
Ameiyeiyin	1	1	2
Bakamin	0	2	2
Taungbyon-Koumyoumin	1	1	2
Talain	1	0	1
Talain-Meingyi	1	0	1
Min Mahagiri	1	0	1
Aloun Boudaw	1	0	1
Boubougyi	0	1	1
Popa Medaw	0	1	1
Tabe	1	0	1
Taungbyon-Ameiyeiyin	0	1	1
Total	55	52	107

Taungbyon Brothers as their fief (see Chapter 8, pp. 131–34), it is not surprising that a plurality of its population should have them as their *mizain-hpazain* nats. The other nats in Table 6.1 are easily traceable, as we have seen, to the regions from which the later inhabitants of the village emigrated.

Not everyone in the village, however, could identify his *mizain-hpazain* nat. More precisely, fifteen people (eight males and seven females)—or twelve per cent of the adult population—were unable to do so. Since these were, without exception, very young and recently married, their ignorance (as we shall see when we examine the ways in which individuals are informed of their nats) is not surprising.

From Table 6.1 it is probably safe to conclude that the *mizain-hpazain* nats are not sex-linked. With a few exceptions, which can undoubtedly be traced to differential places of origin, both sexes may inherit the same nats. More importantly, however, is the discovery that it is possible to inherit two *mizain-hpazain* nats; nine respondents (comprising 9 per cent of the census) have two such nats. These findings are especially important for the light they shed on the mode of inheritance. It has sometimes been suggested (J. Nash 1966:120) that everyone inherits two nats, the *mizain* ("mother's side") nat being acquired through the mother's female line, and the *hpazain* ("father's side") nat being acquired through the father's male line. The fact is, however, as Table 6.1 clearly reveals, that the vast majority have only one nat of this type, and no one has more than two. It might be argued, of course, that in principle each line does contribute one nat, but that this rule is obscured by the coincidence that in most cases marriage takes place between descendants of inhabitants of the same region. And this argument has some empirical support: four of the nine villagers with multiple hereditary nats are children of marriages in which one of the parents was an immigrant from another region, so that each parent inherited a different nat. Unfortunately, however, the bulk of our evidence does not support the argument. In the first place, all nine persons with multiple nats said that, although this is not a hard and fast rule, their own children will inherit only one of their nats—that of the father. More important is the fact, revealed in Table 6.2, that there

TABLE 6.2 *Inheritance of Mizain-hpazain Nats in Yeigyi Village When Parents Have Different Nats*

NAT OF OFFSPRING	SEX OF OFFSPRING		TOTAL
	M	F	
Same as Father	17	16	33
Same as Mother	5	4	9
Combination of			
Father and Mother	2	2	4
	24	22	46

are forty-two other individuals who, although their parents each have different nats, have inherited only one of these nats. In short, it is only in very rare cases—four out of forty-six—that the offspring of parents with different *mizain-hpazain* nats inherit the nats of both parents.

It seems fairly certain, then, that normally an individual inherits only one *mizain-hpazain* nat. It is also fairly certain, as Table 6.2 again reveals, that normally it is the father's nat who is inherited: when the parents have different nats, approximately 80 per cent, both of males and females, inherit the father's nat. It would seem, therefore, that the mode of inheritance is patrilineal. I have no explanation, unfortunately, for the remaining 20 per cent of the cases of matrilineal inheritance; only additional field work can supply the information. Nor can I explain the case (not shown in the table) in which a female respondent could name her father's nat, and yet did not know her own nat (nor that of her mother). If the inheritance rule is patrilineal she should have immediately identified her father's family nat as her own.

It might be wondered why it was not possible to obtain an unambiguous inheritance rule from informants. The answer—and it is partially because of this answer that I attempted to obtain quantitative respondent data— is that informants cannot express a rule. Some can say no more than that the nat descends in the family; others say that they don't know. This would seem to suggest that following the mobility which resulted from the British conquest—and the consequent confusion of descent and residence as criteria for determining one's *mizain-hpazain* nat—no explicit rule has been formulated, different families solving the problem in different ways. In most cases, of course, the problem does not arise. Since marriage most frequently occurs between persons resident in the same region, the heredi- tary principle is never problematic as both parents share a common nat.

There are other curious facts which emerged from the census of these nats. Thus, for example, there are seven cases in which a respondent identified his own nat but could not identify that of his parents. Similarly, there are two cases in which the respondent's nat was different from the nat of either of his parents. These anomalous facts raise immediate ques- tions. Since these nats are inherited, how is it possible to know one's own nat without knowing one's parents'? Moreover, how is it possible for one's nat to be different from one's parents'?

The following data suggest some partial answers to these questions. The seven individuals who did not know their parents' nats had emigrated from their native villages before they were informed of the identity of their nats, and subsequently their parents died. In such cases the identity of the nat is discovered through the aid of a nat medium, or shaman, who obtains the information from her nat-husband. (It is of some interest to note that in almost all cases the nat identified by the shaman was her own nat-husband.) That parents may die before informing children of their *mizain-hpazain* nat is not to be wondered at, for the age at which children discover the identity of their nat ranges, in our sample, from seven to twenty years, the mean age being fifteen. A variety of situations may serve as the occasion for revealing the identity of the nat to the child, and a wide range of kinsmen may serve as the transmitting agent. Thus, in our sample, villagers were informed of their nat by the following: both parents (the usual manner), mother exclusively, father exclusively, mother's brother, father's father's mother, mother's mother, father's father, father's mother. In some cases the person happened to have been with one of the above-mentioned kinsmen when the nat was propitiated, and the kinsman informed him that this was his nat. In other cases the information was obtained when a shaman, called in to diagnose an illness, attributed it to the activity of the *mizain-hpazain* nat. In such cases, then, a person learns the identity of the nat at an early age. But since children have no obligations to the nats, there would be no reason for them to be informed of their *mizain-hpazain* nat until their marriage; until then his propitiation is the responsibility of the adult members of the household. Hence, if a person should emigrate before his marriage, and if subsequently his parents should die, it would be difficult for him to discover the identity of his nat. With marriage, however, and the establishment of an independent household, a person's own responsibility for the nat cultus becomes activated, and it is crucial—lest the nat punish him—that he learn the identity of his *mizain-hpazain* nat so that he may fulfill his obligations. Indeed, the obligation begins at the wedding, when offerings are made to the nats of both bride and groom.[11]

Obligations to *mizain-hpazain* nats not only differ from nat to nat, but they may also differ among those who share a common nat. In the case of the Taungbyon Brothers, for example, different families have different duties and must make different types of offerings. (These will be described in the section on the Taungbyon Festival in Chapter 7.) The basic obligation, however, consists of food offerings (*tin*) to the nat. Typically, the food offering must be made at a nat festival, either in person or by a delegated representative. In some cases offerings are also made on the three holy days of Buddhism—the full moons of Wazou, Thadingyut, and Tagu. These offerings consist primarily of rice, betel, pickled tea, coconuts, and bananas. Flowers, which are food for nats, are also offered. Although chicken and fish are offered to the Taungbyon Brothers, meat is never offered to any of the nats, at least not to those in the Yeigyi sample. Unhappily, I did not inquire for the reasons for the exclusion of meat, an exclusion which becomes all the more significant when it is remembered that animal sacrifice was formerly an important part of the cultus of many of the nats, and that it was not until the sixteenth century that this practice was abolished by the order of King Bayinnaung (Harvey 1925:167). In addition to obligations, there are also taboos related to these nats. Thus, the flesh of the pig is forbidden to those for whom the Taungbyon Brothers are their *mizain-hpazain* nat (because the Brothers were Muslims). The wearing of black clothes is forbidden if Popa Medaw is the family nat.

The attitude toward these nats parallels that toward nats in general. With some few exceptions it is believed that an offering to the nat is a prophylactic against danger, rather than a means for obtaining a boon. If one does not make the obligatory offering, the nat's anger is aroused

---

[11]Lehman (personal communication) believes that this nat type is closely associated with the traditional sumptuary political order, and that it will not be fully understood until the latter is understood.

and he will cause all kinds of trouble, such as illness to members of the family (as well as to their cattle), poverty, and intrafamily quarreling and disputes.

Although the belief in the punitive power of these hereditary nats is much stronger than the belief in their helping power, it is also believed, as we have already seen, that they can be of assistance. When making an offering to them, the Burmese recite a prayer, asking that their income be good, that the members of their family be happy, and that they be free from sickness, danger, and "thorns." The need to render this prayer consistent with Buddhism is felt by many villagers. Typically, after quoting the prayer for me, they would hasten to observe that such benefits could occur only if one's karma were good; if it were bad, the nat's help would be of no avail.

In general, the positive benefits desired from the *mizain-hpazain* nat and, for that matter, from any other nat, are financial. The Taungbyon Brothers are believed to be especially helpful in achieving financial goals, and, as we have seen, it is not uncommon for those who invest in the state lottery to ask for the assistance of these nats, on the condition that should they win they would offer part of their winnings to the Brothers. Gamblers, in general, are devotees of the Taungbyon Brothers. Many wealthy Rangoon and Mandalay businessmen, devoted to horse racing, propitiate these nats before betting on the races. Should their horses win, they offer a substantial share of their winnings to the Brothers at the annual Taungbyon Festival.

PUBLIC WORKS NATS

Every villager recognizes, even when he does not propitiate, the three subtypes of Thirty-Seven nats discussed above—house, village, and "mother's side-father's side." In addition to these, the Burmese propitiate other nats which, although designated as Thirty-Seven nats, cannot be classified in accordance with any of these three types. The propitiation of these nats—in at least the region of Upper Burma in which Yeigyi is found —is contingent upon geographic location and occupation: does one live within the domain of the nat and/or does one work at an occupation associated with the nat? These nats may be viewed as comprising a fourth subtype of Thirty-Seven nats—a type constructed by the anthropologist, not by the Burmese—which, for lack of a better term, can be designated as "public works" nats.

The Burmese, like many other peoples, formerly believed that human beings, if buried alive under the foundations of any construction, would become its guardian spirits. Thus it is well known (Harvey 1925:320–21; Scott and Hardiman 1900:35–36) that when the construction of a Burmese city was completed, human victims were buried alive at the four corners of the city, so that their spirits, known as *myousade*, might protect the city from other evil spirits, as well as human enemies. This custom was practiced as late as the nineteenth century, when, in connection with the construction of Mandalay, fifty-two persons were buried alive beneath its walls and within the palace grounds (Shway Yoe 1896:477).[12] A similar practice was associated with public works, and especially with irrigation works. When the complex and impressive irrigation system of the Kyaukse District of Upper Burma was constructed by the Burmese kings, it was deemed necessary, when any of its constituent wiers was completed, to sacrifice a human victim to serve as its guardian. Associated with many of these wiers is a story of a royal queen who, by throwing herself into the waters, precluded the necessity for any further sacrificial victims. After her death she became the guardian spirit, or Lady (*Thakinma*) of the Wier, for whom an annual festival is held (Brown 1916; Harvey 1925:25).

The wier from which the Yeigyi irrigation canals receive their waters is located at Sedaw village about nineteen miles from Yeigyi. The guardian spirit of the wier at Sedaw is an Outside Thirty-Seven nat, Sedaw Thakinma, The Lady of Sedaw (wier). Her myth (recounted in Chapter 7, pp. 110–11), is almost identical with that recounted by Brown (1916) and by Harvey (1925) for other wiers in the Kyaukse district, whose Lady was the queen of the great Anawrahta himself. As the nat of the Sedaw wier, her domain includes the entire area which is irrigated by its waters. From time to time, various of the inhabitants of these villages, including those of Yeigyi, attend her annual festival (see Chapter 7, pp. 110–12), where they make offerings to her. She has been known to send tigers into those villages which neglect their offerings.

Although she is the nat of the Sedaw wier, the physical jurisdiction of Sedaw Thakinma is not confined to its waters, but extends over a wide tract of land bordering on them. Anyone who enters her jurisdiction without requesting permission is guilty of trespass. Since some of the inhabitants of Yeigyi have occasion to work within this tract—some have fruit orchards within it, others cut bamboo poles in its forests—they are careful always to announce their arrival to the nat and to propitiate her with tea leaves. Since some bring their children with them, the work leader also asks the nat to forgive the children should they offend her by defecating or urinating in the wrong place or by using vulgar language. Should these precautions not be taken, their oxen might lose their way or the workers might suffer injury or accident. One of the work leaders explained the rationale for these precautions in the following way. "It's like a village

---

[12]Stern informs me that as late as 1954 the practice of *myousade* was reported from the countryside in the Burmese press. He also reminds me that the identical custom was practiced in Thailand to produce the Lord Father of the City Post. In Bangkok the shrine for this spirit stands near the royal palace, and in Chiengmai it is adjacent to an old pagoda at the corner of the compound of the American consulate.

headman. It is not very risky to abuse your own headman, but if you abuse the headman of another village, he'll take offense and will punish." Sedaw Thakinma, like the other Thirty-Seven nats, is not only quick to take offense, but she can also be protective. Hence, after making their offering, the people request her to "look upon us as your children; look after us and our oxen." (The latter are used to draw the carts which bring them there.)

The Sedaw wier is not the only public work from which Yeigyi benefits. Part of the Yeigyi paddy fields are included within the former royal fields of Aungpinle, which at one time was converted into a reservoir but which, in more recent times, has been returned to cultivation. The story concerning its nat, Aungpinle Boubougyi, makes no reference to his having been executed in order to serve as the guardian spirit of the reservoir, but this must certainly have been his function—even today he continues to be known as the Yedawshin nat, the "Lord of the water (ruling by royal authority)."[13] Formerly Thihathu, king of Ava, he was killed at Aungpinle while riding on his elephant during the construction of a canal, by a Shan Sabwa, the ruling prince of a Shan state.

Although the reservoir has long been drained, Aungpinle Boubougyi continues to be propitiated as the "Lord of the water" during the same season (the agricultural season) and in the same fields (the Aungpinle tract) in which a female nature nat of these fields, Aungpinle Thakinma, is propitiated (see pg. 49).

Since all the other field nats are female, it is reasonable to assume that this female nat was associated with these fields before the reservoir was constructed, and that she continues, now that the fields are under cultivation, to be associated with them. Although a distinction is made between these two nats—propitiation is performed at different times and consists of different offerings—they are, with the exception of their sex, conceptually indistinguishable.

Aungpinle Boubougyi is propitiated daily during the transplanting and the harvesting seasons, when work is performed within his domain. Before beginning their labor, each work group makes an offering to him of pickled tea and, sometimes, of rice, a coconut, and some jaggery. The offering is made by a female, and, while the other laborers sit behind her, she recites the following prayer (*hsutaung*):

> I respectfully make this offering in this paddy field. If there are insects, snakes or [wild] animals here, please drive them away and divert them.[14]

[13]His myth, recounted to me in Yeigyi, is identical with that of nat number 12 in Temple's list, more formally called Aungpinle Sinbyushin, the "Lord of Aungpinle, Master of the White Elephant."

[14]As far as I know, Aungpinle Boubougyi and Sedaw Thakinma are the only Thirty-Seven nats who are propitiated as part of agricultural cultivation. In addition to propitiating these two nats, it is customary to feed the animals which the other nats ride. The field workers scatter bits of their meals known as *hsinza myinza*, on the ground as food (*sa* = food) for these animals (*hsin* = elephant, *myin* = horse).

In addition to the types delineated in this chapter, E. M. Mendelson (personal communication) suggests that there may be still another type of Thirty-Seven nat, which he terms "occupation" nats. These are (or were) propitiated by all the members of a "guild." According to this hypothesis, Myinbyushin, the village nat represented by a white horse, would have been the nat of those persons (or villagers) who provided the royal cavalry. This very interesting hypothesis requires confirmation by additional research before this type can be added to the present typology.

CHAPTER SEVEN

Thirty-Seven Nats: The Public Cultus

TYPES OF FESTIVALS

The cultus of the Thirty-Seven nats enters into almost all facets of private and public life. Nats are propitiated at various stages of the life cycle as part of *rite-de-passage* ceremonies—notably, at birth, at the boy's Buddhist initiation (*shimbyu*), at marriage, and at death. They are propitiated both to prevent and to cure illness. They are propitiated at various stages in the agricultural cycle, especially during the planting and harvesting seasons. These are all simple ceremonies, privately performed by a family or a small work group, in order to evoke the assistance of some nat or, more typically, to avoid his anger. In general they last but a few moments; their occurrence, even when seasonal, is contingent upon the needs or activities of the participants, and the nat's presence is not required.

In contrast to these simple and essentially private rituals, there are public nat ceremonies, elaborate in form, in which the nat is not only propitiated, but in which his presence is evoked. This type of ceremony is known as a *nat pwe*.[1] In addition to the ordinary participants, a *nat*

---

[1]The Burmese word *pwe* designates a variety of public performances whose object typically is entertainment. Thus, in addition to *nat pwe*, there is *zat pwe*, or the classical drama, *anyein pwe*, or a vaudeville show, and so on. Although the *nat pwe* is entertaining, its avowed purpose is propitiation, and I would assume, therefore, that it is the performance of a dramatic role, or the portrayal of a dramatic character, which is the generic designatum of *pwe*. In the classical drama, or *zat pwe*, characters from the Jātaka stories are the *dramatis personae*. In the *nat pwe*, they are nats.

pwe requires an orchestra, a singer, and a shaman (*nat kadaw*). The presence of the nat is invoked by the singer and orchestra rendering the music and song associated with the nat. The presence of the nat is signaled by the possession of the shaman, whose dancing symbolically portrays the salient features of the myth associated with the nat.

There are two types of *nat pwes*. First, there is the voluntary, non-calendrical, noncyclical ceremony which, though public, is sponsored by a private person or family. Its purpose is to invoke the aid of, or to render thanksgiving to, a particular nat for some specific boon. Very expensive—an orchestra must be hired, shamans paid, the nats provided with offerings, the assembly fed—this type is never seen in the villages, although it occurs regularly in cities. Secondly, there is the prescribed, calendrical, cyclical ceremony, which might properly be termed a "festival." It is the latter type with which we are concerned. Nat festivals can, in turn, be divided into three subtypes associated with three structural levels of public participation—local, regional, and national.

The local festival is performed in, by, and for a village. Lasting only a short time, seldom longer than an hour, its purpose is to propitiate the village and other local nats. Calendrically determined, local festivals are regularly, and at least annually, performed at certain seasons and within specified months. Although occurring at fixed intervals, it is the month, rather than a specific day within the month, which is prescribed.

Regional and national festivals, lasting from one to as many as eight days, are the *nat pwes par excellence*. Occurring on precisely prescribed dates, these are held not only to propitiate a nat whose dominion extends over a large domain—a region or the country—but also to celebrate and commemorate his life and deeds. The festival is *his* festival; its charter is generally embodied in his myth in which, typically, the festival is prescribed by royal command. As a nat enjoying wide dominion, his festival draws upon a large area for its attendance, some participants attending voluntarily, others attending from hereditary obligation. Every famous nat has his regional festival, and traditionally there was a national festival for Min Mahagiri on Mt. Popa. Each of these three types of nat festivals can now be described in detail.

SOME MINOR FESTIVALS

A Local Nat Pwe: Yeigyi

In every Burmese village there is a shrine (*nat sin*) for its village nat, and three times a year he is propitiated at this shrine.[2] Performed during

---

[2]Myinbyushin, as the village nat of Yeigyi, has a public shrine within the village. The flowers in the shrine are watered and changed, the grass about the shrine is cut, and so on, by a committee appointed by the village elders and consisting of three

the months of Wazou, Thadingyut, and Tagu—the same months (July, October, and April) in which the three important Buddhist festivals fall— the ceremony, held at sunset, consists essentially of a ritual offering of food to the nat. This offering, like all offerings of food to the nats, is later distributed among, and eaten by, the participants. The nats, it is believed, consume the spiritual essence of the food by smelling it. Thus the saying, *nathma angwei, luhma atwei,* "a smell (on the part) of a nat (is like) a touch (on the part) of humans."

In addition to the offering of food, candles are lit by the two women in charge of the ceremony before a row of flower pots planted with lilies. While the food and the candles are offered, a prayer is chanted by the local nat expert, accompanied by the village orchestra.[3] The participation of the orchestra, which continues to perform for a half-hour or so after the offerings are made, is explained by the belief that the nats, who died violently, are soothed by music. The lighted candles are explained less satisfactorily: "nats like light." Sometimes nat dancing, as well as cases of nat possession, occur during the playing of the orchestra. The prayer (*hsutaung*) which is chanted with the offering is short. "Please guard and protect from danger all people and cattle [of this village] born on Sunday, Monday, Tuesday, Wednesday, Thursday, Friday, and Saturday."

This, then, is a modest ceremony. The ritual is simple and undramatic. Occuring at the end of a normal workday, it is unaccompanied by the holiday mood that accompanies the nat festivals, a mood that is induced in part by all the conditions absent from this local ceremony—respite from labor, the donning of festive clothes, a plenitude of food and drink, and large crowds.

A Regional Nat Pwe: Sedaw

Sedaw, a village about eighteen miles southeast of Mandalay, is the scene of an annual festival honoring the regional nat of the Sedaw wier, Sedaw Thakinma. Because this wier feeds into the Mandalay canal, the festival attracts from the entire area cultivators whose fields are irrigated by the canal. Held at the end of July (the Burmese Wazou), it falls in the middle of the Buddhist Lent, between the end of the planting and the beginning of the harvesting seasons.

On a hill overlooking the wier, and across from Sedaw village, is a nat shrine, much more elaborate than the typical shrine for a village nat, containing three gilded images: a female in regal costume, flanked on either

---

women and one man who perform these duties. Known as caretakers of the shrine (*nandein*), the women are shamans (*nat kadaw*), while the status of the man, unfortunately, is unknown to me.

[3]The orchestra consists of a deep skin-drum, a xylophone, a clarinet, bamboo clappers, and cymbals.

side by two males in court dress and mounted on horses. The female is Sedaw Thakinma, the Lady of Sedaw Wier, and the two males are her brothers. Her myth, as told by the elders of Sedaw village, is an archetypic Lady of the Wier myth. (Compare Brown 1916 and 1921.) Sedaw Thakinma was formerly the wife of Prince (later King) Minshinzaw, the son of King Alaungsithu of Pagan. On bad terms with his father, Prince Minshinzaw, together with his wife, was sent to the present site of Sedaw to supervise the expansion of the irrigation works first developed by King Anawrahta. Part of his plan was to construct a wier which would feed into the vast royal fields of Aungpinle, bordering on the present Mandalay-Maymyo road. After repeated failures, he was told by his courtiers that to carry out his plan successfully it would be necessary for a member of the royal family to be sacrificed as the guardian of the wier. Undecided about his course, Minshinzaw, after informing his wife of this unhappy prophecy, went to worship at a local pagoda. When he returned, he discovered that his wife, wishing to spare him the distress of choosing a sacrificial victim, had drowned herself in the waters. Later, possessing a member of the royal party, she announced that she had become the nat of the new wier. Her two brothers, recently arrived from Pagan, died from sorrow when informed of her deed, and they too became nats. These are the nats who are propitiated at the Sedaw *nat pwe*.

Arriving in ox carts, on trucks, and by foot, the participants[4] assemble near the shrine while the orchestra plays a repertoire of nat music. Banana offerings to the nats continue to be placed inside the shrine, until there is not room for one more banana. Meanwhile, on a small dance ground before the shrine, a number of people dance before the nats. The dancers, who include female shamans, a few male shamans, and an assorted group, primarily of young men, are spirited, and some are possessed. Most of the new arrivals, however, sit or stand near the shrine, where, watching the dancing, sipping tea, and munching on sweets, they exhibit a festive mood.

Shortly before noon the images are removed from the shrine, raised onto a royal, gilded palanquin, and carried on the shoulders of a large group of men across the wier and down to the river bank. As the procession moves along, the bearers sing nat songs, while others, accompanying the images, dance in front of them. Arriving at the river bank where they are to be ritually bathed, the images are placed on a raft, which is then paddled by two men to the middle of the river. With the banks crowded with onlookers, there then ensues a tug-of-war between two teams, one of men and one of women, for the possession of the raft. Each team, standing chest-deep in water and pulling on long ropes attached to opposite ends of the raft, attempts to pull the raft to its "goal line." In this manner the images are ritually bathed, for while the two teams splash water on each

---

[4]Since Sedaw Thakinma was pregnant when she met her death, pregnant women are not permitted to participate in her festival.

other, the images are thoroughly washed down. The competition is accompanied by much banter and great fun, and the participants become thoroughly soaked.

In the struggle for the raft first one side and then the other seems to grasp victory. When it appears as if the men's team might win, some of its members, ostensibly to prevent the fun from terminating too soon, join the women's team, thus prolonging the struggle. Suddenly, however, the men's team pulls the raft, rope and all, away from the women, and just as suddenly, the latter, having lost the prize, make for the shore. As the women wade from the water, the men, still in high spirits, continue to splash them with water. (Some of the women, now that the competition has ended, evince more than a little annoyance at the men's behavior.)

No satisfactory explanations have been offered for this curious ceremonial struggle. Some informants claim that the tug-of-war is performed "just for fun." Others explain that it is a means for inducing rain. The latter explanation is hardly more satisfying than the former. It is true that a tug-of-war is believed to be an effective means in many parts of Burma for causing rain (cf. Brown 1908:145, 1921:97; Buchanan 1779:193ff.; Htin Aung 1933; Sangermano 1893:18), but it is not at all clear why, in this case, it should be held in the water, and with the nat images, precariously balanced on a raft, as the prize.[5]

Following the tug-of-war the images are brought back to the shore, from where, returned to the palanquin and accompanied by singing and dancing, they are carried back to their shrine. Reaching the far side of the river, and not far from the shrine, the bearers lower the palanquin from their shoulders and proceed to rock it back and forth, very much as one would rock an infant's cradle. After the images are finally returned to their places in the nat shrine, some of the men, accompanied by singing and orchestral music, continue to dance before the nats. A few of them become possessed.

[5]Differing interpretations have been offered for the efficacy of tugs-of-war in inducing rain. Sawyer (Frazer 1913:175) has suggested an interpretation based on imitative magic. "A rain party and a drought party tug against each other, the rain party being allowed the victory, which in popular notion is generally followed by rain." According to informants from Yeigyi, this technique of obtaining rain originated in the Pagan period when a weikza, executed by royal decree, became a nat and, in anger, prevented rain from falling. This nat (Mou-Kyaun-Kyawzaw) was eventually pacified, and it was he who taught the people that rain could be induced by a tug-of-war. Hall, in a gloss on Symes (Hall 1955:253), says the tug-of-war invokes the Pyitsun nat, a special nat "who presides over rain."

Whatever the interpretation of this practice may be, it should be noted that an almost identical practice is part of the ceremonies comprising the funeral of a Buddhist monk. Ropes are attached to his catafalque, "and forthwith all the able-bodied men present commence a frantically contested and uproarious tug-of-war." (Shway Yoe 1896:581). The contest usually lasts for two or three hours, but may continue for as long as three days. In this case the practice is interpreted in Buddhist terms. The winning side has the privilege of carrying the body to the funeral pyre, thereby acquiring "the greatest possible merit." (Ibid.: 582).

A NATIONAL FESTIVAL: TAUNGBYON

The Taungbyon Festival, the most famous nat festival in Burma,[6] is held at the end of August in Taungbyon village, about twenty miles north of Mandalay. Lasting a full week—from the eighth waxing to the full moon of the Burmese month of Wagaung (August)—and occurring in the middle of the Buddhist Lent, this festival is celebrated in honor of the two brother nats, Shwepyingyi and Shwepyinnge, known popularly as the Taungbyon Brothers. Before describing their festival as I observed it in 1961, it is necessary to recount the myth of these nats. Although this myth has frequently been published elsewhere,[7] the present version is worth recounting because, as the variant which some Upper Burmans—those at least who are knowledgeable about nats—know and recount today, it shows the persistence of the myth as well as its variability. On both accounts, it is of special interest to students of Burmese culture.

During the reign of King Manuha, in the year 400 B.E. (A.D. 1038), in the city now called Thaton, a rich merchant, a Muslim from the Malibar coast, arrived with his two sons, Abraham and Ibrahim. The name of the elder brother was Abraham, known as Byatwi, and that of the younger brother was Ibrahim, known as Byatta. They came as traders. During their voyage their ship was wrecked, but the two brothers survived and drifted ashore near Thaton. Near the shore was a monastery, whose monk rescued them and raised them.

Some time before the arrival of the brothers, the monk had acquired the corpse of a hermit magician (*Zawgyi*), which he had preserved for medicinal purposes. One day, during the absence of the monk, the brothers ate the corpse and thereby acquired supernatural powers. They were so powerful that they turned the monastery upside down. When the monk returned he realized, from the condition of the monastery, that the body of the magician had been eaten by the brothers. When King Manuha was informed of their superhuman powers, he instructed that they be seized, and offered a reward for their capture.

The elder was captured by the following ruse. The mother of his sweetheart placed a woman's skirt, worn in childbirth, at the entrance to her daughter's room. When Byatwi walked underneath this skirt he lost his powers (a traditional belief, still found in Burma). He was seized and killed, and his body was dismembered and buried under the palace. His intestines were buried under the four walls of the city, so that he might

---

[6]Descriptions of the festival may also be found in Brown 1915; Enriquez 1921; Ridgeway 1915, section VI and Addenda A.

[7]The *locus classicus*, of course, is Tin and Luce 1960:75–84.

serve as its guardian spirit. The younger brother, however, escaped into the forest.

Meanwhile, in Pagan, King Anawrahta wished to obtain copies of the Tripitaka (Buddhist scriptures) from King Manuha. He sent four soldiers to obtain the Scriptures. On their way they met the younger brother, Byatta. They recognized him, and he agreed to join them. They attempted to invade Thaton but failed because Byatwi, now the guardian spirit of the city, did not let them through the walls. That night, however, Byatwi revealed to his younger brother in a dream that there was a small aperture in one wall, wide enough for a hen to enter. Through this aperture Byatta entered the city, seized the Scriptures, and passed them through to the soldiers. He was taken to Pagan, together with the Scriptures.

For his services the King of Pagan appointed Byatta his flower officer. It was his duty to gather flowers from Mount Popa daily and to take them to Pagan. While performing his duties, he fell in love with an ogress—a flower-eating, not a flesh-eating, ogress—known as Mekuwun.[8] They had two sons, known as Shwepyingyi and Shwepyinnge. Byatta was very fond of his wife and children, and delayed his return to Pagan on several occasions in order to spend more time with them. This annoyed the king, who, in anger, put him to death. After his death, his two sons were raised by their mother, the ogress.

Later, King Anawrahta desired to obtain the Buddha's eyetooth, which was kept in China. Unsuccessful in obtaining the tooth, he attempted to enlist the aid of the two brothers, Shwepyingyi and Shwepyinnge. Their mother, the ogress, refused to part with her sons, and they, in turn, refused to leave their mother. They seized the officer who had been commissioned to bring them to the king and hung him from a cliff by his legs. The officer entreated them to treat him well and they allowed him to return to Pagan. When the king heard this story, he gave his officer a magic rod with which the officer beat the ground at the foot of Mt. Popa, and by this act compelled the ogress and her two sons to roll down the hill. The brothers were seized and taken to Pagan. The mother died of sorrow and became a nat, now known as Popa Medaw, the Mother of Popa.

The brothers then proceeded to China with Anawrahta's army to help seize the Buddha's eyetooth. The tooth was guarded by a Chinese nat (i.e., an image or idol), but the brothers placed a (magical?) mark on the throat of the nat, who, frightened lest he die, passed the tooth over to them. King Anawrahta placed the tooth in a case to be carried by a white elephant. The Chinese authorities persuaded him, however, to leave the tooth in China and, instead, they offered him the case in which the tooth had been enshrined, as well as an emerald Buddha. These were placed on the white elephant to be taken to Pagan. On the return journey, the ele-

---

[8]My wife informs me that in the Burmese movie version of the Taungbyon myth, Mekuwun is played by a beautiful, curvaceous, and gentle actress, "not at all," as a European friend remarked, "what I expected an ogress to look like."

phant stopped and knelt at the present site of Taungbyon village. Taking this as a sign, the king built a pagoda at this site. (It is still standing today.)

At the time of the construction of this pagoda all the soldiers were ordered to share in its construction by contributing one brick each. The Taungbyon Brothers were interested, instead, in playing marbles and did not participate in this task. (To this day two bricks, carefully pointed out to all visitors, are missing from this pagoda.) Kyanzittha, who long bore a resentment against the brothers—for he was the officer whom they had hung by his heels—reported their dereliction to the king. The king ordered that they be punished by being beaten with a small cane. The brothers escaped, but they were later captured in a place not far from Taungbyon. There the villagers helped Kyanzittha to beat the brothers with bamboo poles, but because of their superhuman strength, the beatings had no effect on them. Ultimately, however, they were killed by having their testicles crushed. Thus, they died and became nats, known as *Taungbyon-min-nyi-naung* (the Taungbyon Brother Lords).

Soon thereafter, as the king was returning to Pagan by river, the movement of his barge was suddenly impeded. He beat the waters with a stick, and the two nat brothers appeared. They said they would not let him continue unless he offered them a site in which they could live. The king ordered that a shrine be built for them in Taungbyon, that the Medeia tract be given to them as their fief, and that an annual ceremony be performed there in their honor. These, then, are the nats that are honored at the Taungbyon Festival.

Traveling to the site of the Festival one encounters, both in and near Taungbyon, many evidences of their former lives. On the main road, proceeding from Mandalay, there is a shrine for the female nat Ma U on the northern side of Mandalay Hill. Her image faces in the direction of Taundaw hill, an even larger hill on the road to Taungbyon where, again, she has a shrine. Ma U, an Outside Thirty-Seven nat, is associated mythologically with the elder Taungbyon nat. Sometime after his execution, this nat, Shwepyingyi, was greatly attracted by Ma U, a young woman from Ingyin, a village bordering the hill. Ma U was married and, being virtuous, she repeatedly rebuffed the attempts of the nat to seduce her. In exasperation the nat ordered a tiger[9] to attack her. Seizing Ma U, the tiger dragged her to a cave at the foot of Taundaw hill, near the present site of the images of the Brothers, and devoured her. This cave can still be seen. Proceeding to Ingyin, one can still see, moreover, the site of the house where she was born and in which she lived.

But this is not all. Approaching Taungbyon, one passes through the village in which the Brothers ate their first rabbits, an event which is represented, as we shall see, in an important ritual of the Festival. In Taungbyon itself the pagoda erected by Anawrahta is still standing, with a space

---

[9]Almost all the nats are associated with some animal. The Taungbyon Brothers are associated with tigers, and are usually depicted riding on them.

remaining for two missing bricks. Near the pagoda is the site where the Brothers played marbles, and during the Festival vendors still sell facsimiles of these marbles. At the same site is a "cave" (actually a building) in which the Brothers (although Muslims) had observed the Buddhist Sabbath (*Ubonei*) and practiced Buddhist meditation! This "cave," which is open only during the festival, contains two couches used by the Brothers, and (for reasons I could not discover) a small couch used by the baby-girl nat, Ma Ne.

It must be emphasized, then, that these nats, far from being encapsulated in a dead myth, are constantly animated, as it were, by the power of a living myth. The entire landscape calls one's attention to the important scenes in their drama, scenes which are described in their myth and reenacted in their ritual. This importance of "mythological space," as one might term it—and mythological space pertains not only to the Taungbyon nats, but to many other of the Thirty-Seven nats—for giving life to a myth and its *dramatis personae* cannot be overestimated.

The Taungbyon Festival draws visitors by the tens of thousands each year. Many come because of hereditary obligations to propitiate these nats; and since the original fief of these nats was very large, this motive accounts for a large percentage of the participants. Others, although the Brothers are not their *mizain-hpazain* nats, attend voluntarily. Among the latter group, some attend in order to propitiate the nats. Most of them, however, attend, in the words of a friend in Mandalay, "for jolly sake." Indeed, once they have made their offerings, the others, too, clearly participate "for jolly sake." For this festival is surely one of the most exciting and entertaining events of the Burmese year. With its enormous bazaar, hundreds of shamans available for consultation, exciting sideshows and plays—not to mention the dramatic nat dancing—it is, in some respects, a combination, Burmese-style, of an American state fair and a medieval miracle play. Perhaps a more apt analogy is the Catholic Fiesta in Latin culture.

The organization of a festival of this magnitude requires joint effort by the government, the army and police, and the bus and railroad lines. The complex internal organization of the festival, however, is the responsibility of a hereditary "palace custodian" (*nandein*). U Pou Zoun, the present incumbent, claims that the custodian is merely the administrator for the "keeper of the images" (*nat tein*), the former being a brother (uterine or classificatory) of the latter. These offices, he claims, have been hereditary in his matrilineal line from the very inception of the Festival, the line being descended from two Chinese "queens" that Anawrahta brought back from his Chinese expedition.[10] These two officials receive all the nat offer-

[10]Although U Pou Zoun lives in Mandalay, his sisters continue to live in Taungbyon. In 1931 a dispute between him and his classificatory brother (matrilineal cousin) for the administrative office—of which the emoluments are very considerable —was settled in his favor in the courts.

ings—money, fruit, clothing—which are made during the Festival, as well as the rent which the shamans pay for their stalls in the temporary bazaar, and the fees which they pay for dancing on the main platform. Their expenses, of course, are heavy, but most of these are probably defrayed by the sale of paddy from the ten acres bestowed on this family for this purpose by King Thibaw. In short, the income derived from the Festival by this family is probably, in Burmese terms, enormous.

Although minimizing his financial gains, U Pou Zoun makes no attempt to conceal his financial motives. Observing my tape recorder, he asked if I intended to record the ceremony. When I said that I had hoped to do so, he insisted that I would have to offer five *kadaw pwes* (costing approximately K100) and K300 in cash "to the Nats." (Altogether more than $80.) When I demurred, saying that I was always permitted to record Buddhist ceremonies without payment, he replied acidly, "That's religion; this is business."

Immediately under the custodian in the official hierarchy, and appointed by him, is the "chief shaman" (*nat-ouk*), who, in principle at least, is the head of all the shamans in Burma. Under him, and also appointed by the custodian, are four principle female shamans, known as "Queens" (*mibaya*). They are the principle performers of the dances which, during the ceremony, reenact the main events in the lives of the Brothers. The custodian also appoints four male shamans, known as "royal ministers" (*wungyi*), who serve as the principal male officiants in the ceremonies. All these officials are appointed for life. During the formal ceremonies held in the nat's "palace," they sit on a raised platform with the custodian. It is here that they perform their dances. In addition, they lead all the processions (which will be described subsequently), both on land and on water. At the bottom of the hierarchy are the ordinary shamans who, within the context of the Festival, are known as nat "slaves" (*nat kyun* or *nat kyai*) because it is mandatory for them to attend and to serve the nats by their dancing.

The shrine (*nat sin*) holding the images of the Taungbyon Brothers is probably the most impressive nat shrine in all of Burma. Instead of the usual shrine—a miniature houselike structure attached to a tree or resting on a pole, dirty and unkempt, and more often than not falling apart— this one is an ornate ark, built into one end of a very large open-walled assembly hall called the "nat palace" (*nat nun*), very much like the Ark of the Law in a synagogue. The nat images—again, like the Hebrew Scrolls—are kept inside the ark, which is opened at special occasions only, but which remains open for the duration of the Festival. During the Festival, offerings are placed on an "altar" in front of the ark, and the nat dancing takes place on a raised platform, as well as in the wide hall below it.

Surrounding the palace on all four sides are the stalls of the shamans—

certainly no fewer than one hundred at the Festival I attended—each stall containing, at the least, the image of the nat to whom the shaman is "married," while some contain the images of many, if not all, the classical Thirty-Seven nats. These shamans dance in the "palace," and they are available, for a fee of course, as mediums for any problem believed to be within the competence of the nats—business, illness, marriage, divorce, and so on.

Extending out from the palace, and beyond the shamans' stalls, is a massive temporary bazaar, containing stalls of every kind—food, fruit, clothing, toys, flowers, tools, craft, trinkets—as well as restaurants, snack bars, sideshows, and theaters (for the performance of Burmese drama).[11] Since nat propitiation, like Buddhist worship, is essentially a private matter, taking no more than a few minutes—the core of the propitiation consists of individual offerings accompanied by a short prayer—the average participant, when not watching the nat dancing, spends most of his time in the bazaar, buying or looking, eating and drinking, and carousing. Carousing at Taungbyon is proverbial—the numerous police and army uniforms indicate the authorities' concern that it not get out of hand—something which apparently has happened from time to time in the past[12]—and its leaders are understandably sensitive on this point. U Pou Zoun, in a handbill defending the Festival, notes that "some people" allege that participation in the Festival adversely affects "character and behavior," causing a "loss of the finer feelings." This allegation, he is at pains to argue, is without foundation.

Carousing, despite U Pou Zoun's protestations, is all but inevitable, given the bacchanalian character of the Festival. In the first place, the Festival grounds are filled with (mostly) female shamans, many of whom the Burmese believe to be sexually promiscuous and/or prostitutes, and all of whom are married to, because sexually loved by, the nats. More importantly, their nat-husbands, especially those who play the most prominent roles in the Taungbyon cultus, are believed in their former lives to have been carousers, seducers, gamblers, drunkards. The Taungbyon

[11]Many of the stalls are rented by merchants from the important bazaars in Mandalay (*Zeigyou*) and Rangoon (*Bougyouk*). Others are rented by itinerant peddlers who travel, in an annual cycle, to the many nat and pagoda festivals held in different parts of Burma. Prior to Independence, the stalls were auctioned by the government to the highest bidders; after Independence the entire concession was acquired by an organization, centered in Mandalay, of politically motivated and politically powerful monks, the Young Monks Association (*Yahan-Pyou Apwe*), which, in turn, rents out the stalls. According to U Pou Zoun, the receipts from this venture are approximately K20,000, or almost $5,000. It is this Association which, according to my information, is responsible for many of the attempts in newspapers and magazines to interpret the Taungbyon and other nat festivals as pagoda festivals.

[12]In a decree of King Thibaw, shown to me by U Pou Zoun, the various government officials in the Taungbyon area are ordered "to maintain law and order" at the Festival, and "to prevent the crimes [of the kind] that occurred during the reign of His Majesty, King Mindon." (The nature of these "crimes" is not specified.)

Brothers themselves are known as drunkards, rowdies, and chasers of pretty girls. U Min Kyaw (Min Kyawwzwa in Temple's list), probably the most frequently impersonated nat in the ritual dancing, is notorious for his interest in gambling and cockfighting, and especially for his drunkenness. These qualities are not only known to the participants, but they are the qualities which are emphasized in the dances and stressed by the songs which accompany the dancing. Thus, for example, the song of the elder Taungbyon Brother, Shwepyingyi, ends with ". . . and the pretty maidens have missed us from that day." That of the younger Brother, Shwepyinnge, concludes: "Now all ye maidens love ye us as ye were wont to do while we were alive." Again, U Min Kyaw sings: ". . . many a time did I reel along the streets, drunk . . . and many is the time the pretty little maids picked me up out of the gutter." The sexual proclivities of these nats are believed still to be as strong as ever, and it is not uncommon for women to stay away from the Festival, lest, succumbing to their blandishments to "love ye us as ye were wont to do . . .," they become the nats' "wives."[13]

Taking their cue from the nats, many who attend the Festival view it as an opportunity for eating, gambling, and sex. The incidence of drunkenness, especially among young men, is high. Their (consequent) sexual banter and teasing (involving fairly raw obscenity) as well as sexual fondling (especially of the female buttock) are a traditional feature of the festivities. Since the Festival attracts thousands, and since it is with the greatest difficulty, therefore, that one pushes one's way through the milling crowds, the opportunities, not to mention temptations, for buttock-pinching are omnipresent.

But shopping and carousing in the bazaar are not the exclusive activities of the Festival, whose official purpose, after all, is the propitiation of the nats. Propitiation takes two forms: dancing and other ritual activities performed by shamans, and offerings made by laymen. The latter activity can be simply described. On any day of the Festival, the nat votaries bring their offerings, traditionally prescribed within their family lines, to the shrine. Typically, the offerings consist of coconuts, bananas, cloth, money, liquor, and bouquets of flowers and ferns. While the flowers are placed on the "altar," the ferns are handed to an attendant who, after pressing them against the images of the Brother, returns them—or others which had similarly touched the images—to the offerer. It is believed that power (*mana*) from the image, now transferred to the ferns, will confer good luck (and especially financial benefits) on the possessor. (Some cultivators

[13]Indeed, if my Burmese informants are to be believed, it is not only Burmese women who are susceptible to their powers of seduction. The Burmese tell the "well-known" story of an English woman, the wife of a doctor, who, attending the Festival in 1924, was sought out by the younger Brother, and fell in love with him. Although sent back to England, she could not forget her nat lover and, returning to Burma, she "married" the nat and became a shaman.

believe that these ferns, if placed in the paddy field where the irrigation canal enters the field, can prevent the plants from suffering from blight.)

Tradition not only prescribes for different families the kind and amount of their offerings, but it also prescribes the nature of the nat-human transaction. For some families the offering is merely shown, rather than presented to the nats, the family retaining possession of it. For others the offering is given outright to the nats (which means that it is kept and, in the case of food and other perishables, eventually sold by the custodian). Finally, there are families who, after making their offering to the nats, receive an exchange offering from them. The exchange is determined by tradition: some families receive a gift smaller in value than the value of their offering, others receive its equivalent value, and still others receive more than the value of their offering.

After placing their flowers on the altar, many people join the large groups of people who are already dancing before the nats. This dancing, to be distinguished from the stylized dancing of the shamans, is frequently wild and abandoned, each dancer improvising his own choreography. The dancing, which in some cases leads to possession, is accompanied by shouting and singing. At times these tightly packed dancers attain such a pitch of frenzy that it is a wonder no one is crushed in what seems to be an uncontrollable mob.

Every evening the shamans propitiate the nats. Theatrical in quality, propitiation takes the form of dancing by the "queens," "ministers," and other famous mediums. Dancing in the presence of a huge audience seated in the palace, the shamans, each dancing in turn, perform their dances to the accompaniment of an orchestra. The dances, except for the Taungbyon dancing which requires two shamans, are solo, and they are performed before the nat shrine. Sitting on a platform in front of the shrine are the custodian, members of his family, various members of the official hierarchy, other famous shamans, and important guests (usually heavy donors). The dancing of the shamans is highly stylized, the dancers following the distinctive choreography prescribed for the propitiation of each nat.

These dances have multiple meanings. First of all, the dance is a "command performance," performed at the bidding and for the entertainment of a nat who, in this sense, is its spectator. Since the nats suffered violent deaths, it is believed that the dancing soothes and calms their minds, although the frenetic nature of most of the dances makes it somewhat difficult to understand how this end is achieved. Wearing the nat's costume and reenacting parts of his myth, however, the dancer is not only propitiating the nat, she is personifying him. The dance, then, is not only a performance *for* the nat, but—and this is its second meaning—it is also a symbolic representation *of* the nat. Given the belief, however, that the shaman, while dancing, is possessed by the nat, the dance has yet a third meaning, according to which the nat is not only a spectator of and symbolically represented in the dance, but is also the dancer. Although it is the shaman's body that is dancing, it is the nat who is in fact performing the dance. Like the Catholic priest who, in celebrating the Mass, is both the sacrificer and the sacrificed (Christ), so the dancing shaman is both the propitiator and the propitiated (the nat).

On the palace floor, standing with the orchestra, is a shaman who serves as an "announcer." Preceding each dance, the announcer sings the ode (*nat than*) which, in the first person, recounts the life of the nat about to be impersonated, and which ends with an invocation to the nat to possess the dancer. Following this invocation (*kadaw gan*), the orchestra plays the music of the nat, and the shaman, now possessed, commences her dance. I do not know to what extent the cultural idiom of possession is accompanied by, or is believed to be accompanied by, such psychological states as "trance," "dissociation," "unconsciousness," and so forth. As far as I could observe, only a small minority of the dancers were in trances or trancelike states. Nevertheless, all of them, when queried, insisted that it was not they, but their nats, who were dancing. Some said they were not aware either of going into the dance or of dancing, and it was only when the music stopped, and they in turn stopped dancing, that they again became aware of their surroundings. Although their reports certainly sound like "trance," their behavior, with very few exceptions, did not look like it.

But these exceptions cannot be ignored. I observed cases of nat dancing in which the shamans unquestionably appeared to be in a trance, cases in which the dancers seemed not only to be unaware of their external environment, but in which it seemed as if someone not themselves was in control of their movements. This impression was strengthened by the observation that when the end of the dance was signaled by the final crescendo of the orchestral music, the dancers, obviously incapable of stopping, continued to shake uncontrollably, eyes glassy and unfocused.[14] When this happens another shaman sprinkles water on the dancer, rub-

[14]Despite the many references to shamans in the older literature, there is almost no description of nat dancing, except for such one-word characterizations as "vigorous" or "frenzied" (Scott and Hardiman 1900:18 and 22). Only in one brief description, recorded in the early eighteenth century, does the word "trance" occur. Writing *circa* 1710, the sea-captain Alexander Hamilton (1930:31) writes of a Feast, "called the Collock, [at which] some Women are chosen out of the People assembled, to Dance a Dance to the Gods of the Earth. Hermophradites [*sic*], who are numerous in this Country, are generally chosen, if there are enow present to make a Set for the Dance. I saw nine dance like mad Folks, for above half an Hour, and then some of them fell in Fits, foming at the Mouth for the Space of half an Hour; and, when their Senses are restored, they pretend to foretel Plenty or Scarcity of Corn for that Year, if the year will prove sickly or salutary to the People, and several other Things of Moment, and all by that half hour's Conversation that the furious Dancer had with the Gods while she was in a Trance."

bing her head and back, and sometimes fanning her, until she comes out of trance.[15] It should be observed that all dancers, whether in trance or not, shake at the end of their dancing and are fanned by another shaman. When interviewed, these shamans describe the onset of possession as a highly pleasurable physical act, accompanied by deep and accelerated breathing, palpitations, and tingling of the flesh. The descriptions sounded very much like the description of sexual orgasm, but I could not pursue this line of inquiry because of the near impossibility in Burma of discussing sexual matters with females.

We might conclude this discussion with a description of one dance, that of a Mon buffalo nat, in which the dancer gave every indication of trance. At the completion of the invocation the shaman pounced on the floor and, simulating the movements of the buffalo, groveled before the custodian of the shrine, jumping about madly. Suddenly and unexpectedly, she leaped upon a bowl containing bananas and filled to the top with water. With a jerk of her head, she dipped her face into the water, coming up with a banana between her teeth. After the banana was taken from her by one of the persons on the platform, she repeated this performance until no bananas remained in the bowl.

Although different shamans personify different nats, and some personify more than one, the great majority impersonate the Taungbyon Brothers and U Min Kyaw. That the former are so frequently represented is understandable; after all, this is *their* Festival. I do not know, however, why the latter, among all the other nats, plays such a prominent role.

The dances, as I have already indicated, are a symbolic reenactment of or reference to important incidents in the lives of the nats, or a symbolic portrayal of their salient character traits. Thus, in impersonating U Min Kyaw (he of drinking and gambling fame), the dancer holds a golden cock (U Min Kyaw bet on cockfights) in one hand and a gilded bowl in the other. As the music rises to ever increasing crescendo, the dancer becomes increasingly frenetic in her movements, waving the cock at the Brother images in wide sweeping gestures while the bowl, filled with money contributions, is swung upside down. ("Miraculously" the money does not fall out.) The same dance, incidentally, may be repeated several times. Between each dance, money is put in the bowl by members of the audience; after the dance, the shaman distributes these contributions among the members of the orchestra and among the shamans sitting on the platform.

The dance of the Taungbyon Brothers is performed by two shamans dancing with swords in their hands (the Brothers, it will be recalled, were

[15]The depth of the trance, even in these few cases, does not appear to be as pronounced as in the cases reported from Bali (cf. Belo 1960), or in those which I have observed in Ceylon. I have seen "devil-dancing" in Ceylon which required as long as fifteen minutes of treatment, including the puncturing of the skin, for the dancer to come out of trance.

soldiers). Using the swords as oars, they simulate the paddling of the royal barge whose forward movement, according to the myth, was stopped by the Brothers. Later, walking slowly around two bunches of bananas placed on the floor, the dancers gently poke them with the swords to symbolize the hunting of the hares, which were cooked as a meal for the Brothers. Still later, each dancer pierces one bunch of bananas with her sword and, lifting it in the air, waves it back and forth before the Brother images, thus symbolizing the actual offering of the hares which takes place at the end of the week-long ceremony.

While the shamans are dancing, the audience (in which the women outnumber the men by at least twenty to one) sits quietly on the floor of the palace, showing serious but passive interest in the proceedings and displaying little affect. Periodically, someone will walk up to a dancer to put some money in her bowl, only to return immediately to his seat. On the last night of the Festival which I attended, there occurred, however, an exception to this picture of a passive audience. A group of young men began to dance at the rear of the palace while the solo dancing was in progress. Their dancing soon became reckless, and when it threatened to get out of hand, they were publicly rebuked by the custodian. At one point they even began to move to the front of the palace, where they would surely have disrupted the scheduled dances, and only when forcibly restrained by the police, did they desist.

In addition to the ritual offerings and ceremonial dancing, which occur throughout the eight days of the Festival, there are three other ritual events which take place on the first, fifth, and last days of the Festival, respectively. The first of these rituals consists of the ceremonial bathing of the images of the Taungbyon nats. Carried on royal palanquins and accompanied by the entire official hierarchy dressed in court costume, the images are towed on a royal barge into the Irrawaddy, where they are bathed with water scooped from the river in bowls of silver and gold. Thousands watch the proceeding from the shore, while hundreds more, accompanying the barge in smaller boats, watch from their closer vantage points. There is great merriment in the boats, the riders singing, even dancing, and—in the case of the young men—engaging in sexual banter and shouting obscenities at the girls in other boats. Meanwhile, on the barge itself, the "ministers" and "queens," accompanied by the orchestra, dance before the images. Since the Festival occurs in August, when the plains are flooded by as much as a mile on either side of the river, the procession does not return to shore until mid-afternoon.

On the fifth day of the Festival occurs the second of these three ritual events, the hare-offering ceremony. Since the Taungbyon Brothers ate their first meal of wild rabbit meat in a village near Taungbyon, it is the duty of this village to provide them with wild rabbits at the annual Festival. Each year, on the fourth day of the Festival, the men of the village hunt and kill one male and one female rabbit. On the following day, they bring these sacrificial hares into Taungbyon to be offered to the nat brothers. Arriving in Taungbyon, they first march in procession around the village and then circumambulate the nat palace seven times. The procession is led by a young man specially chosen for this task, who carries the sacrificial hares, one in each hand. Wearing ceremonial costume, and with painted face, he looks as if he were either very frightened, in a state of shock, or in a trance. Following upon his heels is a crowd of rowdy young men, dancing, singing, and shouting obscenities the entire time.[16] Obscenity is explained by the fact that the village which supplies the hares knew the Brothers as drunkards and rowdies. Hence, on this occasion it is appropriate that the young men of the village behave as the Brothers had behaved when the latter were, as an English-speaking monk put it, "young rogues."

Completing their circumambulation of the palace, the procession comes to rest in a shed immediately facing but much below the palace, which is built on a high platform. Facing the palace, the young man who has been carrying the hares swings them back and forth in the direction of the Brother images, thereby indicating to the nats that the animals are being offered to them. In the meantime, the retinue of nat officials, all dressed as courtiers, march seven times down the steps of the palace and into the shed in which the dead rabbits are being swung to and fro; and seven times they march back again, up the steps, and into the palace. Moving in formal procession to the accompaniment of the orchestra, they kiss the dead animals as they enter the shed. For the duration of the procession the rowdy group, which had marched in procession with the hares, remains with them in the shed. Dancing, jumping, shouting, and pushing, they are prevented from breaking out of the shed only by the continuous vigilance of the police. When the nat officials have returned to the palace for the seventh time, the hares are carried into the palace by a surging, milling mob. They are later pickled and eaten by the shamans, who thereby acquire magical power.

On the morning of the last day of the Festival occurs the third of the special ceremonies, the tree-cutting ceremony. Although I did not witness the actual ceremony itself, I did see the dress rehearsal which, except for details[17] omitted at the end, is a faithful facsimile. In essence this ceremony consists of the ritual cutting of two branches, one for each Brother, of the *leinbin* tree, which is planted for this purpose on the very day of the ritual. Many historical and evolutionary speculations have been suggested as explanations for this practice (Brown 1915), but the only explanation that need concern us here is the one which is given by the par-

---

[16]A typical example: "The vagina of the shaman is swollen; she wants to fornicate with a pig's penis."

[17]These details, which I later obtained from informants, are consistent with the published reports in the references cited in footnote 6.

ticipants themselves. King Anawrahta, who had ordered the execution of the Brothers, was himself killed by the nat of the trees, who, in the form of a buffalo, gored him to death. The ceremonial destruction of the tree, so it is explained at Taungbyon, is a symbolic retaliation against the nat.

At the start of the ceremony water is poured on the ground around the "tree" before it is chopped down. Following this ritual watering of the tree, two "queens" and a "minister," each carrying twigs, dance in front of it. Then, with swords in hand, they circumambulate it. Suddenly the chief queen seizes the top branch and cuts off a piece with her sword. Instantly the crowd falls on the tree, tearing it to bits, as everyone tries to obtain a piece, if only a fragment, for himself. These fragments, it is believed, bring good luck and, if planted in the fields, ensure a good harvest.[18]

With the destruction of the tree the Festival is ended. It need only be added that, on the morning of the last day (the day on which the tree is destroyed), 200 monks are fed at Taungbyon from the income of the paddy land owned by the Brother nats. The nats thereby acquire merit. On the last day, too, their images are covered with new gold leaf.

One week after the Taungbyon Festival, the mother of the Taungbyon Brothers is honored at the Yirinaku Festival, celebrated near Amarapura, the former capital of Burma. Popa Medaw (the "mother of Popa") normally resides on Mt. Popa, where she met and married her husband and where she gave birth to her two sons. She visits Taungbyon every year for her sons' festival and, at its completion, she returns to Popa, breaking her journey at Amarapura, where the Yirinaku Festival is held in her honor. Hence, at the end of the Taungbyon Festival her image and those of her sons are carried by ox cart to Amarapura, where, having accompanied her "half-way," the sons take their farewell and return to Taungbyon. Although larger than the Sedaw Festival, the Yirinaku Festival is much smaller and less elaborate than Taungbyon. Its basic ingredients, however, are the same.

---

[18]Although the most dramatic, this is not the only ritual in which a tree branch plays a prominent role. The nat dancers in the palace wave a bundle of sprigs of the *thabye* (Eugenia) tree around their heads, in the belief that the *thabye*, a "victory" tree, will induce possession. While the dancer circles the sprigs around her head, the members of the orchestra sing:

> In order to be victorious,
> Dark-brown colored flowers
> So-called
> Pour the cool, purest water.

CHAPTER EIGHT

The Thirty-Seven Nats: Some Explanations

THE NAT TYPES: A STRUCTURAL EXPLANATION

In Chapter 5 we explored some possible historical bases for the Thirty-Seven nats in connection with a general discussion of the historical context of Burmese supernaturalism. We may now appropriately explore their relationship to the Burmese social structure and, more especially, to the different structural "levels" of traditional Burmese society. This exploration is especially appropriate since the terms by which the main nat types are designated have explicit reference to structural criteria. For one of these types, however—the "mother's side-father's side" nats—the structural variable which is used as the typological criterion is, as we have seen, more than a little ambiguous. It is not clear, for example, whether "mother's side-father's side" refers to a social group (and, if so, to which one), or to the principle—descent—by which this nat is acquired. Equally ambiguous are "house" and "village" in "house nat" and "village nat." Although designating structural entities rather than a structural principle, each may designate not one, but at least four, kinds of entities. This means, if these structural entities are the distinguishing criteria of the nat typology, that these latter types—and, by implication, the former type as well—are associated, not with one, but with different hierarchies of structural levels. This thesis is best explicated with the aid of Charts 8.1 and 8.2.

Typological Criterion	Nat Types		
	House Nat	"Mother's Side-Father's Side" Nat	Village Nat
Unit of cultus-the sociological unit that performs the cultus	Household	Group of agnatically related Kinsmen*	Village
Unit of dominion, social-the sociological unit of the nat's power	Household	Group of agnatically related kinsman*	Village
Unit of dominion, physical-the physical unit within which the nat's power is manifested	House	"Region"	Village
Domain, social-the maximal group over which the nat holds dominion	Nation	Descendants of original inhabitants of "region"	Residents of, and travelers through, the "district"
Domain, physical-the maximal area over which the nat holds dominion	Kingdom	"Region"	"District"
Church-the maximal group that performs the cultus	Nation	Descendants of original inhabitants of "region"	Residents of "district"

*A variable operative primarily in the post-conquest period.

CHART 8.1   Structural variables designated by alternative typological criteria employed for the delineation of the three subtypes of the thirty-seven nats.

"House" and "village" in "house nat" and "village nat" may refer in the first place to the *unit of cultus*, i.e., to the type of social group which performs the ritual for the nat (Chart 8.1, row 1). It is the household that is responsible for the cultus of the house nat, and the village for the cultus of a village nat. By this same criterion, it is a group of localized, agnatically related kinsmen (whose boundaries are highly fluid) which is responsible for the cultus of a "mother's side-father's side" nat. If, then, the unit of cultus is the typological criterion, the structural levels with which these three nats are associated constitutes a hierarchy, in ascending order, of house nat, "mother's side-father's side" nat, and village nat (Chart 8.2, column 1).

Nat Types	Typological Criteria					
	Unit of Cultus	Unit of Dominion, Social	Unit of Dominion, Physical	Church	Domain, Social	Domain, Physical
House Nat	1	1	1	3	3	3
"Mother's side-father's side" Nat	2	2	3	2	2	2
Village Nat	3	3	2	1	1	1

Key: 1 is the lowest structural level

CHART 8.2   Alternative hierarchical orders of the three subtypes of the thirty-seven nats according to the structural variables used as the typological criteria for the delineation of the types.

"House" and "village," however, may refer not to the unit which performs the nat's cultus, but, obversely, to the unit of his protection and punishment, i.e., to the *unit of dominion*. If "house" and "village," taken as units of dominion, designate social groups—so that the typological criterion is the *social* unit of dominion—the structural levels with which the nats are associated remain unchanged (Chart 8.1, row 2), because, for all three nats, the unit of cultus and the social unit of dominion are identical. In short, it is the household, the village, and a group of agnatically related kinsmen who are protected and punished by the respective house, village, and "mother's side-father's side" nats, by virtue of their attention to, or negligence of, their cultus. Since the structural levels with which the nats are associated remain unchanged, the structural hierarchy similarly remains unchanged (Chart 8.2, column 2).

But "dominion" has a physical as well as a social referent: it may designate the physical locus as well as the social unit of power. And, in fact, this is the case in the present situation. For "house" and "village" may refer not only to the social, but also to the *physical* unit of the nat's dominion. It is the case not only that the inhabitants of a house or village, taken as corporate social units, are the objects of protection by the house and village nats, respectively, but that their protection by these nats is confined to the house and the village, taken as physical loci as well. In the case of the "mother's side-father's side" nats, however, the physical unit of dominion is much more extensive. Although centered in his fief— what I am here calling a "region," which corresponds to a large administrative unit in the traditional Burmese kingdom—his dominion is not restricted to it; rather, it extends to any region to which his subjects may choose to migrate. Notice, then, that if the physical unit of dominion is the typological criterion, these three nat types are not only associated with a set of structural units (Chart 8.1, row 3) different from that with which they were associated by the first two criteria but, since the hierarchy of structural levels inherent in this set is different from that of the previous set, this criterion orders the nats in a different hierarchy (Chart 8.2, column 3). Whereas the hierarchy produced by the previous set was, in ascending order, house nat, "mother's side-father's side" nat, village nat, in the present set it is house nat, village nat, "mother's side-father's side" nat.

Let me recapitulate what I have done thus far. For the three nat types with which we are concerned, the distinguishing criterion of the type, explicit in the Burmese terms by which the types are designated, is a structural variable. In two of these three—house and village nats—the variable designated by the term is a structural unit. In the third type— "mother's side-father's side" nat—the variable designated by the type term is somewhat vague. Nevertheless, since nats of this type are also associated with a structural unit, the latter variable, although not terminologically explicit, may be used as the criterion for distinguishing this type as well. Using, then, the structural unit with which each type is associated as the typological criterion, these three nat types can be demonstrated to be associated with three different structural levels of Burmese society, forming an explicit structural hierarchy. This demonstration, however, is not unambiguous, for "house" and "village"—and, by the same token, "mother's side-father's side"—may designaté at least three different types of structural units. Hence, depending on which type of unit is taken as the structural criterion, the nats may be associated with two different sets of structural levels (two of these types yield the same structural set) forming two different structural hierarchies.

But we are not through. Although the structural variable designated by the type terms is a structural unit, the terminology obscures an alternative and perhaps more important structural variable by which these nat types might be distinguished. Rather than distinguishing these types according to the structural units with which they are associated, they might be distinguished by the larger class of which these structural units are members. Thus, instead of unit of cultus, the typological criterion might be the maximum cult group, i.e., the *church*; and instead of the unit of dominion, the typological criterion might be the maximal extension of a nat's dominion, i.e., his *domain*. Analyzed in this way, then, since there is only one house nat for the whole of Burma, his church consists of the entire Burmese nation. By the same token, it is the Burmese nation that is his social domain, and the boundaries of the Burmese kingdom—this analysis is cast in the preconquest period—constitute his physical domain. Any citizen of the Burmese nation, wherever he may reside within the kingdom, is subject to the dominion of Min Mahagiri, the house nat.

This analysis, when applied to the village nat, yields a different picture. Unlike the house nat, there are a number of village nats, and the physical domain of each village nat, as we have already observed, consists of an area defined by a group of contiguous villages. I have arbitrarily termed this area a "district." His social domain, similarly, consists of the residents of the district—they also comprise the church—as well as anyone who may be traveling through it. Anyone leaving the district of one village nat enters the physical domain and, therefore, comes under the dominion, of another village nat.

The situation of the "mother's side-father's side" nats is somewhat more complicated. In the preconquest period, when internal migration was slight, both the church and the social domain of any nat of this type were restricted to the inhabitants of his physical domain, an area—which I am here calling a "region"—coterminous with his fief. That is, since almost all those residing in a given nat's fief acquired, through descent, an obligation to propitiate him, it was they who constituted his church and his social domain. Since, however, the basis for his dominion is hereditary rather than territorial, anyone leaving his fief remains subject to his dominion, even though he has established residence in the domain of another nat. Neither he nor his descendants can leave the church or escape the dominion of their "mother's side-father's side" nat. In short, since both the church and the social domain of these nats consist of the descendants of the original inhabitants of their fiefs, their dominion—following the great population upheavals attendant upon the British conquest—extends to persons living in regions remote from their physical domain. For our analysis, however, we are concerned with the preconquest period, in which both the church and the social domain of these nats consist of the inhabitants of their physical domain.

It is now apparent that church and domain, taken as the criteria by which these nat types are distinguished, not only associate the nats with two new sets of structural variables (Chart 8.1, rows 4–6), but, since these variable sets include a new set of structural levels, they produce a structural hierarchy which is not only different from those inherent in the previous sets, but is actually the reverse of the first two (Chart 8.2, columns 4–6). In short, when structural units are taken as the typological criteria, these nats are associated with the three structural levels of household, kin group, and village, and the nats are thereby associated with a structural hierarchy that consists, in ascending order, of house nat, "mother's side-father's side" nat, village nat. When, however, structural classes are taken as the typological criteria, these same nats are associated with the three structural levels of district, region, and nation, and with a structural hierarchy consisting, in ascending order, of village nat, "mother's side-father's side" nat, and house nat.

We may conclude, then, that depending on the structural variable by which these three nat types are differentiated, they are associated not with one, but with different sets of structural levels, forming differing sets of structural hierarchies. The fact that different hierarchies are possible —whether there is one "true" hierarchy can only be established by more detailed field work—is less important, however, than the fact that, in either case, these nats are associated with various important levels of Burmese society. Indeed, if the personal guardian (*kousaun*) nats— which, it will be recalled, comprise a mixture of Thirty-Seven nats and *devas*—are included within this scheme, and if these structural variables are taken to be inclusive rather than exclusive typological criteria, then nats are associated with, literally, every structural level of traditional Burmese society, beginning with the individual, and proceeding through the ascending levels of household, kinsmen, village, district, region, and nation. According to this analysis there is a perfect fit between the nat structure and the social structure.

THE NAT SYSTEM: A POLITICAL EXPLANATION

Anyone acquainted with the structure of traditional Burmese government (cf. Cady 1958, Chap. 1; Furnivall 1957, Chap. 3; Mya Sein 1938) cannot help but be struck by the obvious isomorphisms between the hierarchy of structural levels with which the nats are associated and the structural hierarchy of the Burmese political system. Traditional Burma was ruled by a monarch whose domain, like that of the house nat, was the Burmese kingdom. Like the house nat, too, the unit of his dominion was the household: the household was not only the unit of taxation and of conscription, but it was also the smallest unit in the administrative hierarchy, ten households being in the charge of a *ywa-gaung* or "ten-household head," the lowest official in the administrative hierarchy.

The kingdom was divided into large administrative units, each headed by a governor (*wun*) appointed by the court. Since the governors, however, resided at the capital, local government was administered by "village circle" headmen (*myothugyi*), a "village circle" consisting of a number of villages within a designated area. These headmen had two types of subjects. One type, the *athin*, was subject to his dominion by virtue of residence in a village within his "circle" of contiguous villages. The second type, a nonresidential group called *ahmudan*, owed him allegiance— usually service (*asu*)—by virtue of descent. Though scattered, the *ahmudan* generally lived within a bounded area recognized as the domain of the headman. Their relationship to the headman has been described as "quasi-feudal, personal, regimental, and tribal" (Furnivall 1957:31). It was for this reason that those of *ahmudan* status who ". . . migrated to regions remote from their original homes did not thereby escape their traditional *asu* [service] obligations or forfeit their personal allegiance to their respective myothugyi chiefs" (Cady 1958:28).

The isomorphism, on the one hand, between the village nat and the *athin* headman, and, on the other hand, between the "mother's side-father's side" nat and the *ahmudan* headman is so obvious that little comment is required. In the first comparison, the basis for dominion is territorial; it is confined to a domain which consists of a district of contiguous villages; and the unit of dominion is the village. In the second comparison, dominion is based on descent; it extends, if necessary, to subjects who emigrate to other domains; and the unit of dominion is a group of kinsmen.[1]

This isomorphism between the structural level of nats and that of political officials extends as well to their respective habitations. As the king has a national capital, so the house nat has his national shrine on Mt. Popa. (But since the household, in both cases, is the unit of dominion, the house nat has a shrine in the house as well). Each village has a shrine for the village nat, and there is often a central shrine for a particular village nat who, like an *athin* headman, holds dominion over a large "circle" although he lives in only one village. There are no local shrines for the "mother's side-father's side" nat, nor could there be, since his subjects do not comprise local residential groups; since, however, this nat, like the *ahmudan* headman, resides in a village within his domain, it is there that his shrine is found.

Given these striking structural similarities between the traditional political system and the nat system, it is hard to escape the conclusion, especially since the fully elaborated cult of the Thirty-Seven nats had developed only after the general pattern of the traditional Burmese state had been established, that the nat structure is patterned after the Burmese political structure. To be sure, both the territorial and hierarchical political structures common to all the Buddhist and Hindu kingdoms of Southeast Asia were themselves modeled after the Hindu-Buddhist picture of the heavenly realm (cf. Heine-Geldern 1942). Based on the magical conception of a microcosm-macrocosm parallelism, the entire kingdom was organized as the cosmos in miniature, with the palace, as its center, representing the mythical Mt. Meru, and the king and his princes representing Indra and the *devas* of the Tavatimsa heaven. The kingdom itself was divided into provinces, each ruled by one of the princes.

Shorto, whose remarkable study I discovered after this section was

[1]It might also be observed that, as in the case of *myothugyis*, these nats are almost exclusively male. Although there are a few cases of female village headmen (*ywathugyi*) in traditional Burma, there were, apparently, no cases of female village circle headmen (*myothugyi*) (Mya Sein 1938:51).

written, goes even farther. In his opinion, the Thirty-Seven nats were Mon nats, brought to Pagan after the sack of Thaton. The Buddhist kingdom of Thaton, based on the traditional Hindu-Buddhist religio-political ideology in which "territorial organization, political hierarchy, and religious cult" are "conjoined in [one] prototype" (Shorto 1963:579), had thirty-three nats, one each for the thirty-two regions (*myos*) into which the kingdom was divided, plus Sakka. But the division of the kingdom into thirty-two regions in itself reflects Hindu-Buddhist cosmology, and specifically, the thirty-two gods (plus Sakka) who reside in the Tavatimsa heaven, located at the top of Mt. Meru.[2] On the one hand, then, the nat order reflected the political order; on the other hand, the latter order—the division of the kingdom into thirty-two *myos*—reflected the supernatural order, i.e., the structure of the Tavatimsa heaven. In short, although the political order was organized as a model *of* the Hindu-Buddhist cosmic order, the political order, in turn, became the model *for* the nat order.

But perhaps even more can be claimed. There are some grounds for believing that the nat structure not only reflects, but was instituted by, the political structure and, more specifically, by the throne (cf. Htin Aung 1962:105). Indeed, if we can accept the historicity of the Burmese chronicles there is explicit evidence, in some instances at least, to support this belief. The cultus of the famous Mahagiri and Taungbyon nats among others, was instituted by this process. (For the former, see Tin and Luce 1960:45–46; for the latter, *ibid.*, 83–84.) This evidence suggests that each of the Thirty-Seven nats acquired an extensive region in fief through a royal edict. The size of this region varied from nat to nat,[3] but in each case, as I have already suggested, it most probably corresponded to the size of, because it was coterminous with, the boundaries of the administrative provinces (*myos*) of traditional Burma. Initially, then, the number of nats included among the Thirty-Seven would have corresponded to the number, still unknown, of administrative provinces in the kingdom, plus, of course, Sakka, the supernatural counterpart of the earthly king. Like the feudal lord of the province (or, more particularly, like the court-appointed feoffee who lived within it), its supernatural lord—nats are addressed as *min*, lord—was authorized by the king to receive annual tribute from the residents of his fief and from their descendants. This

---

[2]Heine-Geldern interprets the structure of the older Pyu kingdom of ancient Burma as modeled after the same religious image. The kingdom's thirty-two "vassals or head of provinces," with the king at the center, correspond to ". . . the thirty-three gods who reside on the summit of Meru and among whom Indra is king. Thus not only the capital city, but the whole empire of the Pyu must have been organized as an image of the heavenly realm of Indra." (Heine-Geldern 1942:19).

[3]In the case of the Taungbyon Brothers, the fief is bounded by the Myinge River (south), the Irrawaddy (west), the town of Madaya (north), and the foothills of the Shan Plateau (east). I suspect, from very scanty data, that this is an especially large fief. The geographic mapping of the domains of these nats, as well as of the village nats, a most important task for the understanding of the nats, is still to be undertaken.

tribute, as we have seen, is still offered to him at the annual festival celebrated at his central shrine. This means, of course, that although thirty-seven nats, or thirty-three, or whatever number, may have been included in the original system of the Thirty-Seven nats, the only nat within this pantheon whom any individual Burman need have attended to was the nat who had been appointed lord of his province. He need no more have propitiated the other nats included in the system than he need have offered tribute to the feudal lord of another province. If this is so, it would follow that the original pantheon of the Thirty-Seven nats consisted exclusively of "mother's side-father's side" nats, and that only later, by a political process still to be described, other types of nats were included within the Thirty-Seven.[4]

I have argued, then, not only that the nat order reflects the political order, but also that the cultus of at least some of the Thirty-Seven nats was established by the political order. Going further, one is tempted, by reading between the lines of the Chronicles, to derive the origin of all these nats from a deliberate reinterpretation by the throne, for its own political ends, of the cultus of the indigenous communal nats (see Chapter 5, pp. 67–68). The Thirty-Seven nats, it will be recalled, are believed to have been identifiable persons who became nats upon their death. Their myths (Temple 1906b) reveal that almost all of them were either persons of royal blood who suffered violent deaths—by accident, by murder, or in insurrection against the throne; or else they were nonroyalty who were put to death because they were disobedient or a threat to the throne. The famous Taungbyon Brothers, for example, were executed for disobeying the king to whom they had sworn allegiance, and their father and uncle before them had also been rebels. Similarly, Min Mahagiri, the most important of the Thirty-Seven, was executed because of his alleged threat to the throne. For a number of reasons—structural, cultural, and administrative—which are irrelevant to our subject, Burmese governments have always been (and to this day continue to be) singularly unstable. Revolt and threat of revolt have been endemic throughout Burmese history. In the early periods of Burmese dynastic history, the kings had always to fear those "mighty men of endeavor" (Htin Aung 1962:62) who, if they could not be incorporated within the regime, were ordered captured and killed. By recognizing them as nats and by prescribing a cultus in their honor—and all the original Thirty-Seven (with the exception of Thagya Min, who is really a *deva*) acquired their cultus by royal command—the throne, whatever its motives, achieved a number of obvious political ad-

---

[4] If nats were apotheosized by the government, it would be expected that, in some sense, they would be subject to the authority of the government. This expectation is borne out, even today, by the seemingly curious belief, which we have already encountered, that government officials (like Buddhist monks) are immune from attacks by nats and that nats must obey their commands.

vantages. On the one hand, the establishment of the cultus could serve to pacify the followers of the actual or potential rebel. On the other hand, it could serve to promote political loyalty. By propitiating a nat whose cultus is prescribed by the king, these erstwhile rebels are symbolically acknowledging the latter's rule.

That the throne might have attempted to manipulate the cultus of the Thirty-Seven for political ends is given more than passing credence by the lyrics (*nat than*) sung by the shamans when publicly invoking the nats at nat festivals.[5] Each of the Thirty-Seven nats has his associated song, which briefly recounts his myth, and almost all of them emphasize the sinful nature of treason, rebellion, and assassination (Temple 1906b: 16). Whether or not they were deliberately intended as instruments of political loyalty, the repetition of these songs could not, and cannot, help but contribute, at least in some degree, to this end. For these songs, be it noted, are more than hortatory. They not only underscore the sinfulness of political rebellion, but they also emphasize its punitive consequences: rebellion leads to execution and, even more disastrously, it may lead to rebirth as a nat, a state which everyone wishes to avoid.

The punitive consequences of political rebellion are emphasized (explicitly or implicitly) not only in nat myths and in their odes, but also in their commemorative rituals. A central rite of the Taungbyon Festival, for example, consists as we have seen in the ritual destruction of a tree. The most frequent interpretation of this rite, offered by the participants in this festival, is that its destruction is a symbolic punishment for the nat of the trees who, in the form of a buffalo, killed the famous king, Anawrahta, by goring him. In short, by emphasizing the punitive consequences of political rebellion, the nat cultus may serve as a deterrent to rebellious tendencies.

Brown has offered still another political interpretation of the Thirty-Seven nats, which, if taken as a functional rather than—as he seems to suggest—a causal explanation, serves to complement the one offered here. He points out that the propitiation of the spirits of political rebels could have afforded their followers—and, it might be added, the potential followers of contemporary rebels—a symbolic expression for otherwise frustrated rebellious tendencies. Since the Taungbyon Brothers, for example, were Muslims, and since, moreover, they were executed for neglecting to assume their responsibility for the building of a royal pagoda, ". . . it is difficult to avoid the belief that they were honored [by the people] for the very reason that they defied the great Buddhist king [Anawrahta]. . . . [The people] resented his proselytizing methods . . . and deliberately honored the rebels for that reason" (Brown 1915:362). More broadly, it might be suggested that by releasing rebellious impulses in politically

[5] The lyrics, characterized by Taw Sein Ko as "odes," have been collected in the *Mahagita Midani* (Scott and Hardiman 1900:17).

innocuous ritual, the nat cultus contributes in yet another way to political stability.[6] Mendelson has suggested a similar interpretation. Court instituted nat cults, by ". . . drawing off living allegiances [of rebel followers to their leader] into the fantasy world strengthened the central authority in the real world" (Mendelson 1963a:787).

It is at the Taungbyon Festival, particularly, that one is struck with this aspect of the nat cult. Here an entire replica of the royal court is reconstituted annually for the sole purpose of doing homage to the Taungbyon nats, homage which is literally fit for a king—a Burmese king. Like the king, the nats live in a "palace," they ride in the royal barge, they are carried on royal palanquins; like the king they possess many "slaves," they are served by four chief ministers, and they are attended by four chief queens. For the seven days of the festival it is as if the entire royal court, except the king, were transferred to Taungbyon. And, although one wonders at first at a royal court without a king, one soon realizes that there is indeed a king. For in this court the Taungbyon nats are kings.

Still, the absence of a human surrogate king serves to point up the complex and conflicting political elements in the nat cultus and the problem of the limits, both of excess and of constraint, which must be established for both the suppression and expression of rebellious tendencies. On the one hand the festival, in a variety of ways, permits the expression of rebellious tendencies. Thus, although the Taungbyon nats, like their father before them, had disobeyed royal authority, they are now being honored; moreover, their votaries, in performing the ritual drama, are suddenly lifted from the ranks of commoners to become members, officials, and nobles of the royal court. On the other hand, rebellious expressions may not go too far. A royal court, even a temporary court, complete with king might imbue the ritual drama with serious overtones. Hence, again, the complexity. There is no king, not only because the Taungbyon nats, the rebels, are surrogate king, but because a human surrogate king would come dangerously close to the limits of permissible excess.

But "mighty men of endeavor" were not the only threat to the state. In addition to these local sources of rebellion, the throne had constantly to cope with the ubiquitous threats to its "empire" from provinces far removed from the capital and its immediate environs (cf., Leach 1960). In a situation of this kind, in which the control of the center over its outlying districts was always tenuous, the nat cultus could be made to serve an important "imperial" end. By propitiating a nat whose cultus was prescribed by the throne, peripheral districts are, in effect, symbolically acknowledging the latter's suzerainty. Here, again, the nat odes sung at nat festivals lend credence to this interpretation. Some of them go out of

---

[6]The resemblance to Gluckman's (1956, Chap. 5) theory of rituals of rebellion as reinterpreted by Spiro (1962) is obvious.

their way to emphasize the wickedness of local rulers, whose territory the royal dynasty had conquered, and to contrast them with the greatness of the king. Thus, after recounting the myth of Min Mahagiri, this nat's ode continues:

> The Glory of His Majesty is that of the sun in all his splendor and magnificence, yet, though he thus shines with refulgence, he beams on the people with a fragrance and a cooling breath like unto a fresh breeze laden with the odors of the wild jasmine. Hence it is that the countries which own his royal sway are many and varied and therefore is his capital happy and prosperous. (Translation by Scott and Hardiman 1900:21.)[7]

But this analysis can be carried yet one step further. The substitution of court-instituted local nat cults for indigenous local cults, their assimilation to the political administrative organization (as in the case of district and regional nats) and their subordination to the royal court—by such techniques as incorporating them into the royal list of the Thirty-Seven nats, granting them fiefs, and prescribing their cultus—all served to strengthen the authority of the throne over individual districts and provinces. The Burmese state, however, not only required the vertical subordination of each district or province to the center, but it also required their horizontal unification. If the local (district and regional) nat cults established by the court served as instruments of political *domination*, it might be argued that the court-established national nat cult (the cult of Min Mahagiri, the house nat) served as an instrument of political *integration*.

When first established, the cult of Min Mahagiri was a local cult, confined to the region of Mt. Popa and its environs. Gradually, however, Min Mahagiri was established as a national nat who, assimilated to the various indigenous, localized house nats, came to be propitiated as *the* house nat in every household in Burma. As a national nat, not only was he propitiated in all the provinces in the kingdom, but his annual festival, although celebrated on Popa, was established as a national festival (Htin Aung 1962:66–67). Here, then, is a nat cultus that not only subordinates every

---

[7]After writing this section I discovered that Mendelson, perhaps our most important Western expert on Burmese folk religion, had independently and sometime previously, arrived at similar conclusions. For reasons which need not detain us, he sees the Burmese state as requiring: "constant buttressing against fissionary tendencies symbolized by particular local spirits—as shown, in my view, by the strong association of many such spirits with disobedience or rebellion against the king in much of *nat* mythology. This buttressing would be achieved by some degree of Hinduization of local spirits, incorporated at a low level in the hierarchy of divinities, and their subordination to the royal power. . . . The result of this would be that a central religious cult would tend often to eschew or even suppress local cults of particular *nats* in periods of royal dominance . . . (Mendelson 1961a:578; see also Mendelson 1963a:780–807; 1963b:112).

Burmese household to the throne, but that unites every household, no matter how far flung, with every other household within the kingdom. Together with Buddhism, the cultus of the house nat is an instrument, *par excellence*, of political integration.[8] It is little wonder that the politically astute U Nu, confronted with serious fissionary problems within the Union of Burma, attempted both to establish Buddhism as a state religion and to strengthen the state's support of the cultus of Min Mahagiri.

Given, then, that the supernatural order exhibits a political structure remarkably parallel to that of the natural order, it is hardly surprising that the Burmese perception of the nats is almost identical with their perception of government. For the Burmese, government—together with fire, famine, flood, and plague—is one of the "five traditional enemies." It may protect its subjects from dacoity and other forms of social and economic disruptions, and indeed it is expected to do so, but in general it is viewed as an exploitative, mercenary power, which one is best advised to avoid. The less one has to do with it, the better. It is understood that one has obligations to government, which, if unfulfilled, will lead to punitive consequences. These obligations, therefore, should be met—hopefully, with the expectation that one will receive benefits therefrom, but, minimally, with some assurance that, having done so, one need not fear its punishment. For some problems—the redress of a wrong, the granting of a loan, the fixing of an irrigation canal—only the government can help, but its help is most readily assured by means of gifts, bribes, and other prestations.

The defining quality of the nats' relationship to the people, like that of the government, is political. This quality is implicit in the entire system of rights and obligations which, as has already been described, governs the interaction between nats and people, and it is explicit in the title *min* by which the nats are addressed. *Min* is a title technically confined to royalty—it is generally translated as "lord"—but it is used, by extension, to refer to all governmental officials, even, if one is inclined to be especially honorific, to village headmen.

Taken, then, as a political relationship, the relationship between nat and people is one between lord and subjects, which, for traditional Burma (and for modern Burma as well) is a despotic relationship. Enriquez fittingly refers to the Thirty-Seven nats as "a divine despotism" (Enriquez 1921). Being despotic they evoke the same sentiments evoked by government. These sentiments can be easily expressed. Since they cause trouble, avoid them; if they cannot be avoided, placate them; if their assistance is desired, bribe (propitiate) them.

---

[8]This interpretation is supported by comparative Southeast Asia materials. In Fu-nan and in Sukhotai it was a mountain-dwelling spirit that became the national god. In Sukhotai this spirit is the Lord of the Mountain-top who, as Coedès interprets him, ". . . symbolized, in magicoreligious terms, the unification of territories conquered and brought together by [King] Rama Khamheng." (Coedès 1966:143).

THE NAT CULTUS: A
MOTIVATIONAL EXPLANATION

If traditionally the central government has manipulated the nat system as a means for controlling rebellious tendencies, one can assume that its *political* motivation (it has had other motivations as well) for perpetuating this system was to maintain and enhance its own power and authority. But among other things, the nats, as I have stressed, symbolize opposition to authority. Hence, in performing their cultus—and, more especially, their public cultus—the people are expressing their opposition to authority. But the nats symbolize opposition not only to political authority; they also symbolize opposition to religious authority. In performing their public cultus, the nat devotees are afforded the opportunity to express their hostility to Buddhism and to satisfy needs which are prohibited by it. Since this hostility and these needs are expressed and satisfied in the nat cultus, we may argue that they constitute important motivational bases for its performance.

Although devout Buddhists, the Burmese frequently experience the austere morality of Buddhism as unduly burdensome. Although they are hostile toward many persons, the Burmese are abjured by Buddhism to love them; tempted by attractive women, Buddhism demands that they avoid them; longing to get drunk, Buddhism prohibits the drinking of alcoholic beverages. This list could be expanded almost indefinitely. Buddhism not only interdicts many of the strongest needs and desires of the Burmese, but its law of karma threatens them with severe consequences should they violate these interdictions. Adultery, lying, drinking, and so on may lead to rebirth as a monster, an animal, or even as an inhabitant of hell. Chafing under these restrictions, and resenting having to pay the consequences of their violation, the Burmese, perhaps unconsciously, may use the nat cultus to express their resentment, and it allows them to satisfy at least some of their interdicted needs. Both of these functions may be readily observed in the Taungbyon Festival (see Chapter 7, pp. 112–25).

In celebrating this festival, it is as if the Burmese are deliberately flaunting most of the values of Buddhism. For instance, in honoring the Taungbyon Brothers, they are honoring two nats whose mythological careers began with their father's and uncle's disobeying the order of a Buddhist monk by eating the corpse of a powerful magician (*wei kza*); they are honoring nats who while alive were Muslim rather than Buddhists; they are honoring nats who became nats because of a crucial act of Buddhist negligence—preferring to play marbles, they neglected to assist in the construction of the Taungbyon pagoda; they are honoring nats who are notorious for their gambling and fornicating; finally, they are honoring nats who, when the gentle Ma U rebuffed their attempts to seduce her, ordered a tiger to kill her. In short, this, the most famous of all nat festivals, honors two nats who personify almost every evil that Buddhism abhors. And the Taungbyon Brothers are not the only nats who, honored at their festival, symbolize opposition to Buddhism. Although some nats, like Ma U, are "pious," many others are famous as gamblers, drunkards, and fornicators. And they, together with the Taungbyon nats, not only are the recipients of the people's offerings, but comprise the *dramatis personae* of the entire ritual drama.

If the nats honored at the festival symbolize an opposition to Buddhist values, so much of the behavior of their devotees at the festival is similarly anti-Buddhist. The celebration of the festival during the Buddhist Lent (*Wa*), a period in which public celebrations are normally prohibited, is in itself an anti-Buddhist act. This is especially evidenced by the saturnalian quality which pervades this eight-day festival. The verbal and gestural obscenities, the indiscriminate sexual caressing, the drunkenness, the all-too-frequent acts of aggression, the general carousing—these are always proscribed by Buddhism, but they are especially prohibited during the Buddhist Lent, a season of sobriety and abstinence. To engage in such activities at any time is to violate core Buddhist values; to exhibit them during Lent is all the more repugnant to Buddhism—or it would be, were it not for the sanctioned license which pervades the nat festival.

The anti-Buddhist quality of the festival is expressed not only in its general saturnalian spirit, but in some of its core rituals as well. The Buddhist prohibition against the taking of life is violated in the dramatic ritual in which a hare is sacrificed and offered to the nats. Even more important, in my opinion, is the tree ceremony in which, in a state of fury, the raging mob literally hacks to pieces the *einbin* tree. Since the tree (especially the sacred bo tree) is taken, in most contexts, to be a symbol of the Buddha, it is at least plausible to suggest that in this context its destruction is symbolic of the people's unconscious hostility to Him and His message.[9] It is significant, then, that soon after this ceremony—and, if this interpretation is correct, almost as an act of penance—200 Buddhist monks are offered a special meal by the organizers of the festival.

Thus far I have been viewing all these activities as symbolically expressing Burmese resentment of Buddhism. Most of them, however, can also be viewed as attempts to satisfy those needs which are normally prohibited by Buddhism. These needs find sanctioned outlet in the activities which comprise the nat cultus. In some cases they are satisfied vicariously

---

[9] It is suggestive that of the three cases of psychopathology observed by me and attributed to nat possession, two of the three patients, while still in trance, shouted "There is no Buddha."

and in fantasy, as when the nats, in their odes, brag about their sexual conquests. In other cases, as in drinking, carousing, buttock-pinching, and so on, they are satisfied directly. The point I would make, then, is two-fold. First, those needs whose satisfaction is normally frustrated because it is prohibited by Buddhism, find satisfaction in the nat cultus. Second and consequently, the desire to satisfy these needs constitutes one of the salient motives for participation in the cultus.

As far as the Taungbyon Festival is concerned, this would account in part for the anticipation with which at least the peasants, look forward to its celebration, and for the obvious excitement and euphoria which it arouses. It is as if they have waited all year for the opportunity to express and to satisfy those needs which, in compliance with Buddhist teachings, they have managed to repress or at least to inhibit. If adherence to Buddhism may be viewed as an institutionalized form of repression, the nat festival may be viewed as an institutionalized form of the "return of the repressed." Symbolically viewed, this function is all the more important because it occurs in the middle of that season, the Buddhist Lent, in which repression is expected to be the most intense. Indeed, one may suggest that this is precisely why so many nat festivals are held during Lent. It would be too much to expect the fun-loving Burmese to abstain from sensual pleasures for a long three-month period. By holding their nat festivals during the Lenten season, they are provided with a period of sanctioned license which permits them to satisfy their prohibited needs without appearing to violate the teachings of Buddhism.

It is not only in Burma, of course, that adherents of ethical religions are provided with periods of sanctioned license, and in a study of the sociology of religion it would be remiss not to allude to cognate phenomena in other cultural traditions. Carnival, that dramatic feature of Latin cultures, is especially apposite in this context, occurring, as it does, in connection with the Catholic Lent. But it is equally important to note two structural differences between the Buddhist and Catholic cases. While Carnival occurs immediately prior to Lent, serving, as it were, to compensate the faithful for the abstentions which are to follow, the nat festival occurs in the midst of Lent, providing them with temporary surcease from their abstentions. While Carnival, moreover, has the unofficial sanction of the Church, so that the actors participate *qua* Catholics, the nat festival is celebrated outside the framework of Buddhism, the actors participating not *qua* Buddhists but *qua* animists.

Closer (both culturally and geographically) to Burma is the Hindu festival of Holi, so vividly described by Marriott (1966). Here the actors are not only permitted a period of moral license, but the very fabric of their social and political structure (the caste system) is temporarily rent apart. Even more than in the Carnival, which has the unofficial sanction of the Church, Holi is an official part of the religion which otherwise interdicts this behavior. It is a Hindu festival. If, then, ethical religions seem to require some such moral safety valve—the social and psychological consequences of Calvinism and Judaism, which offer none, are still to be systematically explored—the nat festival, occurring outside the framework of Buddhism, helps to preserve its "purity." I shall return to this point in the last chapter.

IV

ILLNESS AND
SUPERNATURALISM

CHAPTER NINE

Supernaturally Caused Illness
and Its Treatment

THE BELIEF SYSTEM

Although ghosts, witches, and nats may cause various kinds of suffering, they are especially feared as agents of illness and death. Especially interesting, therefore, given the crucial importance of agriculture in the Burmese economy, is the fact that these supernatural beings do not cause agricultural failure. The latter form of suffering, always assuming that the cultivator has worked his land with skill and energy, is attributed exclusively to such natural phenomena as poor soil conditions, insufficient rainfall, and so on. This is not to say, of course, that supernaturals play no role in Burmese agricultural life, for, as we have seen, a variety of taboos and rituals relating to the nats are practiced in connection with the agricultural cycle. Their observance, however, is believed to affect the health and welfare of the agricultural worker, rather than the success or failure of his work. Thus, under stipulated circumstances, if drums or cymbals are not played when entering a field, or if virgins are permitted to work in a field, or if in general a nat's permission to enter a field is not sought (by means of an offering), the angered nat may, among other things, cause quarrels among the workers, or make them ill, or render their work tiring and burdensome. These consequences of ritual neglect may, of course, importantly affect agricultural productivity, but this economic consequence is a by-product, rather than the intent, of the nat's punitiveness.

Although the malevolence of the supernaturals is primarily expressed in disease causation,[1] it is not the case, despite the fact that certain types of disease are attributed primarily to the action of supernaturals only, that most illness is caused by supernaturals. Burmese traditional doctors estimate that only 25 per cent of all illness is produced by supernatural causes.[2] According to one traditional doctor, supernaturally caused diseases consist preponderantly of eye trouble, intestinal ailments, and "madness." Analysis of more than thirty cases of supernaturally caused illness in Yeigyi—some of which I personally observed, others of which were described for me—supports his generalization.

Table 9.1 classifies the symptoms shown in these thirty cases and cross-tabulates them by type of causal agent (ghost, witch, or nat) and by age of the victim (child or adult). Children's symptoms include prolonged crying, intestinal complaints (stomach aches, diarrhea, dysentery), fever, and body sores. Adult symptoms, many of which are frequently conjoined in the same patient, comprise a much longer list. These include sore eyes, choking feelings, appetite loss, intestinal complaints, fright, madness, and death. "Madness," for the Burmese, refers to the following symptoms: wandering about, unconsciousness, violence, obscenity, fits, and irresponsibility (such as selling of farm animals in order to purchase liquor).

Ignoring symptomatology, Table 9.2 classifies these same cases by cross-tabulating age and sex of the victim with type of causal agent. We cannot place great emphasis on this table because the cases were not collected systematically, and because it excludes encounters with (and even punishment by) supernaturals which did not result in illness. Since most of these encounters are with putative witches, the cases in the witch column of Table 9.2 would have been much more numerous, and the age and sex breakdowns might have come out differently had these cases been included. This table also excludes all cases of supernaturally caused harm other than illness—financial losses, fighting and quarreling, "bad luck," losing one's way, snake bites, etc. Since most of these events are attributed to nats, the nat column in the table would have included many more cases had such instances been included, and the age and sex categories might have been different. Finally, the table excludes those cases of nat possession which are viewed as neither attack nor illness, but rather as a sign

[1]Supernatural causation of disease is, of course, a widely distributed belief, cross-culturally, and it is not surprising that it is found among almost all the peoples, primitive and civilized, Buddhist and non-Buddhist, within the Burmese cultural orbit. Cf. Knox (1911:121 ff.) for the Singhalese; Hackett (1953:558) for the Pa-O (a hill people of the Burmese Shan States); Carstairs (1957:83) for the Rajasthanis (of India); de Young (1955:144) for the Thai.

[2]It is important here to make the implicit point explicit, viz., that in Burmese culture, disease is not linked to notions of sin or morality. To be sure, the violation of the Buddhist moral code has inevitable karmic consequences, which may include illness; but karmic illness in any particular birth is believed to be the consequence of immorality in a previous, not in one's present, birth—a belief which protects the patient from public blame or censure, and which precludes the confession of sins as a therapeutic technique.

TABLE 9.1 *A Classification of Supernaturally Caused Disease Symptoms Compiled from Known Cases in One Burmese Village, Classified by Causal Agent and Age of Victim*

SYMPTOM	SUPERNATURAL BEING		
	WITCH	NAT	GHOST
Babies and Children			
crying	+	−	+
intestinal disorder	−	+	−
fever	−	+	+
body sore	+	−	−
Adults			
eye complaints	+	−	−
choking feeling	+	−	−
appetite loss	+	−	−
intestinal disorder	+	−	−
madness			
wandering	+	+	−
unconsciousness	+	+	+
violence—verbal	+	−	−
—physical	+	−	−
obscenity	+	−	−
fit	−	+	−
irresponsibility	−	+	−
fright	−	−	+
death	+	+	−

of being loved by a nat and, hence, as part of the process of recruitment to the role of shaman. Despite these qualifications, the data in Table 9.2 are instructive to some extent.

It will be noted that all cases of supernaturally caused illness are restricted to individuals under five and over fourteen years of age. On the assumption that a systematic survey woud have revealed some cases within the 5 to 14 age range—and I think this is a reasonable assumption —it is still probably fair to conclude that this, the latency period (as Freud refers to it), is relatively immune to supernatural attacks.

A second conclusion, and one which is consistent with Burmese disease theory, is that infants, both absolutely and relatively, are the most frequent victims of attacking ghosts. (In almost all cases, it is the infant's persistent crying that, perceived as "illness," is taken as a sign of ghostly attack.) Almost all supernaturally caused illnesses of infants are caused by ghosts, and almost all victims of ghost-caused illnesses are infants. By contrast, and this is the third conclusion suggested by Table 2, nats and witches tend to ignore infants and typically select adults as their victims.

It would be illuminating to know the sexual incidence, as well as the

TABLE 9.2 *A Classification of Supernaturally Caused Illness in One Burmese Village According to Causal Agent and to Sex and Age of Victim*

CAUSAL AGENT	AGE AND SEX OF VICTIM												TOTALS
	BABY (0–4)				CHILD (5–14)				ADULT (15+)				
	M	F	?	TOTAL	M	F	?	TOTAL	M	F	?	TOTAL	
Witch	0	1	2	3	0	0	0	0	5	5	0	10	13
Nat	0	0	1	1	0	0	0	0	5	2	0	7	8
Ghost	0	0	9	9	0	0	0	0	1	0	0	1	10
Totals	0	1	12	13	0	0	0	0	11	7	0	18	31

age distribution, of supernaturally caused illness, but the information in Table 2 is either too scanty (for the adults) or nonexistent (for the children) to permit any conclusions. The most that is suggested by this Table, a suggestion that is supported by the reports of informants, is that both males and females are susceptible to attack from all three types of supernaturals. What informants add, however, is that on the adult level females are much more susceptible to attack by both nats and witches than are males. This generalization is consistent with the fact (and perhaps it is this fact that gives rise to the informants' generalization) that the great majority of shamans—a role for which nat possession is a precondition—are women. A Burmese traditional doctor, wise and experienced, proposed what he took to be an obvious explanation for the generalization. In his opinion, the physiological and emotional concomitants of menstruation are interpreted by the women as nat possession or nat attack. Unfortunately, I have no data by which this shrewd hypothesis can be tested.

The supernaturals cause illness, it will be recalled, from either anger or malevolence. Typically, a nat causes illness as retaliation for having been ritually neglected or insulted. (He may also cause illness, however, as an agent of a controlling witch.) Witches, on the other hand, cause illness either from sheer malevolence or because they have been insulted, offended, or frustrated by their victims. (Infrequently, they act on behalf of a client.)

Regardless of their motives, Burmese supernaturals may cause disease in one of four ways: by object intrusion, spirit intrusion, soul interference, and distance attack. In "object intrusion," the typical technique of witch-caused illness, the victim is made to swallow a foreign body or some "poison" food (see above, Chapter 2). In "soul interference," another technique of witchcraft, the victim's soul (*leikpya*) is stolen by the witch. In "distance attack" the supernatural causes illness without any physical contact with his victim, either—in the case of the nats—in a manner which is unspecified, or—in the case of witches—by magical manipulation of the victim's exuviae. "Spirit intrusion" is of two types: in one, the soul (*leikpya*) of the nat unites with the soul of the human; in the other, the nat himself (or the witch), in spiritual form, enters the human. (The latter type, depending on whether the agent is a nat or a witch, is termed *nat pude* or *soun pude*, respectively.) If both types are termed "possession," the former (as we shall see) is possession without trance, while the latter is possession with trance. There are also, to make it even more complicated, cases of trance without possession. These types will be dealt with at greater length in a subsequent chapter.

A NOTE ON MEDICAL PRACTITIONERS

Burma is a society, *par excellence*, of magico-religious practitioners. One expert (Shwe Zan Aung 1912) provides an extraordinarily long list of separate types of specialists in the occult, many, but not all, of whom have some kind of medical skills—as diviners, diagnosticians, therapists, or all three. Viewed in historical perspective, this proliferation of magico-religious specialists is probably a function of Burma's historical role as a mediator of sociocultural currents from indigenous Tibeto-Chinese and Indian traditions.[3] It is probably safe to assume that the astrologer (*nekkhath-saya*), for example, is of Indian origin, that the shaman (*nat kadaw*) is of indigenous origin, that the physician (*hsei hsaya*) represents an amalgam of Indian (Hindu) and indigenous elements, that the exorcist (*ahtelan hsaya*) is an amalgam of Indian (Buddhist) and Tibeto-Chinese elements, and so on. Although all the magico-religious specialists in Burma are concerned with, among other things, supernaturals and supernaturally caused illness, the two most important specialists are the shaman and the exorcist. In addition, there are two important specialists in naturally caused illness—the modern physician (*hsaya wun*) and the traditional doctor or herbalist (*hsei hsaya*).

Even when they know that they are suffering from a naturally caused disease, Burmese peasants, for a variety of reasons not germane to the present discussion, only infrequently consult modern physicians, almost all of whom have their offices in large towns and cities. Instead, they consult a Burmese traditional doctor, usually a resident of their own village. In his practice, the latter not only dispenses herbs and other forms of medicine based on an extensive pharmacopoeia, but he frequently utters some spell or performs some rite as well, over either the medicine or the patient, which enhances the therapeutic efficacy of the medicine. Should the doctor attribute the illness to supernatural causation, however, charms,

[3]Although his claim seems exaggerated, Forschammer maintains that all Burmese science, including medicine, is derived from India. In his famous essay, he writes: "Nearly all technical terms in the Burmese idiom, referring to astronomy, astrology, palmistry, medicinal substances, and therapeutics, are words of Sanskrit, and not of Pali origin. Not a single *original* Burmese work treating of the above subjects has as yet been found." (Forschammer 1885:21).

spells, and amulets—together with herbs—comprise his *materia medica.* Indeed, even in those cases in which the doctor believes the illness to be naturally caused, he may place greater emphasis on the magical aspects of his treatment. In treating a bull for mumps—traditional doctors practice veterinary medicine as well—the doctor in Yeigyi not only administered medicine, but he also recited the "virtues" (*goundaws*) of the Buddha. When I asked him about this, he said that it was the spell, rather than the medicine, which had the greater therapeutic value.

If a Burman initially believes his illness to be supernaturally caused, he will never consult a physician, but will turn at once to one of the three types of indigenous Burmese practitioners. In cases of physical illness, he may consult either a traditional doctor or a shaman. Unlike the former, who heals by means of medicines and charms, the latter, after discovering which nat has caused the illness, prescribes a propitiatory offering by which the offended nat, now appeased, is induced to remove the illness.

If, despite the efforts of doctor or shaman, the illness persists, or if, in the first instance, it is believed to have been caused by witchcraft, or if the illness is a form of psychopathology—and, therefore, surely caused by supernatural possession—the patient consults an exorcist (*ahtelan hsaya*). Often, however, the roles of herbalist and exorcist are conjoined in the same person, who, depending on his diagnosis, performs one or the other therapeutic role.

THE TREATMENT PROCESS

Diagnosis

The first diagnostic task is to determine whether the patient's symptoms are naturally or supernaturally caused, for the therapy differs for each of these broad classes of illness. (Here we are concerned only with illness attributed to supernatural causations.) Often, this part of the diagnosis is simple and does not require the skill of a specialist. Thus, if the patient, encountering a ghost or a nat, is frightened or suffers some harmful consequence, he does not require the assistance of a practitioner to render a diagnosis for him. Then, too, there are those symptoms which are known to be produced only by witches and nats. Just as Western laymen are able to identify obvious symptoms of well known diseases, so the relatives or friends of a Burmese patient are able to identify the more obvious symptoms of supernaturally caused illness. It is common knowledge, for example, that prolonged crying in infants is caused by ghosts. Similarly, although the identity of the supernatural may not be known, behavior taken to be symptomatic of mental illness is immediately identifiable as supernaturally caused. Given the belief in the existence of supernaturals, and given the belief in supernatural possession, certain cues— such as trance or unconsciousness—have become established inductively as obvious diagnostic cues of possession—"obvious" because the diagnoses are usually confirmed in the exorcistic seance, and are confirmed again when, following the exorcism, the symptoms of possession disappear.

But Burmese diagnoses of possession rest not merely on medical experience and the evidence it provides for symptomatic diagnosis; they rest on even more direct indicators in the behavior of the patient. Thus, for the villagers who, with me, observed some of the cases to be described below, the unmistakable proof of possession consisted in the fact that the patients acted in a manner that revealed a conscious will at work, but a will—given their knowledge of the patients—that was clearly not their own. Here were persons who, unbelievably, ordered officials about, behaved aggresively toward relatives, indulged in profane and obscene talk, insulted the Buddha, and so on. These were, for them, startling acts, acts which demanded explanation. And in lieu of an explanation—one based, for example, on a theory of dissociation—the obvious (for them) alternative explanation, based on a theory of possession, is that an alien will has entered into and is in control of the body of the patient.

It is only when the presenting symptoms do not permit an easy diagnosis that the assistance of a diagnostic specialist is required to determine their causes. The specialist, however, given Burmese therapeutic techniques, is confronted with other diagnostic problems. Assuming that the illness is diagnosed as supernaturally caused, he must then determine the type of supernatural agent (witch, nat, ghost, etc.) responsible for the illness, identify the specific member of the type, and—usually, but not always—uncover his motive for wishing to harm the patient.

It is probably not unwarranted to assume that different practitioners, even of the same type, use somewhat different diagnostic criteria. The criteria described here are those used in Yeigyi. In this village, traditional doctors sometimes use a simple hand-trembling test. The patient's palm is examined, and if it shakes in a certain manner, the illness is diagnosed as nat-caused; if it shakes in another manner, as witch-caused; if it does not shake at all, as naturally caused. To test the hypothesis of witchcraft, still other diagnostic techniques may be used. The patient may be instructed to chew on some betel leaf, first on one and then on the other side of his mouth. If the leaf has a sour taste, then, since betel leaf is usually sweet, the illness is probably witch-caused. To further test his diagnosis, and as an essential part of the therapy, the doctor or the exorcist administers a potion, inducing the patient to regurgitate the "poison" (*apin*) by which the witch had worked her evil, and which, if the diagnosis is correct, is still in his stomach.

Having identified witchcraft as the cause of the illness, it is relatively easy to specify the witch by knowledge of the patient's "social history." Since witchcraft is always performed within a localized community—the village, or a group of adjacent villages—the patient's relatives (or the healer, if he lives in the localized community) can always recall some incident by which the patient has become a victim of witchcraft: he was unfaithful to his sweetheart, offensive to his mother-in-law, or in some way annoying to his neighbor. This hypothesis, too, can be tested by inducing the alleged witch to possess the patient, and, using the patient as a medium, questioning the witch.

The specification of a nat requires still other techniques. A shaman attempts to identify the nat by one of two means. Sometimes she discovers his identity by simple questioning of the patient (or his family). Has the coconut for the house nat been changed at appropriate intervals? Has the annual tribute been offered to the Taungbyon nats? Did the patient urinate under a tree possibly inhabited by a tree nat? Were offerings made to the field nat before starting work in a new field? And so on. Sometimes, however, the shaman enters into a state of possession, in which she is informed by her nat-husband that the patient had been neglectful with respect to one of these obligations or taboos. The exorcist, too, can identify the offending nat by the technique of possession, but not his own possession. Inducing the nat to possess the patient, the exorcist then questions the nat.

Therapy

Once the diagnosis of supernatural causation is made, various kinds of therapeutic procedures can be initiated, depending on the nature of the illness and the type of practitioner who treats the case. Basically there are five types of therapy: simple curative propitiation, simple curative magic, a combination of propitiation and magic, exorcism without a seance, and, finally, an exorcistic seance. The first three are used almost exclusively for physical, the latter two for mental, illness. I shall describe each in turn.

Simple propitiation: If a shaman has diagnosed the illness as caused by a nat, angered, let us say, by neglect, the patient is advised to make an offering to the offended nat—the offering may be made for him by the shaman—with the expectation that the nat, appeased by the offering, will remove the illness. Thus, for example, having become bald because he had not offered his annual tribute to his mother's side-father's side nat, Kou Than, at the instruction of a shaman, made an offering to the nat, and shortly thereafter his hair was restored. Here, in a case of minor physical illness, the therapy is correspondingly simple.

The above case, it should be noted, exemplifies two simple generalizations concerning therapeutic functions of shamans: almost without exception, shamans are consulted for cases of relatively simple physical pathology, rather than for psychopathology, and their prescriptions are almost always of a propitiatory type.

Simple magic: If the patient's complaints are minor, and if a ghost is believed to be the causal agent, therapy may consist in the performance of a simple magical ritual. Thus, in treating a baby for persistent crying (which is almost invariably believed to be caused by a ghost) the Burmese doctor—for it is usually to him that complaints of this type are brought— has the baby drink some "medicine" (*hsei*), consisting of water over which he has intoned a magical spell or *gahta*. Usually the *gahta* consists of a Buddhist scriptural passage whose recitation is believed to possess magical efficacy. In other cases, the *gahta* may consist of a Buddhist formula listing the "virtues (*goundaws*) of the Buddha, his teachings, or his monastic order. This "medicine," whose efficacy derives from its magical potency, is not to be confused with physical medicine, whose efficacy resides in its natural, curative properties.

A similar type of magical ritual is employed in the treatment of minor cases of witchcraft. Thus, in treating U Kan's witch-caused eye pains, the doctor bathed the patient's eyes with an amulet (*lehpwe*) which he had immersed in a bowl of water. The amulet consisted of a piece of string over which the doctor had recited the "virtues" of the Buddha. U Kan's recovery the following day was naturally attributed to the power of the amulet.

Propitiation and magic: Should the case be too complex for treatment by simple propitiation or magic alone, but not serious enough to require an elaborate ceremony, therapy may consist of a combination of magic and propitiation. Thus, in a case to be described below in which a teen-age girl was rendered unconscious by the nat Aungpinle Thakinma, the doctor first restored the girl to consciousness by intoning both a prayer (*hsutaun*) and a spell (*gahta*). He then instructed her parents to make an offering to the nat, so that, properly appeased, she would not attack the girl again. The offering comprised a coconut, a bunch of bananas, a small mirror, a bunch of flowers, a comb, a packet of face powder, and a string of woolen yarn.

The prayer and the spell recited by the doctor in this case are variants of many such prayers and spells which are employed to deal with harm caused by witches and nats. The prayer is roughly translated as follows:

> May the five Buddhas, the nats (*devas*), and the Brahmas rest on the forehead (of the patient); may Sakka (Thagya Min) rest on the eyes and ears, Thurasandi Devi (i.e., the Hindu goddess, Sarasvati[4]) on the mouth, and Matali on the hands, feet, and body. May the Buddhas, nats, Sakka, the *devas* and devi rest on these parts of the body, and may they guard and protect me. (This is repeated three times).
>
> May glory (*poun*), grace (*kyethayei*), power (*tagou*), and blessing (*kaungyou mingala*) be my lot, and may all the nats guard and protect me. May I attain peace of mind (*kyanthagyin*) due to the power and glory of all the Buddhas, and due to the effect of their love (*myitta*). (This is repeated three times.)
>
> May immense power, knowledge, and wealth be acquired (by me) as the result of paying respect and showing reverence to the Buddha.

---

[4]Sarasvati is the Hindu goddess of wisdom. In Buddhist Burma, where she is also known as Thuya-Thedi Medau, she is believed to be an important *deva*, a guardian of the Faithful, who will one day be reborn as a male, and then as a Buddha.

May immense power, knowledge, and wealth be acquired (by me) as a result of paying respect and showing reverence to the Dhamma.

May immense power, knowledge, and wealth be acquired (by me) as a result of paying respect and showing reverence to the Sangha.

The spell which accompanies this prayer is merely a shortened version, cast in a different grammatical mood. Thus:

The enemy can be overcome by the power of the all-powerful Buddha.

A good income can be achieved by the power of the all-powerful Buddha.

A goodly group of relatives, companions, and attendants are acquired by the power of the all-powerful Buddha.

May I attain peace, for I am telling the truth, and the above-mentioned facts are true.

Although both the spell and the prayer are either addressed to, or in some form invoke, Buddhist supernaturals and sacra, they are essentially a form of magical ritual; although intoned for the benefit of the patient, they are recited by the doctor in the first person, as if he were seeking assistance for himself. In short, it is the power inherent in the formula, regardless of its normal semantic meaning, which is therapeutically efficacious, and its formulaic power derives from the power of the Buddhist supernaturals which, in some sense, is tapped by its recitation. Moreover, the identical prayer and spell are employed by the doctor for a variety of ends for which their normal semantic meanings are entirely inappropriate. Thus they are recited, not only to cure supernaturally caused illnesses, but to acquire the good-will of other people, to avoid all forms of danger, and to achieve security, both physical and mental. Finally, the power of the formulae is such that if a person repeats them frequently, he loses desire for worldly things and becomes a hermit.

Exorcism without seance: Since this type of therapy, employed in cases of "mental" illness, contains most of the elements of the fifth type (exorcism with seance), only a schematic description is presented here, reserving the details for the description of the exorcistic seance. Having diagnosed the illness as caused, say, by witchcraft, the exorcist administers a purgative to the patient in order that the witch's "poison" (*apin*) be ejected. But this in itself is not sufficient. Since the witch continues to control the patient's behavior, the witch must be exorcised, driven from his body (if he is possessed) or from his immediate environment (if he is not possessed). Hence, the patient must worship the Buddha, and, after making obeisance to the Buddha image, he must vow to faithfully observe the Five (Buddhist) Precepts for the rest of his life. The *devas* are then invoked by the exorcist, and requested to protect the patient from further harm caused by this or by any other witch (and by other evil supernaturals).

Here, again, is a ceremony which, except for the purgative, is almost exclusively Buddhist—the power of Buddhism is assumed to be greater than the power of the supernatural. It is one, moreover, in which the patient, far from being a passive agent in the therapeutic process, takes an active role: he worships the Buddha, and he vows to observe the core elements of Buddhist morality.

Exorcistic seance: Should the patient suffer from a severe case of mental illness—one which has been resistant to an ordinary exorcistic ceremony, or one which is caused by possession—recourse is had to an exorcistic seance. The seance, like ordinary exorcism, is conducted only by an exorcist (*ahtelan hsaya*). Its core element consists in inducing the nat or witch to possess the patient so that, using the latter as a medium, the exorcist may engage the offending supernatural in conversation.

Although different exorcists employ somewhat different therapeutic techniques, because of differences in both training and personality, these differences represent relatively minor variants of a common type. This, at least, is the conclusion to be drawn from the exorcistic sessions which I observed in the Mandalay region of Upper Burma. Table 9.3 classifies the elements that comprised the seances which I attended. This chart, it should be emphasized, is not a summary either of the elements that comprise a seance or of the sequence in which they occur. It is merely a classification of the ingredients from which any seance might be, and is, constructed.

Table 9.3 indicates, then, that there are three elements which comprise any exorcistic seance. One element consists of the performance by exorcist, or by exorcist and patient together, of certain rituals designed to protect the patient from the malevolence of the evil supernatural, to enlist the assistance of benevolent supernaturals, and finally to exorcise the former. Some of these rituals—and all will be illustrated in the seances described in the next chapter—are related to Buddhism, in that it is the power or authority of Buddhist supernaturals and sacra which are tapped to overcome the nat or witch. Other rituals are related to nats or witches who are propitiated with the hope that they will withdraw voluntarily.

A second element consists of the interaction between exorcist and the evil supernatural. Inducing the latter to possess the patient, the exorcist, conversing with the witch or nat who speaks through the patient, pleads, cajoles, promises, threatens. This is the core of the seance and constitutes its primary psychotherapeutic component. It is here that the personality of the exorcist manifests itself strongly, and it is here that differences among exorcists are most pronounced.

The third element of the ceremony consists of the administration of "medicine," whose properties, however, are magical rather than pharmaceutical.

It will be noted, then, that the seance, which is used to treat mental illness, differs from other forms of therapy in two important dimensions: in the presence of the offending supernatural, and in the degree of involvement of the patient. From the Burmese point of view, the efficacy of the

TABLE 9.3 *A Classification of Elements Comprising an Exorcistic Seance*

RITUAL ACT	ACTOR	
	PATIENT	EXORCIST
Buddhist Rituals		
Offering (*kadaw pwe*) to Buddhist supernaturals (Buddha, *weikzas, devas*)		+
Worship/pray to Buddhist supernaturals	+	+
Invoke *authority* of Buddhist supernaturals		+
Invoke *aid* of Buddhist supernaturals		+
Oath to observe Buddhist precepts (*thilas*)	+	+
Recitation of Buddhist precepts	+	+
Dissemination of love		+
Oath of libation	+	
Sharing of merit	+	+
Buddhist-derived rituals		
Drinking of "medicine" containing Scriptural passage (*gahta*)	+	
Drinking of "medicine" containing rune (*in*)	+	
Rituals related to nats and witches		
Offering (*kadaw pwe*) to offending nat/witch		+
Pray to offending nat/witch		+
Pray to other nats		+
Interaction with nat/witch		
Summon to possess patient		+
Possession	+	
Conversation	+	+
Threaten with beating		+
Beat, slap, kick, spit upon		+
Threaten with supernatural punishment (including hell)		+
Promise supernatural reward (including heaven)		+
Make obeisance to exorcist, Buddha *devas*, etc.	+	

seance rests on the same principle as the efficacy of other forms of therapy. In all of them, cures are achieved through the power of Buddhist supernaturals, Buddhist symbols, and Buddhist sacra. ("Buddhist" includes "Hindu," for the Hindu deities invoked in the rites are now, of course, Buddhist.) In short, therapeutic success is achieved by confronting the evil power of non-Buddhist supernaturals with the good, and much stronger, power of Buddhism. In this confrontation Buddhist magic is more powerful.[5]

To inject some life into this skeletal description, it is necessary to describe a seance in detail. For the seance to make sense, however, we must first describe the type of illness—supernatural possession—for which it is designed. Hence in the next chapter we shall deal with possession, deferring a description of the seance for the following chapter.

[5]In Theravada Ceylon, as in Burma, healing rites almost always begin with the worship of the Buddha (cf., Ames 1964:35).

CHAPTER TEN

Possession

A NOTE ON "POSSESSION"

Although physical illness is attributed to natural as well as to supernatural causes, behavior which the Burmese characterize as mental illness is attributed exclusively to supernatural causes. And although there is no ambiguity about the Burmese interpretation of such illness, *viz.*, the patient is under the influence of a maleficent supernatural, there is, at least in my mind, more than a little ambiguity concerning the nature of that influence. In the present state of our knowledge, I can only point to some of the ambiguities, without being able to resolve them.

From the perspective of comparative religion it might be said that, typically, and most strongly, a person is believed to be under the influence of a supernatural when it is thought that he is possessed by it—literally, when the supernatural has entered his body. This condition is generally referred to as "spirit possession." Often, but not always, spirit possession is accompanied by a state of psychological dissociation—alternatively referred to as trance, fugue, unconsciousness, etc. But, of course, supernatural influence, possession, and dissociation can all vary independently of each other (Bourguignon 1965). And part of my difficulty in interpreting the Burmese materials—a difficulty which is derived, in part from fuzzy conceptualization on the part of the Burmese, in part from varying Burmese traditions which have not been integrated, and in part (probably the most important part) from gaps in my field work—resides in the virtual impossibility of sorting these out. In this section I should like to examine some of these difficulties, beginning with the most obvious, the semantic difficulty.

1. The Burmese term *pude* is typically translated by English-speaking Burmans as "possession." Thus, *nat pude* is "nat possession," *soun pude* is "witch possession." If "possession" is taken in the literal sense of body-intrusion, the notion of "witch possession" is a difficult one, unless this expression is taken to mean that the victim is possessed by the spirit of the witch, or by the witch in some spiritual form. If this is not the case, it is possible that "possession" is a mistranslation of *pude*, and that the latter should rather be translated as "coming under the influence of," "attacked by," "enchanted by," and so on. In short, it is not clear that *pude*, whether used for nats or for witches, means "possession," as the latter term is generally defined. However this semantic difficulty is resolved—and its resolution, I think, would importantly contribute to the resolution of most of the other difficulties—there are other problems as well.

2. The relationship between possession and temporary soul loss remains unclear. Permanent soul loss is believed by the Burmese to result in death; temporary soul loss (*leikpya khwade*), however, is believed to result in unconsciousness. In the case of possession, then, does the possessing spirit take the place of the soul? And is it this displacement that results in dissociation? Or is there no relationship between these two events?

3. With respect to nats, possession, in the literal sense of body intrusion, can be of two kinds. (a) When a nat falls in love with a human, it is believed that the nat's soul (*leikpya*) has entered into and has united with the soul of the human. This union may be temporary. If the human, however, becomes a shaman, or spouse of the nat, their souls are formally and permanently "tied" in the wedding ceremony. In one sense, this union may be viewed as permanent possession, unaccompanied by dissociation. (b) When a nat wishes to harm a person, the nat himself enters the body of the human. Similarly, in the exorcistic seance, it is the nat and not his soul whom the exorcist induces to enter the patient. So, too, it is the nat who enters the shaman when she practices divination. (Their souls, of course, are already united or "tied.") In all these cases of temporary possession, dissociation is, or is believed to be, the earmark of possession.

4. With respect to witches, there is only one kind of possession (referring still to its literal sense of body intrusion): the witch herself (probably in some special form), but not her soul, enters the victim to cause harm. In the exorcistic seance, too, it is the witch whom the exorcist induces to enter the patient. In both cases, dissociation is the sign of possession.

5. From the Burmese point of view there may be possession without dissociation; and the scientist, viewing such cases, can only agree that possession or, more accurately, the belief in possession, has occurred

without dissociation. Thus, when human and nat souls are united in marriage, the latter's soul is permanently tied to the human soul. Although the marriage, in Burmese terms, consists of a condition of permanent possession, the human spouse is not in a (permanent) dissociational state.

6. Similarly, from the Burmese point of view, there may be possession with dissociation; and the scientist, viewing such cases, agrees that possession has been accompanied by dissociation. There are cases, that is, in which it is believed that a nat or witch has entered the body of a human, and in which the latter clearly exhibits dissociational states. Dissociation takes two forms, both of which are known as *tekthi*. These are a) unconsciousness, in the sense in which a boxer, when he is "knocked out," is said to be unconscious; and b) trance, in the sense of a temporary psychological state in which ongoing behavior is not subject to recall when the actor emerges from that state. In trance, unlike unconsciousness, the actor behaves, but his behavior is closed to his conscious level of awareness.

As far as I can tell there are, in Burma, four experiences in which possession (more strictly, belief in possession) is accompanied by dissociation. a) In the exorcistic seance, the exorcist induces the offending supernatural to possess the patient, whereupon the latter, going into trance, becomes the supernatural's medium. Here possession is involuntary on the part of the supernatural—he is compelled by the exorcist to possess the patient—and it is voluntary, but not sought, on the part of the patient. b) In divination, the nat is believed to enter into the shaman who, in a state of trance, becomes his medium. Here possession is sought by the shaman and, though not sought by the nat, is entered into voluntarily by him. c) In nat dancing the nat enters the shaman who, in a state of trance, "becomes"—i.e., personifies—the nat. Here possession is sought by shaman and nat alike. d) In certain kinds of illness, the supernatural possesses his victim, thereby causing trance and/or unconsciousness. Here possession is sought by the supernatural, but is involuntary on the part of his victim. From the Burmese point of view, the victim can be cured only when the supernatural is exorcized.

7. From the Burmese point of view there may be supernaturally caused dissociation without possession; and the scientist, viewing such cases, can only agree that, whatever the explanation, dissociation has occurred. Thus, in certain kinds of illness, a person may suffer from states of unconsciousness or trance that are believed to have been caused by a harmful nat or witch, who, although attacking the patient, has not entered his body. From the Burmese point of view, the patient can be cured only by exorcizing the supernatural.

8. Thus far I have been discussing psychological events—trance and unconsciousness—which, though caused by the supernaturals, do not, even

in the case of possession, consist of *encounters* with them. I must finally, therefore, mention those events (some of which have already been discussed) which not only are believed to be caused by spirits, but in which the actor has an encounter with them. From a scientific point of view these encounters can be viewed as either hallucinatory or illusory, depending upon the case. These experiences are not, as I am using the term, dissociative in character—they involve neither trance nor unconsciousness— because the actor is conscious of the experience while having it and is capable of recalling and reporting it after he has had it. Indeed, it is only from his report that we know about it.

The Burmese report three types of such personal encounters with supernaturals. a) There are numerous instances of unsought encounters in which supernaturals are "seen," "spoken to," and so on, much as one would see or speak to another human. Sometimes these encounters are pleasurable (as when a male "sees" a beautiful female nat); sometimes they are frightening (as when one encounters a ghost). In either case the experience may or may not lead to illness. b) There are cases, both sought and unsought, in which nat possession is actually experienced, rather than inferred, as in the dissociative cases, from some kind of dissociational behavior which is taken to be an indicator of possession. The prototypical case is that of the shaman, whose ecstatic experience may include sexual intercourse with the possessing nat. c) In Buddhist meditation, the meditator may enter, voluntarily or involuntarily, into ecstatic states, technically known as *jhānās*, which may consist of visions of supernaturals, both benevolent and malevolent. These visions, however, are of Buddhist supernaturals—those who inhabit one of the many non-terrestrial worlds postulated by Buddhism—rather than of nats. Since these visions are not taken as a sign of illness by the Burmese, they will not be discussed in this chapter.

These, then, are some of the complexities with which we are confronted in attempting to deal with Burmese possession. Given them, the most we can hope for is to resolve the semantic difficulties by some more or less arbitrary decisions. For the purposes of this discussion, then, "possession" will refer to those cases in which it is believed that a spirit or witch has entered the body of a human; "attack" will refer to cases of supernaturally caused illness without possession; "dissociation" will refer to states of unawareness ("unconsciousness") or to behavior which the actor cannot recall after it has occurred ("trance"); "hallucination" will refer to any perception or sensation which, though believed to be veridical by the actor, is illusory from the point of view of science.

With the aid of Table 10.1 we can now attempt to contrast the traditional Burmese notions of mental illness and possession on the one hand, and the scientific notions of dissociation, hallucination, and mental illness on the other. From the traditional Burmese point of view, the first three

TABLE 10.1 *A Comparison of Scientific and Traditional Burmese Interpretations of Possession, Mental Illness, and Hallucination*

SCIENTIFIC INTERPRETATION	EVENT	BURMESE INTERPRETATION	PSYCHIATRIC CONDITION	
			BURMESE	SCIENTIFIC
Dissociation	1. Unconsciousness		1. Pathological	Pathological
	2. Trance behavior		2. Pathological	Pathological
	3. Encounters with spirits	Possession		
?	a. Sensations of (ecstatic) possession		3a. Normal	?
Hallucination	b. Perception of supernatural	True Perception	3b. Pathogenic	Pathological
	1. Pleasant			
	2. Fearful			
	3. Combination			

entries in the table—states of unconsciousness, the acting-out behavior associated with trance, and those encounters with nats reported by the actors as possession—are all viewed as instances of supernatural possession. Since states of unconsciousness are dangerous from the standpoint of Burmese ethnopsychology, and since the acting-out behavior associated with trance is dramatically deviant from the perspective of their ethical norms, both are viewed by the Burmese as pathological. They are not only indicators of possession, but they are also symptoms of illness (caused by possession). Since, however, the nats are believed to exist, and since the actor's behavior in the third type of possession—one associated with the sensation of ecstasy—is neither dangerous to himself nor in violation of any ethical norms, ecstatic possession is viewed by the Burmese as entirely normal.

Turning to the scientific point of view, we can characterize the first two types of events as dissociative states; and since states of unconsciousness and trance behavior are, from a scientific standpoint, clearly abnormal, the scientific view is in agreement with the traditional Burmese view that these dissociative states are symptoms of pathology. They differ only in interpretation: for Burmese ethnopsychology they are caused by possession, for scientific psychology they are caused by inner conflict. The third type of event (the sensation of possession) is, as the question mark in Table 10.1 indicates, not so clear. Hallucinatory behavior, to be sure, is pathological, and if it were the case that the shaman, in a waking state, believed himself to be having sexual intercourse with a physically present nat, there would be no question about the hallucinatory, and therefore pathological, character of the experience. It is more likely, however, that such experiences occur only in dreams, and that ecstatic-sexual experiences in waking states are only later interpreted as consisting of sexual intercourse with a nat. If this is so, then, since the emotional sensation is itself a real experience, the only remaining question is the accuracy of the actor's interpretation. Given the traditional Burmese world view in which it is possible for nats to have intercourse with humans, the actor's interpretation, though scientifically false, is not necessarily pathological. To be sure, the ecstatic experience itself, though nonhallucinatory, may be pathological, but our information about this experience is not adequate for an unequivocal diagnosis. The experience itself, of course, may be symptomatic of some other pathology, but it is at least arguable that the experience represents a resolution, rather than an expression, of pathology. (This question will be discussed at greater length in Chapter 12.)

Proceeding, then, to those experiences in which the actor perceives, rather than is possessed by, a spirit, we again have a difference of opinion between traditional Burmese and scientific points of view. Since, in the Burmese world view, spirits have an objective existence, these encounters represent true perceptions, rather than hallucinations. And since, for the

Burmese, these perceptions are therefore veridical, they do not view these encounters as pathological in themselves. They are, however, potentially pathogenic, for the encounter may be a prelude to an attack by the spirit. If, therefore, the actor falls ill following such an encounter, his illness is attributed to supernatural causation. From a scientific point of view, of course, it is not only the actor's resultant behavior, but his encounter itself, that is properly diagnosed as pathological.

Generalizing, then, from Table 10.1 (as well as from other information about Burmese culture), we can discern both similarities and differences between the criteria used by Burmese ethnopsychiatry for assessing psychopathology and those employed by modern psychiatry. a) Some forms of behavior which modern psychiatry takes to be symptoms of pathology, Burmese ethnopsychiatry considers to be normal. b) Some forms of behavior are considered by both to be symptoms of pathology. They differ only in their interpretation of the cause of pathology. c) There are no forms of behavior (known to me at any rate) which Burmese ethnopsychiatry takes to be symptoms of pathology, but which modern psychiatry views as normal.

With this background, we can now turn to some actual cases of these phenomena, all but one of which are taken from Yeigyi.

SOME CASE HISTORIES

Witch-Caused Illness

Case 1: A seventeen-year-old girl, unmarried, began suddenly to complain of severe stomach pains and for a long period was given to sudden and unpredictable bursts of crying. Shortly after the onset of these symptoms, she began to disappear from her home and was unable, upon her return, to recall where she had been. That she was in a trancelike or fuguelike state during those periods can also be inferred from the fact that often, even while at home, she was subject to spells of unconsciousness. When her family realized that she was "ill" they took her to an exorcist, recognizing (from their knowledge of similar cases) that her illness was probably caused by witchcraft. Their suspicion was confirmed when, in the exorcistic seance, the exorcist was able to engage the witch in conversation.

Case 2: A second case, alluded to previously (Chapter 2) is of unusual interest because it involves multiple bewitchment: four persons were believed to be bewitched simultaneously by one witch. The symptoms from which witch possession was deduced are simply described. Two young men suddenly became "mad," attacking indiscriminately and even attempting to kill anyone they encountered. The other two victims, both young women, also became "mad," but their symptoms were different from those of the men. Painting their faces and wearing fancy dress, they would roam from village to village, all the while remaining absolutely quiet, talking to no one. This double case of *folie à deux* was immediately attributed to witchcraft, and the identity of the witch was soon determined.

Case 3: Less dramatic than the previous case, but in many ways much more interesting, is the intermittent "madness" of a young twenty-seven-year-old man. I first encountered this case when the friends of Maung Oun Yi—for that was the name of the victim—were attempting to obtain an exorcist to treat what was for them an obvious case of witchcraft. That morning Maung Oun Yi had been extremely violent, using abusive and obscene language and indiscriminately attacking everyone with a dagger. At the same time he (or, more accurately, the witch who had possessed him) challenged them to bring in any exorcist they desired, for, as "he" put it, "none can defeat me."

This, however, was merely the last in a set of recurrent episodes that had begun nine months earlier. In the first episode Maung Oun Yi, in a trancelike state, had wandered into the fields after experiencing what he described as a choking feeling which did not permit him to breathe. In this episode, however, he was neither abusive nor violent. The exorcist who was called in to treat him ten days after the onset of the episode diagnosed the illness as witch possession.

His second attack came four months later while working in the fields. Shouldering his tiffin-bowl, he wandered, disorganized and confused, and in a state of great emotional turmoil, about the paddy fields. Sometime—I do not know how long—after the outbreak of this episode, an exorcist was called in and seemed to have cured him. Three months later, again in the paddy field, came his third attack, whose character paralleled the second; again the same exorcist treated him, again with apparent success. Then, seven days prior to my encounter with the patient, he had his fourth attack. At that time his behavior was almost the opposite of what it had been in the previous episodes. Seated in his house in a catatonic-like state, both motionless and emotionless, it was only when the exorcist arrived that he was stimulated to action. He (or rather, the witch who possessed him) again challenged any exorcist to treat him; he would "have his revenge on all of them." All exorcists, he shouted, "are powerless," and he had "no fear" of any of them. Then, for seven days, he alternated between catatonic-like withdrawal and violent acting out against anyone he encountered. On the second day of this episode, another exorcist who happened to be in the village attempted to treat him, but the next day the patient again became violent. On the sixth day the local exorcist attempted to treat him, encountering only abuse, and the patient threatened to smear him with vaginal discharge—a deadly insult in Burmese culture—should he come near him. It was at this point, when he became violent once again, that I was requested to bring his former exorcist to the village.

Nat-Caused Illness

During my residence in Yeigyi I encountered only two cases of psycho-pathogenic nat possession.[1]

Case 4: The first, and relatively simple, case concerns one Kou Nyunt Maung, a young man in his early twenties. Returning from his fields in the late afternoon, and before entering his house, he urinated near the pillar to which the coconut for the house nat is attached. Almost immediately he fell unconscious, and only after being worked on by two masseurs did he regain consciousness. A traditional doctor who was later called to treat him said that he had been attacked by the nat of the trees (Youkhazou), who could be propitiated with a food offering.

A few weeks later Kou Nyunt Maung fell into a trance, running around the village for about an hour until he collapsed. When he regained consciousness he complained of severe stomach cramps. (I do not know how this episode was treated.)

About a month after this second episode, and shortly after his return from the Taungbyon Festival, he again fell into a trance, manifesting the same symptoms. This time an exorcist was called in, and in the seance it was discovered that the patient was possessed by U Min Kyaw, the lusty, liquor-guzzling nat who plays a prominent role in the Taungbyon Festival. At this nat's insistence, Kou Nyunt Maung offered him a bottle of local spirits and a fried chicken. From that time he has had no further relapses.

Case 5: The second, and much more complex case of nat possession, involves a thirty-year-old male who was loved by a spirit known as an *ouktazaun*. Technically, *ouktazauns* are not nats, as I have been using that term, but they elude all other supernatural categories as well. Since Burmese experts disagree on their classification—Htin Aung (1933a) characterizes them as "minor spirits," while Tin (1913a, 1914) classifies them as ghosts—I shall follow the lead of my Yeigyi villagers, who classify them with the "Outside Thirty-Seven nats." From the following description, however, it is apparent that they fall somewhere between nats and ghosts.

Ouktazauns are spirits of either sex (the vast majority are female, however) who guard buried treasure. It is believed that many *ouktazauns* guard the treasures buried in pagodas—gold, silver, jewels, etc.[2]—which

---

[1]Surprisingly there are almost no descriptions of spirit possession in any of the standard works on Burmese folk religion. One of the few exceptions—and it deals with a Mon, not a Burmese, case—is O'Riley's fascinating description of possession in one old woman (O'Riley 1850). The measured and heavy quality of this woman's behavior is in dramatic contrast with the ecstatic, sometimes violent, and frequent possession of older women which Gooneratne (1856), writing in the same period, found in Ceylon.

[2]Wherever possible, pagodas are constructed to hold a relic of the Buddha, of a Buddhist saint, or, at least, of an unusually holy monk. With the relic are buried valuable treasures of the kind noted above.

are to be used at the coming of the future Buddha (the Buddha Maitreya) for the construction of his monastery and pagoda.[3] This role is the karmic consequence of their former, human behavior, which was characterized to the very moment of death by greed for wealth and material possessions. It is their just meet, therefore, that they should now guard this buried treasure.

There are various beliefs concerning the possible fate of an *ouktazaun* (Htin Aung 1933a; Tin 1913a), and, again, I shall describe the one which is found in Yeigyi and its surrounding villages (and possibly in most of Upper Burma). In these villages it is believed that, lonely for human contacts, an *ouktazaun* may employ two strategems to escape her solitary fate. She may attempt, in the first place, to kill a human being, for by doing so she and her victim exchange places: the *ouktazaun* becomes a human and the human becomes an *ouktazaun*. The simplest and most frequent way by which this exchange can be achieved is for the *ouktazaun,* in the guise of a human, to lure her potential victim to a lonely spot by the promise or sight of great treasure, and then to kill him. Periodically one hears of cases of apparently typical human beings, married and with children, who—it later turned out—were really *ouktazauns*. This method of seeking human relationships is limited, however, because the *ouktazaun* can remain in the human abode for only a short time, typically for a twenty-year period, before she must again return to her previous state.

A second technique employed by an *ouktazaun* for establishing a human relationship, one which results in a relatively permanent bond, is to assume the guise of a human being and thereby entice a man into falling in love with her. If, then, she can seduce her hopeful lover, the latter automatically dies and, becoming her spouse, shares with her the task of guarding the treasures.[4] The seductive attractions of the *ouktazauns* are often so great that, despite the victim's knowledge that he will die should he succumb to her charms, he frequently requires the assistance of potent amulets and other forms of magical power to overcome his temptations.[5]

The case we are concerned with here is that of Kou Swe, a man in his early thirties. Walking home alone at dusk, he was passing a hill known to be the haunt of nats and spirits when he saw a beautiful woman wearing a light green blouse. Walking up to her, he put his arms about her waist and then proceeded to caress her, kissing her on the lips and breasts

[3]The Buddha Maitreya (Burmese, Arimadeiya) is to appear, according to Buddhist folk belief, five thousand years after the death of the present Buddha, Gautama.

[4]The belief that illness, if not death, can be caused by the seduction of spirits in the guise of handsome young men or of beautiful maidens is also found in Ceylon (cf. Wijesekera 1949:154).

[5]There is the well known case in Mandalay of a young man who, in order to resist the seductive powers of an *ouktazaun* whom he first encountered a few years ago, wears scores of amulets about his neck and is tatooed with a special protective symbol once every month. His father, a wealthy rice merchant, is a graduate of one of Burma's best mission high schools.

and "touching her all over." They did not, however, have sexual intercourse. While embracing her, Kou Swe developed gooseflesh, and he
thereby realized that, despite her appearance, she was not really human.
Suddenly, in the midst of their lovemaking, she vanished, only to reappear
near the summit of the hill and to beckon him to follow her. When, in
addition to this magiclike disappearance and reappearance, she informed
him that she was the Guardian of the Hill, Kou Swe knew that she was an
ouktazaun, and refused to follow her. Frightened and yet attracted, he
returned to his home, but because of acute embarassment he told no one
of his encounter. It was not until a month later, awakening at night with
severe abdominal pains, and fearing that the *ouktazaun* had stolen his
soul (and permanent soul loss means death), that he went directly to the
local exorcist to recount his story.

But that entire month had been a period of great suffering for Kou
Swe. Unable to forget the *ouktazaun*, seeing her image before him day
and night, and filled with an obsessive desire to make love to her, he was
in constant turmoil. He was unable to sleep, to eat, even to work. Sometimes he would fall into unconsciousness. But there were other signs as
well that he had "become like a madman." To forget her, he turned to
drink, going on a month-long binge. Daily he went to the nearest saloon,
about five miles from Yeigyi, where, either alone or in the company of
friends, he would get drunk. This being an expensive venture—he went
through K130 (about $30) in one month—he was forced to sell his bull
in order to obtain funds for his drinking. A farmer who sells his only bull
is "truly mad." It was not his madness, however, which led Kou Swe to
seek therapy, but his fear that, if he could not extricate himself from the
ouktazaun, he would die.

A MOTIVATIONAL EXPLANATION

Here, then, we have five different cases of obvious psychological disturbance, all believed to have been supernaturally caused. In some cases the
offending supernatural was a witch, in others a nat. In some, the patient's
symptoms were attributed to supernatural possession; in one, to supernatural influence brought about by a physical encounter with the supernatural. In attempting to explain these cases, we must not only attend to
the general question of supernatural attack/possession, but we must consider a number of specific questions. Why, in cases 1 and 4, did the
patients become unconscious and/or fall into simple trance? And why, in
case 1, did the patient, acting as a medium in the exorcistic seance, attribute
her behavior to possession by a witch, while in case 4, it was a practitioner,
rather than the patient—the patient himself could not account for his
behavior—who attributed his behavior to possession by a nat?

Why, in cases 3 and 4, did the patients engage in acts of violence and aggression? And why, in each case did the patient either attribute his behavior to witch-possession, or, when witch-attribution was suggested by others, accept their explanation?

Finally, in case 5, why did the patient hallucinate a nat, female rather than male, who enchanted him with her beauty but who, he deeply feared, would cause his death were he to succumb to her?

It seems obvious from merely raising these questions that the events which we have described do not comprise a unitary phenomenon, and that, correspondingly, they cannot be accounted for by a unitary explanation. It would seem, rather, that these events, which the Burmese attribute to supernatural attack (whether interpreted as possession by, or encounter with, a supernatural), are attributable, psychologically viewed, to a variety of motives. Unfortunately, in most cases my data are too scanty to allow me to do more than offer some tentative suggestions. Thus, for example, I have no physiological measures for the patients whose cases have been presented here—and I assume that susceptibility to dissociational and hallucinatory states is a function of differential physiological thresholds. Moreover, I have almost no data on the early history of these patients— and I assume that these psychic events have their roots in early experience. Finally, and most importantly, I have only the barest information concerning those life-history data which, theoretically, could have been expected to trigger these events. Nevertheless, when these admittedly poor data are filtered through contemporary theories of psychopathology, some tentative explanations at least can be offered for these cases. First, then, I shall outline the motivational theory on which these explanations will be based, following which I shall examine these cases with reference to this theory.

On the assumption that behavior is instigated by some stimulus, any theory of dissociational and hallucinatory behavior must, first, identify the conditions (the stimulus or class of stimuli) by which these types of behavior are instigated and, second, it must indicate how, as responses to these conditions, they enable the personality to cope with them. Whatever these instigating conditions might be, it is obvious a) that in the case of unconsciousness and simple trance the instigations are sufficiently traumatic so that the personality can cope with them only by avoiding them, i.e., by falling into unconsciousness; b) that in the case of trance accompanied by acting-out behavior, they can be coped with only if the actor is unaware of his own behavior, and c) that in the case of hallucination, the actor has no way of coping with them except through fantasy. I would tentatively suggest, then, a) that avoidance (unconsciousness, simple trance) is motivated by intense fear or intense shame; b) that behavior of which the actor is unaware (acting-out in trance) is similarly motivated; that fantasied objects (hallucinations), c) if satisfying, are motivated by needs unsatisfied by reality, and d) if frightening, are motivated by unresolved anxiety.

On the basis of these suggestions, I would interpret both hallucinatory and dissociational behavior as defense mechanisms by which inner conflict is expressed and/or resolved. When forbidden, shameful, or other anxiety-producing stimuli, either external or internal, threaten to overwhelm the personality (usually because the counter, i.e., repressive, forces are not sufficiently strong), there are a limited number of ways in which the resultant trauma can be obviated. Among these are to be included unconscious states, which preclude conscious registration of external stimuli; trance, which permits direct, albeit unconscious, satisfaction of internal stimuli (needs); and hallucination, which allows the needs conscious satisfaction, but only through cognitive distortion (fantasy). Anxiety-arousing hallucinations (encounters with ghosts or evil nats) would seem, at first, to defy this theoretical scheme. If these hallucinations are viewed as projections (externalizations) of inner dysphoric-producing states (guilt, hostility, etc.), however, they can also be encompassed within this scheme: externalized forces are more easily coped with than inner pressures.

This, then, is the general theory on which the following explanations for the dissociative and hallucinatory cases examined in the previous section—and, presumably, for similar cases of psychopathology attributed to supernatural causation—are based. Although the field data, as I have already indicated, are much too scanty to allow a complete explanation of these cases, it is possible at least to indicate the usefulness of the theory in alerting us to those experiences (precipitating conditions) in the lives of the patients which seem to have triggered the onset of illness.

In all five cases described above, the precipitating factor appears to have been frustration, shame, fear, or guilt; and in four of the five, these conditions seem to have been rooted in a sexual relationship. In case 1 (the case of the seventeen-year-old bewitched girl) the witch—i.e., the girl's unconscious—stated during the exorcistic seance that she was angered by the girl's refusal to continue to live with her, and that she was jealous of the new friends with whom the girl now preferred to live. In attempting to reconstruct this case I discovered that the girl had lost her mother when she was only eight years old, and that, following her mother's death, she had been raised by a foster mother, the putative witch. Shortly before her first alleged bewitchment, the girl had decided to move from the home of her foster mother to the home of friends. (During the seance some of the audience insisted that the witch was angered not so much by the girl's departure, in itself, as by her consequent refusal to marry the witch's son. I am more inclined to accept the witch's [the girl's] own explanation). Here, then, we are presented with an explanation consistent with the theoretical model. The girl, guilty because of her ingratitude to her foster mother, fears that the latter, offended by her ingratitude, will retaliate. Gradually, by the process of paranoid projection described in Chapter 5, she begins to perceive her as a witch. This perception arouses in her the most intense fear and, as a defense against her fright, she falls unconscious.

For case 2 (the case of multiple possession) the data are much too fragmentary for more than a guess at an explanation. It seems, however, that a young couple (two of the four patients) had fallen in love with each other, and that another couple (the other two patients) had acted as the intermediaries in their courtship. In the exorcistic seance, the witch (i.e., the patient's unconscious) stated that the patient (the male suitor) had been her lover, and that, from anger and jealousy, she had attacked them all, the lovers as well as their intermediaries. As in the previous case it would seem that the lover, having converted his former mistress into a witch by the process of paranoid projection already described, strongly fears her. As his fear mounts, he attempts to cope with the perceived threat by the defense of identification with the (perceived) aggressor. It is this identification which accounts for his aggression. Identifying with the witch—in witch-possession, the witch controls the behavior of her victim —he commits those very acts which he had imputed to her. (Although this explanation may account, too, for the behavior of his male companion, it does not account for the behavior of the two females, for which I have no explanation.)

In case 3 (the case of the young man who had suffered a multiplicity of attacks by the same witch) the record is much more complete. The patient, Maung Oun Yi, now twenty-seven, was married at the age of twenty-two to a sixteen-year-old girl. As he and his friends tell the story, his wife, after four years of marriage, committed adultery. Maung Oun Yi knew of her infidelity, yet, from shame, said nothing to anyone. His relatives, however, incensed by his wife's behavior, told him in his wife's presence that she did not really wish to live with him, and they accused her of having had two lovers, whom they named. To this Maung Oun Yi replied that, nevertheless, he would not leave his wife, for he believed that she would abandon her "immoral ways." During all of this, his wife denied that she had been unfaithful to him.

Shortly after, about to depart for an extended period of work in the jungle, Maung Oun Yi sent his wife to live with his parents so that they might watch her during his absence. Despite their surveillance, however, she began still another—her third—affair. When he returned from the jungle and was informed of her infidelity, Maung Oun Yi told his wife that, although he would not divorce her—because of his shame that others would learn of her infidelity—he would kill her if he discovered her in an adulterous act. It was almost immediately after this warning that he had his first attack; and it was because she showed no concern for him that his friends and relatives assumed that his wife, wishing finally to be rid of him, had bewitched him.

After an exorcistic seance Maung Oun Yi was cured, but four months later, shortly after his discovery that his wife had again been unfaithful, he had a second attack. (Again, his wife showed no concern for him, either during the attack or during the seance.) His third attack occurred a few months later, and the fourth came after his wife's elopement with one of her lovers and his subsequent engagement to another woman.

When I questioned him, Maung Oun Yi informed me that he and his wife had had no sexual relations between the first and second attacks, and that he had felt no sexual desire for her during that period. Upon inquiry it further turned out that, because of his weak libido, they had never had an active sex life—and it is a probably safe assumption that it was his weak sexuality, among other reasons, that had driven his wife into her adulterous affairs. But there was another, perhaps more important dimension to this case. When I asked Maung Oun Yi why he thought his wife was attempting to harm (bewitch) him, he said it was because she hated him. Only at the end of a lengthy interview did he concede that her hatred may have been provoked, at least in part, by his behavior toward her. Even before his first attack, and despite the earlier picture which he and his relatives had painted of a long-suffering husband, he had, upon learning of his wife's infidelity, beaten her severely, inflicting serious bruises upon her.[6]

Here, then, is a young man who has been rejected by his wife and publicly shamed by her blatant infidelity and the exposure of his own sexual inadequacies. Frustrated and humiliated, he beats her and even threatens to kill her. One can only assume, since his first attack occurred shortly after this threat, that his mounting violence, becoming too much to handle, was, by the paranoid process with which we are familiar, projected onto his wife. This projection of his own rage, together with his fear of her retaliation for his beating, combined to produce an especially virulent witch. As in the previous case, the patient then defended himself against his fear of the witch by identifying with her in his trance aggression. Since, unlike the last case, there are reasonably complete data for this case, we can say more. Identification with the witch not only permits the patient to defend himself against the (perceived) evil witch, but it also permits him to express his aggressive impulses with impunity. Since, that is, his behavior is taken to be the behavior of the witch, he can attack others without censure or blame; it is not he, but the witch, who is in control of his body. Thus, in trance, Maung Oun Yi attacked especially his parents and other close relatives—his earliest important frustrators. His trance-aggression seems to have been overdetermined, stemming not only from his defensive identification with the witch (projected hostility), but also from his repressed hostility to others.

In case 4 (the case of the young man possessed by nats) the precipi-

---

[6]It is at least plausible to assume that his display of aggression was overdetermined. On the one hand, it was certainly a response to the rejection and humiliation he suffered at the hands of his wife. On the other hand his wife's behavior may have evoked memories of the rejection which all Burmans experience in later childhood, and his aggressiveness may then be viewed as a response to this painful memory as well. This would explain why, in trance, his aggression was directed especially to his parents and other close relatives.

tating factor was apparently frustration and/or humiliation. The patient had fallen in love with a girl to whom he eventually became engaged. It was only after their wedding invitations had been sent that his fiancee decided that she did not love him, and then, shortly before their wedding was to have taken place, she eloped with another man. A few days after her elopement, the patient fell into the unconscious state which was interpreted as an attack by a neglected, and therefore punitive, nat. I would explain his unconsciousness and simple trance, rather, as an attempt to block out the pain of his loss and humiliation. It was not he, but a practitioner, who diagnosed his case as caused by nat neglect.

In case 5 (the hallucination of an *ouktazaun*), the precipitating factor seems to have been a combination of sexual frustration and guilt attendant upon an abortive love affair. The patient, Kou Swe, met a woman in Mandalay to whom he was enormously attracted. Although they had a number of private assignations, she discouraged all his attempts to seduce her. Greatly frustrated by her rebuffs, his interest in her had become obsessive: he dreamt of her at night and thought of her during the day. When he first encountered the *ouktazaun*, she looked very much like this woman. It was only when she abruptly disappeared that he realized that he had, instead, encountered a destructive spirit.

This seems to be a fairly straightforward case of hallucination, one, however, which is motivated by sexual frustration and guilt alike. The hallucination of a beautiful maiden, reminiscent of a desired mistress, is an obvious case of wish-fulfillment, motivated by sexual frustration. Not only was the patient able to make love to her, but—as was revealed in the exorcistic seance—instead of rejecting him, the *ouktazaun* (as she turned out to be) claimed to be in love with him, so much so that she refused to leave him.[7] But there is more to this case. Though attracted by the female spirit, and wishing to have sexual intercourse with her, Kou Swe failed in his attempt; and though she claimed that she loved him, she was nevertheless a harmful spirit who, if she succeeded in seducing him, would cause his death. In short, Kou Swe had encountered not only a beautiful, but an evil spirit,

[7]That the hallucination of a beautiful female nat may represent sexual wish-fulfillment, with the nat symbolizing the unavailable love object, is shown in other cases as well. Kou Thwin, for example, when a young man in his teens, was saying his beads late at night, while living on the Yeidigoun hill, which is guarded by the famous female nat, Yeidigoun Thakinma. While in deep concentration, his head bent forward, he became suddenly aware of a most fragrant odor which disturbed his concentration. Raising his head, he saw a beautiful young woman (whose physical appearance, clothes, and jewelry he was able to describe to me in great detail). When she noticed that he was watching her, she disappeared. She was, he said, the Yeidigoun nat. When I asked if she resembled anyone he knew, he said that in both appearance and dress she was almost identical with a young woman in the village, whom he named (and whom I knew). Later I discovered that he had long been enamoured of this young woman, but that he could not woo her because of the great gap in their social positions: he was a landless coolie, and she was the daughter of the wealthiest landowning family in the village.

one whose attraction was fatal. Since Kou Swe was a married man and the father of four children, it is not implausible to suggest that his failure to seduce the spirit, and his hallucination of a punitive spirit, were instigated by the need for punishment stemming from guilt concerning his attempted adultery. Although a frightening hallucination, the projection of an extrapunitive agent of punishment, since it can be exorcised, is a more satisfactory resolution of conflict than its intrapunitive counterpart.

We may summarize these explanations, then, as follows. The dissociative cases (the first four), by blocking out the painful stimuli, are attempts to deal either with the fear of retaliation for an offense committed against another, or with the frustration and humiliation caused by rejection; at the same time, by providing (unconscious) expression for the feelings of aggression and revenge attendant upon these painful experiences, these cases may also be viewed as attempts to cope with those feelings. The hallucinatory case (the fifth) is an attempt to deal simultaneously with the frustration of sexual rejection and with the guilt attendant upon attempted adultery. The first is handled by fantasied satisfaction of the frustrated desire; the second by the externalization of the guilt-produced punishment.

On the basis of this interpretive summary, we may once again compare this explanation with the one offered by the Burmese.

Burmese Explanation	*Scientific Explanation*
1. Mental illness is caused by supernaturals.	1. Mental illness is caused by conflict.
2. Any encounter with a supernatural—possession, perception, etc.—may cause mental illness.	2. Any encounter with a supernatural is an instance of perceptual distortion and/or hallucination. Sometimes it is, in itself, a symptom of mental illness.
3. Any encounter with a supernatural is explained in terms of motivation of the supernatural.	3. Any encounter with a supernatural is explained in terms of motivation of the patient (the desire to reduce conflict).
4. Bizarre behavior following an encounter is explained as instigated by the supernatural; it is interpreted as psychopathology.	4. Bizarre behavior following an encounter is explained as instigated by the patient; although a form of conflict resolution, it is interpreted as psychopathology.

CHAPTER ELEVEN

The Exorcistic Seance

A CASE STUDY

When a patient is believed to be possessed by a punitive supernatural, he is treated by an exorcist (*ahtelan hsaya*). Sometimes, as we have seen (see Chapter 9), exorcism is achieved by ritual alone; sometimes, however, it requires as well a direct confrontation between exorcist and supernatural. To accomplish this end the exorcist induces the supernatural to possess the patient, who then serves as his medium. This chapter examines a series of such ceremonies which were conducted for one patient, Kou Swe, an alleged victim of an *ouktazaun* (see Chapter 10, pp. 165–67 for the details of this case).

To be loved by an *ouktazaun*, it will be recalled, results in the death of her victim should he succumb to her enticements and have sexual intercourse with her. Hence, the exorcistic aim in these cases is to separate the soul of the *ouktazaun* from that of her victim. When this is achieved, the patient is no longer infatuated with her, and his life is spared. When Kou Swe first brought his case to an exorcist resident in Yeigyi, the latter ordered the *ouktazaun* to remain on Kou Swe's palm and not to enter his body, a temporary measure designed to prevent the patient from being seriously harmed until the exorcistic ceremony could be performed. The ceremony took place two days later when the ritual objects, purchased by Kou Swe, were assembled.

The First Ceremony

When I arrived at Kou Swe's home, the ritual elements were arranged on the mat on which the exorcist and his patient were to sit. They included the traditional offering (*kadaw pwe*), a coconut adjoined to two bunches of bananas, a set of fourteen candles arranged in front of the offering, and a cabbalistic drawing (*in*) of the Buddha attached to it—all placed on a white cotton cloth measuring about two yards. The cloth is for the Buddhist supernaturals to sit on when they are invoked.

Upon our arrival, only Kou Swe, his wife, and a friend were present in the house. As time passed and word was received that the exorcism was to take place, others began to assemble, so that by late afternoon, after the ceremony had begun, the house was filled with people and scores of others had to be content with watching the proceedings through the window.

The ceremony began with exorcist and patient making obeisance to the Buddha and then jointly reciting the Buddhist precepts.[1] This was followed by a silent prayer intoned by the exorcist, a public prayer asking that the patient be free from all harm (including the harm caused by witches, nats, and all evil spirits), and then another silent prayer. Then, seizing the hand of Kou Swe, the exorcist spat on it after uttering a spell (*gahta*). Following this, he sought the aid of a number of *devas*[2] and *weikzas*[3] by invoking their presence. When his hand began to shake he knew they had arrived. Assured of the presence of his supernatural helpers, the exorcist placed a small (one to two inches) stone carving of an ox in front of the lighted candles, and then, with a small knife, he ground tiny filings from a small stone bull carving into a cup of water, all the while chanting a spell. Beginning with the magical, *Oum!*, the spell invoked the glory of the five Buddhas (the four who have already appeared, and the future Buddha, Arimadeiya) as protection for patient and exorcist; the assistance of all the *samma devas* was requested with the promise that the exorcist will perform acts of merit; and their combined power was then invoked to destroy and excise all harm caused by "tyrants," "fire," and evil nats.

With the conclusion of the spell, a powerful rite was performed. Lighting a match to the cabbalistic drawing (*in*) of the Buddha which was

[1]The precepts (*thilas*) include injunctions against lying, stealing, killing, drinking intoxicating liquor, and adultery.

[2]In addition to Thagya Min, or Sakka, he invokes the following *devas*: Bezapeteitha, Wirunatha, Idanatha, Ingiratha, Tatayala, Widudaga, Winpaka, and Kuweiri—nine altogether. (Nine is a magical number.)

[3]*Weikzas*, it will be recalled, are humans who have acquired supernatural power of various kinds, including the power of prolonging their lives until the advent of the future Buddha, when they will enter nirvana. In this ceremony, the exorcist invokes sixty-four *weikzas*, including representatives of three of the four major types—*in*, iron, mercury—and also including his own Master, who is now a *weikza*.

attached to the coconut-banana offering, the exorcist collected the ashes in a cup, mixed them thoroughly with his finger, added water, and sprinkled the resulting mixture on Kou Swe while intoning silent spells.[4] The sprinkling of this magical symbol on the patient provided him with a most powerful protective talisman. The exorcist now had the patient drink the cup of water, which was mixed with the stone filings of the bull

[4]This *in* was somewhat different from the usual type, consisting of a drawing of the seated Buddha, made with only nine strokes, each stroke, except for the connecting lines, forming a letter of the Burmese alphabet. Thus his left eye is the letter *da*; his right eye, *da*; his mouth, *ba*; his face, *wa*. The nine strokes represent the nine

FIGURE 3.   *Magical Buddha image constructed by use of nine strokes.*

"virtues" (*goundaws*) of the Buddha. These are: purified of all impurities, a Supreme (in contrast to a silent) Buddha, possessing supernormal powers, blissful, world-knower, pointer of the truth, master of gods and men, supremely enlightened, Lord of the six powers.

But the magical symbolism of this *in* does not end here. In addition, each stroke, beginning with the first and continuing through the ninth, symbolizes the nine sacred objects, each of which exists in multiples of one through nine, respectively. Thus, 1 = Mt. Meru (the center of this world), 2 = the sun and the moon, 3 = the Tripitika (the three "baskets" comprising the Buddhist scriptures), 4 = the four islands (surrounding Mt. Meru), 5 = the Five Buddhas, 6 = the six halos of the Buddha, 7 = the Buzin Sutta, 8 = the Noble Eightfold Path, 9 = the nine virtues (*goundaws*) of the Buddha.

This is a most powerful *in*, so powerful that U Aung, a famous *weikza*, achieved his supernatural powers merely by drawing this magical Buddha and reciting aloud the consonants by which the head alone is constructed.

Ins are used therapeutically in other Asian societies as well. In China, for example, the Changtienssu Taoists employ them as part of a ritual almost identical with the one described here. (Cf. Goullart 1941:142.)

carving. This concoction conferred yet additional magical power on the patient.[5]

When Kou Swe had emptied the cup, the exorcist completed the ceremony with an exorcistic command (known as *ameindawpyan*) by which power the *ouktazaun's* soul is driven from the patient's body.

To all the *samma* and *brahma devas* of the sky heavens; to all the ghosts, monsters, and other evil creatures; to the ogres of the earth; to the master witches and the wizards; to the evil nats and to the *ouktazauns*: I command you to leave. I command you by the glory of the Triple Gems [Buddha, Dhamma, and Sangha].

With the ceremony concluded, Kou Swe appeared to be very tired. When I asked him how he felt he first smiled wanly, then, suddenly, he burst into sobs, thereby indicating (this at least is how it was interpreted) that the ceremony had not been successful, that the spirit was not yet exorcized. The exorcist immediately addressed the spirit: "Why have you come to Kou Swe? There is no basis for a relationship between you. It is now time for you to leave his body. Your love for him is not reciprocated." He ordered her to show a sign that she was leaving Kou Swe's body—the sign being that his middle finger tremble. "Must there be enmity between you and me? Or will you leave voluntarily?" At this, Kou Swe, whose behavior was now taken to be the behavior of the possessing *ouktazaun*, raised two fingers, the index and middle fingers pressed together. This meant, explained the exorcist to the assembled group, that she still loved him; as long as the fingers remain together, the soul of Kou Swe and the *ouktazaun* are united. Only when the fingers separate can it be assumed that her soul has departed.

Since the fingers did not separate, the exorcist announced that he would have to expel her by force. He now ordered all the *samma devas* to drive out the *ouktazaun*, to separate her soul from Kou Swe's. After spitting on Kou Swe's hand, which is a gross insult to the spirit, he repeated over and over again, "Kwe!" "Kwe!"—"Separate," "Separate." Then, after inserting a thin stick between Kou Swe's two fingers—which is taken to mean that the fingers are now separating—he announced that gradually Kou Swe will be alright. To make sure, however, he again asked the *samma devas* to protect Kou Swe, and by reciting the Buddhist statement of faith—"I take refuge in the Buddha; I take refuge in the Dhamma; I take refuge in the Sangha"—he again exorcized all the evil spirits.

While the exorcist was reciting this exorcistic formula, Kou Swe, without warning—and this time obviously in trance—leaped backward from the platform on which he and the exorcist were sitting and fell to the floor.

---

[5]The bull is a powerful figure in Burmese thought. Magical drawings of bulls, placed near the Buddha image in the family shrine, are believed, it will be recalled (Chapter 3, pg. 36), to have great protective powers.

(The men lifted him from the floor, and placed him back on the platform.) With Kou Swe lying on his side, the exorcist, using him as a medium, addressed the *ouktazaun.*

> *Exorcist:* What kind of trouble do you intend to cause? Whatever you have to say, say it now. Are you listening to me? Do you dare to disobey me? Tell me, will you leave this body? I am trying to deal with you gently, softly. I am not trying to harm you. *(This is said in gentle, soft tones, but with an imperative ring.)*
>
> *Patient:* I love Kou Swe.
>
> *E.:* Why don't you go? If you remain you will meet danger, danger of water, of fire, and of all other evils.
>
> *P.:* I love Kou Swe.
>
> *E.:* If you disobey me, I'll have you put to death.
>
> *P.:* I will go back later, but not now. I have something to say before I go.
>
> *E.:* I want no speech from you. Go now. Don't make me angry. Where do you live? Aren't you going to return?
>
> *P.:* I live on Yankintaun hill [the hill near which Kou Swe had first encountered her].[6]

There was a lull in the exchange; Kou Swe continued to lie on his side; neither he nor the exorcist spoke. There was conversation among the spectators, however, who understandably offered various explanations for the events they had just witnessed.

After a few moments, as the exorcist, hoping to resume the ceremony, took a piece of thread and spat on it, the *ouktazaun*, speaking through Kou Swe, began to talk. "I cannot leave here alone. Kou Swe must follow me." "If you take him," the exorcist replied, "I will kill you." Then, after asking all the *samma devas* and the *weikzas* to drive her away, he held the string over Kou Swe's head and spat on the floor. He recited a spell (which I was unable to record) over the string, and then asked the *samma devas* to protect Kou Swe, "as a father protects his child." Spitting again, he tied the string, now an amulet, around Kou Swe's neck.

With this—at 5:45 P.M., and almost one hour and a half after the ceremony had begun—he seemed to have concluded, and all of us began to talk again. (During the conversation the exorcist announced that ordinarily this treatment would have commanded a fee of K70, about $15. Because, however, of his love for Kou Swe, he would charge only a nominal fee.) Our conversation was suddenly interrupted when the *ouktazaun* announced again that Kou Swe must leave with her; at this Kou Swe began to weep. The exorcist said she must go alone, but she said:

> *P.:* I can't go. I love him deeply. How can I go?
>
> *E.:* You must think of him as a brother, not as a husband. Why do you

---

[6]The exchange reported here is a collapsed version of a prolonged and highly repetitious conversation between exorcist and *ouktazaun* from which most repetitions have been eliminated.

love him so much? Separate! Separate! Divorce! Divorce! Separate the souls instantly! *(After asking the* samma devas *to separate the souls, he continues.)* You are an *ouktazaun,* and hence classified with the animals. Kou Swe is a human being; he must observe the Buddhist precepts and protect the Buddhist church. You are classified with the animals, so you do not have these obligations. Go away! All human beings contemplate the glory of the Buddha. You don't. I have been patient with you because of my love [*myitta*]. Everything is impermanent; everything is compounded [two central doctrines of Buddhist ontology]. Though you are an animal, you too know the meaning of the precepts. There is no time: go soon. *(And now the left hand of the exorcist begins to tremble automatically.)*

P.: I am going, but I want to take Kou Swe with me.

With that, with "I want to take Kou Swe with me," Kou Swe became agitated and leaped to his feet. Restrained by the men sitting beside him, he eluded their grasp and attempted to jump through the open window but was brought, struggling, to the floor. As he attempted to go through the window, the exorcist spat on him, ordering the *ouktazaun,* "not only in my own name, but in the names of the Buddha and the *samma devas,*" to leave Kou Swe alone. "Kou Swe is the son of the *devas* and the *weikzas* so why should he follow you?" He then remonstrated with the guardian nats: "Why, Mahagiri (the house nat), do you allow her to enter the house? Why, Myinbyushin (the village nat) do you allow her to come into the village?"

It was now 6:00 P.M. and quiet. Kou Swe turned on his back, and the exorcist told him to give thought to the Buddha and the Buddha image. Kou Swe said that he would like to give his handkerchief, which he had been clutching throughout the ceremony, as a gift to the *ouktazaun.* (The handkerchief, in Burma, is a love symbol. In the Burmese drama, the hero and heroine hold a handkerchief to symbolize their love.) His hand, holding the handkerchief, was trembling acutely. Saying that this is prohibited by Buddhism, the exorcist talked again to the *ouktazaun*: "Don't think about this or that; someday everyone must die. I'm not partial, I'm treating you impartially. But you are an animal, and he's a human being. Kou Swe is in the inner circle of the Buddhist church, but you are an animal." He then chanted the *thamboutei,* a prayer which is believed to possess enormous power.[7] With this, he again ordered the *ouktazaun* to depart.

Kou Swe held up his handkerchief, apparently showing it to the *oukta-*

---

[7]The following is a rough translation: "With bowed head, I do homage to twelve, twenty-eight, one thousand, five thousand, and seven thousand Buddhas; to innumerable Buddhas whose number is as the grains of sand along the Ganges; to the Buddhas, the Conquerors, who have attained nirvana.

"With deep respect, I do homage, too, to the Doctrine and to the Monastic Order.

"By the power of this homage, may I attain the power to discard this body! And (by his power) may all calamities be banished without residue!"

zaun. The exorcist continued: "The Buddha has taught that there should be no attachment of mind. Therefore do not love him, detach yourself! You are spirit, he is a human being. These are the orders of the Buddha." (These sentiments and this command were uttered, more or less in the same form, over and over again.)

Kou Swe covered his eyes with the handkerchief. The exorcist said: "Don't be ashamed. Don't cover yourself with the handkerchief. He is a son of the Buddha, the *devas*, and the Church. The Buddha prohibits him from giving you the handkerchief." When the *ouktazaun* replied that she wanted Kou Swe to return with her, the exorcist, dismissing her request, said, "Think of him as a brother, not as a husband."

It was now 6:15. Again the *ouktazaun* said that she loved Kou Swe and again the exorcist ordered her to depart. He sprinkled more water on Kou Swe and recited yet another incantation. He then informed us that the ceremony would probably continue late into the night, for "it's not a simple case." And he repeated what he had told us earlier, that despite the complexity of the case, he would ask only for a small fee because he loves Kou Swe.

At 6:20 Kou Swe stirred and waved his handkerchief; the *ouktazaun* repeated that she would not leave without him. Suddenly Kou Swe again leaped toward the window, and this time it required five men to hold him down. While struggling the *ouktazaun* shouted, "I won't go without him; I want to live with him." The exorcist asked what she wanted with Kou Swe. Did she wish to give him gold? She replied that Kou Swe wanted no gold. Then she shouted, "There is no Buddha!" And Kou Swe began to weep. The exorcist said, "Kou Swe is married. He has a wife and children. Why do you interfere? Go away; it is not proper for you to love him."

At 6:40 Kou Swe turned from his side to his back, still clutching the handkerchief. Now his hand began to tremble, and he rubbed the handkerchief over the thigh and buttock of the young man sitting next to him, in a manner, I was later informed, suggesting the caress of a lover. Then he waved the handkerchief in the air and touched the ceremonial coconut with it.

At 6:50 he again attempted to leap up—and again he was restrained by force. He shouted, "I want to give her the handkerchief." The exorcist said, "Throw it away. What has she given you?"—that he, Kou Swe, should feel obligated to reciprocate. To this, Kou Swe held up two fingers (indicating that he wished to copulate with her), and he continued to hold them up for almost five minutes, after which he moved, waved the handkerchief, rubbed it on the arm of a young man, and placed it over his eyes. The *ouktazaun* spoke again, saying that she loved Kou Swe—so why would she harm him?—and that she only wanted him to live with her. She concluded by saying that she would call him to her in two months (which meant, in effect, that in two months he must die).

At 7:05 Kou Swe held his abdomen and the *ouktazaun* announced that she had stomach pains. The exorcist said he felt sorry for her, but that nevertheless she must go. She repeated her determination not to go without Kou Swe, and the exorcist repeated his admonition. Kou Swe moaned, waved his handkerchief, and rolled over on his stomach. Again, he waved his handkerchief while the exorcist continued to talk, and again he held up his two fingers.

At 7:10 Kou Swe again tried to leap through the window; again he was restrained by six men; and again the exorcist spat on him. Once more he tried—and once more he was restrained. He repeated his desire to return with the *ouktazaun.*

At 7:15 Kou Swe sat up, and the *ouktazaun* asked him to accompany her to her abode. Kou Swe told her to take his handkerchief, and she muttered, "Suffering, suffering" (*doukka, doukka*). Kou Swe continued to wave the handkerchief while the exorcist asked the *samma devas* to drive the *ouktazaun* away.

At 7:20 Kou Swe once more held up two fingers, and once more the *ouktazaun* said that in two months he would have to follow her. To this the exorcist retorted that Kou Swe is the son of the Buddha, and she cannot do this to him. When she replied that Kou Swe had promised to join her in two months, the exorcist told her that he will prevent this, if need be, by putting Kou Swe into the Yellow Robe. (It is firmly believed that nats and other evil spirits have no power to harm a Buddhist monk.) Kou Swe then held up ten fingers, and the *ouktazaun* said that, if she must return alone, she would not return until 10:00, and if the exorcist wanted her to return now, she would only go if she could take Kou Swe with her. The exorcist then asked her name and age. Her name, she said, is Khindi and she is thirty years old. With this Kou Swe appeared to fall asleep, and there was a brief respite in the proceedings.

During the respite the audience discussed various aspects of the case. There seemed to be consensus within the group that Kou Swe's problems arose at the very onset of his encounter with the *ouktazaun*, when he attempted to embrace her; instead, he should only have asked her for gold. Various and conflicting opinions were expressed about what he did, what he should have done, what he should not have done, and so on. Suddenly, while these discussions were going on, Kou Swe awakened and tried to leap from his mat, but he was restrained by the men sitting at his side.

By this time—7:45—the ceremony had lasted more than three hours, and many people were beginning to express doubts about the exorcist's power to handle this case. A village elder indicated his doubts to the exorcist himself, asking him why he could not once and for all cure Kou Swe. Before the exorcist could reply, Kou Swe attempted mightily to leap up. There ensued a desperate struggle in which, although he was pitted against six men, it seemed as if Kou Swe might break away. The exorcist, in great anger, slapped Kou Swe's head to the floor.[8] (In theory the exorcist, of course, is slapping the *ouktazaun*, not the patient). This served only to intensify the struggle, which continued for another seven minutes before Kou Swe was subdued. While the struggle was going on, the *ouktazaun* turned her wrath on the exorcist: "Who is this exorcist? Beat him! Why did he beat me? Why did he beat me on the head? The exorcist is impious, that's why he commits evil deeds."

It was then that Kou Swe electrified the audience by announcing that the guardian nat of Yankintaun hill had arrived. This meant that the *ouktazaun* herself, and not merely her soul, was present. With this announcement, everyone's mood was drastically changed. For most of the ceremony, even during Kou Swe's violent episodes, the people had shown few signs of awe or fear; they had talked, whispered, and even laughed at some of the conversations between the exorcist and the *ouktazaun*. Now, however, everyone, including the exorcist, seemed genuinely frightened. Some even suggested asking the village monks to intervene in the case. Others said this was too drastic a step, but even they agreed that a more powerful exorcist was now required. The exorcist himself was bathed in perspiration, a sure sign, so I was told, that he was too frightened to continue. Hence, at 8:15, almost four hours after the ceremony had begun, the headman and some village elders asked me if I would drive them to the township seat, about five miles away, to bring a very powerful and well known exorcist into the case. They had already discussed this with the present exorcist and with Kou Swe's wife, both of whom had given their permission. At 8:15 we drove off, and at 10:15 we returned with the exorcist.

Before describing the new ceremony, and in order to place it in context, it is important to relate the events that occurred during the two hours that elapsed between our departure and return. I shall first relate what happened in Kou Swe's house during our absence,[9] and then describe what happened to those of us who went to fetch the exorcist.

During our absence many people went to their homes to await our return, but five or six men (sitting together on one side of the room) and three women (sitting on another side of the room with Kou Swe's wife) remained. Kou Swe, who had now regained consciousness, remained seated on the platform. A small group of women and children remained outside the house, watching through the opened windows. Almost immediately after we left, a cousin of Kou Swe tried to persuade him to become

---

[8]Goullart describes an almost identical scene in a case of Chinese exorcism. Other aspects of the two ceremonies are remarkably similar as well (Goullart 1941:86–89).

[9]These were observed and recorded by my excellent Burmese assistant, U Aung Thein, of Rangoon University.

a monk for two months and thereby gain immunity from the *ouktazaun's* power. (The *ouktazaun*, it will be remembered, said she would call Kou Swe in two months.) So that Kou Swe would not be lonely, he volunteered to enter a monastery with him. Although his wife approved of the suggestion, Kou Swe remained adamant, insisting that since nothing untoward had happened to him, this measure was not necessary. He also said that he had overheard the discussion about the calling of a new exorcist, and that he was opposed to it: he had faith in his own exorcist, and anyway he could not afford any more fees. His cousin advised him not to worry about the fee; it would be taken care of. But to no avail.

As the conversation took a new turn, Kou Swe continued to be agitated. He paced up and down the house for some time before returning to his place on the platform. Standing up, he took some bananas from the ceremonial offering, saying he would destroy them so that the new exorcist would not be able to treat him; he would permit only his own exorcist to treat him. With this, he plucked a number of bananas from their stalk, inviting the people in the house to eat them, while he himself devoured three. The exorcist, too, ate some bananas, saying that, since they were part of the offering, they would protect their eaters from danger. He also explained that having missed his dinner in order to treat Kou Swe, he was now rather hungry. Hearing this, Kou Swe asked his wife if she had prepared a meal for the exorcist. She replied that the food had become cold, and she asked him to wait until she could rewarm it.

While his wife was warming the food, Kou Swe asked what had transpired during those parts of the ceremony for which he had been unconscious. In answering the question, his younger brother stressed especially his violent reaction to being slapped by the exorcist and his personal abuse of him. Kou Swe said he was humiliated at the thought of the pain he had caused the exorcist, and prostrating himself before him three times, he asked his forgiveness. The exorcist said that he had not taken Kou Swe's words as insulting because it was not he, but the *ouktazaun*, who had spoken. He then blessed Kou Swe with the traditional blessing: that he might be healthy and free from evil, and enjoy a long life of honor, fame, and respect.

Kou Swe, obviously touched by these remarks, went to a cupboard and, removing a small bottle and a package, placed them on the table in front of the exorcist. In the package were ten molds (*loun*) used by alchemists for firing their "stones" (*datloun*), and he gave two of these to the exorcist, a part-time alchemist. The remaining molds and the bottle (containing mercury) he would offer, he said, to "his" monk, a serious alchemist. This led to a general discussion of alchemy, which continued for some time while the exorcist ate his meal.

The conversation then returned to *ouktazauns*: what they were like, where they lived, what they did, and so forth. There was an especially prolonged debate as to whether or not an *ouktazaun* might live in a monastic ordination hall (*thein*). The exorcist argued against this possibility, saying that this was why Kou Swe should become a monk for two months.

Kou Swe, in the meantime, was becoming "excited." He paced up and down the house, seemingly looking for something; returned to his platform, where he would stare into the corner; and then walked out of the house—a pattern which he repeated a number of times. His wife, becoming worried, asked his brother to keep an eye on him. When the exorcist walked over to sit next to him, Kou Swe again told him that he wanted to be cured by him alone, and that bringing in another would only complicate the situation. It was at this moment that we returned in the car with the new exorcist.

This new arrival was quite different from his predecessor. Whereas the first exorcist was a mild, insecure-looking man in his fifties, a landless, agricultural worker, the new exorcist was a man in his thirties, a sergeant in the national police force, who gave the appearance of complete self-assurance and confidence. He was greeted with the deference worthy of a man who combines both secular and spiritual power, and who is sufficiently important to have been accompanied by the township officer and his retinue. As he walked into the house, his very costume symbolized his dual source of power and authority. His police revolver dangled from his hip; in his right hand he held the exorcist's wand; and with his left hand he fingered the rosary which hung from his neck. After obtaining permission from Kou Swe's wife and from the first exorcist to handle the case, he proceeded to the platform, where Kou Swe was sitting, to begin the ceremony.

Before describing the ceremony, however, it is necessary to render a brief account of our journey to and from the exorcist's home. While driving to the home of the exorcist, the men expressed persistent concern that the *ouktazaun* might attempt to prevent our safe return. When we arrived at our destination, the exorcist, although agreeing to accompany us, expressed the same concern. Their concern, as we have already seen (Chapter 5, pp. 87–88), was justified: the car in which the exorcist and township officer were riding turned over into a ditch and both men were injured.

The attribution of the accident to the malevolence of the *ouktazaun* was inevitable, reinforcing a conviction already held that we were dealing with an especially powerful and greatly to be feared nat. When we returned, this new encounter with the *ouktazaun* was described to the assembled group, so that it was with heightened feeling and hushed expectancy that, at 10:30—six hours after the beginning of the first ceremony—the new ceremony began.

The Second Ceremony

As the exorcist climbed onto the platform and sat beside him, Kou Swe said he did not want him to treat him; the former said he would make an attempt anyway. Together they worshiped the Buddha, and recited the Precepts. Then, sitting cross-legged before Kou Swe, and with an air of both compassion and assurance, the exorcist placed his hand on Kou Swe's head and instructed him to kneel before him. Kou Swe looked as if he was about to go into trance. The exorcist talked to Kou Swe but received no answer. He instructed the *ouktazaun* to possess Kou Swe, so he might talk with her. Asking her why she wished to harm Kou Swe, he continued:

Exorcist: I will not mistreat you, sister, just tell me the truth.
Patient: I want to call the soul of Kou Swe.
E.: When I call you, sister, can you remain where you are?
P.: No, I must come if you call.
E.: If I mistreat you, is it justified?
P.: No.
E.: By the same token, if you call Kou Swe without the consent of his wife, it is not justified, is it? I am an Embryo Buddha,[10] answer me!
P.: In two months I shall call him to me.
E.: When I offer to share my merit with others,[11] don't you hear me? I always share my merit with others. I have erected a pagoda with jewels in it, and I have shared that merit too. . . . Don't interfere with me in the future [as she did when she caused the auto accident which almost prevented his arrival]. I am an Embryo Buddha; I don't wish to mistreat a spirit. Why did you cause my car to go over the embankment? I am powerful. Do you see all my followers?
P.: I will let Kou Swe send me back, but nobody else [i.e., I shall go back if he accompanies me].
E.: Is that justified? If you really love him, give him your help. Release his soul. (*To this, Kou Swe began making signs with his hands, as if speaking a sign language.*) Don't talk with signs, tell me with your mouth.
P.: I will do what you say.
E.: I will have you drink an oath that you will not return.[12]
P.: I have to think about it.
E.: If you drink the oath, you can attain nirvana. If you will obey me, you can attain nirvana. Before that you will also be able to see the

[10]The Embryo Buddha (*Paya-Laun*) is one who, after numerous rebirths, will achieve Buddhahood. He is, in short, a future Buddha. Although many Burmans aspire to this status, few admit that they are actively striving for it, and fewer would admit that they have achieved it.

[11]At the conclusion of Buddhist ceremonies, by which, of course, the actor acquires personal merit, a ritual formula (known as *amhya wei*) is recited in which the actors share their merit with all creatures, even including nats.

[12]Oaths are sealed in Burma by drinking a cup of water, a process known as the "oath of libation." Once the water is consumed, the oath is sealed, and automatic punitive consequences attend its violation.

Future Buddha. You [as an *ouktazaun*] are not capable of performing meritorious deeds (by which you can achieve a better rebirth).
We [humans] can do so. Therefore obey me so that [sharing my
merit with you] you will be able to go to a better abode. Think upon
the Triple Gems and the nine Virtues [*goundaws*], and do no evil to
human beings. *(Throughout his talk he keeps asking her if she
understands him, if she agrees with him, and to these questons, Kou
Swe consistently nods his head in the affirmative.)* Now, will you
drink this water [by which you take the oath to comply with my
command]?

P.: Yes, I will drink it. *(He nods his head, indicating that he will do so.
Throughout this colloquy, Kou Swe has his hands in front of his
bowed face, the pose adopted when worshiping the Buddha or a
sacred Buddhist object.)*

E.: Faith is for kings, promise is for humans [i.e., you must promise
that you will do so, rather than expect me to accept it on faith]. You
must promise to do so—not to me, but to the Buddha. Do not lie
to the Buddha. *(The exorcist then passes the cup of water to Kou
Swe, who is now swaying back and forth and perspiring profusely.
I was later informed by the men sitting with him on the platform
that, although Kou Swe was dripping with perspiration, his body
was cold—literally, a cold sweat.)* Repeat after me: "I will not interfere with this young man in the future. If I do interfere may I go
to hell, forever. If I keep my promise, then, at the advent of the
future Buddha, may I be the first to worship him." *(The exorcist
recites the promise, sentence by sentence, and Kou Swe—i.e., the
ouktazaun—repeats each sentence after him. The man sitting next to
me observed that each sentence was repeated, word perfect, by the
ouktazaun, except for the warning about hell, when she omitted the
word, "forever.")*

P.: Don't ask me where I live, but tell me: must I change my abode
after drinking the water?

E.: No.

With this, Kou Swe emptied the cup in one gulp, and was then ordered
by the exorcist to do obeisance—to prostrate himself three times—to him
(signifying the *ouktazaun's* recognition of his power and authority), to
Sarasvati—following which the *ouktazaun* said, "Well done, well done"
(*dadu, dadu*)—and to the exorcist's monk. Having done so, the *ouktazaun*
was told by the exorcist: "Now you can go wherever you like. After you
leave, however, Kou Swe will remain in the human world."

At that moment Kou Swe came out of his trance. As his eyes opened,
he saw the exorcist, and, in a startled tone, exclaimed, "Bougyi" (a term
used to refer to an army or police officer), as if he were seeing him for
the first time. After warm greetings had passed between them, the exorcist
told Kou Swe to say his beads, to observe the Precepts, and to share his
merit with the *ouktazaun*—as a protection against her, and as a sign of
his compassion for her. He cautioned him, moreover, to think of her not
as a wife but as a sister. Then, preparing a mixture of water and the

shavings of a "magical" stone, he chanted a spell over this "medicine" and gave it to Kou Swe to drink. And so ended the ceremony.

For one day the ceremony appeared to have been successful. On the night of the second day, however, the *ouktazaun* returned. Shortly after retiring for the night, Kou Swe's wife heard the sound of horses circling their house. Kou Swe, who was awakened by his wife, reported that the horses were ridden by the *ouktazaun* and her assistants, for he, unlike his wife, not only heard the sound of horses' hoofs, but he saw both the horses and their riders. The assistant was a "very ugly" Burman, a male, the same age as himself, of light complexion, and of average size. The *ouktazaun* accused Kou Swe of cruelty toward her (because of the tribulations she suffered during the exorcism) and she asked him to request the exorcist to loosen the power he now held over her. She complained, too, that although she still loved Kou Swe, he no longer loved her. Following this encounter Kou Swe was unconscious for almost twelve hours.

Frightened by this encounter, he sought aid from both the secular and spiritual powers. From the local Buddhist monk he received a spell (*gahta*) which he was to recite daily for protection. (The monk also advised him to don the yellow robe for two months.) From the township officer he received an invitation to live in his house after two months had elapsed —the *ouktazaun* had said that she would return for him in two months— because the nats, so the township officer claimed, had no power to enter government property.

In the meantime the exorcist had not been inactive. For him the return of the *ouktazaun* was a severe blow—his prestige as a healer was at stake —and he decided to conduct yet another ceremony. This ceremony, held two weeks after the first, took place in the morning rather than at night. The ritual objects employed in the first ceremony were used again. Many but not all the people who had attended the first ceremony were present at the second—the core consisting of relatives and friends.

The Third Ceremony

The ceremony began, after the exorcist had placed his rosary on the ritual offering, with exorcist and patient reciting the Buddhist Precepts. After reciting a silent prayer to the Buddha, the exorcist asked Kou Swe for the day of the week he was born. Informed that it was on a Monday, the exorcist told him to concentrate on the episode in the Buddha's life in which, attacked by the Evil One (Mara), He overcame him. The Buddha, he told Kou Swe—who was squatting in the worshipful style, eyes closed, palms pressed together and touching his forehead—defeated the Satanic power because he had faith in his ability to do so. Placing his hand on Kou Swe's head, the exorcist uttered a silent prayer; removing his hand, he continued with the prayer. He then raised his voice, commanding the *ouktazaun* to make an appearance. Receiving no response from her, he again placed his hand on Kou Swe's head and again uttered a silent spell. He then ordered the *devas* to seize her by force and bring her to the ceremony. "Why does it take her so long to arrive? She must come to worship the Buddha. Seize her!" At this, at 10:12, Kou Swe began to cry, a sign that the *ouktazaun* had possessed him.

> E.: My sister, why are you crying? *(As he continued to cry, the exorcist rubbed the back of Kou Swe's neck.)* Why do you cry when you are asked to worship the Buddha? Are you unwilling to worship Him?
>
> P.: I am willing.
>
> E.: You may not go anywhere without my permission. I shall now worship the Buddha; wait here, don't go anywhere. Wipe your nose. *(Kou Swe's nose is dripping.)* Who are you?
>
> P.: Khindi.
>
> E.: Won't you reply? I have love for you; you should have love for me. Concentrate now on my worship of the Buddha.[13]

Then, while Kou Swe remained in his worshipful position, the exorcist, in a low voice, chanted a series of Buddhist "prayers" uninterruptedly for twenty minutes. This melange of prayers, spells, Scriptural passages, and so on, was chanted in the following order. First he recited the "virtues" (*goundaws*) of the Buddha, followed by the ritual formula for the dissemination of love to all creatures,[14] and especially mentioning the *devas* and

---

[13]The similarity to Singhalese exorcism—its rationale, its technique, even the use of sibling terms to refer to the spirit—is remarkable, as the following passage (Sarathchandra 1953:31–32) reveals: "The priest at first attempts to cure the patient by gaining the goodwill of the demons. He addresses each of them in endearing terms, such as *massinē, malliyē* (cousin, brother). Later the priest's tone changes. He no longer adopts a humble and imploring attitude. He begins to threaten the demons and to warn them that they must leave the patient in the name of the Buddha and Vesamuni. He speaks to this effect. 'If it be true that demons must obey king Vesamuni, if it be true that king Vesamuni's power is great, if it be true that the authority of Vesamuni, of the gods, and of the Buddha still prevails in the world, then I command thee, demon, in the name of the Buddha, his priests, and his doctrines, to declare who thou art, and why thou afflictest this human creature in this manner.' Very often at this stage the patient becomes possessed of the demon, that is, the demon who had been harassing the patient enters him. If this does not happen during the incantations, a special ritual is performed in order to force the demon to enter the patient. An arrow (*īgaha*) is placed on the patient's head, and charms are muttered over him, till he gets possessed. Then the patient speaks, and it is believed that the demon speaks through him."

[14]This ritual is known as *myitta* (= love) *pude* (= send). The following translation, with minor changes, is taken from Shwe Zan Aung (1917:131).

"May all creatures, all living things, all beings, all persons, all individuals, all females, all males, all saints, all non-saints, all gods, all mankind, all nats be free from enmity, from care and from oppression!

"May they all carry themselves happily!

"May they all be freed from distress and adversity!

"May they all not fall away from their respectively acquired prosperity!

"May they all help themselves under the law of Karma."

the goddess Sarasvati. He then announced that he had attained special concentration (*samādhi*), so that the *samma devas* will help him to cure the patient; with their help, ordinary medicine will acquire supernormal potency. The presence and assistance of the *samma devas* and the *weikzas* are invoked by reciting the Buddhist Beatitudes, the *Maha-Mangala Sutta*,[15] or, as the Burmese call it, the *Mingala thout*.

Again he recited the ritual formula for the dissemination of love, this time giving special attention to the Thirty-Seven nats, both the "inside" and the "outside." Then, in succession he chanted a number of *Suttas* to enlist the aid of the *devas* and to ensure protection for the patient.[16] Following the chanting of these *Suttas*, the exorcist recited the "Twenty-four Kinds of Mutual Dependence" (*hnase leiba pyissi*), and concluded with the central Buddhist prayer—the famous *Okkatha*—which is recited in all Buddhist devotions:

I beg leave! I beg leave to worship the Triple Gem—the Buddha, the Doctrine, and the Monastic Order—three times, by act, by word, and by thought.

By the merit of this act of worship may I be free from existence in the four miserable planes! May I be free from the three scourges of mankind! May I be free from the eight local faults! May I be free from the five enemies! May I be free from the eight perils! May I be free from the ten punishments! And last of all, may I attain nirvana![17]

With this prayer and expression of faith, the exorcist concluded his chanting, and—at 10:35—he ordered the *ouktazaun* to worship the Buddha. But the *ouktazaun* was silent; Kou Swe, breathing heavily, did not move. The exorcist again began to chant, reciting again the ritual formula

[15]This is a famous chapter from that section of the Buddhist Scriptures known as the *Suttas* (*mingala* = *mangala* = blessing or auspiciousness). This *Sutta* lists thirty-seven moral and spiritual acts which confer blessing on the actor, and it closes with the promise that those who exhibit these acts

On every side are invincible;
They who do acts like these,
On every side they walk in safety;
And theirs is the greatest blessing.

This *Sutta*, together with those listed below, when used in a ritual context, are known as *pareittas*. Their recitation has power to ward off harm.

[16]These *Suttas* are not reproduced here because, intoned silently by the exorcist, their words have little impact on the patient or the audience. Their impact derives, rather, from the knowledge that they comprise a group of Scriptural chapters which, if recited in ritual contexts, possess or enlist the aid of supernatural power.

The *Suttas* recited are the *Metta* (= love) *Sutta, Ahinda* (= Quail) *Sutta, Mora* (= Peacock) *Jātaka,* and *Wuda* (= Quail) *Sutta*. In Burmese these are *Myitta Pareitta, Khanda Pareitta, Mora Pareitta,* and *Wuda Pareitta*.

[17]The translation, with one or two small changes, is that of Shwe Zan Aung (1917:131). Buddhism, as is well known, is given to enumeration, and each class of enumerated evils stipulated in the prayer consists of a specified number. Thus, the "three scourges" are famine, pestilence, and slaughter; the "five enemies" are water, fire, tyrannical kings, thieves, and hateful persons. And so on through the list. Since every conceivable evil is included in these various classes, it necessarily includes evil spirits, witches, etc.

for the dissemination of love and the Love *Sutta*. Following this he asked the house nat and other nats to guard this house, and again expressed his love and compassion for all creatures: "May all creatures who live on the earth, under the water, in the air, etc., all live happily. May all the nats of the earth, the hill, the forest, etc., live happily." The blessing was now extended to include the Eight Planets,[18] the parents of the nats of Mt. Popa, the *ouktazauns* who watch over the treasures of the Buddha, the *weikzas*, Sakka (the king of the nats), all the creatures who live at the four directions, and all who live above and all who live below.

At 10:40 there was still no movement from Kou Swe. The exorcist began to recite his beads to protect himself from the evil spirits. He intoned silently, his eyes closed. At 10:45 Kou Swe—who had remained in a worshipful pose, his eyes closed, unmoving—bowed to the floor, his head in his arms. The exorcist, now perspiring profusely, continued to say his beads. At 10:55 Kou Swe began to sob, and for three minutes his entire body was wracked with his sobbing. At 11:00 the exorcist completed the recitation of the rosary, again recited the formula for the sharing of merit, and then gently poked Kou Swe. The latter sat up, mucus dripping from his nose.

> E.: Who are you?
> P.: Ma Nwei Khin.
> E.: Why don't you speak?
> P.: It's no good.
> E.: What's no good?
> P.: The exorcist is no good for trying to expel my soul.
> E.: If you really cherish Kou Swe it is not proper for you to love him. Leave his body and sit beside him for a moment. I wish to call Ma Saw Khin [a female nat who lives with Ma U, another female nat, on a hill near Taungbyon]. Don't be foolish; leave his body for a while, so that I can call Ma Saw Khin. I've asked several times; I don't want to mistreat you, so I beg you, leave him just for a while.

Kou Swe lifted his head, his eyes closed. He opened his eyes, his face very serious, unsmiling. The exorcist instructed him to worship the Buddha, following which he called Ma Saw Khin to enter him: "Come for a while, I wish to meet you." Ma Saw Khin did not arrive, and the exorcist continued to importune, gently but persistently: "Enter Kou Swe; enter Kou Swe." (It was impossible to record more than one-fourth of his speech to her.) Placing his hand on Kou Swe's head, he chanted silently, then sat back. "Why are you tardy?" he asked. "I want to speak to you." When she still gave no sign of her presence the exorcist became angry, speaking with obvious annoyance. "*Samma devas*: bring her here! I will not harm you. I only wish to investigate this matter between Kou Swe and the *ouktazaun*. . . . Show me a sign that you have entered his body." Kou Swe held out his hand, and the exorcist smiled triumphantly—he had

---

[18]Htin Aung (1962:8–12) enumerates seven or nine, but not eight, planets.

his sign. "Don't do any mischief," he said to her, while pounding the floor with his wand. "Keep hold of her," he told the *samma devas*. Kou Swe swayed back and forth and the exorcist, placing his hand on Kou Swe's head, uttered another prayer. He then questioned the nat.

E.: Who are you?

P.: Nwei Khin.

E.: But I called Ma Saw Khin.

P.: Ma Saw Khin and Nwei Khin are different names for the same person. Ma Nwei Khin is the elder sister of Khind̃i [the name of the *ouktazaun*]; I no longer permit her to live with me.

E.: I called you for a conversation. I regard you as my own sister. Do you agree? [I.e., I want you to understand that I am concerned for you, and bear no malice toward you.] . . . Do not do any harm to your sister. . . . I beg you not to take action against her, only ask her not to trouble Kou Swe. Khind̃i is over thirty years old; she committed adultery with Kou Swe; now call her back to live with you. [Presumably, if she can return to live with her sister, she will release Kou Swe.]

P.: In two months Khind̃i will marry him.

E.: That is not proper. The Buddha is incomparable, and one must always think about him and his teachings. You must think about greed, anger, and lust and [renouncing them] not mistreat Kou Swe. If you do evil you will not enter the higher abodes. Do you want to be an *ouktazaun* or an earthworm?

P.: An *ouktazaun*.

E.: If so, you must learn the meaning of evil. *(He preaches some Buddhist ethical doctrines.)* . . . You must try to be pious so that, when the Buddha's relics recombine to form his physical body, you will be able to attain nirvana. If you commit evil, you will remain a spirit. It is not proper for your sister to marry Kou Swe because, being human, he will die. *(Nwei Khin replies that because her sister has done wrong, she has punished her by not permitting her to live with her.)* . . . I have performed many meritorious deeds. . . . I have built a pagoda in —— [he names a certain village]. Haven't you seen it? *(Kou Swe shakes his head in the negative.)* I want to share my merit with you. I intend to build other pagodas and monasteries, and feed many monks, and the *devas* will know of my piety. All this merit I will share with you. If you need help, I will help you. Only intervene in this case. Let your sister live with you in the treasure house, and tell her not to harm Kou Swe. Tell her to worship the Buddha. I want you also to worship the Buddha. *(Kou Swe prostrates himself in the worshipful manner.)* Will you let your sister return to the treasure house? *(At first there is no response, then Kou Swe nods his head affirmatively.)* I have called you, not to mistreat you, but only to ask you to intervene in this matter. Now worship me. *(Kou Swe prostrates himself.)* Now worship Sarasvati, the guardian of the Buddha's doctrines. *(The patient prostrates himself again.)* Do you know the Dhammazeidi abbot? Or Bou Mingaun, the head of the Mahedi Order [*gaing*] of *weikzas*? I am a member of that Order. Worship my master. *(Kou Swe prostrates himself.)* Although you are my elder, I am a human being. Therefore you must worship me three times. *(Kou Swe prostrates himself.)* May you (as a result of all of this) attain to the higher abodes. Are you willing to come to me if you need me? *(Kou Swe shakes his head in the affirmative.)* If you cannot come yourself, send one of your comrades. *(He nods his head again.)* Go now, if you like, but first worship the Buddha. *(Kou Swe prostrates himself.)*

After remaining for a few moments in the bowed position, Kou Swe sat up, swayed, and fell to the mat. The exorcist ordered him to sit up—which he did—and he said, "Khinɗi, come! Have you come?" Kou Swe sobbed, his face on the mat, and the exorcist continued, "Oh don't cry; don't love him so much." But Kou Swe continued to sob, his whole body shaking. When the exorcist ordered him to sit up, he complied, and the ceremony continued.

E.: Why do you cry? I've spoken with your elder sister and have told her to take no action against you. I now want your promise that you will leave Kou Swe. If you force me to use my power, I shall have to send you to the *samma devas* and the *weikzas* who will really mistreat you. Now, will you forget Kou Swe, or not? *(Kou Swe nods in the affirmative.)* Don't possess him, and don't let others possess him. Will you agree not to harm him again, and not let others harm him? *(There is no response.)* Don't come to him, either in person or in a dream. If you violate your promise, I shall punish you; and if Kou Swe violates his promise, report it to me, and I shall punish him. . . . You are a spirit and cannot perform deeds of merit; Kou Swe, being human, can. So why [since you are members of different species] do you send your soul to his? I do not wish to harm you. . . . Kou Swe is a human being and has a wife and children. You are an adulteress if you take Kou Swe's soul. Kou Swe's wife will be angry with you. If other spirits attempt to possess Kou Swe, and you go to his aid, that is proper, that is real love. Uniting your soul with his is not love. What will happen if you commit adultery, do you know?

P.: I will go to hell. . . . Did my elder sister agree to comply with your instructions?

E.: Yes, she agreed to forgive you, and to let you live with her again. . . . Henceforth don't cause Kou Swe to have dreams [of you]; remain in your own abode and worship the Buddha. *(Kou Swe nods his head in agreement.)* The other day you came with two followers, is it so?

P.: Yes, because I was feeling bored. . . . Will you perform the marriage ceremony for us?

E.: Can't you leave him alone! *(Kou Swe's wife, who had sat passively until now, interrupts to say to the* ouktazaun, *"you can't do it; I have children.")*

P.: Kou Swe said he had no children when he loved me. Now I'm in trouble because I believed him.

E.: Kou Swe is not handsome. He has pock marks all over his face. Why do you love him?

P.: He *is* handsome. . . . He did not say his name was Kou Swe; he said it was Maung Aung.[19]

[19]During the discussion that followed the exorcism, Kou Swe denied that he had told her that his name was Maung Aung.

E.: You have a spiritual essence [*nāma*], he has both a spiritual essence and a material essence [*rupa*]. How can you marry each other?

P.: It can be done.

E.: Listen to my instructions. There are plenty of spirits to love; why love him? . . . He is not Maung Aung, he is Kou Swe. *(Turning to the assembled audience, he asks if the patient is Maung Aung or Kou Swe; they all say he is Kou Swe.)* . . . Now will you go?

P.: . . . I will go, but I want Kou Swe to feed the monks, and to share his merit with me; it should be done at the waning of the moon. *(She and Kou Swe had originally agreed to meet again at the end of the month; now she says she will be satisfied if, instead, he feeds the monks at that time. But, having said this, she now returns to her original stance, insisting that Kou Swe is Maung Aung, that he is a bachelor, and that he has no children; she repeats this over and over, despite the exorcist's remonstrations.)*

E.: You and Kou Swe are both great liars.

P.: . . . I will not harm him, I merely wish to meet him again in two months. We had agreed to meet in two months. I want to ask some questions of Kou Swe.

E.: Don't ask. . . . I have not been harsh with you; I have been kind. And you should obey me. Wouldn't you be frightened if I decided to beat you?

P.: Yes.

E.: I am tired, and I must return to my home. In accordance with your request, Kou Swe and his family will feed the monks, and you must never meet with him again. Don't harm or interfere with him; don't let any other spirit possess him.

P.: Alright.

E.: Next time, should you violate your oath, I will hand you over [for punishment] to the *samma devas*. . . .

As their conversation continued it became established that the *ouktazaun* lived on Yankintaun hill with two sisters. The exorcist told the assembled audience not to betray the sisters' dwelling place to other exorcists, lest, unscrupulous as many of them are, they seek to rob these spirits of the treasure. Similarly, he cautioned them, the members of the audience, to refrain from touching the treasure. He then told the *ouktazaun* that he will help her whenever she needs his help, and that he will share his merit with her and her sisters, but that now she must leave. She said she was ready to go, and would call her elephants to take her back. Before she could call them, however, the exorcist told her to make obeisance, in sequence, to the Buddha, Sarasvatī, the *weikzas*, the Dhammazeidi abbot, and his own Master. Kou Swe made obeisance to each in turn as instructed.

E.: I will always be willing to help all three of you [the *ouktazaun* and her sisters]. Think of me as your brother. Now worship me. *(Kou Swe worships.)* Fine, now you may go.

P.: I will leave Kou Swe.

E.: Abandon all greed, anger, and lust; they only cause trouble.

Silently chanting, the exorcist placed his hand on Kou Swe's head, and then rubbed his neck. Kou Swe moved, prostrated himself, and then sat up. The exorcist fanned Kou Swe's head, saying, "Go out! Go out!" Kou Swe lifted his left arm in the air, dropped it, prostrated himself again. All the while the exorcist was repeating, "Oh this is a most pitiable case." Kou Swe sat up again, quietly. Suddenly, in a startle, his body was propelled forward, his eyes opened, and he saw the exorcist. His look of complete astonishment was followed by a marvelously benign smile, and he sat back. It was 12:20, and the ceremony was over.[20]

It remains to be added that a week or two after the completion of the ceremony, Kou Swe fulfilled his oath to the *ouktazaun*. He offered a special meal to the monks of Yeigyi and two adjacent villages.

A PSYCHOTHERAPEUTIC EXPLANATION

Within the Burmese framework, the exorcist is a religious practitioner, expelling harmful supernaturals from the bodies of their victims through the assistance of benevolent supernaturals. If, following the exorcism, the victim returns to his normal behavior, it is assumed that the ceremony has been a success, i.e., the harmful supernaturals have been expelled. Data on Burmese exorcism are much too scanty to permit any generalizations concerning its efficacy. We do know, both from the skimpy reports in the ethnographic literature and from my field material, that exorcism, in many cases at least, does produce positive results, ranging from marked improvement in the condition of the patient to apparently complete cures. Assuming that these results are not chance phenomena (although in the absence of experimental control this interpretation cannot be positively ruled out), how can we—who believe neither in possession nor in supernaturals nor in exorcism—explain the observed psychological changes that often follow an exorcistic ceremony?

From the naturalistic point of view which has been explicit in this and

[20]Following this ceremony, Kou Swe had two additional encounters with the *ouktazaun*, but neither, so far as I can gather, was traumatic. The first occurred in a dream—but certain dreams are taken by the Burmese as real events—a day or two after the second exorcistic ceremony. In the dream he met her and accompanied her to her residence, or *thaiknan* (*thaik* = treasure, *nan* = palace), where he saw a great variety of Buddha images, and, at her request, did obeisance to these images. Before leaving her, she gave him a bundle of new currency notes. On his way home he found many fish lying along the path, and he picked up as many as he could carry to take home with him. Noticing that the fish were crawling with worms, he took them to the canal to be washed, attempting unsuccessfully to get rid of the worms. (Dreaming of worms or fish—as well as of feces—means, according to Burmese dream theory, that the dreamer will acquire money or wealth in the near future.)

About three weeks later Kou Swe met the *ouktazaun* as he was walking along the canal. Hearing a branch falling from a tree behind him, he turned around to discover her standing about twenty feet from him. When he asked her what she was doing there, she disappeared.

in the previous two chapters, the alleged victim of supernatural possession is mentally ill, suffering from psychological dissociation; the exorcist is a psychotherapist; and the exorcistic seance is a form of psychotherapy. Although modern therapists may be offended by this designation of Burmese exorcism, the exorcistic seance described in this chapter certainly satisfies the minimum definition of "psychotherapy" proposed by some psychiatrists. "Psychotherapy," as defined by Jerome Frank (1961:114), ". . . is a form of help-giving in which a trained, socially sanctioned healer tries to relieve a sufferer's distress by facilitating certain changes in his feelings, attitudes, and behavior, through the performance of certain activities with him, often with the participation of a group."

But having defined the exorcistic seance as psychotherapy, I have merely compounded, rather than solved, our problem. If the seance is psychotherapeutic, it should be possible to identify those of its components which, taken as psychotherapeutic agents, can explain the observed psychological changes in what we would now designate as the psychiatric patient. I should like to point to five factors which, given our present knowledge of psychotherapy, probably play some role in producing the observed therapeutic results of Burmese exorcism. These are group support, patient participation, religious support, the behavior and personality of the exorcist, and patient abreaction.

Group support. The importance of the group in contributing to the therapeutic success of exorcism is at least fourfold. In the first place, the group offers emotional support. Given the Burmese world view, abnormal behavior, however antisocial its manifestations, does not lead to punitive sanctions, to accusations of fault or blame, to attribution of sin or evil, or to physical and social withdrawal. Since the abnormal behavior is caused by nats or witches, it is understood that, although the behavior may be shameful, the actor is not; his behavior may be criminal, but he is not. If abnormal behavior is attributed to supernatural attack, for which the actor has no moral responsibility, the actor himself is viewed as a patient requiring help. For the patient suffering from humiliation and shame, this means that the entire community is ready to help him, thereby providing him with emotional support which at least in part compensates for the feelings of shame which (as I tried to show in the previous chapter) precipitate his dissociation. Similarly, the patient suffering from fear need no longer face his problem in isolation; through his illness, he can mobilize all the resources of his community to assist him in coping with his problem. By the same token, the patient who, in trance, acts out his forbidden impulses is immune to the usual punitive sanctions which similar behavior, exhibited in a normal state, would entail. Rather than being abhorred as a criminal who must be punished or as a moral leper who must be isolated, he is viewed, instead, as a pathetic figure who must be nurtured.

All this suggests that the actor is spared the feelings of guilt, shame, or remorse that are attendant upon a public opinion that accuses, blames, punishes. The actor, if only as a result of his group's perception of him, perceives himself (at least consciously) to be blameless; it is the evil supernatural, not he himself, who is responsible for his behavior.

By interpreting his behavior as supernaturally caused, the group also offers cultural support. If the actor does not initially attribute his behavior to supernatural causation, the group does; and when he does interpret his behavior in this manner, they support his interpretation. In short, though his behavior may be dissensual, its interpretation is consensual: actor and group agree on its meaning. To be sure, the actor's behavior represents deviation from commonly held behavioral norms, but since he is not a deviant from commonly held cognitive norms, he is spared the psychological isolation which inevitably accompanies cognitive dissensus between a social actor and his group.

But we can say more. By identifying the cause of the illness (or by supporting him in his identification of its cause) the group helps, at least in part, to reduce the anxiety which accompanies ignorance of or ambiguity about causation. It is frightening, of course, to believe that one is possessed by a witch or an evil nat; but it is much more frightening to be the victim of a mysterious malady whose cause is unknown. In the latter case one is helpless; in the former case one can at least hope that the putative cause can be dealt with. And in Burma it is believed that the cause *can* be dealt with; there are skilled practitioners (exorcists) whose assistance can be sought and well tried techniques (exorcism) whose efficacy has been established.

In addition to its emotional and cultural support, the group also offers social support. Unlike typical medical practice in Western society—or, for that matter, typical nonpsychiatric practice in Burma—the exorcistic ceremony is always a group ceremony. In addition to the exorcist and the patient, the participants include a large group of other people—kinsmen, friends, and fellow villagers; and the more virulent the case, the larger the group. To be sure, the participation of the group in the ceremony is of a different order from that of the main actors—the exorcist and the patient. Indeed, pursuing the dramatic analogy implied by the term actors, it may be said that if the latter two, together with the invited spirits, constitute the *dramatis personae*, the assembled group constitutes the audience. But this is an active, not a passive, audience. It does not consist, as might be the case in certain theatrical contexts, of jaded spectators, seeking entertainment to shake them from their boredom or to permit them an escape from routine concerns. It consists, rather, of persons who, sharing the same concerns as the actors, recognize that they too are potential actors in the drama that is being acted out before their eyes, a drama in which the forces of Good are engaged in a mighty struggle to overcome the forces of Evil. Identifying with the forces of Good, the members of the audience participate behaviorally as well as emotionally: they make comments, proffer advice, express bewilderment, manifest fear. They may even become members of the cast if the plot demands it. When, for example, the patient becomes violent, members of the audience intervene in order to subdue him. One can properly say, then, that patient, exorcist, and audience constitute one interlocking system. The former two play the more active roles, but their roles interact not only with each other, but are responsive to and produce responses in the members of the audience as well.

Finally, the group offers instrumental support in the form of assistance, sympathy, and encouragement. By participating in the ceremony, the group implicitly renders its sympathy to, and demonstrates its concern for, the patient. Its very presence informs him that it cares, that he has not been abandoned, that he is not alone. More than this, the group members do things for him. Some provide him with the financial assistance—to hire an exorcist, to buy the ritual objects to be used in the ceremony, and to feed the monks following the ceremony, which requires a great deal of money —without which the ceremony could not be performed. Others assist him physically. They seek out an exorcist and bring him to the village, or they go to the market to help him obtain the ceremonial objects. Still others may offer personal assistance. When it was suggested that Kou Swe enter a monastery to escape the clutches of the *ouktazaun*, a friend offered to take the yellow robe with him so that he should not be alone.

Group support, then—emotional, cultural, social, and instrumental—is one of the factors which probably contributes to the efficacy of the exorcistic ceremony, viewed as a psychotherapeutic technique. It is not argued that this support is itself therapeutic, but rather that it provides the patient with a cognitive and emotional context which conduces to successful therapy. Given this context, certain other factors, intrinsic to the exorcism itself, can then make their contributions to the therapeutic process.

Patient participation.[21] The exorcistic seance, unlike other forms of Burmese medical practice, demands active participation on the part of the patient, participation that engages both his mind and his body. In some types of Burmese medical practice the patient is a passive object, being required to do no more, for example, than to swallow some medicine. In exorcism, too, unless it includes a seance, the practitioner may intone spells and prayers which the patient may not even hear: he may be unconscious, for example, or the practitioner may recite the ritual formulae out of his sight and hearing. Since, from the Burmese point of view, the efficacy of the spell inheres in its mere recitation, the presence of the patient is not required; and the fact that some patients do recover under such

[21]For this point, and the two that follow it, a brief restudy of Table 9.3 in Chapter 9, pg. 155, will be useful.

circumstances lends additional credence to their belief in its efficacy. That patient participation does affect the therapeutic process, however, may be inferred from those cases in which an exorcistic seance was successful after other types of therapy, not requiring patient participation, had failed.

"Patient participation" refers to a variety of different activities. First, many of the rituals—rites, spells, prayers, etc.—performed by the exorcist are both seen and heard by the patient. He sees the exorcist perform rites designed to exorcise the supernaturals, and he hears him recite formulae ordering them to depart. Second, the patient himself is instructed by the exorcist to intone ritual formulae, to recite precepts, to invoke the assistance of benevolent supernaturals, and so on. Third, the patient is instructed by the exorcist to *do*, as well as to *say*, certain things. He must sit down, he must stand up, he must worship the Buddha, or he must do obeisance to the exorcist. Finally, and probably most importantly, the patient, when in a trance state, is engaged by the exorcist in a long dialogue, a dialogue in which it is believed that the supernatural, having possessed the patient, is speaking through him. The patient participates, then, while in both a conscious and an unconscious state.

One can only assume, of course, that to the extent that patient participation is a factor in the therapeutic process, the two psychological states of participation, conscious and unconscious, have different effects. The patient's conscious but passive participation (hearing and seeing) serves to inform him of the exorcist's attempts to help, and it exposes him to the cultural symbols, in both their cognitive and affective meanings, in whose transformational potency he himself believes. (How, and to what extent, ritual and verbal symbols have transformational power remains, of course, an unresolved theoretical question.) The patient's conscious and active participation (reciting, bowing, etc.) have some of these same effects, but they presumably have other effects as well. By engaging the patient's mind and body, these acts lead to a heightened concentration; they energize his will to become well, and they impel him to take at least partial responsibility for his own recovery. He cannot merely sit by while the exorcist does the work. Finally, the patient's unconscious and active participation (conversation in a trance state with the exorcist) enables him to release the psychic energies, express the psychic fantasies, and articulate the psychic conflicts whose previous repression may have instigated his illness. This aspect of the therapy will be examined in greater detail below.

But the patient takes an active role not only in the exorcistic rite—he is active both before and after the ceremony. This activity takes him out of his sickroom and mobilizes energy, which would otherwise be channeled into self-preoccupation, for coping with the external world. Thus, before the ceremony takes place a great number of ceremonial objects must be purchased, and since there is no market in the village, the patient may have to travel as far as Mandalay for his purchases. After the ceremony there is almost always some activity to be performed because of a promise made during the ceremony: a nat must be propitiated, monks must be fed, a pilgrimage must be undertaken, etc. These activities, like those preceding the ceremony, require planning and effort.

Religious support. In its essence the exorcistic ceremony is a struggle between the powers of Good and the powers of Evil. It is not only the nat or witch who has harmed the patient who is exorcized. Rather, it is almost as if the offending supernatural were a representative of all evil supernaturals. Thus, in the course of the ceremony the exorcist orders all nats and all witches—and not merely the one who has possessed the patient—to depart; and he orders them all to refrain from harming the patient again. In this struggle to overcome these Evil powers, patient and exorcist are not alone; doing battle for them are all the powers of Good, the Buddhist powers. Indeed, the purpose of the ceremony is to enlist the support of Buddhist power, for it is the power of Buddhism, not the power of the exorcist—except insofar as Buddhist power is vouchsafed to him—which overcomes the Evil power.

The crucial thing to be noted about the confrontation between these two powers is that the outcome of the contest is never in doubt. The power of Buddhism is incomparably greater than all other sources of power. This belief is not merely held by all Buddhists, but, more importantly, it is the belief with which the patient enters the exorcistic ceremony. As a Buddhist he has unquestioned faith in the power of Buddhism, including, if only it can be harnessed on his behalf, its power to cure him. As a patient he participates in rites which are designed to achieve that very end. In the various rituals, prayers, spells, and so on, that comprise the ceremony, he, for himself, and the exorcist, on his behalf, invoke all the powers of Buddhism to align themselves with him. To believe that all this power—including perhaps the power of the Buddha Himself—is on his side, must surely reduce the feelings of lethargy and depression which, stemming from hopelessness, render many therapeutic attempts futile.

The role of the exorcist. There is, of course, an important qualification to this optimistic picture. Buddhist power, to be sure, can overcome any other type of power if there is a confrontation between them; but one can never be certain that this confrontation, which is achieved by inducing the Buddhist supernaturals to intercede on behalf of the patient, will in fact be achieved. Hence, though the patient may have complete faith in the power of Buddhism, he will have little confidence in the chances of his recovery unless he believes that the exorcistic ceremony can mobilize this power on his behalf. And it is here that the exorcist plays a crucial role; for since it is the exorcist who induces the Buddhist supernaturals to enter the case, it is the patient's confidence in the exorcist that determines whether or not he believes that this confrontation will in fact take place.

If the exorcist cannot induce the Buddhist supernaturals to intervene on behalf of the patient, nothing can be done for him. (This, of course, is why Buddhist power is never at issue if the exorcism should fail: therapeutic failure reflects on the power of the exorcist, not on the power of Buddhism.)

The mere fact that the exorcist is willing to perform the ceremony enables the patient to repose confidence in him. That he, the exorcist, is prepared to expose himself to the many dangers inherent in any confrontation with malevolent supernaturals implies that he has sufficient confidence in his own power to risk these dangers, and the implicit self-confidence of the exorcist gives the patient confidence in him. At the same time, the willingness of the exorcist to expose himself to danger on behalf of the patient contains still another therapeutic element. It indicates to the patient that the exorcist cares enough for him and deems him important enough to risk his own security on his behalf.

On the assumption, then, that the patient has confidence in the exorcist, we must examine the ways in which the latter, during the exorcism, exerts therapeutic influence on the patient. Such influence can be exerted in at least three ways: by the rituals he performs; by the manner in which he conducts the seance; and by the kind of person he is—which is to say, by his style and manner, and, therefore, by the image which he projects.

To the extent that he relies primarily on ritual, we would expect the behavior of the exorcist to have, in itself, little therapeutic effect on the patient. This is all the more so if the ritual consists primarily in the recitation of Pali texts which the patient does not understand, or of spells which are semantically meaningless. If, moreover, they are intoned silently, the only impression they can have on the patient is visual. This is not to deny the therapeutic effect of ritual—its efficacy has already been affirmed above—but to indicate that in such cases the therapeutic influence of the exorcist, in contrast to that of the ritual, is limited. Thus, in the case study described in this chapter, the first exorcist emphasized ritual techniques— reciting incantations which, for the most part, the patient did not understand, lighting candles, muttering spells over water, invoking the assistance of the *devas*, etc. The second exorcist, too, employed these techniques— from the Burmese point of view, it is precisely these techniques which exorcize the evil supernaturals—but he performed them in a different manner (which will be noted below) and, more importantly, he placed much greater emphasis on the seance.

The behavior of the exorcist in the seance is his second opportunity for exerting a therapeutic influence on the patient. By establishing a supportive, nurturant environment, the exorcist permits the patient to discuss his conflicts with impunity. To be sure, it is not the patient but the attacking supernatural who is believed to be speaking. But if we assume that this voice, emerging from a patient in a trance, is speaking for that aspect of the patient's personality which, because shameful or forbidden, is normally repressed, the seance can be taken as the pivotal therapeutic dimension of the ceremony. And since, typically, the exorcist does not condemn or punish—on the contrary, he constantly expresses his love and concern— the patient need have no fear of expressing those ego-alien dimensions of his personality which, in the cases we have examined, consisted of sexual or aggressive drives.

The exorcist's sympathetic attitude to the patient's shameful and for- bidden needs is expressed in a number of ways. In the seance described in this chapter, the exorcist persists in referring to the female nat—whom I take to be the personification of the patient's ego-alien drives—as "my sister," a term of endearment. He tells her that he "loves" her, and he says that she should "love" him. He recites for her the "Love" *Sutta*, and he chants on her behalf the ritual formula for the dissemination of love. He asks the patient, while the latter is conscious, to do the same. He tells her that, despite her evil deeds, he will share his merit with her, and he recites the ritual formula (and instructs the patient to do so as well) for the sharing of merit. Throughout, the exorcist is gentle with her, pleading, cajoling, sympathizing, and only rarely condemning.

He is gentle, but he is firm. For although he promises to help her, he yet insists that she depart. And his firmness is concrete; he not only promises, but he threatens. If, despite his concern for her welfare, she remains adamant, he will have no choice, he warns her, but to call upon the *devas* to eject her forcibly; and they, unlike him, will punish her and cause her pain. Notice, however, that even in his threatening demeanor, it is not her past evil for which he threatens her with punishment, but rather her persistent and continuing evil. What she has done, she has done. For that she is forgiven.[22]

The exorcist is therapeutically important, not only because of his role- specific behavior, but because of his personality attributes which find expression in his therapeutic manner, or style. In the case described in this chapter, there was an opportunity to observe two dramatically contrasting manners. The first exorcist, timid and unsure of himself, faced his task

[22]Many of these characteristics of the Burmese exorcist are the attributes which psychiatric thought deems to be of central importance in any type of psychotherapy: concern for the patient, a desire to help him, and an acceptance of him, regardless of his faults, foibles, or problems. Thus, therapeutic success, according to Frank, depends on (among other things) the therapist's "steady, deep interest, an optimistic outlook, and dedication to the patient's welfare. These attitudes enable the patient to talk about any aspects of himself, however shameful they may be, with confidence that the therapist will maintain his interest and concern. . . . In addition the therapist's consistent interest strengthens the patient's self-esteem by implying that he is worthy of the therapist's efforts."

Again, "emotional support, kindly guidance, and the feeling of being accepted by the psychiatrist—qualities related to the psychiatrist's personality rather than his technique—are therapeutically important" (Frank 1961:115, 132).

with anxiety and with little self-confidence. Indeed, at one point his own anxiety became so overpowering that he lost control of himself, undoing whatever therapeutic results he may have already achieved by striking the patient in a fit of anger. The second therapist, though employing quiet, modulated tones, gave the appearance of assurance and force. Almost from the moment he entered the room, one was impressed with his personal magnetism, his sense of self-importance. He radiated a feeling of confidence and communicated a sense of power, almost tangible in their immediacy. "Charismatic" is the label one would prefer to employ, if that word had not been so hopelessly overused. Indeed, I could not help but think, as I watched his masterful performance, that were I to believe in supernaturals and in the power of exorcists to expel them, I would certainly have faith in the power of this exorcist. To the extent that the exorcist has the influence that is suggested by this description, one would expect the patient to establish a positive transference (in the psychoanalytic sense) with him and, from this transference, to find at least some of the energy required to restructure and reintegrate his damaged personality.

A therapeutically effective exorcist, then, is one who has confidence in himself, who believes in his own power, his own authority, his own competence. The timid exorcist, the exorcist dominated by his own anxiety, conveys anxiety rather than assurance to the patient. It is the therapist's self-confidence which, in Lederer's comparative study of psychotherapy, is ". . . the common, basic therapeutic principle."

> This not only renders the therapists able to help others, but gives them the feeling of being themselves relatively safe. They can deal with the unknown, the awe-inspiring, the frightening, because their superior competence in such matters protects them. Thus they, the therapists in each culture, can approach the patient with a minimum of anxiety of their own (Lederer 1959:264).

Patient abreaction. In every seance that I observed, the patient, among other things, shouted obscenities, uttered heresies, insulted the exorcist, became physically violent, and engaged in other forms of "acting-out" behavior. Maung Oun Yi says *he* is not afraid of the Buddha; Kou Swe goes further—he says there is no Buddha. Kou Swe says the exorcist is evil and impious; Maung Oun Yi says he is not afraid of the exorcist whom, should he approach him, he will smear with vaginal discharge. Maung Oun Yi and Kou Swe thrash out at the group sitting at their side. Kou Swe talks about, and makes symbolic gestures of, sexual intercourse —and adulterous intercourse at that. Both in word and in deed they act in ways which in normal contexts are unthinkable.

What we seem to see here, to phrase it in psychoanalytic terms, is almost total victory of the id over the superego, while the ego, rendered unconscious, is quiescent. Normally, the Burman, primarily because of the influence of Buddhism, leads a life of restraint. Although wishing to spend his hard-won earnings on himself, he donates them instead to monks and monasteries; desiring to commit adultery, he refrains because of his Buddhist-derived fear that he will suffer the pains of hell; wanting to get drunk, he abstains, again because of his Buddhist-derived anticipation of punishment. One could go on and on. If Buddhism has been the great civilizing force that many have claimed for it, it is, by that very token, an important frustrating force, and frustration, as we know, breeds resentment and hostility. Buddhism, of course, is not the only frustrating Burmese institution. A number of other institutions—political, economic, kinship —are also sources of need-frustration and, therefore, of hostility-incitement. Normally, however, the forbidden needs whose satisfactions are blocked by these institutions, and the resentment and hostility which attend their frustration, are held in control by the healthy processes of the conscious Burmese ego. But in the seance-induced trance that ego is rendered unconscious, the superego is dissolved, and the usually repressed id emerges triumphant. Concretely, in the course of the seance, resentment which is felt toward Buddhism is expressed clearly and directly; opposition to authority, which is triggered off by an initial negative transference to the exorcist, is also expressed clearly and directly; diffused and impulsive hostility is expressed in diffuse violence; and so on.

But the very expression of these impulses, occurring in this special— ceremonial and sympathetic—context, seems to contain an important therapeutic element: their expression is, at the same time, their abreaction. The patient's bottled-up resentment is now out of his system; his violence ends in physical exhaustion; recriminations end in bitter sobbing, the patient's body wracked with trembling. By the end of the seance he is in a state of physical and emotional exhaustion; and it is at least plausible that, in this state, and with the energy now available through his positive transference with the exorcist, his relatively unstructured psyche is restructured. Proceeding, successively, from conflict, to the repression of conflict, and then to the expression of conflict, the abreactive aspect of the seance enables him, so I am suggesting, to achieve (in some measure) the resolution of conflict. Although the data available to us are not sufficient to permit this analysis to be more than suggestive, the suggestion, I believe, is worth exploring.

V

SUPERNATURAL
PRACTITIONERS

CHAPTER TWELVE

The Shaman

In discussing various aspects of supernatural belief and ritual, we have encountered two supernatural specialists, the shaman and the exorcist. The emphasis in this chapter, which is concerned with the shaman, is on the shaman as a *person*. The next chapter, dealing with the exorcist, emphasizes the exorcist's *role* within the supernatural complex and contrasts it with the *role* of the shaman.

DESCRIPTION OF THE ROLE

Figuring prominently in the cultus of the Thirty-Seven nats is a ritual practitioner whom the Burmese call a *nat kadaw*, and whom I, for lack of a better term, have designated as a "shaman." Despite the conventional meaning of the Burmese term (*nat kadaw* = "nat wife") not all shamans are women; experts at Taungbyon estimate that 3 to 4 per cent are male. Nevertheless, since the overwhelming majority are women, shamans, unless otherwise specified, will be referred to here as female.

The *nat kadaw* is certainly not a shaman in the classical Siberian sense. She does not ascend to the spirit world, nor does she perform other types of "supernatural" feats, nor does she even cure illness. She does, however, display other shamanistic characteristics. She is an oracle, a medium, a diviner, a cult officiant; she performs these aspects of her role in a state of spirit possession. It is not entirely inappropriate, therefore, to refer to her as a "shaman."

Although some shamans—the Queens and Ministers, for example, in the Taungbyon Festival—play a very important cult role, the shaman is not a priestess in the nat cultus. If she dances at a nat festival it is not as an intermediary between the cult members and the nats, but as a nat wife, whose obligation it is to serve her husband (as well as the other nats) by dancing. Cult members who watch the dancing are most appropriately characterized as spectators of, rather than as participants in, a religious performance; they are an audience before whom the shaman dances, rather than a congregation on whose behalf she dances. If, outside the festival, the shaman propitiates a nat on behalf of a client, it is because the latter does not know the ritual, not because he requires an intermediary.

In the absence of survey data, it is fair to assume, based on questioning of shamans at Taungbyon, that there are few if any villages in Burma without shamans. In Yeigyi at the time of our study there was one woman who was a full-fledged shaman; there were two other women who, though not "married" to nats, were "loved" by them; and there was one young man, also "loved" by a nat, who hoped to marry her as soon as he acquired sufficient funds to perform the marriage ceremony. In a village like Yeigyi the activities of the shamans can be easily described. First, the shaman assumes responsibility for the village nat cultus. It is she who arranges for the public nat ceremonies and who makes the offerings to the nats. To the extent, too, that anyone keeps the village nat shrine in good repair, it is she on whom this responsibility devolves. The shaman may dance at the local nat ceremonies, but, as I have already observed, she does so, not as a minister officiating on behalf of a congregation, but from a personal obligation to the nat.

In addition to serving in the village cultus, the shaman may be hired to perform private rites for a client. Younger couples, especially, who do not know the proper ritual for propitiating a nat, invite a shaman to their home to perform the ritual on their behalf. The shaman may also be consulted as a medium. In the village the problem that is typically brought to the medium is illness. As we have already seen (Chapter 9), when a person becomes ill and it is thought that his illness may be caused by a nat, a shaman may be called in, first, to determine which of the nats has caused the illness and, second, to indicate how he must be pacified so that the patient may recover. Sometimes, having discovered that the family had neglected to make an offering to, say, the house nat, the shaman advises them to do so. Typically, however, she invokes her nat "husband," who, having "possessed" her, informs her that the patient had (unwittingly) offended a particular nat. My village neighbor Kou Than, for example, began to develop bald spots at the back of his head. His wife, a firm believer in nats, called in a shaman who, discovering that Kou Than had not been propitiating a certain nat, attributed his baldness to the latter's annoyance with him. At Kou Than's request, she propitiated him on his behalf. Shortly after her intervention his hair grew back.

Shamans may also be consulted about problems which may not be related to the nats, but which, because of their (the shamans') clairvoyant powers, they are deemed capable of solving. Lost objects, for example, might be discovered by a shaman who, as a diviner, informs her client where the lost object may be found.

The shaman who is consulted by a client obtains the relevant information by invoking her nat husband. When she invokes him, he allegedly possesses her, and it is the nat, using the shaman as his medium, who answers the questions and proffers the advice: it is he, not the shaman, who is speaking. Hence during possession some shamans speak in a voice different from their own. The onset of possession is indicated by trembling of the trunk and arms, and the same symptoms mark the nat's departure from the body. Whether possession (assuming that the shaman genuinely believes herself to be possessed) is accompanied by trance is, as I have already suggested in the discussion of nat dancing, a moot question. In mediumship, as in dancing, most instances of alleged possession observed by me showed no indications of trance, and in many cases the culturally stipulated sign of possession—trembling of arms and trunk—appeared to me to have been simulated rather than genuine. Still, I cannot be sure of this.

The shaman, at least in the village, is only a part-time practitioner. Like other village women, shamans are housewives, cultivators, agricultural laborers, and so on. Indeed, the village shaman only rarely has an occasion to activate any of the aspects of her role. Being relatively unknown, she dances only at those nat festivals (usually only one) in which her appearance is mandatory, or which are easily accessible to her village. As a medium, too, she is only infrequently consulted, and this, for at least three reasons. First, the problems for which mediumship may be required are of limited range. Second, mediumship, in its medico-diagnostic aspects, must compete with other, more powerful medical roles (described in Chapter 9). Finally, there is widespread skepticism, as we shall see, concerning the efficacy of the shamanistic role and/or the *bona fide* of its practitioners. It is not surprising, then, that less than 10 per cent of the households in Yeigyi—or, more specifically, only seven of the eighty-two households included in the nat census—have ever used a shaman, either for propitiation or consultation. Consulted infrequently, and receiving small fees —a few pennies in cash, some coconuts or bananas in kind—the annual income of village shamans is negligible.

In the cities, the situation is sometimes rather different. Some urban shamans, enjoying a much wider clientele, devote a large share, and sometimes all, of their working time to this role. If they are well known, occupying important positions in the hierarchy of shamans that is centered in Taungbyon, they are in attendance at all important nat festivals, both in Lower and Upper Burma. Although few are full-time specialists—those I interviewed are bicycle mechanics, food vendors, midwives, shopkeepers, itinerant merchants—some may earn as much as K3000, or more than $600 a year (a very respectable income in Burmese terms), and many may average K100–200 a month. In some instances their income is sufficient to allow their husbands to stop working. The husband of one shaman I know, a clerk prior to his wife's marriage to her nat, gave up his job in order to engage in politics.[1]

The city also seems to differ from the village in the kinds of problems that are brought to the shaman for advice. Although illness is the typical reason for consulting a shaman in the village—if, indeed, she is consulted at all—this does not seem to be the case in the cities. Admittedly based on a very small sample, the nine urban shamans (all from Mandalay) whom I questioned about their clients were unanimous in replying that the problems brought to them are primarily marital or financial in nature. In the former case, the clients are usually women who, believing that their husbands no longer love them and/or have taken mistresses, wish to know what measures they may take to regain their husband's affections. In the latter case, poor people wish to know what they must do in order to overcome their poverty; shopkeepers may wish to know if they should expand their businesses; others seek advice about gambling, the lottery, etc. I met, for example, a number of merchants who claimed that their prosperity was caused by advice obtained from shamans.

RECRUITMENT TO THE ROLE

Although shamans are remunerated for their activities, the financial reward, especially in the villages, is much too small, as I have already observed, for it to be a motivational basis for recruitment to the role. A woman becomes a shaman not at her own but at a nat's instigation; she becomes a shaman because a nat falls in love with her and wishes to marry her.[2] Though she may not marry him, she resists, as we shall see, at her peril. Resistance, however, except for a small minority, is her preference,

[1]The shaman, I suspect, is more frequently employed in the cities than in the villages for the same reason that the nat cultus is taken more seriously in urban than in rural areas (see Chapter 4, pp. 59–63). In the city, where chance and luck play an important role in managing one's life, the divinatory power of the shaman contributes a degree of predictability, and even of control.

[2]Sarah Bekker, whose knowledge of shamanism is unexcelled, writes (personal communication) that in the Rangoon area a person becomes a shaman, "not because of the intensity or variety of his relationship with the nat but as a relationship with the community. *Nat kadaw* as a term . . . means a person whose help may be sought 'professionally' for a fee. . . . The term is applied only to those who arrange nat ceremonies or hold consultations." In Upper Burma, too, the *nat kadaw* is a specialist who performs for a fee, but recruitment to the role requires that a nat inform her of his love for her, and, if possible, that she marry him.

for knowing the low opinion in which shamans are held, she is ashamed to become one.

In general, Stewart's comment of fifty years ago continues to characterize the contemporary attitude toward shamans: "Burmans appear to be contemptuous of them, even while believing in their inspiration" (Ridgeway 1915:393). Unlike Stewart, however, I found that many Burmans do not even believe in their "inspiration." Although U Pou Zoun, the custodian at Taungbyon, estimates that only 10 per cent of the shamans are dishonest, i.e., not "inspired" (possessed), one of the most famous nat dancers in Burma believes that the reverse is the case: for him, only 10 per cent are honest. In Yeigyi almost 60 per cent of the entire male population believe that all shamans are dishonest, another 30 per cent believe that most are dishonest, and only 10 per cent believe that most shamans are to be taken at their word. Although I have no systematic data on the female population of Yeigyi, I suspect that, had they been queried on this point, the figures would have been reversed. The women's greater belief in the integrity of the shamans does not, however, affect their attitude toward them. Like the men, women too, in Stewart's expression, are "contemptuous" of shamans. This attitude is not restricted to Upper Burma. Pfanner (1962: 374) provides similar data for Lower Burma.

There are at least three reasons for the negative attitude to shamans. In the first place, to be loved by a nat often means, among other things, that in some sense the woman has sexual relations with him—at best a shameful thing. Second, shamans are viewed—with or without cause, I cannot be sure—as sexually immoral and promiscuous. Third, shamans dance in public, and dancers (and actresses) in general are viewed in Burma, as they once were in America, as scarlet women.[3] To dance in a state of possession, wildly and with abandon, as the shamans dance, is to compound the shame. It is little wonder, then, that shamans are considered to be, as the village headman put it, of the "lowest type"; that queries about them are invariably met with derisive laughter; that the aunt of the young male shaman in Yeigyi said bitterly, "It is better to die than to marry a nat"; that the mothers of two female shamans told me of beating their daughters in a vain attempt to dissuade them from going ahead with their intended nat "marriages."[4]

---

[3]At least one basis for the traditional Burmese prejudice against actors is that, until recently, the Burmese stage recruited its members from despised pagoda slaves, beggars, and other outcasts (Tha Kin 1923).

[4]It is of interest to observe that, among some hill tribes in Burma, the shaman not only performs the same role performed by the Burmese shaman, but he is recruited to the role in the same manner, and is the object of the same negative and skeptical attitudes. Thus, Chin shamans, according to Lehman, "are needed by the population to divine the causes of illness and the requirements of sacrifice, but few people wish to become shamans themselves, or to have their children become shamans. Their social status is generally low. They claim to travel to the land of the dead and tell what they have seen there, and claim to know about the god or gods; but many Chin profess indifferent faith in these reports . . ." (Lehman 1963:175).

The shamans themselves, interestingly, share these cultural attitudes. Six of the ten shamans whom I interviewed spontaneously expressed shame concerning their calling. When explaining why they had delayed their nat marriages until long after their nats had made their intentions known, each said it was because of the disgrace in marrying a nat. The marriage eventually took place because the pain of not marrying the nat, as the following cases reveal, was even greater.

U Ka, a male shaman in Mandalay, was first loved by his nat, the younger sister of Min Mahagiri, when he was eighteen, but he did not marry her until he was forty-five. Because of this long delay, she not only caused him to lose all his money and property, but she killed his wife as well. To protect himself from further harm, he married the nat.

Daw Pya, a female shaman from Mandalay, was first loved by the younger Taungbyon Brother when she was seventeen. Opposing the marriage, she sought advice from a Burmese doctor about how best to avoid it. That same year she married a human husband and, subsequently, had two children. At thirty-seven, at the insistence of her nat, she divorced her husband. During this long period she was punished by the nat in a variety of ways for refusing to marry him. He caused her not only to lose all her property (she had been a cigar merchant), but also to become ill; her symptoms included long fits or seizures, severe palpitations, vomiting, and inability to digest solid foods. Finally, apprehensive lest she "go mad," she married him. Since then her symptoms have disappeared and she has recovered her property.

Daw Kyoun, a female shaman in Mandalay, married her nat at the age of forty when he first indicated his love. She did not resist him because she feared that she, like her neighbor, would thereby become ill. Her neighbor, wishing to avoid marriage with the nat, had herself tatooed, hoping thereby that the nat would lose interest in her. Instead he punished her by giving her leprosy.

U Ei Maung, a male shaman in Mandalay, was first loved by his nat when he was twenty-five. Although now fifty-six, he has still not married her—he does not have sufficient funds for the wedding—and she still continues to punish him. She beats him on the back of the head with a wooden sandal, forces him to work as a traveling salesman (so that he cannot settle down in any one place), and is "always angry" with him.

These cases are cited to indicate that refusal to marry a nat who is determined to consummate his love is a very dangerous matter,[5] and that the harmful consequences of such refusal is a most important *conscious* motive for nat marriages, one which is stronger than the shame which might be experienced by the recruit.

These shamans, and others whom I interviewed, tend to exemplify the

[5]These dangers have been reported by Taw Sein Ko (Scott and Hardiman 1900: 75, Vol. I) as well.

following generalization of U Pou Zoun, who, as the custodian at Taungbyon, is a recognized authority on shamans. Typically, he says, a shaman
first encounters her nat while in her teens, and marries him between the
ages of thirty and forty. The encounter, however, and the subsequent
relationship between nat and recruit are by no means uniform. Some notion of the variability may be gathered from the following illustrative cases.

U Ka is the "husband" of the nat, Thoun Ban Hla. When he was
eighteen, she announced her love for him by appearing in his dream, and
lying beside him "as a sister." It was only after his marriage to her that
they began (in his dreams) to have sexual relations. Although he was also
married to a human, his nat spouse had no objections to his sex relations
with his human wife.

U Maung Maung was first loved by the nat Ma Ngwei Daun when, at
the age of twenty-five, he attended a nat festival. She appeared in his
dream as a beautiful woman and asked him to have sexual intercourse
with her. Although he had taken a human wife only two months previously,
he divorced her at the bidding of his nat spouse. Ma Ngwei Daun is married to a nat husband, U Min Kyaw, who, although consenting to the
marriage between his wife and U Maung Maung, always interferes when
the latter attempts to have sexual relations with her. U Maung Maung
has still not succeeded in consummating their relationship.

Kou Maung Kou, also loved by Ma Ngwei Daun, first encountered this
nat when, at the age of ten, he was taken ill and shamans were summoned
to propitiate the nats, including Ma Ngwei Daun. That night, after worshiping the Buddha, he fell asleep and a beautiful woman appeared to
him in a dream. She spoke to him as a "bride speaks to a bridegroom,"
telling him of her love. Recounting his dream to a shaman, the latter informed him that the woman was Ma Ngwei Daun. Now twenty-four, Kou
Maung Kou has no human wife because Ma Ngwei Daun has forbidden
him to take one until he marries her.

Daw Pya was sought out by the younger Taungbyon brother after she
attended the Taungbyon Festival when she was seventeen. He appeared
in her dream. He had no objection to her continued relationship with her
husband until, at the age of thirty-seven, she divorced her husband and,
at his bidding, married the nat. Married to him now for six years, she has
not taken another human husband, although her nat husband has no
objection to her doing so.

Daw Kyoun was possessed by her nat husband, U Min Kyaw, at the age
of forty, when, participating in the Taungbyon Festival, she fell into a
trance while dancing. Although she has since married this nat, she has,
nevertheless, remained married to her human husband as well, and, indeed,
she has since borne children by him.

Daw Thi Hla was first loved by the Mahagiri nats (U Tinde and his
sister) at the age of thirteen. For some time she had been emotionally

distraught, weeping and crying without any apparent provocation. A native doctor was consulted, and he informed her that she was loved by these nats. Later, when she was thirty-eight, she was possessed by the younger Taungbyon brother while dancing in the Taungbyon Festival, and married him shortly after. Two years later she married a human husband, but only after receiving permission from her nat husband.

Daw Ei Khin was sixteen when the Mahagiri nats appeared to her in a dream. Five or six years later, she was possessed by U Min Kyaw. Thereafter, as if "deranged," she "drifted about" the village in a trancelike state, barely eating or drinking. Prior to becoming possessed, she had been married and had borne a child, but U Min Kyaw, jealous of her husband, forbade her to resume sexual relations with him. The latter had to become a "servant" of the nat, doing his (i.e., his wife's) bidding. She does not suffer from sexual deprivation because she has sexual relations in her sleep with her nat husband.[6]

Technically, being loved by a nat does not make one a shaman until a formal marriage ceremony has been performed.[7] Many women who have not been formally married are nevertheless called *nat kadaws*, because they are loved by, even if not married to, a nat. Women are loved by a nat, so the shamans claim, because they have "beautiful" souls (*leikpya hlade*). Falling in love with the woman's soul, the nat manifests himself, as we have seen, either in a dream or through possession. In most instances, however, it is a full-fledged shaman who identifies the nat. When

---

[6]It should be noted that, despite the fact that the shaman has sexual relations with her nat husband, there are no reported cases of a shaman's claiming to have had a child by a nat.

[7]The marriage of a human being to a supernatural being is not, of course, unknown in the West. Catholic nuns are Brides of Christ, a state which they achieve by marrying their Heavenly Bridegroom in a formal wedding. Nor is the notion of a sexual relation with a supernatural entirely absent in the West. Although not conceptualized in sexual terms, the experiences of some of the great Christian mystics are unquestionably sexual, both in source and in content, as Leuba, among others, has shown (cf. Leuba 1925:137–55). More explicitly sexual are the ecstatic writings of cloistered nuns. For example: "Mechthild of Magdeburg recounted her love affair with Christ and advised 'all virgins to follow the most charming of all, the eighteen-year-old Jesus, so He might embrace them.' In her *Dialogue Between Love and the Soul*, she wrote, 'Tell my Beloved I am sick with love for Him . . . Then He took the soul into His divine arms, and placing His fatherly hand on her bosom, He looked into her face and kissed her well.' It was not uncommon for many ecstatically adept nuns to determine that they had been embraced by Christ and had conceived by Him. Some of these nuns even sustained false pregnancies as a result of such convictions. It is interesting to note that these sexual religious ecstasies were lent support by the consecration ceremonies of nuns during the Middle Ages, some of which are continued today in certain orders. The young candidate was given a gold wedding ring and called a bride of Christ. One ceremonial response was 'I love Christ whose bed I have entered.' And later in the ceremony they were urged to 'forget there all the world, and there be entirely out of the body; there in glowing love embrace your beloved (Savior) who is come down from heaven into your breast's bower, and hold Him fast until He shall have granted whatsoever you wish for'" (Stark 1965:105–6).

it is definitely established that the woman is loved by a specified nat, the shaman, typically, has the woman drink some "pure water" (*yei zin*), so that the nat will not "disturb" her (in dreams or by possession) too often.[8] Drinking the water symbolizes the woman's formal acceptance of the nat's "proposal." They are now "engaged."

Although engaged, the woman may delay the marriage ceremony, as almost all of those in the cases cited above had done, for many years. This delay is caused not only by the shame which most women feel about becoming nat wives, but also by the heavy expenses of the ceremony. A nat wedding in Taungbyon costs K1500–3000, and even a simple wedding in an ordinary village costs close to K1000 (over $200). Expenses to be defrayed include costumes for the bride, offerings to the nats, payment of the orchestra, construction of a *pandal* (or rental of a nat "palace"), fees for the shamans, feeding of invited guests, and so on. Since the average shaman is a person of modest means, it takes years to accumulate funds sufficient to defray these expenses.

In principle, nat weddings may be held in any month, according to the desire of the "husband." In fact, however, most weddings (at least in Upper Burma) occur in the month of Wagaun (August), shortly after the completion of the Taungbyon Festival. This month, it is to be noted, falls in the middle of the Buddhist Lent, a period in which ordinary human marriages are prohibited. (Nat authorities explain this apparent anomaly by pointing out that the prohibition against human marriages is intended to inhibit carnal appetites. Nat marriages, which are "spiritual," therefore do not come under the interdiction.) The wedding may not only be held at any time, but it may be held at any place. Again, however, just as the month of the Taungbyon Festival is the favorite time, so Taungbyon itself is the favorite site for nat weddings. Despite the greater expense of holding a wedding in Taungbyon, its great prestige as a nat center constitutes a strong inducement.

Wherever it is held, the wedding must be performed either in a nat "palace," such as the one at Taungbyon, or in a temporary structure, a *pandal*. Within the palace or *pandal* the main ceremony takes place in a "ceremonial chamber" (*san khan*), which consists merely of a section of the room, approximately eight feet square, enclosed by a string of cotton yarn. The string, about two feet off the ground, is attached to four *kadaw pwes* (coconut and banana offerings), one at each corner of the square. The central ritual, described below, must take place within this enclosure.

In the wedding which I observed—and presumably in others as well—the ceremony begins outside the "chamber." While the bride sits facing the

---

[8]Unfortunately, I do not know how the water is made "pure." Whatever the process, however, there are some who report that this water may be drunk by laymen as well and that it confers prosperity and long life on the drinker. I never encountered anyone except shamans who had drunk such water.

KEY TO THE SYMBOLS USED IN THE DIAGRAM

A. = A circular offering stand, called 'ka-lat', holding saffron stained uncooked rice.

B. = A blanket.

Br. = Bride.

C. = Comb.

Cu. = Aluminum cooking utensils, and porcelain plates, bowls, cups and saucers.

G. = A small glass bowl holding water and slices of garlic, and spoon.

K. = An offering stand holding coconut and banana, called a 'kadaw-pwe'.

L. = A small looking glass.

N. = A needle with a thread in its eye.

P. = A pillow.

Q. = Chief Queen.

R. = Rice balls in a silver plate.

S. = Circular stone slab, on which a cosmetic is prepared.

Sp. = Silk 'paso' and 'pa-wa' placed on a circular stand ('paso' is a male sarong; 'pa-wa' is a female scarf.)

T. = A piece of cylindrical 'tha-nat-kha' wood which is used in preparing a kind of cosmetic.

W. = A silver cup holding water.

Z. = Position occupied by the caretaker of the Taung-byon nat shrine.

Q.
Br. = The positions taken by the bride and the two Chief Queens when the 'feeding' and the 'leik-pya-theit'
Q.   rites are performed.

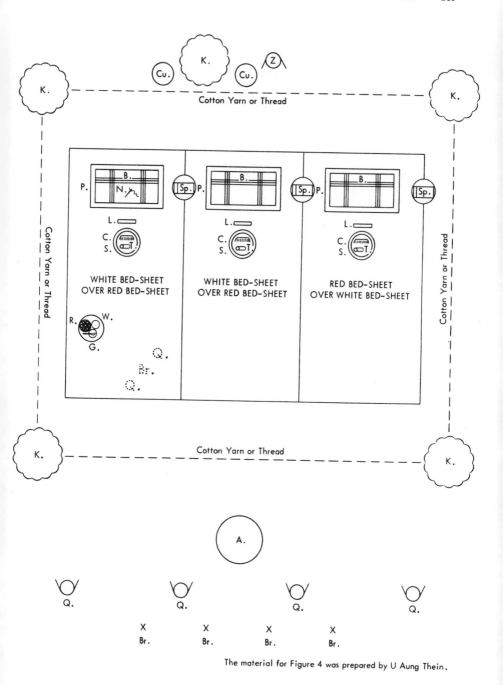

The material for Figure 4 was prepared by U Aung Thein.

FIGURE 4. *Diagram of the ceremonial chamber used for weddings with the Taungbyon nats.*

"chamber," a shaman, married to the nat to whom the bride is to be married, performs the nat's dance, accompanied by an orchestra, while yet another shaman sings the nat's ode. With the completion of the dance, the bride, in preparation for entering the "chamber," changes into her ceremonial costume, the traditional dress associated with her nat. As she is about to step inside this enclosure, her progress is obstructed by two persons (a male and a female), holding a chain, who do not permit her to enter until an entrance fee—known alternatively as a "bachelor's fee" (*lupyou kyei*) or "marriage fee" (*mingala kyei*)—is transferred to them by a member of the bridal party.[9] The amount of the fee varies from place to place; at Taungbyon it is K100, about $20. The fee paid, the bride now enters the "chamber" with two shamans, while the nat husband is invoked by means of the traditional song of invocation, sung to the accompaniment of the orchestra.

In effect the bride and her nat husband have now entered their bridal chamber, for, in addition to various objects used in the ritual, the "chamber" includes two beds (sleeping mats covered with sheets), one for the bride and one for the groom. (When one marries a Taungbyon brother, there is a bed for each of the brothers.) While the music is played a feeding rite takes place in which a shaman, seated on the bride's bed beside the bride, feeds her ritually prepared rice balls and water, seasoned with garlic.

Then follows the core of the wedding, the ceremony of "putting the (bride's) 'butterfly-spirit' (soul) to sleep" (*leikpya theit*). A shaman, holding a mirror in front of the bride, passes it to and fro in front of her face as the bride gazes into it. She then presses another mirror against the bride's back and a eugenia branch against her chest, and slowly moves them over her entire body. Still later the mirror is laid on her head, touching the eugenia branch which has been placed on it. At this time a second shaman ties a cotton string around each of the bride's wrists and ankles, then drapes a long, flowing string diagonally over each of her shoulders, and, finally, inserts a threaded needle into the bride's hair knot. The bride's soul is now believed to be "asleep," and she will soon become the wife of the nat.

The meaning of this rite is obscure. In general it is believed that the butterfly-spirit is fond of roaming and therefore unwilling to establish any permanent tie. Since, technically, it is the bride's butterfly-spirit, rather than her body, which is loved by the nat, it is "put to sleep," i.e., restricted to the bride's body, so that it might then be united with the butterfly-spirit of the groom. It is this union which finally consummates the marriage.[10]

---

[9] In human weddings it was customary to block the path which the groom took to the home of his bride with a strong cord. Until he paid a fee to the young men who put up the cord, he was not allowed to pass (see Shway Yoe 1896:57).

[10] According to Theodore Stern (personal communication), the Karen tie a person's wrists in order to keep his errant soul within his body. Moreover in the Karen wedding rite, the wrists of bride and groom are tied together.

When this ritual is completed, there remains only one more to be performed. A veil is fixed on the bride by the shamans, and flower garlands are draped around her neck. Then, kneeling and still facing the nat shrine, she performs a brief dance while the orchestra plays the music associated with her "husband." When the music stops, an announcement is made that the wedding has been completed, whereupon orchestra and singer burst into the "victory" song. While the nat offerings, which had been displayed all the while in the "chamber," are taken forward to the shrine, the bride rises, dances out of the "chamber," and facing the audience, performs the traditional dance associated with her nat husband. At the conclusion of the dance she is escorted from the hall and taken to a private room where she may rest, for the dancing, usually quite strenuous, leaves her enervated. This was especially marked in one of the four marriages which I witnessed. When the bride rose to dance, she was unable to move, and she staggered, limp, into the arms of two shamans. After much urging from them, she began to dance, only to collapse onto the floor. When, however, they picked her up and attempted to lead her from the hall, she violently resisted their efforts, and suddenly she began to dance. But the dance was not conventional. Instead, she whirled round and round. Several times the shamans caught her, and each time she broke out of their grasp, until finally, seemingly emerging from a trancelike state, she permitted herself to be led away.

Following the wedding the new shaman returns home where, for seven days, she remains secluded with her nat husband. She does not leave her room, and no one else may enter it. At the end of this period of seclusion she emerges to resume her normal life. She is now known, however, as a *nat kadaw*, a nat wife.

A MOTIVATIONAL EXPLANATION OF THE SHAMAN

Having described the shamanistic role and recruitment to it, it remains to provide an explanation for the incumbents of the role and the motivational bases for their recruitment. The obvious datum from which any explanation must take its departure is the claim by the shaman that she is loved, and was chosen, by a nat. Of course, one obvious possibility is to view the shaman as a dishonest person who, for any number of self-seeking motives, falsely makes such a claim. Although this interpretation is applicable, perhaps, to a minority of shamans, it is my opinion that the great majority sincerely believe that they have been loved by a nat, a belief which is based on what is for them a genuine personal encounter—usually in a dream—with their nat spouses. The men of Yeigyi, who impugn the integrity of most shamans, base their skepticism on the demonstrable fact that the clairvoyant power of these women (and men) is found frequently to be wanting. Given the Burmese world view, in which a genuine shaman would in fact possess clairvoyant power, a Burmese villager quite logically concludes that anyone who, though deficient in such power, claims to be a shaman is deceitful. If, however, this world view is rejected, the conclusion can also be rejected: because her predictive power is limited, it does not follow that the shaman's claim to be loved by a nat is spurious.

To argue that the shaman's claim is not spurious does not imply, however, that she is a passive agent in the development of her relationship with her nat. The contrary is the case. That most shamans, on the one hand, accept their calling only after considerable resistance indicates their ambivalence about recruitment to this status. That they feel compelled finally to do so, because of any number of painful experiences attendant upon their refusal, indicates, on the other hand, how strong is their desire for recruitment. From both these facts it can only be concluded that the experience of being loved by a nat is motivated by powerful, unsatisfied needs, that recruitment to the shamanistic role is intended to satisfy those needs, and that the performance of the role, in some measure at least, achieves their satisfaction.

Whatever these needs might be, and we shall examine them below, it must first be emphasized that motivation is not, of course, a sufficient explanation for recruitment, either to this or to any other achieved status. Needs alone do not create the experience of being loved by a nat; this experience, rather, is created by the interaction of the actor's needs with certain cultural beliefs or cognitions. In the Burmese behavioral environment it is taken for granted that nats exist, and that, among their other characteristics, they can fall in love with and possess human beings. These beliefs are learned by the shamans many years before the needs which motivate the experience of nat possession are acquired, or the experience itself is had. These beliefs, though not sufficient, are necessary conditions for this experience, contributing to it in two crucial ways. First, by providing the believer with extra-natural means for satisfying needs, they stimulate him, when under conditions of need-frustration, to seek these means. Second, as part of his cognitive system, these beliefs allow him to interpret (to perceive) some of the psychosomatic consequences of need-frustration—hysterical symptoms, seizures, trancelike behavior, fantasy and vision experiences—as signs of nat possession.

From this discussion, then, there can be seen, in outline, a suggested model for an explanation of recruitment to shamanism. According to this model, shamanistic recruitment requires the interaction of three variables—cognitive, motivational, and perceptual—such that, given certain nat beliefs (cognition), certain experiences, resulting from and/or instigated by need-frustration and the desire for need-satisfaction (motivation), will be interpreted as nat possession (perception). Having already explored in detail these beliefs, and having described, though all too briefly, these perceptions, this section will concentrate on the instigating needs, or motivations.

It should be emphasized from the outset that one would expect a variety of types, rather than one personality type, to be recruited to the shaman-istic role. This expectation is not merely a deduction from the general principle that any role can potentially satisfy a variety of different needs, but it is based, as well, on the character of Burmese nats. The nat pantheon is inhabited by a variety of nats, and different nats would be expected to appeal to different personalities. Whatever needs may be satisfied by being loved, for example, by the mother nat, Popa Medaw, they are surely differ-ent from those which are satisfied by the drunkard, U Min Kyaw. This theoretical expectation is consistently born out by my encounters with shamans: some are rough, some sensitive; some introversive, some extro-versive; some effeminate, others masculine; and so on.

Given that the shaman's role attracts a variety of personality types, it does not follow that recruitment to this status is haphazard or random. On the basis of my (admittedly small) sample, I would suggest that the initial recruitment experience, the experience of being loved by a nat, as well as persistence in it, are both motivated by the desire to satisfy any or all of the following frustrated needs: sexual, dependency, prestige, and, for want of a better term, Dionysian. These needs may be frustrated because, as in some sexual needs, a) the objects by which, or b) the acts in which, they may be satisfied are culturally forbidden; or because, as in some depen-dency and Dionysian needs, c) the drive itself is culturally forbidden; or because, as in some prestige needs, d) the social structure precludes their satisfaction. Unlike other religious means for gratifying forbidden and frustrated needs, in which gratification is achieved in disguised and indirect ways,[11] the performance of the shaman's role usually (but not always) gratifies these needs in an undisguised and, sometimes, in a direct fashion. In short, most of these needs, though requiring substitute (fantasy) satis-faction, entail little or no cognitive distortion, because the shaman's role explicitly permits the expression of needs which are forbidden to non-shamans. These abstract generalizations can be more readily comprehended with the following concrete examples of each of the four needs.

Sexual needs. In most, but not in all, cases, the nat is believed to love the shaman sexually. By substituting a nat for a human being the shaman is allowed undisguised satisfaction, albeit in fantasy, of prohibited sexual needs. "Prohibited," because ordinarily it is forbidden for an unmarried woman to have premarital sexual relations, or for a married woman to have extramarital sexual relations (or to practice polyandry), or for any-one to have homosexual or incestuous relations. And yet these are the very types of sexual relations—the first two quite definitely, the latter two only inferentially—which may characterize the relationship between shaman and nat. The sexually aroused adolescent girl, prohibited from any contact with a male, is possessed by a lusty nat. A married woman, whose husband

---

[11] The monastic role satisfies forbidden needs of Burmese Buddhist monks, for example, but their satisfaction is disguised or distorted. See, for example, Spiro 1965.

has weak sexual interests, or who enters the menopause with heightened sexuality but limited sexual opportunities, is possessed by a nat, well known for his sexual adventures. These two types of heterosexual relationships (pre- and extramarital) are obvious and explicit. The other two types, homosexual and incestuous, are inferential and, without additional data, must remain tentative.

With few exceptions male shamans seem to be either homosexual (manifest or latent), transvestite, or effeminate (and sometimes all three). Their nat, of course, is always female. If the male shaman, either in possession or in a dream, perceives himself as a female or identifies with his female nat, his sexual satisfaction acquires explicit homosexual overtones. To what extent this in fact does happen is, of course, conjectural. What is not conjectural is that the shaman not only is loved by his nat, but that when dancing, he *is* the nat. In the dance, wearing the costume of his female nat, reenacting her life, and in all ways becoming (identifying with) her, the shaman explicitly acts out the feminine components of his personality. If this be so, the male shaman may not be satisfying homosexual needs in the performance of this role, but he is certainly satisfying effeminate needs.

The reverse, of course, is true of female shamans. Although I have never heard of homosexuality or of transvestism among them, many are highly masculine in manner, and many others are married to weak, inconsequential males. If the female shaman does in fact have homosexual needs, they may be satisfied by identification with her nat husband. Some shamans, it should be added, are possessed by the brother and sister (Mahagiri) nats, a type of possession which has even more obvious homosexual possibilities. This is all the more plausible in the light of the apparent bisexuality of some shamans, a characteristic already remarked upon as early as the eighteenth century (cf. Hamilton 1930:31). Finally, as in the case of the males, the female shamans in their dances identify with and personify their nat husbands. At the very least, therefore, the shamanistic role enables a latent lesbian, one with a strong masculine component, to act out her masculine impulses.

The problem of incest arises in connection with the male shamans only, and stems from the fact that some nats may possess them as "mothers" and even as "sisters." (As far as I know, nats do not possess female shamans as "fathers" or as "brothers.") If these relationships include a sexual, in addition to a nurturant dimension, the role permits the satisfaction of incestuous desires, albeit in a disguised fashion (the nat is not taken to be the shaman's real mother).

Dependency needs. Male shamans, as has just been indicated, may be possessed by a female nat in the guise of a "mother" rather than of a "wife." When this happens, regressive dependency on a parent or any other adult, which is ordinarily denied to normal adults, is permitted undisguised satisfaction in fantasy to the shaman. If some shamans *satisfy* their dependency needs by leaning on a nat mother, such as Popa Medaw, others *express* such needs in a highly regressive identification with the baby girl nat, Ma Ne. By identifying with this nat child, and personifying her in the dance, the shaman expresses his dependency, making claims, as it were, on the nurturance of all who watch him.

Prestige needs. In Burma, as in all societies, many people suffer frustrations, not because of cultural prohibitions, but because of social structural or physiological impediments. Women may feel status-deprived because of their low position in the social hierarchy; the poor may feel of little consequence because of their humble position in the economic hierarchy; the unattractive may feel inferior because of their inferior status in the sexual hierarchy; and so forth. By "prestige needs" I refer to these and all other needs which have to do with esteem, either in one's own view or in the view of others. Any number of such frustrated needs may find undisguised, substitute gratification in the shaman's role. For some, being loved by a nat—though a poor substitute, perhaps, for being loved and cherished by another human being—is certainly better than not being loved at all. For others, to be loved by a nat is a much greater enhancement of one's self-esteem than to be loved by a human. The nat, after all, is a "god," who, when he was human, may even have been a prince of the royal blood. It is surely no accident, when looked at this way, that only a small minority of shamans are of upper-class origin. Although U Pou Zoun, the custodian at Taungbyon, estimates their number as 10 per cent of the total, other informants believe that the proportion of upper-class shamans is much smaller than that. My own impression is that they comprise no more than 1 or 2 per cent.

Being loved by a nat is not the only source of ego gratification afforded by the shamanistic role. For a retiring person, essentially unrecognized but with a desire for recognition and attention, the shaman's role is a dramatic means to that end. Not only do people come to the shaman for consultation or for nat propitiation—the shaman, unskilled at anything else, is a recognized expert in something—but, when dancing at nat festivals, the shaman is the center of attention for hundreds, sometimes thousands, of spectators. That the shaman, as we have seen, is often an object of derision and contempt, does not disconfirm this argument. For a person with strongly deprived status needs, any kind of attention, even notoriety, is to be preferred to the ignominy of being ignored.

If being loved by a nat brings esteem, at least in his own eyes, to the shaman, then this must have important effects on his sense of identity. Indeed, it might be suggested that recruitment to this status is motivated by (among other things) an attempt to resolve an identity problem. Thus, for example, a member of the lower class, discontent with his class position, can acquire an entirely different social identity by becoming the spouse of a royal nat. Similarly, unhappy with, and in conflict over, his sexual identity, a latent homosexual can resolve his identity problem by identification with his nat of opposite sex. The shamanistic role allows the recruit to act out many identity problems of this kind.

Dionysian needs. As Buddhists, the Burmese are constrained to act in measured ways, taking their enjoyments in moderation and renouncing the orgiastic in all forms. (Even in their secular dances, these constraints are not removed. The dancer performs in a long skirt, reaching to the ankles, the movements of her legs and feet being circumscribed by the width of the skirt.) Chafing under such restrictions, the shaman, in behavior prescribed by her nat, is provided a sanctioned outlet for otherwise repressed Dionysian impulses. In possession she is permitted to lose ego control; in the dance she may move with wild abandon; in impersonation of the nat, she may guzzle alcoholic drinks, brandish a sword, cavort like a buffalo. In short, being loved by a nat permits her, openly and without disguise, to perform orgiastic acts that are otherwise absolutely tabooed.

These, perhaps, are some of the needs which motivate recruitment to the shamanistic role, or, more specifically, which provide the motivational basis for the belief that one is loved by a nat. It is the interaction of these needs with culturally acquired cognitions about nats which, I have argued, allows the shaman to interpret or perceive certain of his experiences as nat possession. The remaining question then is to account for these experiences —i.e., to identify the stimulus conditions that evoke the kinds of emotional experiences which, when had by individuals with the cognitions and needs already outlined, are perceived as nat possession. A complete answer to this question requires richer and more detailed data on a larger sample of shamans than I now possess. Nevertheless, there are sufficient data to provide at least some clues for the beginning of an explanation. The basic clue lies in the fact that, instead of occurring randomly, the first experience of nat possession—as far at least as the shamans in my sample are concerned—occurs during or immediately following a nat festival, or during or immediately following some traumatic experience. Let us examine each of these contexts separately.

Some nat festivals, such as Taungbyon, are so strongly conducive to possession that some women, it will be recalled, refuse to attend the festival from fear (as they conceptualize it) that a nat will fall in love with them. This fear is well grounded for, somewhat differently conceptualized, it may be said to contain an essential psychological truth, *viz.*, that it is the configuration of stimuli comprising the festival that triggers the experience of nat possession. The heightened emotionality produced by large, milling crowds, the imbibing of intoxicating liquor, the exposure to sexually arousing verbal and physical stimulation, the witnessing of orgiastic dancing, the hearing of songs recounting the sexual prowess and appetites of the nats who, moreover, invite the females "to love them now as they had loved them when they were alive"—all of this occurs during the Buddhist

Lent when sensuous pleasures have been muted by religious proscription. And it follows the planting season when these pleasures have already been reduced by the reality of hard work and rigid schedules. Such is the context in which, or immediately following which, nat possession occurs. More accurately, this is the sociocultural configuration which produces those psychophysiological states—trance, hysteria, intoxication, etc.—which are taken to be symptomatic of possession.

It is obvious, of course, since most participants in a nat festival do not become possessed, that this context is not a sufficient condition for the possession experience. Seeking a more comprehensive explanation, we are aided by some additional clues, the most important being that possession is not randomly distributed within the population. Restricting this discussion to female shamans, it will be recalled that, typically, females are possessed by a nat, and/or decide to marry a nat who had previously possessed them, either in adolescence or in or near menopause. These are females, in short, who are either first experiencing the mounting pressures of sexual desire and therefore—especially in Burma, where any physical contact with the opposite sex is prohibited—of sexual frustration, or they are females who, at menopause, are experiencing a heightening of their sex drives combined with the fear of losing their sexual attractiveness. The attendant frustration of the menopausal females is further intensified (in a large percentage of cases) by marriages with socially weak and sexually inadequate husbands. Add to this a previous observation, *viz.*, that the majority of those possessed, being of lower-class origin, are also suffering from status deprivation, and it then becomes at least plausible that one explanation for the differential effect of nat festivals is differential drive-intensity. That is, it is the women with the strongest frustrations (sexual, prestige, etc.) who are most susceptible to possession.

But differential drive strength is not enough. Even among the women whose frustrations are especially strong, only a small number become shamans. We must look therefore for additional explanatory variables. If differential drive strength provides part of the explanation, differential cognitive strength must surely provide yet another part. Here again two observations come to our assistance. It is striking that a large proportion of shamans, according to informants, are the daughters of shamans. It is also striking that villages which are situated near nat centers—such as nat shrines, sites of nat festivals, areas historically associated with the life of some nat, and so on—seem to have a disproportionately large percentage of shamans. In Yeigyi, for example, there is only one full-fledged shaman, while in the much smaller village of Ingyin—the village in which the nat Ma U was born and lived, until killed by the Taungbyon Brothers—there are eight. It is reasonable to assume that environments in which nats are a constant and vivid feature of a growing girl's daily experience provide an unusually strong experiential basis for the cognitive affirmation of the reality and importance of nats. Given the greater cognitive strength of their nat beliefs, it is not surprising that they exhibit a greater tendency to perceive such psychophysiological phenomena as trance, hysteria, and so on, as symptoms of nat possession.

Differential drive strength and differential cognitive conviction are, then, two of the factors which help to explain differential recruitment to the status of shaman. But these factors only narrow the field; they hardly exhaust it. Most women with the drives and needs, the cognitions and beliefs described here, do not become shamans even when exposed to the stimulation of nat festivals. Clearly, then, there remain still unknown factors which, finally, distinguish female shamans from other women.

In my sample all but one of the females first experienced nat possession at nat festivals, whereas all but one of the males had their first experience of possession following trauma. Whether this is an artifact of a small sample, or whether it is a valid generalization about sex differences, I cannot tell. Rather than speculate, therefore, on the possible meaning of this sex difference,[12] I shall turn to some concrete cases.

In one case the death of a young man's mother was followed by his experience of being loved "as a mother" by Popa Medaw, the mother of the Taungbyon Brothers. In another case it was during the Japanese bombing of Mandalay in World War II that the shaman experienced the love of the baby girl nat, Ma Ne. In still another case the precipitating crisis was illness. As a child, the shaman—an adopted son of a shaman—while being treated for an illness by nat propitiation, was possessed in his dream by Ma Ngwei Daun.

In all three of these cases there are still other factors that are probably related to the possession experience. The shaman who lost his mother had been deeply attached to her and, while still in mourning, had gone to "worship" the relics of a famous monk.[13] It was on that occasion that he was "told by the monk" to propitiate Popa Medaw. Shortly after propitiating her, she appeared in his dream, telling him that she loved him, "as

[12]This difference in instigating conditions may also relate to the great disparity in the sexual incidence of shamanism—women, it will be recalled, outnumber men by a very wide margin. Again, however, in the absence of data, this problem cannot be handled here. At least three factors, none of them mutually exclusive, may be related to this problem, however. a) There are systematic, sex-linked, constitutional differences which render Burmese females more susceptible to possession. b) Burmese males suffer from less intense conflict than females, with respect at least to those needs which are importantly satisfied by the shamanistic role. There is some evidence that this might indeed be the case. c) There exist for Burmese males, but not for the females, institutional alternatives which serve as functional equivalents for the shamanistic role. The monastic role, for example, may satisfy at least some of the same needs that are satisfied in shamanism. For the females there is no structural alternative; the nunhood, for example, is (in most cases) the last refuge for the unsuccessful and unwanted.

[13]The remains of famous monks are buried in urns, often within their monastic compounds, and sometimes shrines are built over them. Believed to possess magical power, these enshrined relics are often "worshiped."

a mother loves her son." Today, as a shaman, when he is about to dance, he longs for, and feels compassion for, her as he thinks "about her tragic life." It requires little insight to see in Popa Medaw a mother surrogate for this man. The latter two cases are the reverse of the first case. Orphaned as very young children (in one case both parents had died; in the other, the mother only), they were brought up, first by one set of relatives, and then by another. Without stable or nurturant maternal environments, it is not implausible to assume that both were seeking mother figures.

As in the case of the female shamans, these precipitating factors hardly comprise a sufficient explanation for the inception of shamanism in these males; many nonshamans, too, have experienced similar life crises and personal traumata. As in the case of the female shamans, however, it is possible here to further narrow the explanatory net. Male shamans differ from their female counterparts in that, with some exceptions, the males tend to be bachelors, while the females tend to be married. Male shamans, as has already been indicated, are usually highly effeminate, often practicing transvestism, in private if not in public, and giving the strong appearance of latent, if not active, homosexuality. Indeed, some of them are alleged to be practicing homosexuals. Although homosexuality and transvestism are both found in Burma outside of shamanism, they are viewed, in these other contexts, with disdain. Practiced as part of the shamanistic role, however, they are accepted, if not approved. Similarly, although there are no formal sanctions which discriminate against bachelors in Burma, it is taken for granted, and indeed expected, that a "normal" male will marry. The male shaman, though a bachelor, can escape the onus of "abnormality" by his claim that his nat prohibited him from marrying, or, if married, that she ordered him to divorce his wife. This is exactly what two male shamans, highly effeminate and obviously uninterested in women—and whose claims I take to be sincere—have claimed. One said he could not marry until his nat gave him permission, and the other, who had been married, divorced his wife at the instigation of his nat, only two months after his human wedding.

This explanatory model, then, though not unproblematic, has enabled us to point to a number of variables which serve, in part, to elucidate the problem of shamanistic recruitment. To be sure, there remain still unknown, and probably idiosyncratic, factors which have eluded our explanatory net and which, finally, distinguish shamans from nonshamans. I would suggest that these are of two types. In the first place, there may be a host of experiences in the life history of shamans which either renders this role more congenial than any of its possible functional alternatives, or which precludes the availability and/or viability of these alternatives. In the second place, there may be a number of constitutional variables—genetic, temperamental, etc. —which are related to susceptibility to suggestion, trance, hysteria, and so on; and it is difficult to believe that differences in the occurrence of possession at nat festivals or during emotional crises are not importantly related to constitutional differences in the tolerance thresholds for these psychosomatic phenomena. Since both suggestions, however, require additional research, it is more profitable, in the absence of further data, to turn from the problem of role recruitment to that of role persistence.

If, as our data suggest, the shaman is recruited to her role by a number of unresolved conflicts and painful frustrations, it is not unlikely that she remains in this role because of its continued capacity to satisfy these, as well as other, needs. I can merely touch upon some of the latter needs. For the shaman who despises her husband, it is convenient to be able to explain her treatment of him as a servant as obedience to the command of her nat. For the shaman who wishes to break up her marriage, it cannot be long before she believes that it is her nat husband who insists that a divorce be obtained. Unable to settle into a sedentary, "normal" existence, the male shaman attributes his restlessness to his nat, who desires that he move from one nat festival to the next. And so on. Thus, the shaman is not only spared the pain of self-criticism, but she is also spared the criticism which, were she not a shaman, her behavior would evoke from others: because her behavior is prescribed by the nat, it can be exhibited with impunity.

The latter statement holds not only for deviation from norms of morality and etiquette, but for deviation from norms of psychological normality as well. Although I have been arguing that shamanism represents a resolution of conflict—and I shall return to this thesis again—there are nevertheless some few shamans whose conflicts are not resolved in their role performance. The latter, unlike the majority who, in my experience at least, appear to be quite normal, suffer from extreme psychological disturbance. For them, the psychopathological elements in their role behavior—which for most shamans is confined to, because temporarily resolved by, the intermittent activation of the role—spill over into other aspects of their lives. Their transvestism or homosexuality, for example, are manifested outside of possession as well as during it. Their speech and thought processes are disorganized and schizoid in ordinary discourse, as well as in their trancelike states. I have met only two of the latter types, one male and one female. Looked upon by their fellows as "crazy," their strange behavior is accepted with mingled amusement and sympathy because it is attributed to the nats. Interestingly enough, the one abnormal male shaman whom I know well not only is viewed by others as "crazy," but views himself so. Explaining his abnormality as a punishment (by his nat) for having neglected to arrange for their marriage, he is confident that it will disappear once the wedding is performed.

This leads to my last observation concerning shaman personality. When confronting the events which precede shamanistic recruitment, as well as the emotional states which both precede recruitment to the role and accompany its performance, one cannot help but be struck by the similarities between Burmese shamanism and Burmese psychopathology (see Chapter 10). In both cases we observe symptoms of physical (psychosomatic?) illness—intestinal pains, palpitations, and so on; both are characterized by dissociational states; and both are believed to be caused by supernatural possession. And yet I agree with the Burmans in viewing most shamans as normal, and most nonshamans who exhibit these same characteristics as abnormal. This seeming paradox demands an explanation.

For me, an explanation was first suggested while pondering an important ethnographic fact about possession. In nonshamanistic dissociation, the actor must be freed from the supernatural who has possessed him; he remains ill until the supernatural is exorcised. In shamanistic dissociation, the contrary obtains. It is the actor, attempting to free himself from the supernatural, who becomes ill; he becomes well only when he agrees to permanent possession by the supernatural—when, that is, he unites ("ties") his soul with that of the supernatural in marriage. In short, from the Burmese point of view, possession, for the nonshaman, is the cause of illness; for the shaman, it is its cure. Although the Burmese could probably not explain why it is so, this thesis is, I believe, profoundly true. In our terms we would say that the dissociational states that accompany nonshamanistic possession are an expression of, and an unsuccessful attempt to resolve, conflict, while in shamanism these states result in the reduction, if not in the resolution of conflict.[14] This thesis is best explicated by reference to some ethnographic data, already presented, and in the light of the general theory of dissociation formulated in Chapter 10.

In the first place, it will be recalled that the illness which precedes shamanistic recruitment is believed to be caused by a benign nat. The nat, usually in a dream, informs the recruit of his love for her, and it is only because the latter declines to marry him that he attempts to goad her into marriage by causing her to suffer various troubles, including illness. Having once declared his love, the nat may continue to appear to the future shaman in her dreams, or he may possess her during nat dancing—and in both cases the experience is always pleasant, if not ecstatic. Nonshamanistic illness, on the other hand, is always caused by a punitive nat, a ghost, or a witch. Angered because neglected (nat) or harmed (witch), or from sheer malevolence (ghost), the supernatural is motivated by malice rather than by love. He possesses the actor with the intention of harming him. It is not surprising, then, that the dissociative behavior of the patient is either harmful to himself (in cases of unconsciousness, simple trance) or to others (in cases of trance aggression). Nor is it surprising that (in dissociation) the experiences of possession or (in hallucination) the encounters with the supernatural are ones of great fear and anxiety. (We

[14]Ackerknecht, in a comparative study of shamans, states categorically that ". . . shamanism is not disease but being healed from disease" (1943:46).

have already noted that hallucination, an obvious symptom of pathology, is not a characteristic of the shaman. He either interprets certain sensations as indicators of possession or, if he perceives the nat, it is while dreaming.)

These reported phenomenological differences between shamanistic and nonshamanistic possession are related systematically to differences in their instigating needs. Shamanistic possession, as I have suggested, is motivated by the desire to satisfy frustrated sexual, dependency, and prestige needs. Unable to satisfy these needs by other means, the shamanistic recruit hopes to satisfy them through the shaman's role. In conflict between the desire to become a shaman and the public shame attendant upon the performance of this role, she resists marriage with the nat who has declared his love for her, and this conflict is expressed in various psychosomatic symptoms. As her tensions mount, she succumbs to her persistent, barely repressed desire to marry—i.e., to become possessed by—the nat. In so doing her conflict is reduced, if not resolved, and her frustrated needs are satisfied, at least in part.

The dissociational and hallucinatory experiences found in nonshamanistic possession and attack are, in general, motivated by a different set of instigating needs, which might be grouped together as moral anxiety. Having committed some offense or harm, either against the attacking supernatural or someone else, the actor becomes a victim, either of his own intrapunitive needs or of his fear of retaliation, which he has externalized in the form of attacking supernaturals. Unlike shamanistic possession, then, nonshamanistic possession expresses conflict, rather than reducing or resolving it. Dissociative and hallucinatory behavior are thus symptoms of pathology requiring therapy.

One might say, then, that shamans are recruited from persons suffering from either pathological or at least pathogenic symptoms, and that it is by becoming shamans that they are saved from psychopathology. By resolving their conflicts and satisfying their frustrated needs, this culturally sanctioned role spares them the emotionally disruptive consequences of continuous conflict or the repression of their unsatisfied needs, and hence, of continued frustration. They are spared, too, the cognitively disorienting consequences of resolving their problems by means of privately constructed, idiosyncratic symbol systems. Some of these needs, to be sure, are satisfied in dissociative experiences, associated with the shamanistic role. But occurring, as they do, only intermittently and in culturally patterned, culturally induced, and culturally controlled contexts, they can hardly be considered in themselves to be pathological. On the contrary, by satisfying the shaman's frustrated needs, these experiences serve to contain these pathogenic stimuli. It should also be noted that the cognitive distortion which is characteristic of hallucinatory experiences (and which is surely a sign of pathology) plays no role in the shaman's behavior. The shamanistic role, in short, functions as a culturally constituted defense, which, by satisfying the shaman's frustrated needs and thereby precluding the need for idiosyncratic defenses, serves to avert the outbreak of psychopathology.[15]

It need not be emphasized that in resolving the personal conflicts and gratifying the personal needs of the shaman, this role serves important social functions as well. In the absence of this or of some functionally equivalent role, the shamans, whose forbidden desires are now satisfied by their role performance, would remain frustrated; and it is not hard to imagine that they would then become agents of discontent and unrest. Provided with an outlet, these potentially disruptive needs—being contained by, because satisfied in, the shamanistic role—have little if any adverse affect on the normal working of Burmese society.

[15]Although there appear to be some minor differences between us, my views concerning shaman personality are very similar to those propounded by Devereux in his very important contribution to this subject. Devereux (1956:30) views the shaman's conflict as ". . . *located in the unconscious segment of his ethnic personality, rather than in the idiosyncratic portion of his unconscious.* . . . [Therefore], he can express, control, and redirect his impulses and conflicts by using the many—usually ritualized —devices which each culture places at the disposal of those whose conflicts are of the 'conventional type.' " For Devereux, however, these culturally constituted defenses, though allowing the shaman to function, do not conceal the fact that he remains a neurotic or psychotic. For him, the shaman ". . . is simply in remission" (*Ibid.*, 32).

I agree with Devereux that the shamanistic recruit suffers from a neurotic conflict; I am even prepared to agree that shamanism represents not a cure but a "remission." But to the extent that his new role permits him to reduce, if not to resolve, his conflict, I would argue, in the case of the Burmese shaman at least, that his neurosis, if not cured, is at least "contained." As long as he remains a shaman, his pathogenic needs are satisfied within a culturally acceptable role, so that he is a problem neither to himself nor to society. To be sure, were he deprived of this culturally constituted defense, his conflicts would again overpower him. But, on this score, I see little difference between the shaman and the rest of mankind. Without culture and the defenses which it provides we would all be conflict-ridden. The only difference, then, between the shaman and the rest of us is that our conflicts, being less intense, require cultural defenses which, commensurately, are less dramatic.

CHAPTER THIRTEEN

The Exorcist

DESCRIPTION OF THE ROLE

The Burmese call the supernatural practitioner with which this chapter is concerned an *ahtelan hsaya* ("Master of the Upper Path"). Among the many components which comprise the role-set of this practitioner, we are concerned here primarily with its exorcistic component. Among other things, the *ahtelan hsaya* possesses the power to expel harmful supernaturals from those whom they have possessed (see Chapters 9 and 11). Here, then, is a salient difference between the exorcist and the shaman. The shaman propitiates the harmful supernaturals, the exorcist (in principle, if not always in practice) controls them. The *ahtelan hsaya*, however, is not the only practitioner who possesses power to control harmful supernaturals. The same power is exercised by the *aulan hsaya* ("Master of the Lower Path"). The latter, it will be recalled (see Chapter 2), is a master witch who achieves his malevolent ends by compelling harmful spirits to execute his intentions.

Although this chapter is concerned with exorcistic power of the *ahtelan hsaya*, it should at least be noted that his power to control spirits is but one aspect of his more general power. Every *ahtelan hsaya* is a member of one of many quasi-Buddhist sects (*gaings*), all of which share the common aim of acquiring magico-religious power.[1] In some instances it is

---

[1]Mendelson, whose knowledge of these *gaings* is unexcelled by any Western writer, prefers to call them "Messianic Buddhist Associations." For a detailed description of some specific *gaings*, as well as of their generic attributes, his articles (Mendelson 1960, 1961a, 1961b, 1963a) are indispensable.

religio-political power, to be attained through the restoration of the mon-
archy, which is sought. But in most instances what is sought is the power
to become a *weikza*, the power, that is, to prolong life indefinitely, or at
least until the arrival in 2500 years of the future Buddha, Maitreya. Just
prior to his arrival, the relics of the present Buddha, Gautama, will be
recombined to form his physical body. By worshiping him, the *weikza*
will automatically achieve nirvana. In the meantime, he has not only
achieved a partial immortality, but he has acquired power to perform
numerous supernatural feats.

The crucial means for becoming a *weikza* is through the practice of
alchemy, and different sects specialize in different alchemic practices. The
ahtelan hsaya, therefore, devotes much of his time and most of his economic resources to this occult practice. Although his *materia alchemica*
may still be insufficiently powerful to enable him to become a *weikza*, they
are yet powerful enough to combat harmful supernaturals. The *ins*, *datlouns*, and other objects used in the exorcistic seance (see Chapter 11)
are key ingredients of the *ahtelan hsaya*'s alchemic kit. Moreover, it is the
power acquired from the alchemic (and other occult) practices of his sect,
as well as the power derived from the *weikzas* associated with his sect,
which, in part, permit him with impunity to have traffic with harmful
supernaturals.

But his alchemic and occult practices are not the only source of his
power. The *gaing* is a "quasi-Buddhist" sect, not only because one of its
goals is the attainment of nirvana—and, in some instances of Buddhahood—but because initiation into the sect requires a commitment to
Buddhist discipline. The sect member must observe the moral precepts
of Buddhism; he must practice Buddhist devotions; and he must engage
in Buddhist meditation. These activities are not only the necessary—
though not sufficient—means for the achievement of *weikza*-hood, but they
are also a means for achieving control over harmful supernaturals.
Through them he acquires the power which renders him less susceptible,
if not immune, to attack from these malevolent beings. Moreover, by these
activities he comes under the protection of the Buddhist "gods" (*devas*),
and it is with their assistance that he is able to defeat the harmful supernaturals.

Exorcism, then, is but one of the occult powers which is acquired by
membership in one of these sects. Not every sect member is an exorcist,
but every exorcist is a member of, and acquires his power through membership in, a sect. Since only the exorcistic role of the *ahtelan hsaya* is
relevant to our discussion of Burmese supernaturalism, I shall refer to him
simply as an "exorcist."

Like the shaman, the exorcist is a part-time practitioner. Since, however, many exorcists are also traditional doctors (*hsei hsaya*), and since
many combine both types of medical practice with astrology and other

occult practices, it is possible that some urban exorcists are full-time practitioners. The city, whose population base provides a potentially large clientele, might well enable some exorcists who combine all of these therapeutic skills to devote full time to the practice of medicine and the occult.[2] All the exorcists whom I know, however, both in rural and urban areas—even when they are also native doctors—are part-time specialists, deriving their main income from other occupations. These include, in my sample, an agricultural laborer, a canal guard, a night watchman, a truck driver, a police sergeant, and a Buddhist monk. In addition to these, I know two exorcists, both living in Mandalay, who, claiming to be *weikzas* as well as being claimants to the throne, are supported by the offerings of their followers.

Unlike the shaman, the exorcist, *qua* exorcist, does not participate in any cultus, nor is he an officiant of one. He may, *qua* animist, participate in the nat cultus; and he most certainly, *qua* Buddhist, participates in the Buddhist cultus. As an exorcist, however, he is exclusively devoted to the treatment of supernaturally caused illness and, particularly, of possession.

Although practiced as a part-time specialty, the exorcist role exhibits, if only in nascent form, most of the characteristics of professionalization. It not only requires specialized, achieved skills but it is also, in the words of contemporary role theory, functionally specific, affectively neutral, client-oriented, and universalistic. Since all but the last of these criteria have more or less the same meaning in any sociocultural context, it is only the latter, the universalistic, criterion which I should like briefly to discuss. This criterion, uniquely, raises certain moral dimensions of a professional relationship which can be culturally variable. Among these dimensions I should like to examine, through some simple examples, only four which arise in the exorcist-patient relationship.

The first dimension concerns the exorcist's responsibility for the patient. Here an unqualified rule is expected to govern the exorcist's behavior. Although an exorcist may refuse with impunity to treat a patient, once he has entered a case he must, unless he knows that he is inadequate to the task, see it through to completion. Let us take, as an example, the case of Kou Swe, the young man who was possessed by an *ouktazaun* spirit (see Chapter 11). After four hours of exorcism, it became apparent, to both the assembled group and the exorcist himself, that some dangerous forces had been unleashed which were too powerful for him to cope with; he was clearly frightened. Despite his fear, however, it was his professional duty to continue with the treatment, a duty which placed him in a painful dilemma. If he fulfilled his moral obligation and continued with the treatment, he would expose himself to serious physical danger. If, however, he

---

[2]Although proscribed by monastic rules, some Buddhist monks also serve as exorcists. It is to be noted, however, that no monk ever serves as a shaman, nor, consistent with the differences between them, does an exorcist.

discontinued the treatment on those grounds, he would lay himself open to the charge of unethical practice; and if he discontinued it on the grounds of inadequacy, he would be admitting his incompetence. Fortunately, his dilemma was resolved, and he was allowed to save face, when the headman and elders recommended that the most famous exorcist in the area be called into the case. With respect to the moral issue, theirs was a face-saving recommendation because it was not he, but they, the village authorities, who decided that he withdraw. Moreover, by recommending that a most distinguished exorcist be called in, his competence was not uniquely impugned; it was as if an ordinary physician in our society, faced with an especially vexatious case, were to turn for assistance to a famous specialist. (This attempted face-saving was not entirely successful. A few weeks later the exorcist informed me that he was forsaking exorcism—this, after I had heard a number of people suggest that he was, indeed, not very competent.)

A more serious example (already alluded to in Chapter 2, pg. 31), in which an exorcist was in fact charged with unethical practice, arose in the case of Kou Aung (described in Chapter 10), who was bewitched by his former wife. A few nights after an apparently successful exorcism, Kou Aung again became exceptionally violent, attacking even his friends and kinsmen with fists and knife. In great fear, his relatives invited his exorcist, who lived in another village, to resume his treatment. When they described the symptoms to the exorcist, it became quite obvious to me— I had driven them to his home—that he was as frightened as they. Saying that he could not resume his treatment unless the date were astrologically auspicious, he entered his house to consult his calendar. Emerging after a long delay, he reported that he could not accompany them to the patient's home because, according to his calendar, that day and the next were inauspicious; were he to treat the patient, both he and his patient would suffer serious trouble. He could, however, he hastened to add, return on the third day. In the meantime, he would give them some medicine which they could administer to the patient, and he would lend them his exorcist's wand by which they would be able to subdue the witch. Taking the medicine and the wand out of courtesy, Kou Aung's relatives returned to the car. As we drove away they all agreed that the exorcist's astrological explanation was a ruse, and that by not accompanying them he had violated his professional duty. Regardless of the danger or inconvenience to him, the exorcist "must first of all have compassion (*myitta*) for the patient." Never again would they turn to him.

But the exorcist has still another responsibility to a patient. Just as he may not abandon a patient once he has begun the treatment, so—and this is the second rule—he may not commence treatment without permission of the patient or, if the latter is incompetent, of a responsible kinsmen. Thus, in the case of Kou Swe, his exorcist, a close friend, could not treat him until he gave his consent. When a second exorcist was called into the case, he took no heed of Kou Swe's insistence that he did not wish to be treated by him—Kou Swe was in a state of great agitation and, hence, incompetent—but he would not proceed until he had first obtained permission from Kou Swe's wife. To treat a patient without permission would be laying oneself open to the charge of practicing the black arts, of being an *aulan hsaya* rather than, or in addition to, an *ahtelan hsaya*.

As the exorcist has a responsibility to the patient, the latter has a responsibility to the exorcist. Thus a third rule governing the exorcist-patient relationship is that a patient may not, in the course of treatment, seek a second exorcist without obtaining the permission of the first. And, as a corollary, there is still a fourth rule, one which governs the relationship between exorcists: one exorcist may not enter a case which has been, or is being, treated by another exorcist without the latter's consent. Thus, in the case of Kou Swe, it was necessary to obtain the permission of his first exorcist in order to bring in a second. And, when the latter arrived, he asked the former if he had his permission to enter the case. Similarly, in the case of Kou Aung, when his exorcist refused to treat him for three days, he made it clear that if this were not satisfactory, he would release the patient so that his relatives would be free to seek another therapist. When, in fact, they did obtain another, they immediately informed him that Kou Aung had been released by his former exorcist.

RECRUITMENT TO THE ROLE

Not having conducted a systematic census of exorcists, I cannot say how prevalent they are, either within and among villages, or within and among regions. In the Yeigyi region, exorcists are to be found in some, but not in all villages, and in Yeigyi itself, a village of five hundred people, there are two. Although the average exorcist does not, *qua* citizen, enjoy exceptional prestige, neither does he suffer the mild contempt that is frequently the fate of the shaman. Moreover, there is less skepticism concerning his skills, for only half of those in Yeigyi who expressed skepticism about the power of shamans were skeptical of the power of exorcists. And there is also a greater demand for them—while only seven Yeigyi households (out of eighty-two) had used shamans, thirty-three had used exorcists.

Putting it more positively, it would not be inaccurate to state that the exorcist, *qua* exorcist—here, again, he differs from the typical shaman—enjoys the respect of his fellows. In the case of a famous exorcist, the respect is commensurately greater. This is not surprising when it is remembered that almost all the elements in his elaborate symbol system are Buddhist, and that with these symbols the exorcist has the ability to tap the great reservoirs of beneficent power contained in Buddhism. Symbolic of this respect is the obeisance which the patient, in the form of ritual prostration, offers him during the ceremony. In Burma, this is the highest possible form of respect.

This is not to say that all exorcists are viewed as powerful or that all are regarded as equally powerful; it is to say, however, that there is very little skepticism about the efficacy of the role. Thus, in the case of Kou Swe, although there developed considerable skepticism concerning the power of his first exorcist, skepticism of the man generated no skepticism concerning the role: instead of suggesting that some alternative technique be used to deal with the case, it was suggested, rather, that a more powerful exorcist be called in. Moreover, when an exorcist in whom people have faith meets with apparent failure, they are prepared to follow him in attributing the fault to some technical error in the performance of the role rather than to question its efficacy. Thus, when the *ouktazaun* returned to haunt Kou Swe only a few brief days after a second exorcist had conducted an apparently successful ceremony, the villagers agreed with the exorcist that the ceremony had not, after all, been entirely unsuccessful because, although the *ouktazaun* had returned, she was obviously afraid to enter Kou Swe's house. They also accepted as reasonable the exorcist's explanation for his partial failure, *viz.*, when he ordered her not to return, he neglected to include her subordinates in his injunction. (It was the latter who had returned on horseback to Kou Swe's house.) In his second attempt, he would—and, in fact, he did—forbid her subordinates, as well as the *ouktazaun* herself, to return.

It is fair to say, then, that whatever may be the impediments to recruitment to the exorcist's role, they do not consist of negative cultural evaluation, of skeptical attitudes, or of the absence of a clientele.

On the other hand, although not suffering from social or cultural disabilities, neither does the exorcist, *qua* citizen, enjoy any special prestige. The respectful attitude shown him while performing his professional role does not spill over into his nonprofessional life. Except for very famous exorcists, whose fame is a tribute not only to their exorcistic skills, but also to their general reputation as powerful *ahtelan hsayas*, the position of the exorcist in the prestige hierarchy of the village is unaffected by his professional role. Typically, as we shall see below, village exorcists are recruited from humble stations in the social structure, and their relatively low prestige—as day laborers, tenant farmers, and so on—is not enhanced by their practice of exorcism.

Although the exorcist, *qua* citizen, receives no special respect by virtue of his occult skills, he is nonetheless treated somewhat differently from his fellows. Since the power of the exorcist to control nats or witches is morally ambiguous—the same power that can be used to protect people from their harm can be used to compel them to harm people—one can never be entirely confident that an exorcist, appearing to be an *ahtelan hsaya*, is not really an *aulan hsaya* (see Chapter 2, pg. 29). And, indeed, at least some villagers believe that the two exorcists in Yeigyi practice both roles. Few people, therefore, would wish to insult an exorcist or to incur his anger. In general, it is deemed wise to be somewhat circumspect in his presence, to treat him with a certain amount of deference.

Although the ambiguity of magical power is conducive to a certain ambivalence toward the exorcist, none of the exorcists whom I know viewed this as a deterrent to their own recruitment to the role. Hence, unlike the shaman who is involuntarily recruited to her role by being "called" by a nat who has fallen in love with her, the exorcist enters his role entirely voluntarily. And, unlike the shaman, for whom spirit possession is a necessary qualification for role recruitment, the exorcist is recruited by studying as an apprentice at the feet of a Master.

At this point, unhappily, my data almost completely fail me; I know next to nothing about this apprenticeship. The following meager information must suffice. If the apprentice lives with his Master, he can acquire the necessary knowledge within six months; otherwise it may take many years. During his apprenticeship, he not only learns the techniques of exorcism, but he becomes subject to Buddhist discipline as well. He must practice meditation, recite and observe the Buddhist precepts, say his beads, and so on. At the same time, he acquires magical power by making and swallowing many *ins*, and by becoming tatooed (which, in effect, means covering parts of his body with *ins*). He is also instructed in the various taboos which as an exorcist he must observe. Among other things he may not eat beef; he may not eat food used either in a funeral or at a wedding feast, or which has been offered to the nats; he may not drink intoxicating liquor; he may not walk under a ladder or under a house in which a woman is in labor.

Upon satisfying his Master of his competence, the apprentice, before he is permitted to practice, must be able to answer the following questions in the affirmative and to swear that his answers are true. "Do you believe in the Buddha unconditionally? Are you willing to eat the food granted to you by the Buddha? (I.e., will you remain content with whatever you may have?) Are you willing to go anywhere the Buddha may direct you? Can you remain anywhere the Buddha may send you?" If the recruit can truthfully answer these questions in the affirmative, all that remains before he can begin his practice is the ritual laying on of hands, by which the magical power of the Master is transferred to the apprentice. When this is completed, and with the acquisition of the exorcist's wand, the apprentice has become an exorcist.

A MOTIVATIONAL EXPLANATION OF THE EXORCIST

Although the exorcist is remunerated for his work, typically the fee is too small and his practice too limited for economic considerations to play an important part in his recruitment motivation. There are, of course, exceptions to this generalization, and these exceptions, as in the case of affluent shamans, are found in urban areas. I know Buddhist monks who —or whose monasteries—have become wealthy through their exorcistic practice. I know, too, of at least one layman, a bus driver, whose monthly income from his practice is K300 (about $65), a substantial income in Burmese terms. In the typical rural case, however, the exorcist's income does not exceed a few kyat a month.

What then are the motives for recruitment to this role? In some cases the decision to become an exorcist is based on the experience of having been cured from a psychopathological episode. The case best known to me is that of a Yeigyi exorcist who, at the age of thirty-two, suddenly went "mad." Stripping off his clothes, he ran through the village, nude, shouting, "Buddha, Dhamma, Sangha." Following successful treatment by an exorcist, he decided that he, too, wished to become one, and he apprenticed himself to the exorcist who had cured him. Such cases, however, do not seem to be prevalent.

On the basis of my very limited sample, I would suggest that the two dominant motives for recruitment to the exorcist role are status anxiety and power. Almost without exception, the exorcists I have known were recruited from humble origins and from occupations yielding low incomes and little prestige. Many of them, moreover, suffer from some kind of physical disability; they tend to be very short or very ugly or partially lame or partially blind. It would seem, then, that this role serves as a compensatory mechanism for feelings of social and/or physical inferiority. To be sure, a lowly night watchman, although an exorcist, remains (as we have seen) a lowly night watchman. But in performing his professional role, he has his brief moment of glory. He may, as did the watchman whom I know, allude to his humble occupation even during an exorcistic ceremony—"I am not a Master, I am only a watchman"—but nevertheless it is he who continuously occupies stage front and center. Indeed, the allusion to his humble, nonceremonial status may be interpreted in two ways: on the one hand it betrays his status anxiety—"I am merely a humble person"—but on the other hand it reflects his momentary triumph —"although I am a mere watchman, it is I to whom you have come for assistance."

The exorcist's desire for esteem and admiration is satisfied not only during the ceremony, but also in its prelude and aftermath. When he talks, everyone listens; what he says is attended to with care; when he shares his esoteric knowledge—"There are six types of wishes, and each type, in turn, has eleven subtypes"—they are visibly impressed. Outside of this context, he may be nothing.

But power must surely be as strong as prestige in the exorcist's motivational system. From his normally humble position, the exorcist can seldom command; and if he commands, he is seldom obeyed. In the exorcistic ceremony, however, it is he who dominates the situation throughout. What he asks for, he is given; when he tells the patient to prostrate himself before him, it is done. And his power, unlike the power of even political authority, extends to the supernaturals as well. They too must obey him. When he orders them to leave the patient, they leave. It is little wonder, then, that the exorcist, *qua* exorcist, exhibits a manner, a flourish, and a confidence that is lacking in his role as cowherd, transplanter, or guard.

Although this sketch of the exorcist personality is not fully satisfactory, it cannot be taken farther without more research. Rather than speculate about the many points on which there is no information, I shall turn instead from the psychological characteristics of the exorcist to the cultural attributes of his role.

A CULTURAL-HISTORICAL EXPLANATION OF THE EXORCIST ROLE

Historical Reconstruction of the Role

In attempting to elucidate the "meaning" of the exorcist role, viewed within the entire context of Burmese supernaturalism, we must note the curious fact that this role has apparently ("apparently," because our historical information is unsatisfactory) undergone, even within the brief span of the last one or two hundred years, some important changes.

Sangermano, one of the few early writers to describe Burmese exorcism, refers to the exorcist as a "physician," a neutral term which tells us nothing about his therapeutic technique. Sangermano does tell us, however, that in some cases the "physician" would invite a shaman to enter a case which he was treating. Bidding her to perform a ritual dance (a "devil dance"), she would become possessed by the nat who had victimized the patient, and, using her as a medium, the "physician" would then interrogate the nat. "For this purpose," writes Sangermano (1893:172),

> a middle-aged woman, to whom they give the name of wife of the Natzo, must dance, and go through a number of contortions, to the sound of a drum or some other musical instrument, in a tent erected for the occasion, in which is placed a quantity of fruits and other things as an offering, but which turn to the account of the dancing girl. By degrees she feigns to become infuriated and utters some incoherent words which are regarded as the answer of the Nat, who has been thus consulted with regard to the conclusion of the malady.

Thus in this earlier period, in contrast to the contemporary scene, it was a shaman, rather than the patient, who served as the exorcist's medium.

Sir George Scott, writing about one hundred years later, gives two accounts of exorcism and the exorcist. In one account (Scott and Hardiman 1900:74, Vol. I) the exorcist is called a *hmaw saya*; in another (Shway Yoe 1896:410–417) he is referred to, alternatively, as a *hmaw saya*, a *baydin saya*, and a *weikza*. To refer to the exorcist as a *weikza* is most certainly wrong. The other two terms may well be used, even today, in Lower Burma, from which most of Scott's information derives. More-over, *hmaw saya*, according to Mendelson (personal communication), is used in Central Burma as a general term for magical practitioners. (He also suggests that Scott's *baydin saya* may be a *bada saya*, i.e., a mercury *weikza*.) In any event, the term, *ahtelan hsaya*, is found in neither of Scott's accounts. According to his later account, the exorcist achieved his aims by beating the supernatural (i.e., by beating the patient, whom the super-natural has possessed), by choking him with a rope, or by threatening to kill him. If none of these techniques was effective, the exorcist called upon a shaman who, by her dancing, induced the supernatural to leave the body of the patient and to enter her body. It was then that the exorcist ques-tioned the supernatural in order to discover what might be done to appease him. Again, as in Sangermano's description, is was a shaman, rather than the patient, whom the exorcist used as his medium.

Turning to a description of healing ceremonies among tribal societies in Burma and in traditional Burmese Mon society, one might speculatively reconstruct three historical changes in Burmese exorcism. These putative changes consist in a shift from the importance of the shaman to the im-portance of the exorcist, and, with that, in a shift from practitioner-possession to patient-possession, and from an animistic emphasis to a Buddhist emphasis. Let us first, however, look at these additional data.

Among certain of the hill tribes in Burma (those in the "northern divi-sion"), when illness is caused by spirit possession, a "spirit medium" is called upon to treat the patient. Then, according to Scott (1921:396),

a bamboo altar is constructed in the house, and various offerings, such as boiled fowls, pork, plantains, cocoa-nuts, and rice, are placed on it for the *nat*. The celebrant then takes a bright copper or brass plate, stands it up on edge near the altar, and begins to chant, keeping at the same time a close eye on the polished copper, where the shadow of the *nat* is expected to appear. When this appears the medium begins to dance, and gradually works herself into a state of ecstacy. The state of tension produced fre-quently causes the patient to do the same thing. This, naturally, has definite results, either in the way of recovery, through excitement or col-lapse through exhaustion. If as sometimes happens, the invocation of the possessing spirit is carried on for two or three days, it is very certain that something must happen, one way or the other. [The use of a mirror to perceive the spirit is a technique also found in Ceylon.—M.E.S.]

Here then, it is a shaman, not an exorcist, who performs the ceremony; moreover, it is the shaman who goes into trance; and, finally, if the patient goes into trance, it is spontaneous, rather than deliberately induced by the practitioner.

Among the Talains (the Burmese Mon), the preferred treatment was for the patient himself, rather than the shaman (but at the instigation of the shaman, or "spirit doctor," as O'Riley designates her), to perform the "spirit dance." Only if the patient was too old or too sick did the shaman perform the dance. (For a marvelous description of this dance, see O'Riley 1850:594–95, 596–97.) Again, as in the case of Burmese tribal societies, it is a shaman rather than an exorcist who performs the ceremony, but, as in the case of contemporary Burmese exorcism, it is preferably the patient, rather than the practitioner, who becomes possessed.

On the basis of these data, one might offer the hypothesis that contemporary techniques of Burmese exorcism represent relatively recent innovations, and that the exorcist as we know him—the *ahtelan hsaya*—is a relatively recent phenomenon in the history of Burmese psychotherapy. Using some (but not all) Burmese tribal practice and Mon historical data to establish a historical baseline for a historical reconstruction, one might speculate that exorcism was initially practiced in Burma by female shamans. From the former, but only to some extent from the latter, data, it might be suggested that the therapeutic technique consisted in inducing the offending spirit to leave the patient and to possess the exorcist himself. If this is, in fact, a true baseline, then, on the basis of the meager historical evidence available to us at this time, it can be inferred that three significant changes have occurred in the historical development from shamanistic to exorcistic therapy. First, there has occurred a change in the sex of the therapist from female to male. Second, there has occurred a change in therapeutic technique—from a self-induced trance in, and thereby possession of, the therapist, to a therapist-induced trance in, and thereby possession of, the patient. Third, there has occurred a change in the cultural content and meaning of therapy—from expulsion of the offending spirit by the power of the therapist, to exorcism of the spirit by the power of "Buddhism."

Since shamanism continues to exist—although the shamans have been stripped of their former exorcistic function—it would seem that the roles of shaman and exorcist represent parallel historical developments. That is, although the exorcist appears to be a later development than the shaman, it seems that rather than evolving from the shaman, he, instead, superseded the shaman. It is also clear from eighteenth-century Mon data, as well as from nineteenth-century Burmese data, that this supersedence was gradual rather than sudden, and that the consequent changes in therapy—from female to male therapist, and from therapist possession to patient possession—did not occur simultaneously. Thus, in the case of the Mons, although exorcism was conducted by a female shaman, preferred practice was to have the patient rather than the therapist become possessed. In the case of the Burmese, even after the male exorcist superseded the female shaman, therapeutic practice, in difficult cases at least, consisted in the exorcist's inducing the offending spirit to possess a shaman of his (the exorcist's) choosing. But whatever the details of the historical sequence may have been, the following broad trend may be suggested: originally the function of the (female) shaman, the treatment of supernatural possession has become the exclusive monopoly of the (male) exorcist.

If, in cultural terms, the ascendance of the exorcist over the shaman represents, as I think it does, the triumph of magical Buddhism over magical animism, in therapeutic terms it represents the triumph of verbal over ecstatic, and of patient-centered over practitioner-centered therapy. It is not at all clear, however, why these different therapeutic roles could not have existed side by side. In Ceylon (like Burma, a Theravada society) both types of therapists, the shaman and the exorcist, exist side by side.[3]

Cultural Status of the Role

Although the above reconstruction of the historical relationship between the shaman and the exorcist, being highly speculative, is open to many questions, there is little question about the contemporary cultural relationship between these two roles. The cultural features which characterize the exorcist as a type are readily distinguishable from those which characterize the shaman as a type, and these distinguishable features offer some important insights into the cultural status of the exorcist, especially within the context of a Buddhist culture.

In a series of very important papers, Mendelson (1960; 1961a; 1961b) has suggested that the quasi-Buddhist Burmese sects (*gaings*) to which all exorcists belong represent an interstitial magico-religious area which both separates animism from Buddhism and, at the same time, bridges the gap between them. Following on Mendelson's thesis, I would suggest that the exorcist, who as we have seen learns his role in the process of acquiring membership in one of these sects, is an exemplification of his thesis. Just as the belief system of the sect bridges the gap between animism and Buddhism, so the exorcist, whose therapeutic role, it will be recalled, is but one component of the role-set of the *ahtelan hsaya*, is the cultural mediator who bridges the gap between the animistic practitioner (the shaman) and the Buddhist practitioner (the monk). Indeed, speculating somewhat beyond the available data, it might be suggested that the exorcist, standing between the shaman and the monk, represents those Hindu-Mahayanist elements which, even today, continue to inform much of the (Theravada) Buddhism of Burma.

Let us turn, then, to those cultural differences between the shaman and

[3]In Ceylon some cases of spirit possession are brought to a (male) shaman, known as a *kattadiya*, and, as is the case among Burmese tribal societies, it is he who performs an exorcistic dance and becomes possessed—the theory being that the demon leaves the patient and possesses the exorcist (Pieris 1953:115–16). Other cases, however, are brought to a practitioner known as a *kapurala*, who is similar to the Burmese exorcist. When a *kapurala* treats a patient, it is the latter (as in Burma) who becomes possessed (Pieris 1953:115). It should be noted, however, that in Ceylon (unlike Burma) both types of practitioners are male.

exorcist which, in their configuration, serve to distinguish these two magico-religious types. These differences include their relationship to, and their method of interacting with, the nats, the *devas*, and Buddhism.

Relationship to the nats. For the shaman, nats are powerful beings whose power, with respect to human beings, is ambiguous. On the one hand, the nats can be solicited for various kinds of human benefits; the shaman officiates in a cult, both private and collective, which invokes their assistance. On the other hand, the nats may also harm human beings, and their malevolent power cannot be countered; one can only acquiesce in it. Hence, the shaman performs propitiatory rituals which, rather than combating their power, attempt to induce the nats to remove their harm.

The exorcist, like the Buddhist monk, seldom seeks the assistance of the nats. Unlike the monk, however, who is prohibited from any traffic with nats, the exorcist interacts with the nats, without, however, acquiescing in their power or attempting to propitiate them. Instead, he engages them in combat, attempting not only to remove their harm, but also, unlike the shaman, to drive them away or to exorcise them. And this latter feat he accomplishes by the use of Buddhist power. Here, then, one clearly sees the interstitial position of the exorcist. Like the shaman he recognizes the power of the nats, but like the monk he does not invoke it. Like the monk, too, he recognizes the superior power of Buddhism, but unlike the monk he utilizes this power to counter the nats.[4]

It should be added, of course, that the shaman, having no access to

---

[4]The indifference of the monks to nats and their power is a normative rather than an empirical description. By the rules which govern the monastic order (the *Vinaya* rules), monks are prohibited from any traffic with the occult or the supernatural. In fact, however, many monks engage in some kind of occult activity—alchemy being the most frequently practiced—and some monks, primarily in the towns and cities, practice exorcism. Even when they do not practice exorcism, some monks are turned to for charms and talismans which are believed to cure and/or prevent supernaturally caused illness. Thus, when the *ouktazaun* spirit returned to plague Kou Swe, the latter sought assistance from the village monk, who wrote out a typical Buddhist-derived incantation (*gahta*) which, he said, could offer protection against any kind of danger, whether emanating from nats or from bullets. This incantation, which Kou Swe was to recite daily, and as frequently as possible, can be translated as follows:

> Oum! For the Buddha in the East, the Dhamma in the West, the Pyisiga [Silent] Buddha in the South, the Rahandas [Saints] in the North. Observe: I am in the Center. Protect me, so that all harm directed against me may vanish.
> Oum! The [sacred] Bo Tree, and the Buddha's Golden Throne. When the Buddha attained Nirvana, he was protected by [the *deva*] Sakka. So too, may he protect me.
> Oum! Ten impurities are destroyed by [the power of] the Buddha. May the Samma Devas protect me.
> Oum! May I be cured by the power of the Triple Gems.

Monastic involvement with magic and supernaturalism is not, I hasten to add, a recent phenomenon. Almost seventy years ago it was observed that ". . . many of the most noted seers, necromancers, and tatooers are *pôngyis* [monks]" (Scott and Hardiman 1900:81, Vol. I).

power other than that afforded by animism, has no choice but to acquiesce in the power of the nats. The exorcist, in whose role a variety of historical traditions intersect, has access to many different sources of power. This was dramatically symbolized in the example of the exorcist described in Chapter 11 (pp. 184–94). Arriving for an exorcistic seance, he was dressed in white to symbolize both his strict observance of the Buddhist precepts and, implicitly, the power of these precepts. Strapped to his side—he was a police sergeant—was a police revolver, symbolizing the power of the state. In one hand he held his exorcist's wand, which contains occult power, while with the other he fingered his rosary, which contained Buddhist-derived power. Armed with these different kinds of power, he then proceeded to invoke still another source of power, that of the Hindu-derived *devas*, in order to do battle with the evil nat.

Method of interacting with nats. Although both shaman and exorcist are specialists in dealing with troubles caused by nats—the former by acquiescing in their power, the latter by combatting it—their ritual methods of interacting with nats are quite different. The shaman, concerned to know the reasons for an offending nat's anger, asks her nat spouse to possess her, and while she is in a trance state, she serves as his medium. The exorcist, wishing to speak with an offending nat, asks him to possess the patient, who, while in a trance state, serves as the nat's medium. Employing Loeb's distinction, it may be said that the shaman is a person *through* whom the nats speak, while the exorcist is one *with* whom they speak.[5] Although differing, then, from the Buddhist monk, who does not engage in any traffic with nats, the exorcist differs from the shaman, as well, by eschewing a shamanistic (ecstatic) technique, and by adopting a Buddhist (verbal) technique in his interaction with the nats.

Relationship to the devas. In addition to the power he acquires through Buddhist magic, the exorcist most importantly attempts to acquire the assistance of the benevolent Buddhist supernaturals, or *devas*. Although all *devas* enjoy their present celestial bliss by virtue of good karma acquired in former existences, Buddhists, it will be recalled, distinguish between a large class of unnamed and undifferentiated *devas* who do not interact with the human world, and a small class of named, individualized *devas* who render assistance to human beings. The latter class comprises the gods of the Hindu pantheon—which the Buddhists can and do identify as Hindu gods, and it is the *devas* of this class who, by name, are invoked by the exorcist. Just as it is true that these *devas*, having been incorporated into the Buddhist cosmological system, are part of Buddhism, so it is also true that to ritually invoke their aid clearly reflects a Hindu, rather than a Buddhist, conception and practice. Nevertheless, since, on the one hand, the shaman,

[5]Loeb (1929) proffered this distinction to differentiate two types of practitioners whom he calls "shamans" and "seers."

as an animistic practitioner, recognizes neither Buddhism nor its Hindu-derived elements, and since, on the other hand, the exorcist believes that by invoking the *devas* he is invoking Buddhist power, the exorcist again occupies an interstitial, essentially Hindu, position between animism and Buddhism.

Relationship to Buddhism. Here the difference between the two roles is clear-cut. The exorcist qualifies for and practices his role as a devout Buddhist. He must not only practice Buddhist precepts in his daily life—should he violate them, the *devas* will not render their assistance—but the content and symbolism of the exorcistic ceremony, as we have already seen (Chapter 11), are almost exclusively Buddhist. The recitation of the Buddhist precepts, the Buddhist rituals of the dissemination of love and of the sharing of merit, the worship of the Buddha, and so on, constitute the core of the ceremony. None of this holds for the shaman. Shamanistic performances are devoid of Buddhist content or of Buddhist symbolism; they are exclusively animistic. Indeed, the shamanistic performance is not only devoid of Buddhist elements, but the shaman and her performance alike may violate important Buddhist precepts. Thus, the consumption of liquor is a prevalent feature of shamanistic performances, and the sexual "immorality" of shamans is common gossip. In short, whether in the performance of her role or in her personal life, the shaman violates, or is believed to violate, two of the five Buddhist precepts.

Here, as in the first three features by which the exorcist is distinguished from the shaman, the role of the exorcist in mediating the difference between animism and Buddhism is salient. As a salvation religion, Buddhism is exclusively concerned with otherworldly goals. All Buddhist discipline—morality, meditation, and ritual—has as its aim the attainment of nirvana; and, in normative terms, the Buddhist monk practices this discipline exclusively for the attainment of this otherworldly goal. Like the monk, the exorcist, too, practices Buddhist discipline, but his aim—unlike the monk's, but identical with the shaman's—is the attainment of this-worldly rather than otherworldly goals. Hence, in combining the goals of animism with the discipline of Buddhism, the exorcist again exemplifies his interstitial position between these two traditions. In using Buddhist rather than animist means for the attainment of his goals, he asserts the primacy of Buddhist over animist power. At the same time, since his goals are those of animism, he subverts the essence of these Buddhist means by converting them from religious discipline into magical technology.

On all these dimensions, then, the exorcist stands midway between the shaman and the monk. Neither sacred nor profane, he is rather sacred *and* profane; neither this-worldly nor otherworldly, he is both this-worldly *and* otherworldly; neither Apollonian nor Dionysian, he is both Apollonian *and* Dionysian. In short, by incorporating both animist and Buddhist elements within one role, the exorcist has become the cultural mediator between the polar cultural traditions of Buddhism and animism. As a mediator one might suggest that he has been an important factor in maintaining their polarity. For just as the public nat cultus may have served to protect the integrity of Buddhist worship from the incursions of Tantric elements (see Chapter 14, pp. 279–80), so the exorcist may serve to protect the integrity of the Buddhist monk from the incursions of shamanistic practices.

VI

CONCLUSION

CHAPTER FOURTEEN

Supernaturalism and Buddhism

Since the Burmese system of supernatural beliefs and practices described in the previous chapters exists in a society which proudly proclaims its faith in Buddhism, and since I have frequently, especially in the last chapter, touched upon the relationships between Burmese supernaturalism and Buddhism, these relationships must be explored in a systematic fashion. In order to simplify the task, this exploration will be devoted exclusively to the relationship between Buddhism and the nat cultus.

Despite the fact that the vast majority of Burmese Buddhists also participate in the nat cultus, most of them concede that these two systems exist in a state of tension. Indeed, this tension has always been apparent to the Burmese and, from the earliest encounters of these systems, attempts have been made to resolve the tension by providing the nats with Buddhist legitimacy. Thus, from the very beginning, the imported Buddhist supernaturals, the *devas*, were classified, together with the indigenous Burmese supernaturals, as "nats." In one sense, this is hardly surprising. Since the only term for "supernatural being" in the aboriginal religion was "nat," if the supernatural beings of Buddhism were to be classified at all, they could be classified only as "nats." Moreover, the *devas* were and are differentiated from both the earlier conception of the indigenous nats and

247

their later reinterpretations by being designated as "good" or "Buddhist" nats, while the latter were designated as "evil" (*meihsa*) nats. Nevertheless, this lexical incorporation of the *devas* into the indigenous religious terminology has undoubtedly had important consequences for the entire nat system. By classifying the *devas*, who are clearly part of orthodox Buddhism, as nats, and thereby assimilating them into an indigenous cognitive structure, the aboriginal nats, too, were provided with Buddhist sanction.

This thesis is best exemplified in the case of the *deva* Thagya Min—the Lord, Thagya—or, as he is called in Pali, Sakka. Sakka is referred to as the "king of the nats," a statement which is highly ambiguous. On the one hand, he is the king of the *devas* who, residing in the Tavatimsa heaven, descends to the earth on the Buddhist New Year (*Thingyan*). On the other hand, he is the king of the Thirty-Seven nats, superseding Min Mahagiri, who had formerly been first in the royal list of the Thirty-Seven nats. In addition to his origin, which in itself places him in a separate category—that Sakka is the Hindu god Indra is well established—it is clear that structurally and functionally he does not belong with the latter nats. He has no mythological biography, no special cultus or specialized practitioners, no special shrine (*nat sin*). Although he is invoked at certain nat festivals, he has no shamans to whom he is married, nor does he possess anyone else. Unlike the other Thirty-Seven nats, he is benevolent; he figures prominently in Buddhist rites and, indeed, he is preeminent in the Buddhist New Year festival. Here, then, is a nat who, though included among the Thirty-Seven nats, is clearly a Buddhist *deva*. That this difference was recognized from the very first may be inferred from the early differentiation of Sakka from the other Thirty-Seven nats. Thus in 1059, when the images of the original group of Thirty-Seven nats were placed in the Shwezigon pagoda in Pagan by King Anawrahta, Sakka's was separated from all the others—thereby providing all the more reason to believe that by conferring upon this explicitly Buddhist "nat" the title of "king" of the Thirty-Seven nats, these non-Buddhist nats were, and are, invested with Buddhist legitimacy.

The ambiguity in the classification of Sakka points to yet another example of a probable attempt to "Buddha-ize" these nats. According to Buddhism (again under Hindu influence), Sakka is the king of thirty-three *devas*. As we have already observed, the original royal list of the Thirty-Seven nats (whose images are in the Shwezigon pagoda) comprised exactly thirty-three nats—thirty-two non-Buddhist nats, plus Sakka. It is hard to believe that this number, especially when these thirty-three nats are presided over by the same *deva* who presides over the original Hindu list of thirty-three *devas*, was determined by chance. And if it was not by chance, then it is at least plausible to assume that this represents still another attempt, witting or unwitting, to provide the indigenous nat system with Buddhist sanction.

There are other relationships between Buddhism and the nat cultus which are suggestive of early attempts to Buddha-ize the latter, or, at least, to assert the subservience of animism to Buddhism. Often, for example, nat rituals are followed almost immediately by the performance of a Buddhist ritual; and since there is good reason to believe that the nat rituals in question preceded the introduction of Buddhism into Burma, it is almost as if the nats were simultaneously being recognized by, as well as being rendered secondary to, Buddhism. Thus, during the harvest season certain nats are propitiated in the paddy fields for protection against snakes. Characteristic of the nat cultus, this ritual is almost always performed by one of the females in the work group. Then, immediately following this offering, one of the men leads the group in the worship of the *Nagayoun* Buddha, which is found in a pagoda in the nearby village of Lethit. This image, which depicts the Buddha hooded by a *naga*, a mythical dragon, is believed to have the power to cure snake bites. After reciting the Five Precepts, the group offers flowers and cooked rice to the image, and a prayer for protection from snakes is recited.

This same dual function—the conferring of Buddhist legitimacy on the nats while at the same time asserting their subordination to Buddhism—is also suggested by certain types of physical relationships that obtain between Buddhism and the nat cultus. Thus, there are many places which serve as devotional centers for both. Mt. Popa, for centuries a national center for the nat cultus, is also the seat of numerous Buddhist monasteries and pagodas. (See also Mendelson 1963a.) At the foot of Mandalay hill, sacred to Buddhism, there is an image of Mandalay Boudaw, the nat of Mandalay town, on the southern side of the hill, and one of Ma U, a female nat associated with the Taungbyon Brothers, at the northern side. This physical juxtaposition of nats and Buddhism is found in hills of lesser importance as well. The two most famous nat festivals in Upper Burma, at Taungbyon and Yirinaku (near Amarapura), are held immediately adjacent to pagodas. At the latter festival, it is necessary to go through the pagoda compound in order to reach the nat shrine. At the former, part of the temporary bazaar which is constructed for the festival is erected inside the pagoda compound, and the participants move back and forth from the nat to the Buddhist domains. In both cases the division between domains is symbolized by the removal of footgear when entering the pagoda compound.

Just as in some cases (such as the Yirinaku Festival) one must go through the pagoda compound in order to reach the nat shrine, so, in other cases (such as the Sagaing hills) one cannot approach a Buddhist shrine without first encountering a nat shrine. Thus, for example, in approaching the famous Hall of the Fifty Sitting Buddhas, one must pass the shrines of the hill nat and of the tree nat. More interesting is the situation at Taundaw Hill, the hill of the nat Ma U, about six miles north of Mandalay. At the bottom of the hill are the images of the Taungbyon

Brothers, each riding a tiger; at the top are images of Ma U and of other lesser nats. In between, however, are eight or nine level places which break the winding, ascending path to the top. At the first level there is a huge Buddha image, and at each of the succeeding ones there is a small pagoda with images of the Buddha at the corners. The path, literally, leads from the nats through the Buddha images to the nats.

This physical juxtaposition of Buddhist and nat symbols can probably be explained in a number of ways. Since Buddhism, like the nats, is also used for the attainment of mundane ends, this common function provides one explanation—offerings and prayers can be made to nat and Buddha images at the same festival or at one pilgrimage. There are other possible explanations as well, and I should like to underscore the one which is consistent with the general thesis of this section. Since the nat cultus preceded the introduction of Buddhism into Burma, it is not farfetched to assume that all these "high places," originally shrines for nat propitiation, only later became places of Buddhist worship, so that this juxtaposition of the two systems, with the consequent necessity of worshiping the Buddha either prior or subsequent to propitiating the nats, was intended to serve two functions. In the first place, it served to Buddha-ize the nats and, in the second place, served—and serves—to remind the nat devotee that his primary loyalty was—and is—to Buddhism. As one villager put it, "Pagodas are always erected near a nat shrine so that people should not forget the Buddha even if they come to propitiate the nats."

Despite these and other attempts to Buddha-ize the nats, the Burmese continue to recognize that a tension exists between animism and Buddhism. Since this tension is felt even by peasants (Chapter 4, pp. 57–58), it is not surprising that it is felt by intellectuals as well. Thus, in the course of my field work in 1961, many Burmese language newspapers carried articles, during the famous Taungbyon and Yirinaku nat festivals, critical of nat propitiation. Many of them claimed that these two festivals had had their inception as pagoda festivals and should again be treated as such. Commenting on the Yirinaku Festival, one editorial writer, for example, had the following to say.

> Once popularly known as a nat festival, it has now come to be known as a pagoda festival. Every Buddhist should welcome this change. . . . [Beginning as a pagoda festival] the nat festival was developed later [to be held] at the same time. In consequence, the name, pagoda festival, had undergone a change to nat festival. It is a pity!
>
> The nat festival was instituted by the younger brother of a Queen of King Bagyidaw. He was also responsible for instituting the nat festival held simultaneously with the Pagoda Festival at Taungbyon . . . for the amusement of the people. . . . As a Buddhist I am saddened that the nat festival has taken precedence over the pagoda festival.
>
> Buddhism has now been made a State Religion. . . . [Hence] it has come to pass that the nat festival has receded to the background and

the pagoda festival has once again come to the fore (*Bahosi,* September 4, 1961).

Although this editorial writer does not stipulate the grounds for his uneasiness concerning nat propitiation, other Buddhist intellectuals view the nat cultus as a form of "superstition" which, they claim, is in direct conflict with Buddhist rationalism. The following extract of a letter, published in an English language newspaper, is an accurate reflection of this statement.

We true *theravadis* [Southern Buddhists] firmly believe that our religion is a perfectly rational one without any touch of the supernatural or mysterious and that . . . [nat worship] is an incomprehensible degradation of it. And if we see in . . . [government leaders] any public preoccupation with personal deities, with witchcraft, with the mumbo jumbo of charms and magical ritual and all manners of superstition . . . we will never forget the harm and damage done to the cause of Buddhism (*The Guardian,* May 22, 1961).

Like the writer of this letter, most Western commentators on Burmese nats point to the incompatibility between Theravada Buddhism and nat beliefs on precisely the same grounds. In both cases, however, these criticisms are misplaced. Far from denying the existence of supernatural beings, canonical Buddhism, as we have already seen, explicitly affirms the existence of a variety of spirits, both good and evil. The good spirits, of course, are the *devas,* whose existence and whose power to help man are explicitly affirmed both in Scripture and in early Buddhist sculpture (cf. Colston 1910) alike. The scripturally based evil spirits range from Mara, the Evil One who confronted the Buddha himself, to a host of lesser spirits including the *yakkhas, asuras, rakkhasas, petas,* and others (cf. Ling 1962, Chap. 1).

But Scripture goes even further. The belief in the existence of evil spirits not only enjoys canonical sanction, but Scripture teaches that these spirits may be coerced and exorcised by the recitation of certain Suttras. This *pareitta* ceremony, as it is called, which is still performed today in all Theravada countries, was already performed by the Buddha's "right hand" disciple, Maudgalyayana (Waddell 1911:572). As La Vallée Poussin (1917:210) has put it, ". . . the ancient Buddhists were concerned with the raksasas and the yaksas just as Burmese monks are nowadays concerned with nats. . . ." (He is wrong, however, in his characterization of contemporary monks.)

Contrary, then, to some Buddhist intellectuals and to most Western critics of Burmese nats, animistic beliefs, as well as ritual, are perfectly compatible with orthodox Buddhism, even with the Buddhism of the Pali Canon. Their alleged incompatibility stems from the false assumption that "pure" Buddhism is—or, at least, in its original form, was—an exclusively ethical system, devoid of supernatural beliefs and rites. But if this assumption does not even hold for canonical Buddhism, it most surely does not hold for contemporary Buddhism, which includes a host of animistic beliefs and a plethora of magical technology. Let us merely note some of these supernatural elements, without elaborating on them.

The recitation of *pareittas* to ward off evil continues to be an important function of Buddhist monks. In addition, some monks are famous as exorcists (*ahtelan hsaya*). The aim of both ceremonies is to tap the power inherent in Buddhist texts (*gahtas*) and to invoke the assistance of benevolent Buddhist supernaturals (*devas*), in order to exorcise nats and witches, and to avoid disaster. These twin beliefs concerning the magical power of Buddhist sacra and the supernatural assistance of the *devas* are widespread, and they are activated in a variety of situations. I have already referred to the famous prayer, the *thamboutei*, by which the assistance of the *devas* is invoked in case of trouble. In some cases, moreover, the Buddha Himself is worshiped in order to obtain release from ills of various sorts. I have referred, for example, to the worship of a special Buddhist image (*Nagayoun*) which protects the victims of snake bites. The Buddhist rosary is frequently used as a talisman, and the saying of one's beads is deemed especially efficacious as a means of warding off evil spirits. The yellow robe of the monk is extremely powerful, and the most effective way of escaping from attack by evil supernaturals is to don the robe, which means becoming a temporary monk. Buddhist relics, of course, have great protective power. The building of sand pagodas of specified dimensions is a means of averting collective disaster. Although the catalogue could be extended at least tenfold, this list will suffice to document the thesis that supernatural beliefs and magical practices are not absent from contemporary Buddhism, any more than they were from early Buddhism. One can only conclude that if Burmese animism is in conflict with Buddhism, the conflict, surely, does not consist in the supernaturalism of the one versus the naturalism of the other.

This is not to say, however, that there are no grounds on which Buddhism and animism are incompatible. For although the criticisms of Western scholars may be misplaced, there are grounds for conflict between these two systems, and there is abundant evidence that the Burmese themselves, at least the more introspective ones, are aware of such a conflict. That almost half the male population of Yeigyi expressed some degree of skepticism concerning the nats (see Chapter 4, pp. 56–59), however much their skepticism may be only verbal, must surely indicate that even on the peasant level, the Burmese are caught up in some kind of conflict concerning their nat beliefs. This conflict is even more acute among sophisticated Burmans. Their conflict was most dramatically articulated by a well known Buddhist scholar in Rangoon. When I first called on him, he characterized the nats as being of historical interest only, referring to them as "something the Burmese had formerly believed in." A few days later, when showing me his copy of Temple's classic work on the nats, he commented: "But after everything is said, we still believe in them [the nats]. Even we [i.e., intellectuals] do. They're part of us, they're in our system. We simply can't get rid of them."

But if he and the professed skeptics in the village cannot "get rid" of nats, why, as they are attempting unsuccessfully to do, should they try? The answer, I think, is clear—the attempt to get rid of the nats is an attempt to resolve their own inner conflicts concerning nat beliefs. For some (the educated city dwellers), this conflict is induced by a perceived incompatibility between their scientific world view and their nat beliefs (see Chapter 4, pp. 62–63); for others, it is induced by a perceived incompatibility between Buddhism and nat beliefs. The incompatibility with which we are concerned here has two dimensions. One dimension, which the Burmese themselves articulate, is doctrinal, referring to the obvious incompatibility between nat belief and practice, on the one hand, and the Buddhist doctrine of karma (Pali, *kamma*; Burmese, *kan*), on the other. The second dimension, though equally obvious and, if anything, even more important, is infrequently articulated. This refers to the polar opposition in ethos between these two systems. Each of these dimensions will be dealt with separately.

THE DOCTRINAL CONFLICT

According to Burmese interpretations of karma, one's this-worldly existence, and all of one's future existences, is inexorably determined by the merit (Pali, *kusala*; Burmese, *kudou*) and demerit accumulated from all prior existences. This accumulation comprises one's karma, and whatever happens in the course of one's life, both good and bad, is a consequence of this karma. Hence if a person's karma is good, it follows that nats and other evil spirits cannot harm him—for their power is less potent than the power of karma—and to propitiate them is wasted energy. To be sure, the nats will respond to any offense or neglect with punitive action—they may attempt to cause illness, for example—but their success in carrying out their intentions is a function of the karma of their intended victim. If his karma is good, their attempts are abortive; if they succeed, it is because his karma is bad, and they are merely the agents, as it were, of his unfolding karma. In short, given the doctrine of karma, the propitiation of the nats is futile: they cannot harm a person whose karma is good, however much he may offend or neglect them; and while propitiation may induce them to refrain from harming him, if his karma is bad he will suffer harm in some other manner.

For the same reason, attempts to seek the assistance of the nats are as futile as attempts to avoid their harm. If a person's karma is good, he will enjoy his just deserts, regardless of the intervention of the nats; if it is bad, propitiation of the nats may incite them to come to his aid, but their efforts will be of no avail. From the Buddhist point of view, therefore, one is better advised to simply ignore the nats, and to devote one's energies, instead, to the building of good karma through the performance of meritorious deeds; for it is the action of karma, rather than the action of the nats, which accounts for the vicissitudes of life. To attribute these vicissitudes to the nats, and to believe that their propitiation (or lack of propitiation) can in any manner influence one's life-fate, is to implicitly deny the omnipotence of karma, a doctrine which constitutes the very core of Buddhist teaching.[1]

Keenly aware of the inconsistency between the doctrine of karma and the propitiation of nats, the Burmese make many attempts to resolve it. Their attempts, obvious rationalizations, fall very short of being satisfactory. Thus, after recounting the ills which the nats might perpetrate if not properly propitiated, the Burmese will then observe—this refrain is almost ritualized—that while the nats cannot harm those whose karma is good, they can wreak harm on those whose karma is bad. Similarly, after recounting the advantages to be gained from nat propitiation, informants add that the nats can render aid only to those who are pious or whose karma is good. To the twin objections that bad karma will inevitably result in pain—if not administered by the nats, then by some other agents —and that the consequences of good karma do not require the agency of the nats for their expression, there is never a satisfactory answer.

Since the above discussion is a distillation of interviews with Buddhist laymen, it is of more than passing interest to compare their views with those of Buddhist monks. Monks themselves do not—or at least, according to the monastic regulations, they ought not—propitiate any spirits, including the nats. Moreover, as "Sons of the Buddha," they are superior to the nats and therefore immune to their power. In a sample of twenty-four monks, whose nat beliefs were obtained through interviews, one-fourth either denied the existence of nats, or, adopting the classical Buddhist distinction between the religious (*lokuttara*) and the worldly (*lokika*) points of view (in essence the distinction between reality and appearance) they argued that although from a religious point of view (reality), the nats do not exist, from a secular point of view (appearance) they do.

This argument, a species of legerdemain, and one which is also propounded by the more sophisticated village laymen, runs something like

---

[1]Because this dilemma is clearly recognized even at the village level, it is all the more surprising to discover that, according to La Vallée Poussin (1917:210), offerings to evil spirits were not interdicted by early Buddhism—the attitude being that these are "mere trifles" which "cannot endanger the normal and energetic endeavor of the saint walking in the Path." Interdicted or not, it is to be noted that the inconsistency between the doctrine of karma, on the one hand, and the belief in the efficacy of spirit propitiation, on the other, is rooted in early Buddhism itself, rather than a result of the interaction of Buddhism with an indigenous Burmese religion. The *pareitta* ceremony which, as we have seen, is prescribed by the Canon itself, is an example of this thesis.

this. According to Buddhism, there can be no nonmaterial entities, for everything is compounded of four physical elements—earth, air, fire, and water. Hence, if the nats are nonmaterial, they cannot exist; conversely, if they do exist, they must be material. Now from a worldly (*lokika*) point of view, since they give the appearance of being material—they have been seen, touched, heard, etc.—they exist. In reality (*lokuttara*), however, their materiality is an illusion; from a religious point of view, they do not exist. This, then, is a facile technique—one which I encountered frequently—for resolving the conflict between what one believes and what one ought to believe. By invoking this distinction between appearance and reality the Burmese can hold both horns of their dilemma: the existence of the nats is only apparent, not real; but since one must live in the world of appearance, it is expedient to act as if they existed.

The majority of monks in my sample, however, did not invoke this argument. For them the nats do exist, and, according to them, it is proper to make offerings to them, as long as the offering is conceived as charity (*dāna*), rather than as propitiation. Even on this latter point, however, some of the monks claimed that nat propitiation was proper if it were intended to protect small children, who are especially vulnerable to their harm. All agreed, however, that the nats have no power to render help, although almost half of them were of the opinion that, if one's karma were bad, they could cause harm.[2] In any event, whether or not they believed in the existence of nats, the monks, like the laymen, agreed that the belief in the causal agency of nats and the performance of nat ceremonies as a means for influencing their behavior are clearly inconsistent with the Buddhist doctrine of karma.

It is their conscious awareness of this inconsistency[3] that is one of the

[2]Although the majority of these monks agreed that it is improper to propitiate the nats, monks do not go out of their way to criticize their propitiation by laymen. One layman, a former monk, insisted that monks refrain from criticism from fear that they will incur material privation because of diminished support from wealthy laymen. I have no evidence, positive or negative, which bears on this contention. In some instances, it should be added, monks encourage nat propitiation. Those monks, for example, who practice native medicine or exorcism often diagnose the complaints of their patients as having been caused by nats. The following case is especially interesting because of its ironical conclusion. The mother of a monk who lives in a forest retreat near Yeigyi took ill, and she consulted a monk in Mandalay who is renowned for his medical skills. He informed her that her illness was caused by her "mother's side-father's side" nat, as a punishment for having neglected her food offerings to him. If she were to get well, she would have to resume her offerings. Since, however, she lives in her son's monastic compound, in which it is forbidden to propitiate nats, she had to arrange for a shaman to make the offering on her behalf.

[3]Here we find an important difference between the ethnic Burmese and the less sophisticated Buddhist hill peoples. The Pa-O of the Shan Hills also employ the two explanatory systems of nat intervention and karmic influence, and, although they will offer a rationalization for this inconsistency when pressed by the ethnographer, it occasions little if any cognitive conflict for them (Hackett 1953:551–52). For the Burman, even at the village level, conflict is aroused by the perceived inconsistency.

bases for the Burmese inner conflict concerning their nat beliefs and practices. For, although as Buddhists they profess to believe in the karmic law —and, indeed, they perform numerous meritorious acts with the intention of enhancing their karma—as nat cultists they deny, at least by implication, its inevitability. That they should refuse to accept the consequences of the karmic doctrine is not surprising. Since, according to this doctrine, present suffering is the karmic consequence of previous sinning, one can do nothing to avoid it. If, on the other hand, suffering is caused by nats and other harmful supernaturals, one can combat suffering, rather than acquiescing in it, by proper propitiation of these supernaturals. In brief, the belief in nats permits the Burmese to obviate the painful consequences of a consistent belief in karma.

Note then, the dilemma of the Buddhist. Should he repudiate the doctrine of karma, he not only repudiates Buddhism (a horrible thought!), but, since the doctrine of karma provides him with the means for acquiring a better future, he also repudiates his only hope for avoiding future suffering (another horrible thought!). Should he, on the other hand, repudiate his belief in the causal agency of nats and in the efficacy of nat propitiation as a means of avoiding suffering, he repudiates his only hope for resolving present suffering (an equally horrible thought!).

This dilemma, and part of the inner conflict which it entails, was poignantly expressed by one informant when he said, "As Buddhists we should not propitiate the nats, but out of fear, we must." He need only have added, ". . . and out of hope we must," in order to complete the expression of the conflict. "Out of fear"—because if the nats exist, and if we offend them, then, karma or no karma, they will harm us unless we propitiate them. "Out of hope"—because if the nats do not exist, and all suffering must be attributed to karma, there is nothing we can do to combat it. In short, when religious norms, however sacred, are inconsistent with personality needs, it is the latter, however strong the resulting conflict, which prevail. This is one of the reasons that neither Buddhist knowledge nor (see Chapter 4, pp. 60–63) higher education nor Christianity have much effect on the Burmese conviction concerning the role which nats and other spirits play in human affairs. On the other hand, since the Burmese commitment to Buddhism is as strong as the need to avoid a consistent commitment to the doctrine of karma, their conflict remains. Rather than resolve this conflict by solving their dilemma, the Burmese prefer to hold on to both its horns—they propitiate the nats *and* they remain Buddhists.

It should be added, in order to round out this picture, that certain Buddhist beliefs have been modified by the Burmese reluctance to accept the full implications of the karmic law. In theory, those acts which increase one's store of merit yield their karmic consequences in one's next existence. However, when faced with trouble, the Burmese perform meritorious acts with the hope not merely of affecting their future karma, but also of altering their present karma. Although the latter, having been determined by one's past actions, is unalterable in principle, the Burmese venerate relics, worship the Buddha, say their beads, offer food to monks, and so on, with the expectation that the good karma which is thereby accumulated will nullify the bad karma which is responsible for their present ills.[4] This attempt to acquire "instant kan," as Nash styles it (M. Nash 1965:309), reflects the same reluctance to face up to the orthodox doctrine of karma as does the belief in nats. Although Buddhism, with its doctrine of karma, is, as someone has put it, a heroic religion, few people are sufficiently heroic to act in accordance with this doctrine.

THE CONFLICT IN ETHOS

Since logical rigor is not a dominant feature of any people's mentality, it is implausible to believe that doctrinal inconsistency between Buddhism and the nat cultus is the sole ground for the Burmese inner conflict concerning nat propitiation. And, indeed, it is not. Between Buddhism and animism there exists another conflict, a conflict in ethos. It should certainly be apparent by now that, on whatever dimensions they may be compared, the Buddhist and nat systems represent, in their ideal-typic forms, opposite orientations to the world. These orientations may be labeled as Apollonian and Dionysian, respectively.[5] This thesis can be easily documented by reference to but some of the dimensions in which, ideal-typically, these systems differ. It need not be emphasized that ideal-types refer neither to concrete behavior nor to real persons; rather, they are constructs which, created by the researcher, refer to the abstract roles and the formal statuses specific to a circumscribed system. Thus, as Buddhists and as citizens of Burma, shamans of course comply with the values of Burmese society and the Buddhist religion to the same degree that other Burmese Buddhists do. But shamans, *qua* shamans, subscribe to a set of values associated with a non-Buddhist system. Hence, in contrasting shamans with monks I am not contrasting two groups of people, but two (pure) structural and cultural types. This same method is used in delineating the other differences between Buddhism and the nat cultus which are outlined in Table 14.1.

[4]The Taungthu, a Buddhist people in the Shan Hills, have modified the doctrine of karma in exactly this same manner. See Hackett 1953:553.

[5]It was Ruth Benedict (1934), it will be recalled, who first introduced these terms into anthropology, having borrowed them from Nietzsche's classification of Greek tragedy (1924). Benedict employed the Dionysian-Appollonian dichotomy in an attempt to distinguish and characterize total cultures. I am using it, as did Nietzsche, to distinguish two orientations within the same culture.

TABLE 14.1 *A Comparison of Some Salient Dimensions of Buddhism and the Nat Cultus, Viewed as Ideal Types*

DIMENSION	BUDDHISM	NAT CULTUS
morality	moral	amoral
sensuality	ascetic	libertarian
reason	rational	non-rational
personality	serenity	turbulence
society	otherworldly	worldly

Morality. Buddhism, like all the great religions, is a religion of morality. The minimum definition of a practicing Buddhist is one who observes the five moral precepts incumbent upon all laymen, and who, on Buddhist holy days (Sabbath, Lent, Festivals, etc.), observes an additional three or five precepts. Morality (including acts of charity) is not only required by Buddhism, but it is the only Buddhist means by which one's future lot can be improved. It is through morality that one increases one's store of merit; it is one's merit that determines one's karma; and it is one's karma that determines one's rebirth.

If morality is required of the Buddhist layman, it is doubly incumbent upon the Buddhist monk, the very personification of Buddhism. The rules governing the monastic order (codified in the *Vinaya*) include not five, but 227 precepts. To be sure, many of them are concerned with the legal and ritual dimensions of monastic life, but a very large percentage are concerned with its moral dimensions, often delineated in the smallest detail.

Compliance with the moral code of Buddhism, whether it be the lesser code of the layman or the more stringent code of the monk, is the mark of the Buddhist because this code, the Burmese believe, was first discovered, and then revealed, by the Buddha Himself. Liberation, the Buddha taught, can be achieved only by walking the Noble Eightfold Path, a Path which includes "right intentions," "right speech," "right conduct," "right livelihood," and other values. Morality, then, is inextricably associated with Buddhism. It was taught by its Founder, it is transmitted by his "Sons" (as Buddhist monks are called), it is the indispensable requirement for a better rebirth. In short, not only do the Buddhist sacra stand for and symbolize the moral order, but Buddhist doctrine (and especially the doctrines of merit and karma) serves to sustain that order. Even on the level of popular Buddhism it is believed that Buddhist magic (the recitation of prayers and spells, the saying of beads, etc.) is efficacious only if the actor observes the Buddhist precepts. Otherwise, all his ritual and acts, which are intended to achieve supernatural assistance or power, are in vain.

Unlike Buddhism, Burmese animism is, at best, amoral in its behavior and its spirit. The nats neither symbolize nor sustain the moral order. In their human lives, nats were neither consistently moral nor immoral: some were one, some were the other, some were both. In any event, their moral qualities were entirely irrelevant to their becoming nats. Similarly, morality is entirely irrelevant to their present existence as nats—some nats are believed to be moral, others are believed to be immoral—as it is irrelevant to their interaction with humans. Nats are indifferent to the moral conduct of their votaries, and morality is totally absent as a dimension of the nat cultus. Nats punish those who offend them or who neglect to make offerings to them, and they assist those who propitiate them and who make offerings to them, regardless of their moral state. The criminal who propitiates a nat will be the object of his favors, and the saint who neglects him will be the victim of his punishment.

Morality, in sum, is not a mark of Burmese animism. The nat cult neither symbolizes the moral order nor is it concerned with it. The nat world is an amoral world; the nat cultist, *qua* cultist, is an amoral person; the nat practitioner, the shaman, neither represents nor transmits a moral tradition. Shamanistic recruitment does not require compliance with a moral code, and shamanistic role performance is governed by no moral rules. A shaman may lie and cheat, drink and fornicate, for these are irrelevant to the requirements of her role, to her influence on the nats, or to her success in obtaining clients.[6]

Sensuality. Buddhism, as is well known, teaches that desire is the cause of suffering, and that suffering can be eliminated only by the elimination of desire. The entire Buddhist discipline—charity (*dāna*), morality (Burmese, *thila;* Pali, *sila*), meditation (Burmese, *bauwana;* Pali, *bhāvanā*)—is a means to the twin ends of first realizing the truth of the basic Buddhist insight, that desire is the cause of suffering, and then of achieving that state of desirelessness by which suffering can be escaped. It is only by the elimination of desire, or clinging (*tanhā*), that the ultimate Buddhist goal, nirvana (Burmese, *neiban*; Pali, *nibbāna*), can be achieved. The Buddhist life, *par excellence*, is the life of asceticism, a life in which the passions are subjugated, controlled, and finally eliminated.

This message of Buddhism is found not only in Buddhist Scriptures, but it is symbolized in and exemplified by the two most sacred of Buddhist symbols, the Buddha and the monk. Every Burmese schoolboy knows the story of the prince Gautama, who attained to Buddhahood only by abandoning the pleasures of an oriental palace and becoming an ascetic mendicant. Every Burmese schoolboy, too, emulates the Buddha when, as part of the most sacred of all Buddhist ceremonies (the *shimbyu*), he reenacts this archetypic myth of Buddhism. This ceremony begins with the boy's

[6]In Thailand, too, Textor has distinguished between amoral animism and moral Buddhism (Textor 1960).

playing the role of a royal prince, and it ends with his entering the monastery and donning the robes of the ascetic monk.

If the Buddha symbolizes the One who has succeeded in overcoming the passions and their impurities (Burmese, *kilitha*; Pali, *kileisa*), the monk symbolizes the one who is striving to achieve this goal. The high prestige (*goun*) which attaches to the monk, and the great veneration which he is afforded are a direct function, as all the interviews indicate, of his attempts to subjugate his physical passions. Subjugation of the passions, then, is the earmark of all three of the Sacred Gems of Buddhism: the Buddha (who exemplifies its attainment), the Teaching or Dhamma (which emphasizes its paramount value), and the monastic order, or Sangha (which represents the striving for its attainment). This theme is reiterated daily when the Buddhist recites his confessional formula: "I take refuge in the Buddha! I take refuge in the Dhamma! I take refuge in the Sangha!"

If Buddhism represents the subjugation of the passions, the nat cultus represents their indulgence. Both as humans and as supernaturals, the nats, with some few exceptions, exemplify craving, clinging, desire—for power, for glory, for material pleasures. Some of the more famous nats, as we have already observed, are notorious for their indulgence in sensual pleasures—in food, in liquor, and in sex. Their festivals are bacchanalian in spirit, marked by feasting, drinking, obscenity, and lewdness. Unlike the holy days of Buddhism, which require abstention from food, sex, and other sensual pleasures, nat festivals are often an opportunity for sensual gratification, if not license.[7]

As the monk is the exemplification of the ascetic spirit of Buddhism, so the shaman is the exemplification of the libertarian spirit of the nat cultus. Like their nats, shamans gratify rather than subjugate their passions. Physical pleasure is believed to be their primary aim. Sexuality, both heterosexual and homosexual, is their badge. Ornamental and colorful dress is their costume. The guzzling of liquor is often a requirement of their ritual performances. Sexual experience is the very core of their role recruitment. Unlike the monk, who must renounce sex as a condition for assuming his office, shamanistic recruitment requires that the shaman (during possession) have sexual intercourse with her nat as a condition for assuming her office.

Reason. Buddhism is a religion of reason. There are two senses in which this is the case. Rejecting both faith and ecstasy—the two typical, and usually alternative, religious orientations—its truths are to be accepted, rather, on the basis of reason (applied to experience), and its goal (nirvana) is to be attained by the intellectual process of meditation.

---

[7]Although this description characterizes nat festivals, it does not hold for other types of *nat pwes*, in which sensual, let alone obscene, features are missing. Sarah Bekker has observed (personal communication) that in some *nat pwes* "any obscenity or any sexual irregularity, even the touch of a hand, is absolutely taboo and can spoil the success of the *nat pwe*."

Although the basic Buddhist truths were taught to the world by the Buddha, the supremely Enlighted One, these truths were not acquired by Him through some revelation, nor are they dogmas to be accepted by His followers on faith. For the Buddha, empirical observation of the human situation was the mother of these truths, and His analysis of man's condition was their father. Having concluded, on the basis of his own observations, that suffering, for example, is an inevitable characteristic of sentient being, intellectual analysis led Him, step by step, to the discovery of the cause of suffering in desire. Proceeding, then, from observation to generalization (induction) and from generalization to analysis, He arrived at the obvious deduction: if desire is the cause of suffering, suffering can be eliminated only by the elimination of desire. Putting this deduction to the empirical test, He was able to confirm its truth: by eliminating desire He attained nirvana, a condition characterized by the total absence of suffering.

Although the truth of suffering (*dukkha*), as well as the truths of impermanence (*anicca*) and of no-self (*anatta*), are the central doctrines of Buddhism, the Buddhist is not asked to accept these truths on faith. Rather, these are truths which he can, and which he is expected to, confirm for himself. Contrary to Tertullian, the Buddhist is expected to believe, not because his beliefs are "absurd," but because they are rational, i.e., because they can be confirmed by experience. Since ordinary experience, however, is chaotic and deceptive, Buddhism provides a means—meditation—by which insight (Burmese, *wipathana*; Pali, *vipassanā*) into these truths can be obtained. Whatever differences there may be among the various techniques of meditation, they all entail "mindfulness"—that is, concentrated attention to various bodily processes, conscious awareness and noting of these processes, and detailed analysis of the sensations attendant upon them (cf. Nyanaponika 1962).

But meditation is not merely a technique for discovering the Buddhist truths for oneself; it is the indispensable means for the attainment of nirvana. Since desire produces action, and action produces karma, and karma produces rebirth, the only escape from the round of births and rebirths (*samsāra*) is to uproot its cause, viz., desire. And it is only through meditation that this can be achieved. Through meditation one discovers for himself that suffering, impermanence, and no-self are indeed the essential attributes of being; having made this discovery, one loses all desire; and having lost desire, one satisfies the basic requirement for the attainment of nirvana. In short, in theory and in practice Buddhism stresses the life of reason. Mindfulness and awareness, attentiveness and concentration, consciousness and meditation—these are the characteristic features of the Buddhist way.

If Buddhism stresses the rational, the nat cultus stresses the nonrational. If reason is the foundation stone of the former, emotion is the basis for the latter. Nat propitiation is motivated by fear; nat truths are discovered through possession. The desired psychic state of the nat devotee is ecstasy. Thus, unlike the Buddhist monk, who seeks Buddhist truth through study and meditation, in consciousness and self-awareness, the shaman achieves her revelations by means of nat possession, in states of unconsciousness and trance. If insight is the product of meditation, dissociation is the product of possession. If mental concentration (Burmese, *thamata*; Pali, *samādhi*), achieved in solitude, is a necessary condition for meditation, emotional intensity, stimulated by group interaction, is a prerequisite for possession. Alcoholic intoxication, group contagion, bacchanalian music, abandoned dancing—these set the stage, individually and severally, for the experience of possession. In sum, although the nat cultus is not opposed to reason, it is most certainly indifferent to its demands. It not only emphasizes the emotional, but it requires the abdication of the rational.

Personality. Since Buddhism has as its goal the elimination of desire and, hence, of suffering, it is no accident that serenity is the characteristic feature of the Buddhist personality ideal. Free from passion and conflict, yet characterized by tenderness and compassion (Burmese, *myitta*; Pali, *mettā*), the ideal Buddhist personality is calm, peaceful, imperturbable. These, of course, are the characteristics of the Buddha, as He is portrayed in both myth and sculpture. There are few Buddha images, however poorly executed, that do not convey this feeling of serenity and inner peace. These, too, are the characteristics aspired to by the Buddhist monk. And, though seldom achieved, these are the characteristics which mark his professional persona. Inevitably, when making a public appearance, his walk is measured, his demeanor calm, his expression impassive, his gestures balanced. He is the very personification of sobriety, of inwardness, of calm.

The nats and their shamans personify the contrary traits. Turbulence, not serenity, is the outstanding attribute of the nat cultus. If inner peace is the prerequisite for Buddhahood, violence is the prerequisite for nat-hood: it is because of their violent deaths—by burning, drowning, murder, and so on—that they became nats. In their cultus they are associated with turbulence, both physical and emotional. Frenzied dancing, dithyrambic music, angular gestures, shouting and screaming—these are the characteristics of nat festivals. Physical violence and verbal abuse are the typical symptoms of nat-caused illness. It is entirely appropriate, then, that the professional persona of the shaman is the opposite of that of the monk. Possessed by her nat, the shaman may charge like a bull, gesticulate like a drunkard, brandish a sword like an executioner. She expresses inner turmoil, not inner peace; agitation, not calm.

Society. Taking "society" to mean the secular socio-cultural system— "the world," as Christian theology refers to it—the orientations of Budhism and the nat cultus are diametrically opposed. Buddhism, it will be recalled, draws a radical distinction between *lokika* and *lokuttara,* between the worldly and the otherworldly. The former is mere appearance (illusion); the latter is reality. The former represents *saṁsāra*, the wheel of rebirth; the latter represents *nirvana*, the escape from rebirth. The former stands for the material, the latter for the spiritual. The former symbolizes desire, the latter the absence of desire. The former entails suffering, the latter the absence of suffering. The former constitutes the great obstacle to salvation, the latter constitutes its attainment. Attachment to the world implies continuous involvement with all those impurities that preclude the possibility of salvation, especially the three cardinal impurities of greed (*lobha*), anger (*dosa*), and delusion (*moha*). As a religion of radical salvation, therefore, the Buddhist attitude to the world is unambiguous—the world is to be renounced. Salvation, for Buddhism, means salvation *from* the world.

World-renunciation is the message of the Dhamma, it was practiced by the Buddha, and it is exemplified in the Saṅgha. The latter, the monastic order, is the continuous symbol of this, the basic Buddhist message—the world and all its works are vanity. Abandon the family, renounce the desires for wealth and glory, reject the quest for pomp and power; retire from the world, don the yellow robe, and enter the monastery.

The nat cultus turns this message on its head. It is with *lokika*, not *lokuttara,* that it is concerned. Nats are propitiated for worldly ends. Like Buddhism, the nat cultus, too, is concerned with suffering and the release from suffering, but its concern is to avoid suffering while remaining in the world. Far from rejecting the world, the nat cultus embraces it. In this sense the shaman is the perfect foil for the monk. The shamanistic role, both in its trappings and in its goals, symbolizes all the desirable attributes of the world: wealth and power, pomp and circumstance. At the Taung-byon Festival, for example, the shamans are royal queens and court ministers; they perform in a royal palace; they ride on a royal barge; they exercise dominion over their subjects. The message is clear. Accept the world; exploit it for your satisfaction; strive for its rewards.[8]

On all these dimensions, then, the ethos of Buddhism and the ethos of the nat cultus represent conflicting and incompatible orientations. One is Dionysian, the other Apollonian; one represents impulse, the other represents its control; one symbolizes the id, the other symbolizes the superego.[9] This radical incompatibility between the value orientations of Buddhism and Burmese animism is a second basis, then, for the Burmese inner conflict concerning their participation in the nat cultus.

[8]The shaman-monk bifurcation is not, of course, unique to Burma. It is found in other Theravada societies, such as Ceylon (cf. Ames 1964; Yalman 1964), and it finds its analogue in the Hindu priest-shaman bifurcation in India (cf. Berreman 1964).

[9]Leach has shown similar distinctions in Ceylon between Buddhism and the cult of Pulleyiar (Leach 1962).

TWO RELIGIONS

The Burmese awareness of the inconsistency between animism and Buddhism has not led to any diminution in the intensity with which they hold their nat beliefs, nor in the frequency with which they perform nat rites. As far as one can tell, the nat cultus is as strong today as it was when it first encountered Buddhism more than a thousand years ago. Those historical scholars, like Ray, who argue that Buddhism has "replaced" the nats (Ray 1946:263), are either unacquainted with the contemporary Burmese scene, or they are the victims of their own wishful thinking. But if the nat cultus continues to flourish in the context of a self-professed Buddhist culture, how are we to interpret the relationship between these two systems?

Logically, there are four possible interpretations of this relationship. First, it might be argued that these two systems are hopelessly intertwined, forming a syncretistic religion, whose separate components can be distinguished only analytically. Second, and in opposition to this first argument, it might be argued that these systems are, in fact, empirically distinguishable, and that they comprise two separate religions. The second argument, in turn, has three logically possible subtypes with respect to the relative importance of these systems. It might be claimed, first, that these systems are of equal importance; second, that the nat cultus enjoys primacy over Buddhism; third, that Buddhism enjoys primacy over animism.

Except for the first subtype of the second argument, which no one, at least to my knowledge, has put forward, and the last subtype, which I shall put forward, each of the other arguments has had vigorous advocates. Thus, adverting to the first argument, we may refer to a modern anthropologist who, noting the similarity in offerings made to Buddhist monks and to the nats, writes as follows:

> Here again the behavior patterns related to Buddhism and animism are essentially the same, and while the schooled Buddhist may find us guilty of confusing distinctive forms of behavior, the burden lies with him for proving distinctive motivation among the peasant supplicants who seek to improve their lot (Brohm 1963:165).

For Brohm, then, Buddhism and the nat cultus do not comprise a substantive, but rather a conceptual, syncretism. Buddhism, he argues, is conceived animistically, and the conceptions underlying Buddhist worship are essentially the same as those underlying nat propitiation. More recently, a philosopher who has also observed the Burmese religious scene at first hand has argued for a substantive as well as a conceptual syncretism between these two systems.

In Burma the host of Indian deities was merged with the local nature spirits or nats. To Indian wisdom was added Burmese folk-lore. And the whole of it came to be known as Buddhism! (King 1964:62)

If some contemporary writers argue for a syncretistic relationship between Buddhism and animism, an earlier generation argued that these systems are distinctive and that animism is the "real" religion of the Burmese, while Buddhism is merely a "veneer," possessing little depth. It was Eales, in the 1891 Census Report, who first characterized Burmese Buddhism as "a thin veneer of philosophy laid over the main structure of shamanistic belief" (quoted in Government of India 1902:33). A decade later, in the 1901 Census, we are told that "inwardly in their hearts the bulk of them [the Burmese] are still swayed by the ingrained tendencies of their Shamanistic forefathers, in a word are, at bottom, animists, pure and simple" (quoted in Government of India 1902:33). Temple, in his classic work on the nats, paraphrases Eales when he writes that the Burman "is at heart an Animist, his professed faith [Buddhism] being little more than a thin veneer of philosophy . . ." (Temple 1906b:2). Quoting Lowis, the 1911 Census Report again restates the primacy of animism in the Burmese religious mentality. Buddhism ". . . has done all that a polish can do to smooth, to beautify, and to heighten. . . . [But] let but the veneer be scratched, the crude animism that lurks must out. Let but his inmost vital depths be touched, the Burman stands forth an Animist confessed" (Government of India 1912:94). Even Scott, perhaps the most sensitive and knowledgeable interpreter of traditional Burma, considers it to be an "indisputable fact" that the "vast body of the [Burmese] people are really animists pure and simple, and that Buddhism as a religion is merely the outward label. . . . Buddhism is merely a sounding brass and tinkling cymbal, an electro-plating, a bloom, a varnish, enamel, lacquer, a veneer, sometimes only a pargeting, which flakes off, and shows the structure below" (Scott 1921:389–90).[10]

"But if we can lead them to talk of their crops, and houses and illnesses, and of the births and deaths that have occurred in their memory, we shall find that we are in a world of demons, who give trouble and must be driven away, who are sometimes seen with fatal consequences in the jungle,—a world in which tribute must be paid to the goddess of disease, and to the far away deity of Kattragama; in which scarcely anything happens by direct human or natural agency, but all by virtue of charms and omens. The old monk up there casts horoscopes, it is true; but for all practical purposes a 'kapurala'—an exorcist or devil-priest in the next village—is the pastor of the flock. The whole home life is haunted by a sort of religion, but Buddhism is almost as completely outside it as the British Government." (Copleston 1908:465).

[10]Foreign observers in other Buddhist societies generally view the Buddhist-animist relationship in the same way. In the following quotation, a close and not unsympathetic observer of late nineteenth-century Ceylon could have been writing of Burma, both in his description, as well as in his evaluation.

Although the nats are deeply engrained in Burmese thought and behavior—were this not so, one could hardly justify the writing of this study—the opinions quoted above are, in my judgment, either misleading or false. Far from being a veneer, Buddhism is deeply embedded in Burmese culture and deeply rooted in Burmese personality. And rather than being indistinguishable, Buddhism and the nat cultus are in most, but not in all, respects distinctive systems. For as a salvation religion Buddhism is entirely unaffected, even in the case of the most ardent believer in nats, by the nats and their cultus. On the crucial dimension of salvation the distinction between these systems is absolute.

Between the nat cultus and Buddhism there exists a very clear division of labor. The nats have jurisdiction over those mundane matters (the domain of *lokika*) which are absolutely irrelevant to Buddhism, whose concern, on the Great Tradition level, is almost exclusively with supermundane matters (the domain of *lokuttara*). Nats are propitiated, either to avoid dangers or to solicit boons in the present mundane existence. As a salvation religion, Buddhism is not concerned with the mundane world, characterized by impermanence and suffering. The Buddha is worshiped and His Path is followed in order to transcend the mundane world and to attain nirvana, goals which are of no concern to, and beyond the power of, the nat cultus.

In agreement with the Buddhist Great Tradition, the Burmese believe unqualifiedly that Buddhism alone is the exclusive means for the achievement of otherworldly goals. The desire to avoid rebirth in any of the lower abodes, or the desire for rebirth in the human world or in the *deva* heavens, or the desire to escape from the round of rebirths (*samsāra*) and to achieve nirvana—any of these goals can be achieved by Buddhist means only. Propitiation or nonpropitiation of the nats cannot, in the slightest degree, affect their attainment. On this point every Burman, whatever his place of residence, social status, or educational level, will unqualifiedly agree. On this point there are no ifs or buts. I have never encountered a Burman, peasant or sophisticate, who believes that propitiation of the nats has the slightest influence on his chances of salvation, whether the latter be conceived as a better rebirth or as the attainment of nirvana.

It must be admitted, however, that the contrary is often the case. Consistent with the Great Tradition, but going much beyond it, most Burmese, as was emphasized in a previous section, also use Buddhism for the attainment of certain mundane goals. Indeed, Buddhist and nat rituals, although separately performed, may both be employed by the same person for the attainment of the same worldly goal. And this, the subversion of Buddhism for mundane ends, the conversion of Buddhist *sacra* into instruments of magical technology, not only constitutes a genuine problem for Buddhist orthodoxy but qualifies my contention that Buddhism and animism exhibit a clear division of labor.

Despite this overlap, however, Buddhism and animism remain distinctive systems. For, although Buddhism may be used for the attainment of worldly goals, the nats are never used for the attainment of otherworldly goals. Here the distinction between these two systems is absolute. If the Burmese believed that nats and other spirits influenced one's karma and, therefore, one's chances for salvation, and if, consequently, the nat cultus were based on the former premise and motivated by the latter, it could then be legitimately claimed that Buddhism and animism constitute one undifferentiated, syncretistic system. But this is most definitely not the case. For the Burmese karma can only be affected—and, hence, salvation can only be attained—by the practice of Buddhism, i.e., by following the three Buddhist techniques of charity (*dāna*), morality (*thila*), and meditation (*bauwana*). For the Burmese these three techniques are Buddhist acts, *par excellence*, and these acts alone are instrumental for the attainment of salvation. The nats and the nat cultus are wholly excluded from these acts and this goal. It is for this reason, among others, that the Burmese exclude the nat cultus from the category of *Boudaw patha*, the Burmese term for Buddhism.

It may be concluded, then, that the Burmese clearly distinguish Buddhism from the nat cultus. For the Burmese these are separate and distinctive systems, differing both in their means as well as in their ends. Although they may overlap in some respects, they are substantively and conceptually distinct. For the Burmese, the basis for this distinction is self-evident: Buddhism is religion, while the nat cultus, whatever else it may be, is not religion. It will be recalled, for example, that when I asked the director of the Taungbyon Festival why it was necessary to pay for the recording of nat, but not of Buddhist, ceremonies, he replied, "That [i.e., Buddhism] is religion, this [i.e., the nat cultus] is business." Not all Burmese would agree that the nat cultus is business,[11] but they would certainly agree that, unlike Buddhism, it is not religion. For the Burmese, religion means the Path to salvation, and the nats are totally and completely irrelevant for even finding, let alone walking along, that Path. On this score, the humble and the exalted alike are in agreement. Indeed, the following words of the former Prime Minister, U Nu, express the sentiments of any peasant in Yeigyi.

Of course as Buddhists we believe in the existence of the nats—they do exist. And we propitiate them, i.e., we offer them food, just as I offer you food or tea if I would like you to do something for me. But the nats have nothing to do with religion, that is, with the release from suffering

[11] I should note, however, that all the shamans, including two male shamans who became my personal friends, with whom I discussed nat problems always ended our conversations with the hope (and prayer) that I might become rich.

and rebirth. Only the Buddha, Dhamma, and Sangha are for that" (Personal interview, August 6, 1959).

That the Burmese, given their definition of "religion," refuse to characterize the nat cultus as one, need not blind us to the fact that the nat cultus, given an alternative conception of religion, may very well be one. Indeed, given *my* definition, the nat cultus is very much a religion. Thus, although I disagree with the distinguished English historian, D. G. E. Hall, that ". . . animism is the true cult of the great mass of the [Burmese] people," I strongly agree with him that in Buddhism and the nat cultus we witness ". . . the existence of two religions . . . not only side by side in the same community, but in the same individuals . . ." (Hall 1942:13). In short, my disagreement with many contemporary Western writers on Burma is not with their inclusion of animism, together with Buddhism, within the Burmese religious domain, but with their argument that these systems comprise an indistinguishable, syncretistic Burmese religion.

To ignore the systemic differences between Buddhism and the nat cultus —differences which, as we have seen, are very clear to the Burmese themselves—is to force these two religious systems within the procrustean religious framework of most non-Buddhist cultures. Since in most cultures the practice of religion is intended to achieve both mundane and supermundane goals, it is assumed that both types of goals, and their related practices, must always form part of one system. And from this assumption it is then concluded that Buddhism and the nat cultus comprise a single religion. Since in Burma, however, as in most other Buddhist cultures,[12] this assumption is false, the conclusion is similarly false. For the Buddhist, the function of "religion" is primarily the attainment of supermundane goals. Hence, any action system such as the nat cultus, whose primary function is the attainment of mundane goals, is, *ipso facto*, a distinct and separate system. Whether the latter system is also a religion, as I think it is, or whether it is something other than religion, as the Burmese believe it to be, is, as far as this argument is concerned, beside the point. For, in

[12]This distinction between the functions of animism and Buddhism is found in most, if not all, Theravada societies, as well as in some Mahayana countries. As early as the eleventh century, when Anawrahta's mission to China (Nanchao) inquired about the huge image of a god called *Sandi*, the Chinese primate replied: "We have two religions, one of this world, and the other of the next world. For this life we worship the idol Sandi; for the next life we worship Buddha" (Harvey 1925:30). More recently, Levenson has distinguished the worldly orientation of Confucianism from the otherworldly orientation of Taoism in traditional China (Levenson 1964).

In contemporary Thailand it is "as a means for storing up merit for life in the next world [that] the villager turns to Buddhism; for protection in his present world, the peasant looks to the host of good and evil spirits that affect his every undertaking" (De Young 1955:140). In Ceylon, too, as Pieris has shown, non-Buddhist cults have arisen to attend to those mundane concerns to which normative Buddhism is indifferent (Pieris 1952). These cults, as Ames has shown, are to be clearly distinguished from Singhalese Buddhism (Ames 1964).

either case, it can be agreed that Buddhism and the nat cultus constitute two distinguishable systems.

Although arguing that Burmese Buddhism and the nat cultus are distinctive religious systems, I do not intend to imply that the former is (as many Burmese claim it to be) pure Theravada Buddhism. Since such an inference would most certainly be false, it would be misleading to conclude this section without at least indicating that although structurally distinct from the nat cultus, Burmese Buddhism shares some of its important characteristics. (A more extensive treatment of this subject must wait for a separate monograph.)

I have already pointed out above that although Buddhism may be used magically for the attainment of worldly goals, a practice which in itself constitutes a corruption of Buddhism, the nat cultus is never used for the attainment of otherworldly goals. The latter goals are the province, uniquely, of Buddhism. But even with respect to otherworldly goals—and this is a second and even greater corruption—Buddhism shows affinities with the nat cultus. When used within a Buddhist context, the English word "otherworldly" is highly ambiguous. In Western terms "otherworldly" refers to those concerns which transcend the present existence. In Buddhist terms, however, only the concern with nirvana, the state of nonexistence, is truly otherworldly, for Buddhism postulates the existence of thirty-one abodes, all of which come within the realm of lokika, or the worldly. Only nirvana is truly otherworldly (lokuttara), because nirvana means the extinction of existence—the "extinction" at least of the two modes of existence characteristic of any of the thirty-one abodes in which rebirth takes place—the nonmaterial (nāma) and the material (rūpa) modes. Since, for Buddhism, all of the thirty-one abodes are characterized by suffering and impermanence, the Buddhist goal is the transcendance of all these abodes by escaping from the wheel of rebirth (samsāra).

Although normatively, then, Buddhism is alone the means for the attainment of otherworldly goals (in both the Western and the Buddhist meanings of "otherworldly"), and although Burmese opinion is consistent with this normative belief, most Burmese are not so much concerned with the transcendance of all existence as they are with the attainment of a better rebirth in their next existence. Although paying lip service to the desirability of nirvana, they prefer to remain in samsāra, hoping to be reborn either as wealthy humans or, even better, as blissful devas in one of the heavenly abodes. Contrary to Buddhist teaching, in which these pleasurable states are but temporary way stations on the Path to its ultimate goal, most Burmese take these way stations as their ultimate goal. And although it is only through Buddhist means that they attempt to achieve their goal, their orientation is a corruption of the normative goal orientation of Buddhism. And as a corruption, it should be noted, it is similar to the normative orientation of the nat cultus. The goal of the nat cultus is the attainment of a more pleasurable existence, and to the extent that this is also the goal of a corrupt Buddhism, their goal orientations are identical. They differ only in the locale in which the goal is sought. For the nat cultus, the goal is sought in this birth, whereas for Buddhism it is projected into a future birth.

But it is not only in the corruption of its goal orientation that Burmese Buddhism shows affinities with the nat cultus. Even when its goal orientation is retained, non-Buddhist means, similar to those employed in the nat cultus, may be employed for its attainment. Thus it is widely believed in Burma that nirvana may be achieved not only through the arduous practice of Buddhist discipline, but also through the magical practices associated with those quasi-Buddhist sects known as *gaings*. Through membership in one of these sects various magical techniques, both alchemic and cabbalistic, are learned for becoming a *weikza*, and thereby extending the duration of one's present existence at least until the coming of the future Buddha. Now, taking their professions at their face value—i.e., granting that they wish to prolong their lives only that they may meet the future Buddha, and granting that their desire to attain nirvana is the desire for the cessation of all rebirths—sect members wish to live till the coming of the Buddha so that, having worshiped the recombined relics of the present Buddha, they will immediately attain nirvana.

Notice again the affinity of Buddhism, this time an instrumental affinity, with the nat cultus. Rather than attain their goal by the religious techniques of morality and meditation, they hope to attain it by the magical technique of worship. It is "magical" because it is not conceived, as it is in normative Buddhist worship, as an expression of veneration; it is conceived, rather, as it is in normative nat propitiation, as instrumental for the attainment of a goal. It is, moreover, purely mechanical, the mere performance of the act guaranteeing its success. Although the forms and symbols used by the *gaing* are all Buddhist, their spirit and substance are animist. Ironically, the Buddhist power which is believed to be inherent in the symbols is used for the subversion of Buddhism. Nevertheless, just as the exorcist may be properly conceived as the mediator between monk and shaman, conceived as polar types of Burmese religious practitioners (see Chapter 13, pp. 241–45), so the *gaings* may be viewed as mediating between the polar Burmese religious systems of animism and Buddhism.

Here then is a complicated picture indeed. On the one hand, we see the nat cultus with its magical means and its worldly ends. On the other hand, as its polar opposite, we see Buddhism with its religious means and its otherworldly ends. For the Burmese there is no question about what is Buddhism and what is animism. Still, though they are committed Buddhists, the Burmese are yet drawn to both the goals and the means of animism. Using Buddhist means, they pursue natlike, non-Buddhist ends; cathecting Buddhist goals, they attempt to achieve them by natlike, non-

Buddhist means. In short, between the polar extremes of animism and Buddhism, we see a continuum of beliefs and practices which show attributes of both systems.

It was Mendelson who, as we have already seen, first introduced the notion of a continuum in Burmese religion, with animism and Buddhism representing the poles of the continuum which are linked by the *gaings*, those quasi-Buddhist sects which he characterizes as "Messianic Buddhism" (cf. Mendelson 1960). I disagree with Mendelson, however, in his conception of this continuum. For him this continuum represents one system which he calls Burmese religion. For me—for the reasons given above—the poles of the continuum represent two distinctive religions, despite the fact that Mendelson is undoubtedly correct in arguing (Mendelson 1963b) that for many Burmese even meditation is a means for the acquisition of power (an animist notion) rather than wisdom (the Buddhist notion).[13]

THE PRIMACY OF BUDDHISM

Agreeing that Burmese animism and Buddhism are separate systems, an earlier generation of Western scholars concluded, as we have seen, that the former was the "true" religion of the Burmese. It is primarily because Buddhism, at least in its Great Tradition aspects, abdicates almost all concern for worldly goals, that they mistakenly (in my opinion) perceived Buddhism to be nothing but a veneer. Scott, for example, had no doubt but that this was the case because, he observed, when a Burman

wants to build a house, launch a boat, plough or sow his fields, start on a journey, make a purchase, marry a wife himself, or marry his daughter to another, bury a relation, or even endow a religious foundation, it is the spirits he propitiates, it is the nats whom he consults (Scott 1921:390).

Although Scott's generalization is true, his conclusion is false. For the Burman consults the nats, not in *defiance* of Buddhism, but in *default* of Buddhism. Orthodox Buddhism, neither as a philosophy nor as a religion, has anything to say about these mundane matters. Since the world and its affairs have nothing to do with salvation, Buddhism, as a salvation religion, has nothing to do with them. The fact that the Burman consults the nats in these matters does not indicate, therefore, that Buddhism is a veneer; it merely indicates that in the pursuit of non-Buddhist goals, the Burmese employ non-Buddhist means. Indeed, far from agreeing that Buddhism is a veneer in Burma, I would insist, rather, on its primacy, not

[13]Mendelson's historical argument concerning the relative strength of animism and Buddhism on a national political level seems to me to be sociologically very sound. In essence he argues that the national strength of Buddhism is positively related to the strength of royal authority, while that of animism is negatively related to royal authority (Mendelson 1963b).

only because on the crucial problem of salvation there is not even a contest between the two systems, but for a number of other reasons as well.

In the first place, viewed purely in physical terms, the amounts of energy, thought, time, and wealth which are expended on the nats are insignificant compared to those devoted to Buddhism. Indeed, the Burmese concern with Buddhism (at the village level, at least) is almost obsessive. It would be difficult to exaggerate this concern. Endless conversations are devoted to discussions of Buddhist ethics, Buddhist ideology, and even Buddhist metaphysics. A Westerner is astonished at the spectacle—what else can he call it?—of uneducated peasants discussing such arcana as the distinction between appearance and reality, matter and spirit, form and content, subject and object, and so on, and their relevance for behavior, motivation, and moral judgment. Buddhism is not only an endless topic of conversation, but Buddhist activities, voluntarily engaged in, take up inordinate amounts of time. Feeding of monks, planning for a son's ordination as a novice (the *shimbyu* ritual), organizing a pilgrimage, arranging for a ceremony, preparing for a holy day—these and similar activities occupy the bulk of a Burmese villager's free time. And, it should be added, these activities are not only time-consuming, but they are also very expensive. Yeigyi families, for example, spend annually an average of K200 (about $45) on Buddhist activities; the nat cultus consumes less than one-tenth that amount. In short, although space does not permit me to pursue these details any further, it is a matter of simple observation that Buddhism takes priority over the nats on any quantitative dimension— physical energy, emotional cathexis, material sacrifice, etc.—on which they might be compared. Detailed proof for this assertion can be produced, of course, only in a full-length study of Burmese Buddhism.

A second reason for insisting on the primacy of Buddhism is cultural. The values embedded in Burmese culture and internalized in the personal value system of the typical Burman are the Buddha's, not the nats'. Again, since this statement, too, requires a full-length study of Burmese culture, I shall merely explicate its meaning, without attempting to prove it.

In stating that Burmese values are Buddhist values, I do not mean to suggest that the Buddhist ethos is the only, or even the primary, ingredient of Burmese personality. On the contrary, we have already seen that Burmese personality expresses the ethos of the nat cultus at least as strongly, if not more strongly, than it expresses the ethos of Buddhism. But "personality" is a differentiated, not a homogeneous, concept. If, on a cultural level, Buddhism, as I suggested above, symbolizes the superego and the nat cultus symbolizes the id, this is because the former, I believe, represents, or is embodied in, the Burmese superego, while the latter represents, or is a projection of, the Burmese id. To put it differently, although Burmese needs and drives are more often consistent with nat values than with Buddhist values, Burmese values are more often consistent with Buddhist values than with nat values. Hence, although the Burmese may not always want to do what their Buddhist values tell them they ought to do, there is no question in their own minds about what it is they ought to do; and although they may often act upon their desires rather than upon their values, they are aware of, and experience conflict over, this inconsistency. This conflict, of course, is a measure of the degree to which they have internalized the values of Buddhism.

Another, more easily demonstrable, measure of the primacy of Buddhist values is the veneration accorded to those whose lives exemplify these values. The typical Burman may desire riches or sensual pleasures or worldly goals, and he may admire those who possess wealth or power or worldly success. His veneration, however, is reserved for those who have eschewed the world, together with its wealth and its sensuous pleasures. The world-renouncing monk is the most venerated person in Burma, and the greater his renunciation, the greater is his veneration. The Burmese admire political power, but they (literally) worship the monk (among other reasons) precisely because he disdains such power. They seek to indulge their sensual appetites, but they worship the monk precisely because he has subdued these appetites. They wish to be reborn in the physical world, but they worship the monk because he seeks in nirvana to transcend the physical world.[14]

Another way of stressing the primacy of the Buddhist over the nat value system is to say that Buddhism stands to the nat cultus as the sacred to the profane. For most Burmese, animism is a concession to human frailty; Buddhism is a striving for human nobility. Animism represents man's natural fears and desires, Buddhism symbolizes his highest ideals and aspirations. Animism presents man as he is; Buddhism indicates what he *ought* to be (and can become). One worships the Buddha because He is holy; one propitiates the nats because it is expedient ("out of fear we must").

The differences in the attitudes and sentiments which these systems evoke, indeed the differences in the very vocabulary by which they are described, reflect this sacred-profane dichotomy. Let us take the word "worship," for example. It is misleading to use "worship," as most Western writers do, in reference to both nats and the Buddha. The closest Burmese equivalent for "worship" is *shikkou*, which, literally, refers to the act of physical obeisance or prostration. For a Buddhist, there are five "objects [worthy] of worship": The Buddha, His Teaching (Dhamma), the Monastic Order (Saṅgha), his parents, and his teachers. Worship of the Buddha is *Paya shikkou*. (*Paya* = Buddha; *shikkou* = worship). The expression *nat shikkou* is never used in reference to the nat cultus; indeed, a Burman would be shocked by the juxtaposition of these words. The

---

[14]The primacy of Buddhist over animist values has been noted for Lower Burma (Pfanner 1962:401–3) and Ceylon (Ames 1964:26) as well.

Burmese do not "worship" (*shikkou*) the nats. They either "feed" (*tinde*) them, or "make offerings" (*puzo patha*)[15] to them; sometimes, too, they even "pay respect" (*kou gwede*) to them. Never, however, do they "worship" them. The Buddha, who is revered, is worshiped; the nats, who are feared, are pacified or propitiated. Following Burmese usage, I have throughout this volume referred to the "propitiation," never to the "worship," of the nats.

Because Buddhism, as an ideological system, is sacred, no one—at least no one whom I ever encountered—expresses skepticism concerning the ideas, values, and norms which comprise it. Many Burmans express intellectual difficulties either in understanding or in accepting one or another of the component elements of this system, but they always interpret these difficulties as reflecting the limitations of their own intellectual attainments, rather than constituting a challenge to the truth of Buddhism. In short, if there are Buddhist skeptics, I never met or heard of any. Indeed, on the peasant level, a skeptic would meet with such severe censure, if not revulsion, that his continued presence in the village would be impossible.

This is not the case with respect to animism. Not only are some people skeptical of the nats, but, as far as social sanctions are concerned, skepticism can be expressed with impunity. To be sure, a wife may be frightened by her husband's expressions of skepticism because his consequent neglect of the nats might offend them, thereby arousing their wrath. To reject the nats, given their demonstrable potency, may be a sign of rashness, even stupidity. But no one views the nat skeptic with distaste or opprobrium; on the contrary, he is admired for his courage and for his piety. To reject Buddhism, on the other hand, is a sign of degeneracy. The apostate may remain a man, but he is no longer a Burman.

The primacy of Buddhism is demonstrated not only by its sacred quality, but by its normative role. Since, for the Burmese, the truth of Buddhism is self-evident, in any confrontation between Buddhism and some competing system, it is the latter system, never the former, which is usually on trial. As a normative system, Buddhism is the measure of all things; it is the criterion by which all ideas, all values, all behavior are to be judged. This is as true in the realms of science or politics as it is in the realm of religion. Conflict between Buddhism and any of these other systems is never resolved by raising questions about the truth of Buddhism; it is resolved, rather, by attempting to render these other systems compatible with Buddhism. Buddhism is not only the criterion by which all else is judged; it is the criterion by which, in case of doubt, all else must be justified. To justify a Buddhist idea or a Buddhist practice by reference to some non-Buddhist criterion would strike any Burman as strange indeed; to

---

[15]*Puzo* is the Burmese corruption of the Pali *puja*—"to do homage"—and the synonym of the Burmese *patha*, "to offer." For the Burmese "to do homage" and "to offer" are equivalent acts.

justify them by reference to an animistic criterion would strike him as monstrously bizarre.

It is for this reason that so many Burmese, as we have already observed, are deeply troubled by the incompatibility between animism and Buddhism. For this incompatibility does not merely arouse the intellectual discomfort of sustaining inconsistent belief systems, but, even more importantly, it arouses the emotional discomfort (anxiety) which is induced when a profane belief system contradicts a sacred one. It is precisely because Buddhism, rather than animism, is the sacred and, hence, the normative system that so many Burmese are disturbed by the implicit threat which animism poses for Buddhism, while so few—are there any?—are troubled by the implicit threat that Buddhism poses for animism.

Attempts to deal with the animistic threat to Buddhism can be classified, as we have already observed, into two types. One type faces the threat squarely and rejects either the existence or the power of the nats. The other type, equally aware of the threat and yet incapable of rejecting the nats, argues that the nat cultus is really not incompatible with Buddhism. That most Burmans reject attempts of the first type indicates how strong is their reluctance to accept the full implications of the doctrine of karma, and how deep-seated are the needs which are given expression in the nat cultus. On the other hand, the frequent occurrence of attempts of the second type, and the lengths to which they will go, is an unambiguous index of the intense anxiety aroused by a knowing violation of a Buddhist norm or value. Throughout this book we have encountered many instances of simple peasants, aware of the inconsistency between nat and Buddhist beliefs, attempting to justify the former. The government itself, cognizant of the strong hold of Buddhism on the Burmese masses, has felt constrained to justify its support of the nat cultus. Sensitive to the Buddhist-inspired criticism of its 1961 decision to construct a new shrine for the Mahagiri nat, the government, through its Directorate of Religious Affairs, issued an official statement defending the project. (See *The Nation*, December 10, 1961.) Having consulted some "leading monks," it was the government's opinion that nat propitiation did not "amount to heresy if it is conducted in accordance with Buddhist regulations." This being the case, and seeing that the new shrine would contribute "towards prosperity of the country," the statement urged that "Buddhists should not sneer" at the project.

No group is more cognizant of the normative role of Buddhism than the leaders of the nat cultus, and in assessing the relative importance of Buddhism and animism as normative systems, it is important to underscore the great pains which they take to provide a Buddhist justification for animism. That the leaders of the nat cultus should feel the need to emphasize the Buddhist legitimacy of animistic beliefs and practices is a strong measure of the hold which they believe Buddhism to have over the

Burmese masses to whom their appeals are directed. These efforts, which would be somewhat superfluous if Burmese Buddhism were merely a "veneer," are but another indication of the importance of Buddhism as a normative system, and its obvious primacy over animism.

A most dramatic instance of such an effort occurred, during the course of my field work, when the nat cult, as we have seen (see pp. 250–51), came under strong attack from certain elements of the press. In attempting to counter this attack, the leaders of the Taungbyon Festival published a widely circulated pamphlet defending the nat cultus against its critics, but mentioning none of its "negative" features—those which are potentially inconsistent with Buddhism, and for which Buddhist justification would be difficult to find. Thus, for example, nothing is said about mandatory propitiation, about the punishments meted out by the nats for nonfulfillment of hereditary obligations, or about the nats' role in causing illness and other forms of pain and trouble. Although stressing only its positive features, the authors are yet careful to differentiate the nat cult —they concede that it is not a "noble thing"—from Buddhism, while, at the same time, providing it with goals which would appeal to the average Burman. Thus, they wrote:

> We do not believe that it is a noble thing to propitiate the Nat Brothers, but we claim that it is not a wrong belief to do so. [The nats are propitiated] so that we may live long, be protected from all evils, and enjoy greater prosperity. When we propitiate them we do not do anything [as the critics had claimed] that adversely affects [our] character or behavior. . . . Those who propitiate them, as we do, will enjoy health, wealth, and prosperity.

But this argument, the authors obviously felt, was not compelling in itself. For instead of leaving it at that, they proceed to justify the goals of the cultus and the means—nat propitiation—for their attainment by reference to a Buddhist charter. First, the authors list five types of beings, similar to the Burmese nats, who are explicitly recognized by the Buddha himself. Second, they point out that the goals of nat propitiation, the attainment of health and prosperity, have an unambiguous Buddhist sanction. Third, they cite many instances, from the Jātakas and from early Pagan history, in which pious Buddhist kings (including the Buddha himself in previous incarnations) sought to achieve these two ends by enlisting the assistance of nats.[16]

Recognizing the overwhelming importance of Buddhism for the Burmese,

---

[16]They also, incidentally, appeal to political as well as to Buddhist sanctions. First they quote a decree, issued by King Thibaw, informing the family of the present director of the Taungbyon Festival that it is exempted from normal taxes and the corvee, because of its responsibilities connected with the festival, and commanding them to continue the festival as usual. They also quote a more recent decree from a former British Commissioner, exempting the family which traditionally organizes the festival from the capitation tax.

some leaders of the nat cult, attempting to render it compatible with Buddhism. go so far as to portray the nats as pious Buddhists concerned with promoting Buddhist values. Shamans, for example, will often say that a portion of their fees is required by the nats who wish to offer alms (*dāna*) to the monks and thus acquire merit. Indeed, two hundred monks are fed at the conclusion of the famous Taungbyon Nat Festival from the proceeds of the paddy land owned by the Taungbyon nats, so that they (the nats) might acquire merit. In the same vein, during the 1960 Festival it was widely reported in the Burmese press that the Taungbyon nats, disguised as humans, had offered robes, an umbrella, and sandals to the most famous monk in Burma, the Weibu Sayadaw. During my stay in Burma, the Burmese papers reported that U Nu, while meditating on Mt. Popa, was given copies of the Buddhist Scriptures by the mother of the Taungbyon nats, Popa Medaw.

Some nat-cult leaders go so far as to claim that nat propitiation is not only compatible with Buddhist goals and values, but that it is an important means for their attainment, as well. The logic underlying this thesis, as propounded by the director of the Taungbyon Festival (in a personal interview), is ingenious indeed. Nat propitiation, to be sure, is not to be confused with Buddhist worship—Buddhism is for nirvana, the nats are for worldly prosperity. Nevertheless, these two systems are related, he argued, as means are to ends. In order to enter nirvana, one must give charity; but, he asked triumphantly, how can you give charity unless you are prosperous? By making you prosperous, the nats enable you to attain nirvana! In short, nat propitiation, far from being inconsistent with Buddhism, is an instrument for the attainment of its *summum bonum*. And, indeed, there is ethnographic truth to his argument. It is easy to cite many instances of Burmans who propitiated the nats in order to acquire the necessary funds for holding some Buddhist ceremony, including the most sacred and meritorious ceremony of all—the monastic ordination.

Propitiation of the nats is justified by still other nat-cult leaders who claim that at least some of the nats are really Buddhist gods (*devas*). Thus in discussions with other shamans at the Taungbyon Festival, I pointed out that certain nat skeptics argue that since, according to Buddhism, all beings in the Wheel of Life (*samsāra*) must be reborn, the nats, too—even if they had once existed—must have long ago been reborn into some other abode. Taking up this Buddhist challenge, the shamans had a ready Buddhist response. The nats do indeed change their abodes, and in some cases, at least, this is all the more reason to propitiate them. Thus, the Taungbyon nats, according to the director of the Taungbyon Festival, are now *samma devas*, inhabiting the Buddhist Satumahayit heaven. (Their rebirth as *devas*, which, he claimed, was first revealed to King Mindon by a group of Buddhist monks, is consistent with a "rumor" [!] reported to me by a Buddhist monk, that the elder Taungbyon nat had become a *deva.*) They will remain in this heavenly abode until the coming of Arimadeiya (the future Buddha) when, after erecting a golden monastery in his honor, they might even enter nirvana. In the meantime they, like all *devas,* are Guardians of the Buddhist religion (*Sāsana*). What greater Buddhist sanction might one desire?

Thus far, then, I have argued that Buddhism, clearly and unambiguously, enjoys primacy over animism in Burma because the Burmese invest large amounts of psychic energy in Buddhism, they view Buddhist values as sacred, and they accept the teachings of Buddhism as normative. I should now add still another, and final, reason for the primacy of Buddhism—power.

I have already observed that although the nats are never used for the attainment of supermundane goals, Buddhism is often used for the attainment of mundane goals. Since, except in certain circumscribed cases, such practice has no scriptural sanction, it represents a deviation from Buddhist norms. By the same token however, it indicates that, for the Burmese, Buddhism possesses greater power than animism. When the nats are impotent, Buddhism is called upon.

Since Buddhism is enormously more powerful than animism, in any confrontation between Buddhism and animism, it is an unquestioned assumption on the part of the Burmese that its power can always overcome nat power. This assumption is implicit, as we have observed, in all therapeutic and prophylactic ceremonies (Chapter 11), whose efficacy rests on the belief that nats (as well as witches and other supernatural beings) cannot withstand the power of Buddhism. Thus, as has already been noted, Scriptural recitation (*pareittas*) will protect a potential victim from an attack by nats; the invocation of Buddhist gods (*devas*) will exorcise them; Buddhist worship will render one invulnerable to them. Anyone who recites his rosary and worships the Buddha is immune to the influence of nats (and other supernaturals), and if he recites the nine "virtues" (*gunas*) of the Buddha he is doubly immune. As the folk saying has it, "Anyone who regularly recites the *gunas* [of the Buddha] is like a pagoda"—i.e., nothing can harm him. Buddhist morality has similar consequences: by observing the Buddhist precepts, one is assured of the constant protection of the Buddhist gods (*devas*), and they, as has already been indicated, are more powerful than any of the spirits. It is for all these reasons that monks, as "Sons of the Buddha," need have no concern for the nats and do not propitiate them. Being superior to the nats, the latter, rather, must worship them.

A man's power in relationship to the nats (as well as to ghosts, witches, and so on) is in inverse proportion, therefore, to his Buddhist piety. Those who are truly pious are more powerful than the nats and may ignore them with impunity. Those, however, whose piety is in question are most vulnerable to their attacks. Thus the Burmese distinguish three types of Buddhists, each type having a different status vis-à-vis the nats (and other evil spirits). The first type consists of pious Buddhists, those who are in complete possession of the "Triple Gems" (the Buddha, His Teachings, and His Monks). Since they are protected by the *devas* they can ignore the nats. Persons of this type are known as *kalyana* ("good worldlings"). The second type consists of those who, although good Buddhists, pay only intermittent attention to the Buddha and His teachings. These are known as *ale ala* ("average worldlings"). The nats cannot harm them but, unless propitiated, they will not protect them. Finally, there are the *anda puhtuzin* ("blind worldlings"). They know nothing about Buddhism and observe few of its precepts. It is they who must propitiate the nats lest they be harmed by them.[17]

In conclusion, then, there is little justification for regarding Burmese Buddhism as a veneer, barely concealing their real religion of animism. On any of the dimensions examined here—time, energy, capital, sanctity, normative quality, and power—Buddhism enjoys unambiguous primacy. But primacy is not monopoly. If the nats represent the Dionysian aspects of Burmese personality, they, or some functional equivalent, will probably occupy a prominent role in Burmese culture as long as the Burmese remain Burmese, which is to say, as long as the Burmese remain human. Indeed, it might be argued even further that the nat cultus, at least in its Dionysian dimensions, is important not only for the Burmese but also, to return to the central concern of this chapter, for the persistence of Buddhism in Burma. This turns the usual argument, that Buddhism with its other-worldly ethos creates a need for the nat cultus and its worldly concerns, on its head. For if it is true that Buddhism makes the nat cultus necessary, it can also be argued that the nat cultus renders the persistence of Buddhism possible. Without this animistic system, it might be argued, the Burmese hostility to the repressive features of Buddhism might have resulted either in its overthrow, or in the incorporation by Buddhism of those anti-Buddhist needs which are now expressed in the former system. This, indeed, is what has happened in the Tantric Buddhism of the Himalayas. In Burma, however, the bacchanalian needs, prohibited by Buddhism, have been drained off into the nat cultus, thereby obviating the necessity either of opposing Buddhism or of corrupting it.

By providing the Burmese with a non-Buddhist institution for the expression of those needs that are prohibited by Buddhism, the nat cultus

[17]Professor U Ko Ko of Mandalay University tells me that the technical meaning of these terms in the Pali texts is somewhat different from these colloquial meanings. In the texts there are two types of "worldlings" (*puhtuzin*), i.e., those who have not yet found the Path leading to nirvana. The first type (*kalyana*) comprises those who, very close to the Path, have a good chance of speedy Liberation. The second type *(anda)* comprises those who are far from the Path and who will remain in the cycle of rebirths for a very long time. The Burmese not only added a third type (*ale ala* = middle) as intermediate between these two, but they also, as we have seen, assigned them somewhat different meanings.

enables Buddhist institutions to remain uncontaminated by them. This has the effect not only of maintaining the integrity of Buddhism, but also of strengthening it. For by insulating Buddhism from those "impure" needs that are associated with the nat cultus, these two systems have not only been kept distinct, but they have become (and they remain) polarized, with the result that Buddhism has become highly idealized. If, in psychological terms, therefore, the nats represent the projection of the "impure" impulses of the Burmese, Buddhism represents the projection of their "ideal" impulses. Buddhism, as the object of these ideal projections, is thereby conceived to be free from all impurities. Hence it is that Buddhism and the monks in which it is personified receive the intense veneration which only highly idealized objects are capable of eliciting (and worthy of evoking). Psychologically viewed, it is this veneration which gives to Buddhism the inordinate strength which it possesses in Burma.

References Cited

ACKERKNECHT, ERWIN
 1943 "Psychopathology, Primitive Medicine, and Primitive Culture."
  Bulletin of the History of Medicine, 14:30–67.

AMES, MICHAEL
 1964 "Magical-animism and Buddhism: A Structural Analysis of
  the Sinhalese Religious System." *Journal of Asian Studies*,
  23:21–52.

BA U, U
 1959 *My Burma, the Autobiography of a President*. New York,
  Taplinger.

BELO, JANE
 1960 *Trance in Bali*. New York, Columbia University Press.

BENEDICT, RUTH
 1934 *Patterns of Culture*. Boston, Houghton Mifflin Company.

BERREMAN, GERALD
 1964 "Brahmins and Shamans in Pahari Religion." *Journal of Asian
  Studies*, 23:53–70.

BIGANDET, P.
 1912 *The Life or Legend of Gaudama, The Buddha of the Burmese*.
  2 vols. London, Trübner.

BOURGUIGNON, ERIKA
1965   "The Self, the Behavioral Environment, and the Theory of Spirit Possession." In *Context and Meaning in Cultural Anthropology*, Melford E. Spiro, ed. New York, The Free Press of Glencoe, Inc.

BROHM, JOHN
1963   "Buddhism and Animism in a Burmese Village." *Journal of Asian Studies*, 22:155–68.

BROWN, R. GRANT
1908   "Rain-Making in Burma." *Man*, 8:145–46.
1915   "The Taungbyon Festival, Burma." *Journal of the Royal Anthropological Institute*, 45:355–63.
1916   "The Lady of the Weir." *Journal of the Royal Asiatic Society*, pp. 791–96.
1921   "The Pre-Buddhist Religion of the Burmese." *Folklore*, 32: 77–100.

BUCHANAN, FRANCIS
1779   "On the Religion and Literature of the Burmas." *Asiatick Researches*, 6:163–308.

CADY, JOHN
1958   *A History of Modern Burma*. Ithaca, Cornell University Press.

CARSTAIRS, G. MORRIS
1957   *The Twice Born*. London, Hogarth.

COEDÈS, G.
1966   *The Making of South East Asia*. Berkeley and Los Angeles, University of California Press.

COLSTON, E.
1910   "Discussion" (of R. C. Temple, *The People of Burma*). *Journal of the Royal Society of the Arts*, 58:695–710.

CONDER, JOSIAH
1826   *A Popular Description of Birmah, Siam, etc.: Geographical, Historical and Topographical*. London, J. Duncan.

COPLESTON, REGINALD S.
1908   *Buddhism, Primitive and Present in Magadha and in Ceylon*. London, Longmans, Green & Company, Ltd.

CRAWFURD, J.
1834   *Journal of an Embassy from the Governor General of India to the Court of Ava in the Year 1827*. 2 vols. London, Henry Colburn.

CUMING, E. D.
1893   *In the Shadow of the Pagoda*. London, W. H. Allen.

DANIÉLOU, ALAIN
1964   *Hindu Polytheism*. New York, Bollingen Foundation.

DEVEREUX, GEORGE
1956   "Normal and Abnormal: The Key Problem of Psychiatric Anthropology." In *Some Uses of Anthropology: Theoretical and Applied*, Joseph Casagrande and Thomas Gladwin, eds. Anthropological Society of Washington.

DE YOUNG, JOHN E.
1955 *Village Life in Modern Thailand.* Berkeley, University of California Press.

DUROISELLE, M. CHARLES
1921–22 "Wathundaye, The Earth Goddess of Burma." *Annual Report, Archaeological Survey of India*: 144–46.
1922–23 "Four Burmese Saints." *Annual Report, Archaeological Survey of India*: 174–76.

ENRIQUEZ, MAJOR C. M. (THEOPHILUS)
1921 "A Divine Despotism." *Journal of the Burma Research Society*, 11:5–9.

EVANS-PRITCHARD, E.
1937 *Witchcraft, Oracles and Magic Among the Azandi.* Oxford, Clarendon Press.

FIELD, M. V.
1960 *Search for Security: An Ethnopsychiatric Study of Rural Ghana.* Evanston, Northwestern University Press.

FORSCHAMMER, EMMANUEL
1885 *An Essay on the Sources and Development of Burmese Law.* Rangoon, Government Printing.

FRANK, JEROME
1961 *Persuasion and Healing.* Baltimore, Johns Hopkins University Press.

FRAZER, JAMES G.
1913 *The Golden Bough,* vol. 9. London, Macmillan & Co., Ltd.

FURNIVALL, JOHN SYDENHAM
1911a "Harvest Home in Burma." *Journal of the Burma Research Society,* 1:92–95.
1911b "Matriarchal Vestiges in Burma." *Journal of the Burma Research Society,* 1:15–30.
1913 "Powers of Heaven and Earth." *Journal of the Burma Research Society,* 3:80–83.
1957 *An Introduction to the Political Economy of Burma.* Rangoon, Peoples' Literature Committee and House.

FYTCHE, ALBERT
1878 *Burma, Past and Present with Personal Reminiscenses of the Country.* 2 vols. London, Routledge & Kegan Paul, Ltd.

GLUCKMAN, MAX
1956 *Custom and Conflict in Africa.* New York, The Free Press of Glencoe, Inc.

GOONERATNE, DANDRIS DE SILVA
1866 "On Demonology and Witchcraft in Ceylon." *Journal of the Ceylon Branch, Royal Asiatic Society,* 4:1–117.

GORER, GEOFFREY
1943 "Burmese Personality." New York, Institute for Intercultural Relations (Mimeograph).

GOULLART, PETER
  1941   *The Monastery of Jade Mountain.* London, John Murray, Publishers, Ltd.

GOVERNMENT OF INDIA
  1902   *Census of India, 1901.* Vol. XII, Part 1 (Burma Report). Rangoon, Government Press.
  1912   *Census of India, 1911.* Vol. IX, Part 1 (Burma Report). Rangoon, Government Press.

HACKETT, WILLIAM DUNN
  1953   "The Pa-O People of the Shan State, Union of Burma." Ph.D. Thesis, Cornell University.

HAGEN, EVERETT
  1962   *On the Theory of Social Change.* Homewood, Illinois, Dorsey.

HALL, D. G. E.
  1942   "Burmese Religious Beliefs and Practices." *Society for the Study of Religions,* 40:13–20.
  1955   (Editor) *Michael Symes: Journal of His Second Embassy to the Court of Ava in 1802.* London, George Allen & Unwin.

HALPERN, JOEL
  1964   *Government, Politics, and Social Structure in Laos.* Monograph Series #4, Southeast Asia Studies, Yale University.

HAMILTON, ALEXANDER
  1930   *A New Account of the East Indies.* 2 vols. London, Argonaut Press.

HARVEY, G. E.
  1925   *History of Burma from the Earliest Times to 10 March 1824, the Beginning of the English Conquest.* London, Longmans, Green & Company, Ltd.
  1946   *British Rule in Burma, 1824–1942.* London, Faber & Faber, Ltd.

HATT, G.
  1951   "The Corn Mother in America and in Indonesia." *Anthropos,* 46:853–914.

HEINE-GELDERN, ROBERT
  1942   "Conceptions of State and Kingship in Southeast Asia." *Far Eastern Quarterly,* 2:15–30.

HILDBURGH, W. L.
  1909   "Notes on Some Burmese Amulets." *Journal of the Royal Anthropological Institute,* 39:387–407.

HITSON, HAZEL MARIE
  1959   "Family Patterns and Paranoidal Personality Structure in Boston and Burma." Ph.D. Thesis, Radcliffe.

HTIN AUNG, MAUNG
  1933a   "Some Inferior Spirits." *Man,* 33:61–62.
  1933b   "Burmese Rain-Making Customs." *Man,* 33:133–34.
  1962   *Folk Elements in Burmese Buddhism.* London, Oxford University Press.

KARDINER, ABRAM
  1945   *The Psychological Frontiers of Society.* New York, Columbia University Press.

KING, WINSTON L.
  1964   *A Thousand Lives Away.* Cambridge, Harvard University Press.

KNOX, ROBERT
  1911   *An Historical Relation of Ceylon.* Glasgow, James MacLehose and Sons.

LANGHAM-CARTER, R. R.
  1934   "Lower Chindwin Nats." *Journal of the Burma Research Society,* 24:105–11.

LA VALLÉE POUSSIN, LOUIS
  1911a   "Cosmogony and Cosmology, Buddhist." In *The Encyclopedia of Religion and Ethics.*
  1911b   "Blest, Abode of the Buddhist." In *The Encyclopedia of Religion and Ethics.*
  1916   "Magic, Buddhist." In *The Encyclopedia of Religion and Ethics.*
  1917   "Nature, Buddhist." In *The Encyclopedia of Religion and Ethics.*

LEACH, E. R.
  1960   "The Frontiers of 'Burma.'" *Comparative Studies in Society and History,* 3:49–68.
  1962   "Pulleyar and the Lord Buddha: An Aspect of Religious Syncretism in Ceylon." *Psychoanalysis and the Psychoanalytic Review,* 49:81–102.

LEDERER, WOLFGANG
  1959   "Primitive Psychotherapy." *Psychiatry,* 22:255–65.

LEHMAN, F. K.
  1963   *The Structure of Chin Society.* Urbana, Illinois, University of Illinois Press.

LEUBA, JAMES HENRY
  1925   *The Psychology of Religious Mysticism.* New York, Harcourt, Brace & World, Inc.

LEVENSON, JOSEPH R.
  1964   "The Humanistic Disciplines: Will Sinology Do?" *Journal of Asian Studies,* 23:507–12.

LING, T. O.
  1962   *Buddhism and the Mythology of Evil.* London, George Allen & Unwin.

LOEB, E.
  1929   "Shaman and Seer." *American Anthropologist,* 31:60–84.

MANDELBAUM, DAVID G.
  1966   "Transcendental and Pragmatic Aspects of Religion." *American Anthropologist,* 68:1174–1191.

MARRIOTT, McKIM
    1966   "The Feast of Love." In *Krishna: Myths, Rites and Attitudes*, Milton Singer, ed. Honolulu, East-West Center Press.

MENDELSON, E. MICHAEL
    1960   "Religion and Authority in Modern Burma." *The World Today*, 16:110–18.
    1961a   "A Messianic Buddhist Association in Upper Burma." *Bulletin of the School of Oriental and African Studies, University of London*, 24:560–80.
    1961b   "The King of the Weaving Mountain." *Royal Central Asian Journal*, 48:229–37.
    1963a   "Observations on a Tour in the Region of Mount Popa, Central Burma." *France-Asie*, 179:786–807.
    1963b   "The Uses of Religious Skepticism in Burma." *Diogenes*, 41:94–116.

MIDDLETON, JOHN, AND E. H. WINTER
    1963   *Witchcraft and Sorcery in East Africa*. London, Routledge & Kegan Paul, Ltd.

MONIER-WILLIAMS, MONIER
    1891   *Brahmanism and Hinduism*. London, John Murray, Publishers, Ltd.

MYA SEIN, DAW
    1938   *Administration of Burma*. Rangoon, Zabu Meitswe Pitoka Press.

NASH, JUNE
    1966   "Living with Nats: An Analysis of Animism in Burman Village Social Relations." *Anthropological Studies in Theravada Buddhism*. Cultural Report Series No. 13, Yale University Southeast Asia Studies.

NASH, MANNING
    1965   *The Golden Road to Modernity*. New York, John Wiley & Sons, Inc.

NIETZSCHE, FRIEDRICH
    1924   *The Birth of Tragedy*. New York, The Macmillan Company.

NYANAPONIKA, THERA
    1962   *The Heart of Buddhist Meditation*. London, Rider.

O'RILEY, EDWARD
    1850   "On the Spirit (Nat or Dewah) Worship of the Talines." *Journal of the Indian Archipelago and Eastern Asia*, 4:591–97.

PERTOLD, O.
    1929   "Foreign Demons: A Study in the Sinhalese Demon Worship." *Archiv Orientalni*, 1:50–64.

PFANNER, DAVID E.
    1962   "Rice and Religion in a Burmese Village." Ph.D. Thesis, Cornell University.

PFANNER, DAVID E., AND JASPER INGERSOLL
    1962   "Theravada Buddhism and Village Economic Behavior." *Journal of Asian Studies*, 21:341–61.

PIERIS, RALPH
    1952   "Society and Ideology in Ceylon During a 'Time of Troubles,'
             1795–1850." *University of Ceylon Review*, 10:79–102.
    1953   "The Brodie Papers on Sinhalese Folk Religion." *University
             of Ceylon Review*, 11:110–28.

PYE, LUCIAN W.
    1962   *Politics, Personality and Nation Building: Burma's Search for
             Identity*. New Haven, Yale University Press.

RAY, NIHAR-RANJAN
    1946   *An Introduction to the Study of Theravada Buddhism in
             Burma*. Calcutta, Calcutta University Press.

RIDGEWAY, W.
    1915   *The Dramas and Dramatic Dances of Non-European Races
             in Special Reference to the Origin of Greek Tragedy*. London,
             Cambridge University Press.

RYAN, BRYCE (in collaboration with L. D. Jayasena and
             D. C. R. Wickremesinghe)
    1958   *Sinhalese Village*. Coral Gables, Florida, University of Miami
             Press.

SANGERMANO, VICENTIUS
    1893   *The Burmese Empire a Hundred Years Ago*. Westminster,
             A. Constable.

SARATHCHANDRA, E. R.
    1953   *The Sinhalese Folk Play*. Colombo, Ceylon University Press
             Board.

SCOTT, SIR JAMES GEORGE
    1918   "Indochinese Mythology." In *The Mythology of All Races*,
             Louis Herbert Gray, ed. Boston, Marshall Jones.
    1921   *Burma: A Handbook of Practical Information*. 3rd Edition.
             London, Alexander Moring.

SCOTT, SIR JAMES GEORGE, AND J. P. HARDIMAN
    1900–01 *Gazeteer of Upper Burma and the Shan States*. 5 vols. Ran-
             goon, Government Printing.

SEIN TU, U
    1955   "Ideology and Personality in Burmese Society." Cambridge,
             Harvard University (Mimeograph).

SHORTO, H. L.
    1963   "The 32 *Myos* in the Medieval Mon Kingdom." *Bulletin of
             the School of Oriental and African Studies*, 36:572–91.

SHWAY YOE (JAMES GEORGE SCOTT)
    1896   *The Burman: His Life and Notions*. London, Macmillan &
             Co., Ltd.

SHWE ZAN AUNG, MAUNG
    1912   "Hypnotism in Burma." *Journal of the Burma Research So-
             ciety*, 2:44–56.
    1917   "Buddhist Prayer." *Journal of the Burma Research Society*,
             21:52–56.

SMART, R. B.
    1931   "Burmese Birth Customs." *Journal of the Burma Research Society*, 21:52–56.

SPEAR, RAY FORREST
    1928   "The Syncretism of Animism and Buddhism in Burma." Ph.D. Thesis, Northwestern University.

SPEARMAN, HORACE R.
    1880   *The British Burma Gazeteer*. Rangoon, Government Printing.

SPIRO, MELFORD E.
    1952   "Ghosts, Ifaluk, and Teleological Functionalism." *American Anthropologist*, 54:497–503.
    1953   "Ghosts: An Anthropological Inquiry Into Learning and Perception." *Journal of Abnormal and Social Psychology*, 48: 376–82.
    1962   "An Overview and a Suggested Reorientation." In *Psychological Anthropology*, Francis Hsu, ed. Homewood, Illinois, Dorsey.
    1964   "Religion and the Irrational." In *Symposium on New Approaches to the Study of Religion*, J. Helm, ed. Seattle, University of Washington Press.
    1965   "Religious Systems as Culturally Constituted Defense Mechanisms." In *Context and Meaning in Cultural Anthropology*, Melford Spiro, ed. New York, The Free Press of Glencoe, Inc.
    1966   "Religion: Problems in Definition and Explanation." In *Anthropological Approaches to the Study of Religion*, M. Banton, ed. London, Tavistock (Monograph #3, Association of Social Anthropologists).
    in press   "The Psychological Functions of Witchcraft." In *Mental Health in Asia and the Pacific*, William Caudill and Tsung-Yi Lin, eds. Honolulu, East-West Central Press.

SPIRO, MELFORD, AND ROY D'ANDRADE
    1958   "A Cross-Cultural Study of Some Supernatural Beliefs." *American Anthropologist*, 60:456–66.

STARK, RODNEY
    1965   "A Taxonomy of Religious Experience." *Journal of the Scientific Study of Religion*, 5:97–116.

STERN, THEODORE
    1962   "Language Contact Between Related Languages: Burmese Influences Upon Plains Chin." *Anthropological Linguistics*, 4:1–28.

STEELE, JAMES
    ms.   "A Preliminary Analysis of the Burmese Rorshachs."

TACHIBANA, S.
    1926   *The Ethics of Buddhism*. London, Oxford University Press.

TAW SEIN KO
    1893   "The Spiritual World of the Burmese." *Transactions of the Ninth International Congress of Religion*. London.
    1913   *Burmese Sketches*. Rangoon, British Burma Press.

TEMPLE, R. C.
1906a   "A Native Account of the Thirty-Seven Nats." *Indian Antiquary*, 35:217–27.
1906b   *The Thirty-Seven Nats*. London, W. Griggs.
1911   "Burma." In *The Encyclopedia of Religion and Ethics*.

TEXTOR, ROBERT
1960   "An Inventory of Non-Buddhist Supernatural Objects in a Central Thai Village." Ph.D. Thesis, Cornell University.

THA KIN, MAUNG
1923   "Depressed Classes of Burma—a Further Note." *Journal of the Burma Research Society*, 18:139–43.

THOMAS, EDWARD J.
1920   "State of the Dead, Buddhist." In *The Encyclopedia of Religion and Ethics*.

TIN, MAUNG
1913a   "Burmese Ghosts." *Journal of the Burma Research Society*, 3:65–68.
1913b   "Burmese Ghost Stories." *Journal of the Burma Research Society*, 3:183–85.
1914   "Burmese Ghost Stories." *Journal of the Burma Research Society*, 4:53–56.

TIN, PE MAUNG AND G. H. LUCE, eds.
1960   *The Glass Palace Chronicle of the Kings of Burma*. Rangoon, Rangoon University Press.

TRANT, T. A.
1827   *Two Years in Ava from May 1824 to May 1826 by an Officer on the Staff of the Quarter Master General's Department* (Trant). London, John Murray, Publishers, Ltd.

VOSSION, L.
1891   "Nat Worship Among the Burmese." *Journal of American Folklore*, 4:1–8.

WADDELL, L. A.
1911   "Demons and Spirits (Buddhist)." In *The Encyclopedia of Religion and Ethics*.

WEBER, MAX
1946   "The Social Psychology of the World Religions." In *From Max Weber: Essays in Sociology*, H. Gerth and C. Mills, eds. New York, Oxford University Press.

WIJESEKERA, N. D.
1949   *The People of Ceylon*. Colombo, Ceylon. M. D. Gunasena.

WINTER, CHRISTOPHER TATCHELL
1858   *Six Months in British Burmah; or, India Beyond the Ganges in 1857*. London, Richard Bentley.

WIRZ, PAUL
1954   *Exorcism and the Art of Healing in Ceylon*. Leyden, Brill.

YALMAN, NUR
1964   "The Structure of Sinhalese Healing Rituals." *Journal of Asian Studies*, 23:115–50.

Index

A

Ackerknecht, Erwin, 227n
Ahtelan hsayas (*see* Exorcists and exorcism)
Alaungpaya, King, 85n
Alaungpaya dynasty, 70n
Alaungsithu, King, 111
Alchemy, 36, 183, 231, 242n
Ames, Michael, 42n, 156n, 263n, 268n, 273n
Amulets, 29, 35–36, 166n
   (*see also* Tattooing; *Ins*)
Ananda, 44
Anatta, 69, 70
Anawrahta, King, 45n, 52, 96n, 105, 114–15, 116, 125, 135, 248, 268n
Ancestor worship, 69n–70n
Apin, 28
Apollonian-Dionysian traits
   (*see* Dionysian-Apollonian needs, traits)
Ariyas, 44n
   Specific Ariyas
      Shin Angulimala, 44n
      Shin Peindola, 44n
      Shin Thiwali, 44n
      Shin Upagok, 44n
Astrology, 148, 190
Aulan hsayas (*see* Witches and witchcraft; Master witches)
Aungpinle, 106, 111
Aung Thein, U, 18, 182n

B

Babies (infants), 34–35, 83, 146, 147, 152 (*see also* Children)
   cradle ceremony, 94
Bagyidaw, King, 250
Bali, 122n
Ba Thaw, U, 18
Ba U, U, 88–89

Bayinnaung, King, 103
Bekker, Sarah, 19, 33–34, 44n, 53n, 98, 208n, 260
Beliefs, 71–89
   cognitive explanations, 80–89
   motivational explanations, 76–80
   perceptual explanations, 71–76
Belo, Jane, 122n
Benedict, Ruth, 257n
Berreman, Gerald, 263n
Bigandet, P., 71n
Bilus (*see* Ogres)
Bodawpaya, King, 52
Bourguignon, Erika, 157
British, the, 10, 11, 99, 101, 130
   Anglo-Burman war, 37n, 85n
Brohm, John, 264
Brown, R. Grant, 33n, 55n, 105, 111, 112n, 113n, 124, 135
Buchanan, Francis, 112
Buddha, 29n, 41, 51, 57, 175–76, 180, 186ff, 231, 250 (*see also* Buddhism)
   embryo, 185
   eyetooth of, 114
   Gautama, 44n, 166n, 231, 259
   Maitreya, 175, 231, 278
   Nagayoun, 249
   "virtues" of, 45n
   Withoudaya myth, 29n, 46
Buddhism, 2–3ff, 67ff, 70–71, 88–89, 231, 234ff, 247–80 (*see also* Buddha; Monks; Sangha)
   and ghosts, 37–38, 71
   and nats, 40–46ff, 63, 67ff, 71, 86, 87, 110, 113ff, 132–33, 138ff, 175ff, 222–23, 242–46
   conflict with, 247–80
   conflict with, doctrinal, 253–57
   conflict with, in ethos, 257–71
   conflict with, primacy of Buddhism, 271–80
   visions, 160
   and witchcraft, 21n, 29, 71, 82

293